POST-COMMUNIST RESTITUTION AND THE RULE OF LAW

POST-COMMUNIST RESTITUTION AND THE RULE OF LAW

CSONGOR KUTI

CEU PRESS

Central European University Press
Budapest New York

Published in 2009 by
CENTRAL EUROPEAN UNIVERSITY PRESS

An imprint of the
Central European University Share Company
Nádor utca 11, H-1051 Budapest, Hungary
Tel: +36-1-327-3138 or 327-3000
Fax: +36-1-327-3183
E-mail: ceupress@ceu.hu
Website: www.ceupress.com

400 West 59th Street, New York NY 10019, USA
Tel: +1-212-547-6932
Fax: +1-646-557-2416
E-mail: mgreenwald@sorosny.org

ISBN 978-963-9776-40-1

LIBRARY OF CONGRESS CATALOGING-IN-PUBLICATION DATA

Kuti, Csongor.
Post-communist restitution and the rule of law / Csongor Kuti.
p. cm.
Includes bibliographical references and index.
ISBN 978-9639776401 (cloth : alk. paper)
1. Restitution—Europe, Eastern. 2. Europe, Eastern—Claims. 3. Confiscations—Europe, Eastern. I. Title.

KJC7521.R48K88 2009
341.6'6--dc22

2009002733

Printed in Hungary by
Akaprint Nyomda

Table of Contents

Introduction

It was a long time ago, even before I got admitted to the law school, when I had my first encounter with property. My grandmother, she decided to submit her claim for my great-grandfather's 3 hectares land, taken by the communist authorities sometime in the foggy 50's. Great-grandfather had, besides his land, four children—some of them passed away in the meantime—each with numerous offspring on their turn. So it proved to be a truly painful experience to contact everyone, to clarify the succession and to nominate a common representative. Especially, that there was a deadline for submitting such claims, a deadline fortunately manifold prolonged by our government. All in all, a rather boring story, and if I could have read Penner then, I would most probably agree with him: property is a bore.[1] Of course, none of us had, thus the only thing we read was the confusion on each other's faces, when the mayor of a dusty village in a God-forgotten corner of Transylvania told us that there is no available land to restitute anymore. And even if there would be any, it is impossible to identify the old boundary signs. Something smelled fishy: as if the government wanted to restore a landscape that did not exist anymore.[2] A quick family council decided that we can live very well without those 3 hectares, as the costs of a legal action would most probably exceed the worth of the land. Obviously, my family is not exactly an idealist type. If it were to be so, it could have happily filed one of the about 1 million lawsuits generated by the Romanian land restitution scheme.[3]

---

[1] Katherine Verdery, *The Vanishing Hectare: Property and Value in Postsocialist Transylvania*, Cornell University Press, 2003, p. 79–93.

[2] J. E. Penner, *Property in Law*, Oxford University Press, 1997, p. 1.

[3] *Ibid.*, p. 97.

I have less dramatic experiences with property from earlier times. Not that we did not come across it often enough: as we quickly learned, almost everything belonged to the people: the buses, the school benches, the forests, the entire country. Who exactly were "the people", it remained a mystery, but one thing was sure: clearly, it was none of us. Everything was everyone's and no one's in the same time: why bother than?

1. On restitution and the rule of law

If one looks for writings on post-communist restitution in a library, one may find a decent number of recent publications in the field of anthropology[4] or economy,[5] but—surprisingly—very few in legal scholarship.[6] On the contrary, there are plenty of books on historical justice–related restitution (in former colonies, Holocaust reparations, or other post-conflict situations). Is this a sign of caution, or simply a lack of interest on behalf of legal scholars? In the following passages I will present three different arguments: one maintaining that other questions of transitional justice, especially the one relating to its retributive aspect, appeared more acute, or dramatic, as they concerned the faith of persons, rather than of objects (through lustration and decommunization), while the other two arguments are built on the special characteristics of the communist era takings. First, it is argued that the nature of the takings themselves is problematic, as the bulk of the nationalization was carried out by means of law, or "in the shadow of law";[7] therefore, their legality is difficult to challenge. Second, the

[4] See, for example: Verdery, *op. cit.*; Chris Hann, *The Postsocialist Agrarian Question*, Lit Verlag Münster, 2003.

[5] See, for example: Johan F.M. Swinnen (ed.), *Political Economy of Agrarian Reform in Central and Eastern Europe*, Ashgate, c1997; Henri A.L. Dekker, *Property Regimes in Transition: Land Reform, Food Security and Economic Development: A Case Study in the Kyrgyz Republic*, Ashgate, 2003; Hella Engerer, *Privatization and its Limits in Central and Eastern Europe*, Palgrave, 2001.

[6] See, for example: A.L. Cartwright, *The Return of the Peasant: Land Reform in Post-Communist Romania*, Ashgate, 2001 (a work of socio-legal scholarship).

[7] I borrowed this suggestive expression from Grażyna Skąpska, "Restitutive Justice, Rule of Law, and Constitutional Dilemmas," in Czarnota, Krygier, and Sadurski (eds.), *Rethinking the Rule of Law after Communism*, Central European University Press, 2005, p. 215.

passage of a relatively long period of time—during which some of the former owners passed away, taken properties were reassigned, modified, or destroyed, evidence of the initial title might have been lost, the structure and composition of society has significantly changed—raises a number difficult questions.

Deprivations of property during the authoritarian regimes were neither the sole, nor—arguably—the most important losses that had to be endured. Real and presumptive opponents of the emerging communist regimes, entire social classes categorized as enemies, and in certain cases the entire population, suffered serious limitations upon their right to life, security, privacy, freedom of movement, speech, religion, etc. This made opponents of property restitution schemes argue that there are no reasonable justice considerations that may validate compensations for certain losses, while others are left unaddressed.[8] Consequently, a major dilemma for transition governments was to handle somehow the legacy of the past: "violations of human rights, travesty of legality, pervasiveness of collaboration with the secret police [...] outright crimes conducted for political reasons."[9] The problem, which occurred as most acute, was the fact that perpetrators of the above acts, the former oppressors, often managed to position themselves in the halo of the emerging political elite, and the need for a purge, for a settling of accounts was intensely felt. The "settling of accounts" differed in form and intensity from country to country, but it managed to raise the same host of moral, political, and legal controversies, and became, as Sadurski labeled it, "one of the most vexed and divisive questions of post-communist transition."[10] In Czechoslovakia, the notorious "Lustration Law," providing for the exclusion of former secret police members and collaborators from public offices, was upheld in part by the Constitutional Court, in one of its most famous decisions. In Hungary, also through a much-cited decision, the Constitutional Court dismissed

[8] See, for example: Offe and Bönker in "A Forum on Restitution: Essays on the Efficiency and Justice of Returning Property to Its Former Owners," *East European Constitutional Review* 2 (1993), p. 31; see: Chapter 2, *infra* for more details.

[9] Wojciech Sadurski, "'Decommunisation,' 'Lustration,' and Constitutional Continuity: Dilemmas of Transitional Justice in Central Europe," European University Institute, Florence, EUI Working Paper Law No. 2003/15, p. 2.

[10] *Ibid.*, p. 3.

a bill that would have created the possibility of prosecuting those involved in the suppression of the 1956 revolution and the repression that followed it, grounding its view on rule of law considerations.[11]

The entire process of breaking with the past is extremely difficult to deal with in an uncompromising manner within a democratic framework. Moreover, law itself can hardly be regarded as the right instrument for performing a symbolic rupture: classical liberal regimes are characteristically abstaining from performing symbolic or didactic actions in order to conserve their highly praised ideological neutrality.[12]

In the defense of property restitution programs it can be argued that large-scale expropriations during authoritarian rule did not have solely an economic (reform of ownership structures) or a punitive (e.g., taking of dissident property) feature, but represented much more than that. In the context of the Holocaust, expropriation of Jewish properties appears as part of the genocidal project,[13] while communist nationalization targeted the eradication of the entire system of private property,[14] and by that the (at least political and economical) annihilation of "exploitative classes."[15]

Another possible—hopefully not too far-fetched—explanation for a relative caution in addressing the question of mitigation of property injustices might be found in the nature of the initial takings themselves. As it will be explained in this book, restitution policies rely heavily on considerations of justice and legality. Restitution aims to correct past injustices and to consolidate the moral foundations of the system.[16] The problem, however, can be the aforementioned past wrong itself. It is easy to identify such injustice in the case of colonization, where the preexisting social organization was simply wiped out, or in the case of

---

[11] Ruti Teitel, "Post-Communist Constitutionalism: A Transitional Perspective," in Sadurski (ed.), *Constitutional Theory*, Ashgate, 2005, pp. 465–6.

[12] Sadurski, *op. cit.*, pp. 5–9.

[13] Christopher Kutz, "Justice in Reparations: The Cost of Memory and the Value of Talk," *Philosophy and Public Affairs* 32.3 (2004).

[14] Hungarian Constitutional Court (hereinafter HCC), AB 27/1991, 91/E/1990.

[15] Skąpska, *op. cit.*, p. 215.

[16] The re-establishment of a private property system, as a precondition of a market economy, was also an important goal of post-communist restitution schemes, and it will be discussed extensively in Chapter 2, but it is less relevant for the present argument.

Nazi or other war-related takings, but it is slightly more complicated to point to an injustice in the case of communist nationalization (collectivization).

Writing about collectivization of land, Verdery notes[17] that except for the Soviet Union—where collectivization took place with terrible violence, famine, and massacres—the methods adopted in the rest of the communist countries were less extreme. Roughly two main methods can be identified: taking through confiscation (especially in the case of those labeled "enemies of the regime" or of "the nation": those charged with war crimes, etc.) or through donations and exchanges. In the former case, it is perhaps slightly easier to point to an injustice, especially if the confiscation was the outcome of a conviction for political beliefs, or if the authorities "forgot" to provide for compensation. However, many formal requirements were still respected as to uphold as much as possible the impression of legality. As to the latter case, "donations" were the usual method of forming the collectives—procedural requirements insisted on witnesses and signatures to demonstrate free consent. Simultaneously, land exchanges had to be made between the newly constituted collectives and the neighboring non-members, so as to form compact plots. Cartwright notes—writing about Romania—that forcing through the exchange (despite the protests of the non-member landowner) was not decreed as lawful until 1951, even though the practice started much earlier.[18]

The fact that a certain appearance of legality was kept—takings usually took place within the framework of a so-called land reform and/or procedural formalities were used to demonstrate the former owners' free consent—makes it difficult from both justice and legal perspective to point to and to prove a past wrong. The variations in the preexisting property regimes, in the character of the takings, and in the diverging methods applied even within each type of taking,[19] lead to important

[17] Verdery, *op. cit.*, p. 46.

[18] Cartwright, *op. cit.*, p. 83; see also: Chapter 1, n. 21.

[19] For instance, there were significant differences between the methods used for land collectivization in the Soviet Union, Hungary, or Romania, or for instance Poland, which renounced collectivization early on. Similarly, as it is shown below, the takings of land in New Zealand were based on the Waitangi Treaty, while no such instrument was employed in the neighboring Australia.

differences in the outcome of restitution processes; therefore, their importance cannot be overlooked in the analysis of restitution methods and policies.

Finally, the problems raised by the passage of time can—with a little exaggeration—be captured in the question: who should compensate whom, for what, and at which costs? As the book argues, restitution schemes failed to offer convincing arguments upon their choice in answering these questions, and thereby raise doubts on one hand as to the justness of the programs, and on the other hand as to their ability "to fulfill promises of the rule of law."[20]

The compensating agent—*prima facie*—is the state, which carried out the takings, although this is slightly more complicated in the case of Jewish and repatriated persons' properties. (In the former case, compensation may be granted by a foreign government, for example, in the Hungarian Golden Train case, discussed in Chapter 2, *infra*. In the latter, for example, the Hungarian Constitutional Court held that the state's obligation exists only in those cases in which it gave up through international agreements its claims to repatriated citizen's properties.[21]) Nevertheless, the compensating government is certainly not identical with the one that caused the injustices that are remedied. This is especially true for takings affected during military occupation (notably the cases of the Baltic States and of the German properties expropriated during Soviet occupation). As it is argued in Chapter 2, there is no such clearly formulated obligation in international law that would require successor governments to remedy property losses caused to the citizens by their predecessors. (This obligation nevertheless is recognized as existing with respect to the properties of foreign citizens.[22]) Further, traditionally, domestic constitutional law does not know restitution as a remedy for wrongful seizure. Finally, a formalist approach—fashioned by the European Court of Human Rights, or the UN Human

[20] Skąpska, *op. cit.*.

[21] HCC, AB 45/2003, 960/B/1995 part II/B, para. 7. The Court also stressed that the Hungarian state has no obligation to compensate property losses of Hungarian citizens, caused outside the boarders of Hungary by foreign states, on the basis of the 1947 Paris Peace Treaty (see also: HCC, 1043/B/1992).

[22] European Court of Human Rights (hereinafter ECHR), James and Others v. United Kingdom, Application No. 3/1984/75/119, Judgment of 22 January 1986.

Rights Committee, as discussed in Chapters 2 and 4, *infra*—may lead to the inadmissibility of complaints about restitution, as the relevant international provisions entered into force after the violation in question has occurred.

Determining the beneficiaries of the compensation program has never been an easy exercise, as it proved to be a powerful means of exclusion or inclusion, creating or perpetuating discrimination and class injustice, raising the question of intergenerational equity. Through drafting the pool of possible claimants, the claimable items, and the temporal limits of the program (cut-off dates), the restitution schemes demonstrate their preference to certain generation (*ancién régime*'s *status quo*) social group, or institution. As it is argued in the subsequent chapters of the book, the programs created winners and losers of restitution. In certain cases they preferred the majority over certain minorities, churches over other civil organizations or one church over another, landowners over other owners, victims of communist takings over victims of Nazi takings, etc.

Finally, the governments pursuing a restitution program were faced with the problem of costs. In fact, the given financial capacities of the state presented a core argument in justifying limited compensation. Albeit, if remedying past property losses is thought of in terms of justice, reliance on limited financial capacities—although it is an objective fact—does not appear as a convincing argument for denying (even the theoretical) chance to full compensation. However, restitution programs were closely linked with economical reform, and had the—sometimes declared—twin goal of undoing past injustice and creating the preconditions of market economy. This duality made more plausible those economical reasons invoked for sustaining the limited character of restitution, and also permitted—as it was the case in Hungary—to ground the entire program not on the subjective right to remedy, but on governmental gratitude.

* * *

Due also to the problems that were sketched above, facing the past represents a serious test for the new democracies in—as Skąpska's stylish expression states—fulfilling the promises of the rule of law. From the above passages it already may be inferred that addressing the question of property injustices is a problem at least as relevant in its implications and consequences as the question of lustration and de-communization.

Writing about the essence of the rule of law, Raz notes that law should be able to actually guide human conduct.[23] This view is nicely completed by Teitel, who argues that in periods of political upheaval, the rule of law serves to mediate the normative shift in justice. For natural lawyers, continues Teitel, the predecessor regime's immorality determines the necessity for a "fresh start," for the rule of law to be grounded in something else than adherence to the preexisting law.[24]

The commitment to processes that "allow property rights to be secure under legal rules that will be applied predictably [...] is the essence of the rule of law"—Cass tells us.[25] The question that arises than is the following: were restitution laws "good laws"? One must note that modern theories of the rule of law deny its moral features. Raz and Rawls speak about a legally good system, instead of a morally good one.[26] Neumann adds that rational people need a predictable, not a fair system: "[w]e know that life is not fair and we plan our lives accordingly [...] it matters not at all whether this unfairness is found inside or outside the courtroom, so long as it is predictable."[27] Moreover, law is essentially good, because there are good reasons to have law and be governed by it—adds Marmor.[28] At most, it might be argued that the rule of law—although representing basically functional values—also promotes additional goods (beyond functionality), such as impartiality, transparency, etc., and these contribute to the popularity of the rule of

[23] Joseph Raz, *The Authority of Law*, Oxford University Press, 1977, pp. 211–2.

[24] Ruti G. Teitel, *Transitional Justice*, Oxford University Press, c2000, pp. 11–27.

[25] Ronald A. Cass, "Property rights systems and the rule of law," Boston University School of Law, Working Paper Series, Public Law and Legal Theory Working Paper No. 03-06 2003, available online, at http://ssrn.com/abstract_id=392783, p. 2.

[26] Michael Neumann, *The Rule of Law: Politicizing Ethics*, Ashgate, 2002, pp. 1–20.

[27] *Ibid.*, p. 45.

[28] Adrian Marmor, "The rule of law and its limits," USC Public Policy Research Paper No. 03-16, available online, at http://ssrn.com/abstract=424613, p. 53.

law ideal.[29] Albeit, as Rosenfeld stresses, it is unclear even within a single tradition of the rule of law, whether its first and foremost concern is predictability or fairness.[30]

Given all the theoretical controversies, it is perhaps not too difficult to imagine the sort of problems which national courts had to face when dealing with reparation cases. They were facing the task of flashing out a concept of the rule of law—which was regularly asserted to be a cornerstone of the new system in post-communist constitutions—and almost concomitantly, they had to deal with reparation claims within this new conceptual framework. The cases cited in this book are an illustration also of this problem. Albeit this is not to say that judges and courts of "established democracies" would have had a much easier time in dealing with restitution issues. The jurisprudence of the European Court of Human Rights in restitution matters gives a telling account in this respect. It is extremely exciting to see the anguish of the Strasbourg court to conciliate reparation-related claims with its own vision of the rule of law (and how transitional problems influence this view). As the cases presented in this book demonstrate, the Court's vision can be easily categorized neither as predictability, nor as fairness-centered, although there are commentators who argue that the Court is reluctant to inquire into the actual circumstances of the loss of property or of the reparation claim, preferring to foster the stability of property relationships.[31] What arguably follows is that not even the European Court of Human Rights could convincingly solve the problem of matching the specific problems of transition with the inner logic of the right to property.

2. What is it all about?

The central argument of the book starts from the idea that property restitution schemes do not have an exclusively reparative nature; moreover, restitution was deliberately linked with structural reform, and

[29] *Ibid.*, p. 10.

[30] Michel Rosenfeld, "The Rule of Law and the Legitimacy of Constitutional Democracy," Cardozo Law School Working Paper Series No. 36 (2001), p. 5, available online, at http://papers.ssrn.com/paper.taf?abstract_id=262350.

[31] Tom Allen, "Restitution and Transitional Justice in The European Court of Human Rights," *The Columbia Journal of European Law* 13.1 (2007), p. 45.

due to this duality, the scheme features a mixed distributive-reparative character. This, however, represents a real problem for the rule of law, as, according to Hayek's remark, "any policy aiming directly at a substantive ideal of distributive justice must lead to the destruction of the Rule of Law." According to Hayek, the rule of law is inherently leading to economic inequalities, but this inequality is acceptable, until it is not deliberately produced, and until it consists in the differentiated treatment of the different persons, that is, objective equality of opportunities is preferred to a subjective equality.[32]

Building on this finding, the book explores whether the Central and East European restitution programs manage to live up to the Hayekian requirement of offering objectively equal opportunities to those placed in an equal situation. However, the analysis demonstrates that the various limitations that are placed on restitution (person-related, temporal, quantitative, and property-based) betray concerns towards substantive equality, which in practice resulted in unjustified inequalities, producing arbitrary outcomes.

But even if one endorses a minimalist reading of the rule of law, as proposed by Raz, according to which the rule of law needs not to produce just outcomes,[33] and accepts the functionalist view which expects not more and not less than (restitution) laws to be predictable, coherent, and consistent,[34] one may find that the post-communist schemes fall short in some aspects (quantification, deadlines, evidence) from the requirements of this thin version of the rule of law, too. Conclusively, whatever role it is considered that the rule of law may have during transition, the consequences of these restitution policies reach far beyond the transition period, as in the same time they perpetuate old, and create and entrench novel, property injustices.

Perhaps readers of this book will find it intriguing that the political process analysis was deliberately avoided. This was not done out of shortsightedness: the enormous influence of politics on the entire reparation procedure is unquestionable, and the political dimension of the problem is not less fascinating then the legal one. However, the

[32] F. Hayek, *The Road to Serfdom*, University of Chicago Press, c1991, p. 59.

[33] Joseph Raz, "Rule of Law and Its Virtue," in Cunningham (ed.), *Liberty and the Rule of Law*, Texas A&M University Press, 1979, p. 4.

[34] See also: Neumann, *op. cit.*, p. 45.

intention was to demonstrate that even such a highly politicized matter can be dealt with as a strictly comparative constitutional and jurisprudential issue, using the tools of legal analysis, without having to face the danger of collapsing law into politics. Hopefully, this approach will be regarded as a strength, rather than a weakness of this project.

The book is structured in four chapters, out of which the first one is dedicated to the drafting of a background theory of property, while each of the following three chapters consists of the detailed discussion of an element of the above-explained argument.

Accordingly, the intention of the first chapter is to provide a background, against which restitution schemes fashioned in Central and Eastern Europe can be assessed. The chapter is broken down into six subchapters. The first one deals with classical theories of property, departing from the late Middle Ages and ending with the great thinkers of Enlightenment. The focus is on John Locke, the changes in thinking that preceded, were caused by, or followed him, its subsequent critique and refinement (Rousseau, Hume, the utilitarian theories). Arguably, the influences of the Lockean, pre-political conception of property are the most significantly felt in the restitution schemes of post-socialist Central and Eastern Europe. Feldmann speaks about privatization as a process by which "natural right to private property gains recognition and the incentive quality of private property becomes effective" in the transition countries,[35] while Engerer also found that "possessive individualism" represents the "philosophical background of the kind of market economy taken as model by Central and Eastern European countries."[36] The rest of the chapter briefly presents the neoclassical theories, and the Nozickean and Rawlsian concepts.

Chapter 2 discusses the relationship between justice and reparations. Departing from Raz's argument, according to which justice is an ideal distinct from the rule of law,[37] and also endorsing Radbruch's view of the relationship between these two ideals as an antinomy be-

[35] Horst Feldmann, *Die Eigentumstheorien Lockes und Humes und ihre Lehren für den Aufbau privatwirtschaftlicher Eigentumsordnungen in den Transformationsländern*, Tübingen, 1993, p. 15, quoted by Engerer, *op. cit.*, p. 41.
[36] Engerer, *op. cit.*, p. 40–1.
[37] Raz, *op. cit.*, p. 4.

tween two essential elements of legality,[38] the first subchapter argues that this contrast is most difficult to deal with in regime change contexts. The following two subchapters briefly discuss the role of the rule of law in transitions, and attempt to explain the goals attached to post-communist restitution. In the following, an overview of the main forms of justice, and correspondingly, of the forms which various restitution policies embraced, is given. The bulk of this chapter, represented by subchapter six, is dedicated to the two fundamental justice problems that transitional property reparation schemes have to answer: why property injustices have to be mitigated, and why former property owners enjoy a privileged status in comparison with other victims of past injustices. The analysis concludes that although neither international law, nor general principles of justice, not even domestic constitutions recognize a general right to restitution, in a number of exceptional cases (illegal or unconstitutional takings, lack of compensation), a solid argument may be made for the existence of such a right. Under the second question, three possible arguments that may justify property restitution are presented: recognition and protection of rights, past harm, and political persecution. Albeit none of them can adequately explain why former property owners are preferred to other victims. Therefore, subchapter seven argues that transitional compensation schemes have a pronounced distributive character, which, taking into consideration the fact that material justice is the archenemy of formal rationality, constitutes a serious threat to the rule of law.

Chapter 3 focuses on the pool of beneficiaries, arguing that even those who had been placed in an equal situation—that is, all suffered past property injustices—are not offered an objectively equal opportunity to claim redress. The argument developed in this chapter maintains that due to the fact that the schemes addressed restitution—at least in part—from a distributive perspective (which resulted in an attempt to create a substantive equality between victims), the result that they achieved was objective inequality, as everyone was entitled to restitution between the same limitations, while everyone suffered losses of different extent. Here, each subchapter is dedicated to a different

[38] Gustav Radbruch in Csaba Varga, *Law and philosophy: selected papers in legal theory*, Project on Comparative Legal Cultures of the Faculty of Law of Eötvös Loránd University, Budapest, 1994.

limitation. Consequently, the first subchapter deals with person-related limitations (citizenship and residence), the second with quantitative (caps), the third with temporal (cut-off dates), while the fourth with property-based limitations (distinctive treatment according to the nature of the lost property: movable or immovable, various immovable, commercial, religious, and communal). The chapter concludes that these differences in treatment between various former owners are mostly arbitrary, and in certain cases deliberately introduced so as to produce inequalities, and thereby meet the Hayekian concerns as far as they produce results that conflict with the idea of the rule of law. The analyzed provisions of the restitution schemes lead in practice to exclusion, to the creation of winners and losers of restitution, to a breach of the idea of formal equality before the law.

Finally, in the conditions in which according to the conclusions of the previous chapter restitution schemes fall short from a thick conception of the rule of law (justice, rights, or objective equality), chapter four investigates whether requirements of a thin reading—focusing on foresight, clarity, and consistency—were still met by post-communist property redistribution. However, as the problems analyzed in the three subchapters (valuation, time limits, and probation) demonstrate, the restitution programs' provisions are not beyond criticism. As what concerns valuation, certain cases' entitled persons were brought in a situation in which it was impossible for them to exercise their right, in other cases international agreements were disregarded, or subsequent norms altered the initially established entitlement. Further, compensation through vouchers demonstrated incoherence in practice (especially as what concerns the vouchers' future utilization), and constituted mostly a theoretical, rather than an actual compensation. Time limit related concerns are pertaining to the submission deadlines, which almost in every analyzed example had to be extended, in certain cases even several times, and to the length of proceedings, which in some cases were considered as leading to a breach of right to remedy, or amount to an unconstitutional omission. Evidence-related problems arose with regard to the number of documents required, or the conditions attached to their use, which made their employment impossible in practice.

The inquiry uses a comparative perspective, which on one hand focuses on the analysis of nine different post-communist restitution schemes: the Czechoslovakian (and subsequently Czech and Slovak),

Estonian, German, Hungarian, Latvian, Lithuanian, Polish, and Romanian ones. On the other hand, the post-communist schemes are contrasted—where appropriate, and to the relevant extent—with experiences from around the world, such as the indigenous claims in Australia, New Zealand, United States, and Zimbabwe; the Holocaust restitution in United States and some West European states; and the Croatian apartment cases.

A comparative standpoint—which attempts to draw conclusions upon the comparison of different approaches to restitution—has necessarily to presume a "significant degree of congruence between problems and their possible solutions across the spectrum."[39] Of course, similarities and differences need to be evaluated with due care: for instance, in the Holocaust restitution, the need for a corporate body to administer restituted goods was based on a completely different reason than in the case of the Maori. Or, in the case of Croatia, international pressure for the restitution of pre-war real estate was arguably exerted neither with the desire to engender the rule of law, nor with the intention to support the emergence of market economy, as was the case in the rest of Central and Eastern Europe, but primarily out of a very pragmatic attempt to resettle refugees and displaced persons.

There is an obvious difference in Western and Eastern approaches to restitution. However, as such dichotomies "over-simplify complexity,"[40] value judgments are to be avoided, and due care is given to the backgrounds that generated the different approaches to restitution. Moreover, even within Central and Eastern Europe, the diversity of the factors affecting restitution policies was so significant that broad conclusions may be drafted only with peculiar care. (For instance, under communist regimes, in most of the countries in the region a very limited private possession of land was tolerated, while in Poland there was no collectivization.)

However, comparative knowledge might prove its worth by contributing the specific and difficult problem of property restitution. What this book aims at is not a solution which "can be fitted with an

[39] Norman Dorsen, Michel Rosenfeld, András Sajó, and Susanne Baer, *Comparative Constitutionalism: Cases and Materials*, West Group, 2003, p. 4.

[40] Günther Frankenberg, "Critical Comparisons: Re-thinking Comparative Law," *Harvard International Law Journal* 26 (1985), p. 411.

adapter and plugged into"[41] any chosen system; rather, it will seek for a deepened understanding of the problem. "Comparative law"—writes Glendon—"helps us to understand the dynamics of social, as well as legal, change."[42] Comparative analysis has the capacity "to push analytic categories to higher levels of abstraction in order to bridge differences and similarities observed"; moreover, "it holds the potential to help us better understand law and legal systems."[43]

[41] Mary Ann Glendon, Michael Wallace Gordon, and Cristopher Osakwe (eds.), *Comparative Legal Traditions*, West Publishing Co., 1994, p. 10.

[42] *Ibid.*.

[43] John C. Reitz, "How to Do Comparative Law," *American Journal of Comparative Law* 46 (1998), p. 617.

CHAPTER 1

Theories of Property

I have described briefly in the Introduction my personal, somewhat boring encounters with property, but for the innocent bystander, property is simply the right to a thing: land, house, and movables. Pipes reminds us that the American revolution was carried out for the protection of property, and quotes Adams, who argued that the term "happiness" in the Constitution's Preamble conveyed "property," and this is the reason why the normative part of the Constitution contains no express provision on the sanctity of property.[1] For a first-year (civil) law school student, it is the Holy Trinity of *jus utendi, fruendi et abutendi* or *usus, fructus et abusus*—a curious incantation in a long-dead language—from which, in the ideal case, it may be deduced that property is a bundle. But no one can convincingly establish whether property is the sum of the elements of this bundle, or only of some of them, and in any event, how many pieces can be taken from the puzzle without ruining the picture. Underkuffler argues that theory is unable to advance a definition of property beyond mere description, and doubts whether property is a coherent idea in law.[2] Others, more plastically, talk about an "identity crisis."[3] Theorists emphasize that the modern regulatory (welfare) state, which creates a "strain between property's protective ideals and the exigencies of modern governance,"[4] contributes es-

[1] Richard Pipes, *Property and Freedom*, Vintage Books, 2000. According to this argument, the pursuit of happiness was closely related to the acquisition of property.

[2] Laura Underkuffler, *The Idea of Property: Its Meanings and Power*, Oxford University Press, 2003, pp. viii–ix.

[3] Penner, *op. cit.*.

[4] James W. Ely, Jr., *The Guardian of Every Right: A Constitutional History of Property Rights*, 1992; cited by Underkuffler, *op. cit.*, pp. 1–3.

sentially to the erosion of property that not so long ago provided the boundary of the legitimate scope of government.[5]

In spite of all these problems in coming to grasp property, the restitution fever that burnt in the former socialist part of Europe reflected the firm belief that property would advance democracy and markets. The Hungarian Compensation Law's Preamble spoke about the creation of an efficient market economy,[6] the Estonian Supreme Court identified a similar goal of the ownership reform,[7] while other courts in Poland and Lithuania emphasized the positive social aspects of property reform.[8] For the post-socialist elite, property became also a question of justice, symbolizing—together with accountability—a commitment to instituting the rule of law. The already mentioned Hungarian preamble and the Estonian decision both mention the building of a rule of law regime amongst the goals of property restitution or compensation. Justice and accountability bore heavily on the legitimation of the emerging order.[9]

Seemingly, there is a slight paradox: property—not only as a right, but also as a value—was in the focus of the discourse, while there was hardly any consensus as to what property meant—both as a right and value. Of course, lack of consistency has never been a problem in political discourse.[10] But there is more behind this than mere cynicism. According to Engerer, the issue of property can be reduced to three major questions: evolutionary (emergence and transfer), justification,

[5] Jennifer Nedelsky, *Private Property and the Limits of American Constitutionalism: The Madisonian Framework and Its Legacy*, University of Chicago Press, 1990.

[6] Law No. XXV of 1991, Preamble, available online, at http://www.complex.hu/kzldat/t9100025.htm/t9100025.htm.

[7] Estonian Supreme Court (hereinafter ESC) Decision 3-4-1-10-2000 of 22 December 2000, available online, at http://www.nc.ee/english.

[8] Polish Constitutional Tribunal (hereinafter PCT), K 2/04, Judgment of 15 December 2004; Lithuanian Constitutional Court, "On restoration of citizens' ownership rights to land," Decision of 8 March 1995.

[9] Verdery, *op. cit.*, p. 79.

[10] For instance, in 1990, the prime minister of Romania at a parliamentary debate found himself speaking about the necessity of the "prevent[ion of] the concentration of land in the hands of one proprietor, for that would discourage the formation or preservation of village communities as spaces of the authentic national spirit." Quoted also by Verdery, *op. cit.*, p. 77.

and functional (functions performed).[11] Departing from this classification, she argues that in Western legal thought, the functional aspect formed the essence of the discourse, as in the established democracies the existence of private ownership and the separation of private and public sectors is seen as a basic fact that requires no justification. Quite the opposite, in the Central and Eastern European discourse, the evolutionary and justification aspects—how property emerges, how it can be justified, and how the state redefines its role within the new property rights system—occupy a central place.[12] The Hungarian Constitutional Court, for example, considered that the scope of the constitutional protection of property must be considered within the framework of public and private law restrictions, and it must take into account the subject, object, and function of competing private and public claims.[13]

The question that arises then is the following: how does the post-socialist experience contribute to property's "identity crisis"? Can we really speak about a genuine difference in approach? If we turn to Posner and Vermeule, we may learn that there is no essential difference between East and West in terms of goals: each approach attempts to minimize uncertainty about property rights.[14] Engerer observes that transformation (transition) is not a process following given rules, but rather a process producing them. Therefore, neoclassical, contractarian, and monetary theories may not thoroughly explain property rights in transition. She argues that, except maybe for institutionalism, there is a certain vacuum of theory in this field.[15] Verdery notes that from the restitution process one may learn that obtaining property rights is far less important than controlling the context in which these rights could be exercised.[16] In any event, conclusions should be drawn with

[11] Hella Engerer, *op. cit.*, p. 12.

[12] *Ibid.*.

[13] Decision "On the Freedom of Enterprise and on the Licensing of Taxis, No. 24/1994"; and Decision "On the Local Government Apartments, No. 64/1993"; quoted also by Underkuffler, *op. cit.*, p. 146.

[14] Eric A. Posner and Adrian Vermeule, "Transitional Justice as Ordinary Justice," *Harvard Law Review* 117 (2004), pp. 762–5. (The article is also available in form of a Working Paper at the University of Chicago's website, Public Law and Legal Theory Working Paper No. 40, March 2003, at http://www.law.uchicago.edu/faculty/posner/resources/eapav.transitional.pdf.)

[15] Engerer, *op. cit.*, pp. 104–5.

[16] Verdery, *op. cit.*, p. 20.

due care: the troubled waters of property rights transition have barely started to settle.

This chapter is dedicated to the presentation of the most important theories of property, to explore what lies—in terms of theory—behind the apparently straightforward quest of "getting one's things back" so popular in most of the post-socialist countries of Central and Eastern Europe for over a decade. The text is broken down into subchapters, each of them dedicated to different theories, and to their reflection in various instances and aspects of post-communist restitution programs.

1. Classical theories

It might seem somewhat strange today, but much more than one would actually think changed in the way we perceive the world along the breaking lines of the chasm whose first crack was caused by Luther's *Manifesto*, and what we know as Reformation. Up until then, private property was regarded by the church as a consequence of the Fall of Man, whose depravity was reflected in the division into mine and thine.[17]

The early Christian Church accepted private property as a fact of life, and exhorted the faithful to engage to the maximum extent possible in charity.[18] Matthew 19:16–21: when someone asked Jesus how to attain eternal life, He told him to obey the Commandments, and that if he wished to be perfect, he should sell his possessions and give the proceeds to the poor. Still, a balance had to be found between Christian ideals and mundane reality: after all, what would happen, if everyone gave his possessions to charity? Augustine came up with the solution, arguing that a property-free society is only possible in Paradise because it demands perfection. He viewed property as a responsibility, a kind of "trust" held by the individual for the public good:[19] "the evil uses good gold for evil, and the good uses good gold for good."[20] Tomas

[17] Ingo Böbel, *Eigentum, Eigentumsrechte und institutioneller Wandel*, Berlin, 1988; quoted by Engerer, *op. cit.*, note 11, p. 14, n. 7.

[18] Pipes, *op. cit.*, pp. 13–4.

[19] *Ibid.*, p. 15.

[20] Cited in Alfons Heilmann (ed.), *Texte der Kirchenväter*, Vol. III, Munich, 1964, p. 208; quoted by Pipes, *op. cit.*.

Aquinas in *Summa Theologica* put property in a justice context, where justice is the "perpetual and constant will to render to each one that which is his." Personal possession is good, because it has an educative effect: it teaches man to praise both work and the goods, which are its results. Moreover, argued Aquinas, private property creates an incentive for man to be preoccupied with his own affairs, which would have a beneficial effect on peaceful co-existence.[21] However, God is the sole owner, man, against all appearances, only uses the goods. Aquinas showed—borrowing the idea from Aristotle—that property enables charity, which is a Christian obligation, thus the rich are obliged to give their superfluous wealth to the poor.[22]

Although "veneration of property" was considered a heresy, the Christian Church did not venture beyond voluntary renunciation of one's own wealth. Pope John XXII for instance crushed the Franciscan "Spirituals," who advocated renunciation of all possessions. Over one hundred of them were burnt at stake. He issued a bull in 1323, declaring it a heresy to deny that Christ and the Apostles had had possessions. Six years later, in a new bull, the pope asserted that property of man over his possessions does not differ from that of God over the universe, which He bestowed on man; property is, therefore, a natural right, predating human law.[23]

Later, Reformation refined this view. Especially Protestants, on the basis of the seventh commandment ("thou shall not steal"), argued that property is a right created by God, thus private, instead of communal property was willed for man.[24] Calvin wrote approvingly of industry and trade, rejecting the medieval prohibitions on usury. There are theorists who argue that Calvinism did a great deal to foster capitalism.[25] This change of paradigm did not solve the problem, only reversed the question of justification: now the obviously existing communal property needed to be explained somehow. In the late Middle Ages, when secular authorities began to assault church properties,

[21] Manfred Brocker, *Arbeit und Eigentum, Der Paradigmenwechsel in der neuzeitlicher Eigentumstheorie*, Darmstadt, 1992; quoted by Engerer, *op. cit.*, note 11, p. 14, n. 7.

[22] Pipes, *op. cit.*, p. 16.

[23] *Ibid.*, p. 17.

[24] Brocker refers to Melanchthon; quoted by Engerer, *op. cit.*, p. 15.

[25] Pipes, *op. cit.*, p. 17.

the Catholic church turned to defend property on a principled basis, and started to gave up viewing it as an unavoidable reality. To protect church goods from seizures by the crown, theologians began to speak about the inalienable right to property. (This idea was later on picked up and built upon by Grotius.)[26] The ground for such a discourse was also prepared by the rediscovery of Roman Law, which began to be taught in the early 12th century at Italian universities.[27] This quarrel between church and state firmed the status of property as "sacrosanct," even if the parties of the dispute traced the justification of ownership to different sources. According to the Second Vatican Council,[28] private property (understood as the right to dispose over material goods) is part of the expression of the personality, and makes possible the fulfillment of the individual's social role. Therefore, it is extremely important for both individuals and communities to hold possessions. Private property should be regarded as a sphere of autonomy, an extension of human freedom, and one of the conditions for civil liberties. Moreover, goods should be transferred to the public domain only through the acts of a competent authority, according to the requirements, and within the limits of the common good, and upon fair compensation.[29]

In spite of the Church's obvious concern for property and its role in society, it was the Enlightenment that brought with emphasis the question of property into focus. Theorists argue that while the absolutist monarchies of the Middle Ages justified political power by the principle of hierarchy—supreme power was God-given, and transmitted through descent—this theory did not fit the diversified and already complex distribution of property.[30] With the surge of commerce, property also came to mean capital.[31] The rising "middle class" of merchants, manufacturers, and intellectuals has outgrown the feudal social structure, and it desperately wanted its share of fortune (property) and

[26] *Ibid.*, p. 17–8.

[27] *Ibid.*.

[28] 1962–5.

[29] A II. Vatikáni Zsinat Dokumentumai, Szt. István Társulat, az Apostoli Szentszék Könyvkiadója, Budapest, 2000, Gaudium et Spes, p. 716.

[30] Böbel, *op. cit.*, and Niklas Luhmann, *Gesellschaftsstruktur und Semantik. Studien zur Wissensoziologie der modernen Gesellschaft*, Vol. 3, Frankfurt am Main, 1993; quoted by Engerer, *op. cit.*, note 11, p. 15.

[31] Pipes, *op. cit.*, p. 25.

fame (political power).[32] It is the utterly material universe of Descartes and Newton in which these processes take place: property is things, and the right to as many things as possible is the goal of everybody, because property and power are perceived as being directly proportionate. Harrington argued that he who controls the country's wealth controls its politics, as the latter depends on armed power, and mercenaries have to be paid.[33] On the other hand, "[p]olitical power [...] I take to be a right of making laws [...] for the regulating and preserving of property," writes Locke right in the introduction of the *Second Treatise*.[34] There was a long way, however, from Thomas Aquinas to John Locke, and before getting to him, some other thoughts about property need to be explored. On the one hand, communal well-being became the sum of individual happiness, while property was now seen as a reward of a rational life. Many 16th–17th century writers approve the pursuit of private interest.[35] On the other hand, beginning with the Renaissance, theorists started to seek a more rational justification for worldly authority than the will of God as revealed in the Holy Scriptures, and this justification was found in reason. This view came to dominate Western thought in the 17th–18th centuries. Grotius, in *Rights of War and Peace*, discusses the origins of property, and asserts that the "right of first occupancy" occurred before there were states.[36] Law of nature is "so unalterable that God Himself cannot change it."[37] This necessarily leads to the inviolability of property. Arguably, one side effect of the subjects'

[32] However, not everybody believed in the sanctity of private property. For instance, Winstanley and his "Diggers" movement advocated a communistic theory, according to which neither land, nor its fruits should be marketable commodities; interestingly, they were equally hostile to intellectual property and criticized savants for monopolizing learning just like landlords monopolized the soil. Beer, *British Socialism*; Manuel and Manuel, *Utopian Thought*, both referred to by Pipes, *op. cit.*, p. 37.

[33] James Harrington, *The Commonwealth of Oceana* and *System of Politics* (1656); in Pipes, *op. cit.*, p. 32.

[34] John Locke, *Treatise of Civil Government and a Letter Concerning Toleration*, Appleton-Century, 1965, p. 4.

[35] It is enough to point for example to Spinoza's *Ethics* or the Preamble of the U.S. Constitution.

[36] Jeremy Waldron, *The Right to Private Property*, Clarendon Press, Oxford, c1988, p. 154.

[37] Grotius, *Rights of War and Peace*, Vol. II; quoted by Pipes, *op. cit.*, p. 29.

right to undisturbed possession justified denying them political rights—on the ground that reciprocity demanded the subjects to leave the sovereign full power to run the affairs of the state.[38]

Grotius also departed from the mirage of a Lost Paradise, where everyone lived in a peaceful community of goods. According to him, private property emerged as a response to the inevitable shortage of resources that subsequently occurred, by way of contract, an implicit or explicit agreement that led to the division between mine and thine. This is important, because, as theorists emphasize, as long as private property is man's creation, it remains revocable.[39] From a theoretical perspective it is extremely interesting to note that in the case of the indigenous people, variations of the natural rights theory (what Frame calls "the imperial export model")[40] were employed both to justify and—later, after decolonization—to condemn the taking of their lands.[41]

---

[38] *Ibid.*.

[39] Brocker; quoted by Engerer, *op. cit.*, p. 18.

[40] Alex Frame in Janet Mclean (ed.), *Property and the Constitution*, Hart Publishing, 1999, p. 226.

[41] In Blackstone's words, property is "[t]he sole and despotic dominion which one man claims and exercises over the external things of the world, in total exclusion of the right of any other individual in the universe" (William Blackstone, *Commentaries on the Laws of England*, II.1; quoted by Frame, *op. cit.*, p. 226). He viewed property in land as a "transient" property, acquired through first occupancy, and lasting as long, as the first occupier was effectively using it. However, when the number of potential first occupiers increased, conceptions of "more permanent dominion" were entertained, and individuals appropriated not the mere use, but "the very substance" of the thing (*Ibid.*, II.3; also quoted by *Frame*, *op. cit.*, p. 227). Examined from the colonies' perspective, the Blackstonian definition looked unsatisfactory. Maclaurin, a New Zealand-raised scholar, came up with the idea of a "hierarchy of agricultural development," structured on multi-tiered scale, from the lowest to the most evolved, and naturally finding fully matured property solely at the top of this ladder. His hierarchy looks as it follows: 1. Bushmen of South Africa: wandering hunters; 2. Australian Aborigines: defined hunting grounds belonging to clans; 3. Maories of New Zealand: primitive agriculture; 4. village community with intensive agriculture, arable land divided among families, pastures held in common (R.C. Maclaurin, *On the Nature and Evidence of Title to Realty*, Clay & Sons, 1901; also quoted by Frame, *op. cit.*, p. 227). As it naturally flows from the above presented, that which is below the top level is something less than property, and therefore indigenous lands could

Hobbes went one step further than Grotius did, and asked what would happen, if, in spite of the initial contract, man would still infringe on the property of his fellows. For him, breaches of the contract appeared as inevitable; therefore, he argued that an authority had to be created to guarantee exclusion. Interestingly, Hobbes reached back for the Aquinean phrase *suum cuique tribuere* ("to render to each one what is his," see *supra*),[42] and translated *suum* as "propriety." But one may find hints in this direction also in Grotius, who divided one's belongings into "alienable" and "inalienable," stressing that certain goods, as "life, body, freedom, honor" are attributes of personality sanctified by the law of nature, and can not belong to others.[43] The representatives of the tumultuous English political life quickly picked up these notions: in 1646, a Leveller argued that "by natural birth all men are equally and alike born to like propriety, liberty and freedom."[44]

Hobbes followed Grotius' footsteps, but he did away with the original happy community, and considered more likely a *bellum omnium in omnes* ("war of every man against every man") for domination.[45] To put an end to anarchy, man transferred to a group of persons their natural rights. Thus it is possible to consider the state as the sole owner, who grants to its members a right of use. This way, the individual's undisturbed possession is safeguarded from other individuals' attacks, but not from the state, which is free to do what it pleases, until it does not encroach on the individuals' right to self-preservation.[46]

---

be considered "unoccupied" or "legally vacant," and taking them into possession was a fairly decent thing to do for the European colonists. In these conditions the "courts of the conqueror" found it extremely difficult to uphold indigenous claims to restitution. A telling example in this sense is the U.S. Supreme Court decision in the Tee-Hit-Ton v. United States (348 U.S. 272 [1955]), in which the Court held that if the tribes did not have a deed for their ancestral land, they did not own it in a constitutional sense (Nell Jessup Newton, "Indian Claims in the Courts of the Conqueror," *American University Law Review* 41 [1992], pp. 822–3).

42 The phrase is actually attributed to Plato; its Latin translation is credited to Cicero, Pipes, *op. cit.*, p. 30.

43 Grotius, *Jurisprudence of Holland*, Vol. I; quoted by Pipes, *op. cit.*, pp. 30–1.

44 *Ibid.*.

45 Engerer, *op. cit.*, p. 18.

46 Thomas Hobbes, *Leviathan*, ed. by C.B. Macpherson, Penguin Books, 1968, p. 188.

Undoubtedly, the most prominent and influential thinker for the Enlightenment in the field of property rights was John Locke. One must note that his famous *Two Treatises of Government* were an overt critique of Filmer's royalist work, *De Patriarcha*, and at the same time, less directly, of Hobbes's *Leviathan*. Locke rejects Filmer's and Hobbes's theory of permanent war, and imagines a happy community of freedom and equality. However, man has to give up this idyllic condition for the sake of property, threatened by greed and discord, after the apparition of money and development of trade: thus the state came into being to safeguard property. In this way, unlike in Hobbes, property predates sovereignty, and is the source and justification of government.[47] "The great and chief end, therefore, of men's uniting into commonwealths, and putting themselves under government, is the preservation of their property"—writes Locke.[48]

One of the fundamental questions in understanding Locke is to determine precisely what he means by "property." The two most significant chapters in the *Second Treatise* which deal with the question of property are Chapters 5 ("On Property") and 9 ("On Government"), but only in the latter explains Locke that "lives, liberties and estates [...] I call by the general name, property."[49] It is at least questionable whether in Chapter 5 he uses the term in the sense indicated above, or in the more restricted understanding of "estate." Still, one must remember that this was written in the age of Descartes and Newton, when it must have been extremely difficult for a reasonable man living in a mechanical universe to understand property as something else than "things." As it was shown above, Grotius distinguished freedom from estates when talking about one's belongings. What Locke does is exactly the opposite: he ties estates to freedom; furthermore, arguably he deduces freedom from estates. According to him, man owns himself, and by extension, everything that he produces. His famous theory of labor argues that by mixing work with nature, the resulting goods will necessarily belong to the worker. Some commentators argue that the idea of owning oneself entails liberty: the liberty of disposing of oneself, which is the mean-

[47] Locke, *op. cit.*, "An Essay Concerning the True Original Extent and End of Civil Government."

[48] Locke, *op. cit.*, Chapter 9, § 124.

[49] *Ibid.*, p. 82.

ing of freedom.[50] To make himself even less understandable, Locke toys around a bit with words, and uses the expression "workmanship" when speaking about the creation of man. Thus, if we are to take seriously his labor theory, in the case that man is the product of God's "workmanship," then man is necessarily the estate of God and private property a mirage or a nightmare, depending on how one looks at it.

Madison distinguished "rights of persons" (liberties) from "rights of property" (estates), which were both considered as cardinal objectives of government. Nedelsky, in her seminal account of the history of American constitutionalism,[51] showed that property (in the sense of estate) was important for the exercise of liberty, and liberty required the free exercise of property rights. Inevitably, this led to an unequal distribution of property (estate), which required protection from those who had less or none.[52] Thus, according to her, this inequality was the central problem for the Republican government, and Madison made sure that the participation of the people (in the government) was rendered as safe (i.e., ineffective) as possible.[53] Property somehow became part of liberty, or at least the free exercise of unequal faculties for acquiring property, a function of liberty.[54] Indeed, according to other interpretations of Madison, he did not regard property as a natural right, but as a by-product of the freedom of action, which in its turn was an essential part of liberty.[55] This (civic Republican) concept of property that can be traced back to Madison and Jefferson constitutes a very different

[50] Waldron, *op. cit.*, pp. 181, 398.

[51] Jennifer Nedelsky, *Private Property and the Limits of American Constitutionalism: The Madisonian Framework and Its Legacy*, University of Chicago Press, 1990.

[52] Harrington's theory of political "balance" winks at us from behind the Federalist papers.

[53] Nedelsky, *op. cit.*, Chapter 6.

[54] Locke can be hijacked in many ways: his labor theory was turned inside out by socialists and anarchists, who argued that in capitalist production schemes workers do not earn the fruits of their labor, and hence, the means of production should be nationalized (Beer, Driver, and Hearnshaw [eds.]; quoted by Pipes, *op. cit.*, p. 36).

[55] Treanor, "The Origins and Original Significance of the Just Compensation Clause of the Fifth Amendment," *Yale Law Review* 94 (1985), p. 694; as quoted by Laurence H. Tribe, *American Constitutional Law*, The Foundation Press, Inc., 1988, p. 608.

tradition in American constitutional philosophy, a tradition that denies the natural rights approach and represents the basis of serious debates. According to the positivist (legal realist) view, property is a creation of the state and has nothing inherent in it. Property represents the basis of participation in civic life: it is essential for the exercise of constitutional and political rights.[56] Thus, the right to property features in the end social and public characteristics.[57] The modern version of the civic Republican concept regards property as the secure baseline, which ensures anyone's voice in the political order; thus, property contributes to the maintenance of the political and social order.[58] Ownership then is a tool, granted by the state to the individuals for promoting the common good; and the state's role is to ensure its proper redistribution.[59]

However, this does not mean that the government may dispose at will of private property: as Tribe argues, constitutional norms, described through notions as regularity, autonomy, and equality confer protection to private property interests (expectations) against governmental power.[60] The U.S. Supreme Court has acknowledged that because the Constitution did not create any property rights itself; property is, essentially, what the state says it is.[61] However, at the same time the Court also identified some limits to this governmental power by

---

[56] Obviously, at the time of the Founding Fathers this necessarily translated into the self-sufficient white male landowners' (the yeoman farmers') right to political participation.

[57] Carol M. Rose, "Property as the Keystone Right?" *Notre Dame Law Review* 71.3 (1996), pp. 329–65; Gregory S. Alexander, *The Global Debate Over Constitutional Property*, University of Chicago Press, 2006, pp. 4–5.

[58] The social aspect of property was an important theme of reparations, as it will be argued *infra*.

[59] Joseph L. Sax, "Some Thoughts on the Decline of Private Property," *Washington Law Review* 58 (1983); Rose, *op. cit.*; Alexander, *op. cit.*, p. 222; Frank I. Michelman, "Property as a Constitutional Right," *Washington and Lee Law Review* 38 (1981), pp. 1097, 1112; Akhil Reed Amar, "Forty Acres and a Mule: A Republican Theory of Minimal Entitlements," *Harvard Journal of Law and Public Policy* 13 (1990), pp. 37, 38–42.

[60] Tribe, *op. cit.*. Elsewhere, Tribe also speaks about "intuitive notions of private property [that] place limits on the positivist power of the state to redefine property rights" (Tribe, *Constitutional Choices*, Harvard University Press, 1985, p. 170).

[61] Webb's Fabulous Pharmacies, Inc v. Beckwith, 449 U.S. 155 (1980).

stating that the state can take property neither without compensation,[62] nor—except for "extraordinary situations"—without hearing the concerned owner.[63] The attitude of the Hungarian Constitutional Court towards the compensation scheme resembles in a way the positivist view presented above, to the extent that—explaining the theoretical grounds of compensation[64]—it considers that property as an institution is the creation of the state. Albeit, as long as for the American theorists it is clear that the state's role is limited to the creation of the institution while being barred from deciding about the beneficiaries (owners),[65] in the Hungarian Court's reasoning this distinction is blurred, enabling it to consider governmental benevolence as the sole ground for compensation.[66] During the transition period in Central and Eastern Europe the relationship between property and political rights was arguably less relevant in reparations than in the privatization process, during which the governing elite attempted to satisfy its economic appetite in order to lay the foundations for successful party financing in the future.

As the property restitution or compensation schemes that will be discussed in this book demonstrate, property may survive changes of regimes and even of legal systems: ownership rights can be revitalized and brought to a new life even centuries after their formal "extinction." The language employed by certain restitution schemes reflects this idea (regardless of what has been achieved in practice): the Latvian program is talking about the "renewal of property rights,"[67] while the Lithuanian scheme uses the expression "restoration of ownership rights."[68] More importantly perhaps, the approaches to restitution denote a largely prepolitical, more-or-less Lockean conception of property. As Waldron

---

62 *Ibid.*.

63 Fuentes v. Shevin, 407 U.S. 67 (1972).

64 For a more detailed discussion of the "novation" theory, see: *infra*, Chapters 2 and 3.

65 See: Tribe, *American Constitutional Law*, *supra*.

66 The HCC spoke about the state's sovereign decision as to the form of reparations, and the decision between "reprivatization," privatization, or compensation was considered to be grounded on the state's owner status (AB 27/1991, 91/E/1990).

67 Law "On the Land Reform in the Republic of Latvia Rural Regions," 1990; Law "On Land Privatization in Rural Regions," 1992.

68 Law No. I-1454 "On the Procedure and Conditions of the Restoration of the Rights of Ownership to the Existing Real Property," 1991.

notes (referring also to Nozick's *Anarchy, State and Utopia*), Locke's theory of property is a theory of "historical entitlement": ownership rights are established "contingently and historically as the upshot of what individuals have done, therefore it is not open to us to abrogate or reorder them on the basis of what we think society ought to do."[69] Property is prior to the establishment of government, and governments are established to protect property: "government has no other end but the preservation of property."[70] An interesting example in this sense is the formulation used by the Lithuanian Constitutional Court, which literally stated that "[t]he right to possess property is one of the most significant human natural rights."[71] Alas, as it will be seen later on, this discovery did not bar the legislator from enacting (and the Court from generally sustaining) a rather restrictive approach to what they called "restoration of citizen's ownership rights." The latest revision of the Romanian restitution scheme enunciated the principle of complete restitution (*restitutio in integrum*). During the constitutional (preliminary) review of the act, the government's representative argued—and the Court endorsed this view—that respecting the right to property is incompatible, save for certain public interest considerations, with "proportionate" exercise, thus limited restitution is unacceptable.[72]

Locke's labor theory had adepts also in France, where the Physiocrats advocated every man's exclusive property of his person and of all things acquired by his labor. Interestingly, this influential school regarded land as the most authentic form of property, and therefore argued that the state should be governed by landowners, as only they possessed the fatherland—by a curious abstraction they equated fatherland (*patrie*) with patrimony (*patrimoine*).[73] The 1789 revolutionaries were considerably influenced by the Physiocrats: property rights were consecrated as sacrosanct to justify the abolition of feudal rights;

[69] Waldron, *op. cit.*, p. 138.

[70] John Locke, *Two Treatises of Government*, Dent, c1924, pp. 163–4.

[71] Lithuanian Constitutional Court (hereinafter LiCC), Ruling of 27 May 1994.

[72] Romanian Constitutional Court (hereinafter RCC), Decision No. 375 of 6 July 2005, part II, para. 8.

[73] Jean Touchard, *Histoire des Idées Politiques*, Vol. II, Paris, 1956; Gide and Rist, *Histoire des Doctrines Économiques*, Vol. I, Paris, 1947; both quoted by Pipes, *op. cit.*, p. 43.

moreover, the Declaration of Rights of Man and the Citizen declared property rights as "natural and imprescriptible." Still, their enthusiasm was not reflected in the common legislative practice, as Mirabeau, for instance, declared in 1791, that property was a social creation and therefore society is entitled to determine its uses.[74] The theory of "imprescriptible" property was voiced, for instance, at a certain moment by the Romanian Constitutional Court, which held that unlawful acts could not have extinguished the individual legal rights and therefore the state could not have acquired title to the respective property.[75] A somewhat contrary view can be attributed to the Hungarian Constitutional Court, which, although it found a number of nationalization norms unconstitutional and consequently annulled them, at least did not exclude the possibility of compensation on a common, *ex gratia* basis for all past property grievances.[76] The annulment of these norms—as the Court explained—did not bear on the validity of those legal relationships that came into being before the publication of the Court's decision; consequently, the state's ownership rights over the unconstitutionally expropriated items were left untouched.[77] The social aspect of property rights—mentioned by Mirabeau—came forward even more preeminently in most compensation or restitution schemes. As it will be presented in the following chapters, the social dimension of private property was a central theme for instance in Estonia, Lithuania, Poland and Hungary.[78]

The most influential albeit inconsistent[79] French thinker of the Enlightenment, Rousseau, elaborated a theory of property based on first occupation justified by labor. He held that the first appropriation is mutually recognized, and that unequal distribution is due to the differ-

[74] Pipes, *op. cit.*, p. 44.

[75] RCC, Decision No. 73 of 19 July 1995, published in the *Official Gazette*, No. 177, 8 August 1995.

[76] HCC, AB 27/1991, 91/E/1990.

[77] *Ibid.*, part III, para. 5.

[78] See: *infra*, Chapter 2, section 3.

[79] In his *Discourse on the Origin of Inequality* (1755), he held that "the fruits of this earth belong to all and the earth to no one"; in *The Discourse on Political Economy* (1755) he called the right of property "the most sacred of all citizens' rights, and more important in certain respects than liberty itself"; in the *Social Contract* (1762), he wrote about the communities' right to all, to which the individual's right is always subordinated.

ent abilities of man.[80] This is largely in line with Locke's ideas; however, Rousseau departs from the Englishman, by assuming that shortage and unequal distribution will result in conflicts. To put an end to this Hobbesian "free for all," the people conclude a social contract, which also regulates appropriation. Thus, Rousseau does not attach too much importance to who owns what: he is more interested in the fact that the individual acknowledges exclusion.[81] Exclusion, however, cannot be guaranteed in the state of nature, and the French philosopher ends up with creating a strong state, which subordinates individual rights of ownership to the community, and the state becomes the sole owner. This resembles Hobbes's *Leviathan*, but it can be distinguished by the fact that according to Rousseau, the state represents the general will of its citizens, and its main objective is to oppose inequality.[82] The ideal of a strong state preoccupied with enforcing exclusion (the existing *status quo*), rather than with the justness of possessions, is mirrored by the counterrevolutionary "Chartre Constitutionelle" of Louis XVIII. The document provided for the inviolability of the legally acquired properties during the revolutionary period.[83]

There was also an Englishman, who although he had more faith in human nature than Hobbes did, rejected fair and square the idea of natural rights, arguing that rights are not derived from nature, but from "artifice."[84] David Hume[85] believed in individuals' tendency to respect each others' rights, but at the same time he pointed to selfishness as another key aspect of human nature. Unlike Hobbes, Hume considered that "conventional wisdom" could be the source of the laws of justice that could solve the problems of the state of nature.[86] Sened argues that Hume, without the technical tools of contemporary game

---

80 Engerer, *op. cit.*, p. 28.

81 *Ibid.*, p. 29.

82 *Ibid.*, pp. 29–30.

83 Robert A. Kann, *The Problem of Restoration: A Study in Comparative Political History*, 1968, p. 331; quoted by András Sajó, "Preferred Generations: A Paradox of Restoration Constitutions," *Cardozo Law Review* 14 (1993), p. 861.

84 Itai Sened, *The Political Institution of Private Property*, Cambridge University Press, 1997, p. 19.

85 David Hume, *A Treaty of Human Nature*, ed. by David Fate Norton and Mary J. Norton, Oxford University Press, c2000.

86 *Ibid.*, pp. 19–20.

theory, managed to recognize the multitude of a possible social equilibrium and the consequent fragility of any such equilibrium, and thus came to the conclusion that ideas of mutual respect for property are bound to fail. Therefore, the weakness of human nature requires governmental guardians who can enforce conventional wisdom's imperatives. Still, Hume admits that "[a]lmost all governments [...] have been founded originally either on usurpation or conquest or both, without any pretense of a fair consent or voluntary subjection of the people."[87] Other authors interpret and give to Hume a utilitarian reading, considering him as the "initial utilitarian theorist of property."[88] Understanding utility as common interest, it both explains and justifies in Hume the origins and the institution of property. Hume's social equilibrium is based on the stabile possession of things. What make possession stabile are conventions: people recognized that it is in their interest not to disturb others' possessions, provided that the others do not disturb their own possessions. Over time, these conventions lead to a coordinate behavior, and the individual expectations based on them confer stability to possession.[89] The idea of stabile possession as a factor essential to carve out and maintain a social equilibrium was also mirrored by the pro-restitution or compensation arguments. Certainty in possessions was largely considered as a precondition for creating a functional market economy,[90] while the unclarity regarding the property titles or the perpetuation of what was considered to be a "historical injustice" was deemed to affect the rule of law.[91]

Before addressing the thoughts of utilitarianism's main figures, Mill and Bentham, it is necessary to make a short detour, and revisit the remarkable Jean Jacques Rousseau. For he is the one who, somewhat like Martin Luther in the late Middle Ages, marked a substantial divide, true, of a much lesser amplitude, this time only between continental and Anglo-American political philosophy. The liberal school

[87] *Ibid.*, p. 21.

[88] Stephan R. Munzer, *A Theory of Property*, Cambridge University Press, 1990, p. 194.

[89] *Ibid.*.

[90] See: *infra*, Chapter 2, section 3.

[91] Argument voiced by the representative of the Romanian Government before the RCC, in Decision No. 375 of 2005, published in the *Official Gazette*, No. 591, 8 July 2005.

of the social contract attempted to reconcile individual autonomy with the need for centrally enforced law and order.[92] After Rousseau's dismissal of individual autonomy in favor of the awkward ontological entity that embodied the "general will," continental philosophers became more concerned with the grand principles of social life. In the meanwhile, English and American scholars focused on the autonomy of the individual, at the expense of a comprehensive theory of government.[93] As Rawls put it, "the tradition associated with Locke [...] gives greater weight to [...] 'the liberties of the modern,' freedom of thought [...] basic rights of the person and of property, and the rule of law [while] the tradition associated with Rousseau [...] gives greater weight to [...] 'the liberties of the ancient,' the equal political liberties and the values of public life."[94]

Thus, English utilitarianism can be said to return attention to the individual, pursuing the acts that would bring the most happiness to the greatest number of people.[95] According to Bentham,[96] happiness can be translated into the language of pleasure and pain: in this equation happiness equals pleasure. Further, Bentham believes that happiness can be measured in terms of wealth: more goods will produce more happiness.[97] (One might also remember Adams's theory, mentioned in the Introduction, which argues that "happiness" in the Preamble of the U.S. Constitution can be understood as "property.") Property is defined in terms of expectations,[98] the expectations of deriving some kind of advantages from the things one possesses. Because unlike animals, humans are able to anticipate the future,[99] they are able to experience pleasure when their expectations are fulfilled. Thus, if utility

---

92 Sened, *op. cit.*, p. 26.

93 *Ibid.*.

94 John Rawls, *Political Liberalism*, Columbia University Press, 1993, pp. 4–5.

95 George Sher, *Introduction to J.S. Mill*, Hackett, 1979, p. 8; quoted by Sened, *op. cit.*, p. 27.

96 Jeremy Bentham, *An Introduction to the Principles of Morals and Legislation*, The Athlone Press, 1970, pp. 11–2.

97 Alan Carter, *The Philosophical Foundations of Property Rights*, Harvester Wheatsheaf, 1989, p. 52.

98 Munzer, *op. cit.*, pp. 194–5.

99 This is a quite problematic statement today, as contemporary research has shown that certain primitive communities have a completely different notion of time, into which "future" can hardly be fitted.

is pleasure, then utility will be promoted when securing the individuals' expectations with respect to the things they possess.[100] The most important objective for legislation is, therefore—argues Bentham—, security: "assure to the cultivator the fruits of his industry, and perhaps in that alone you will have done enough."[101] Besides security, three other ends are enumerated as conducive to the increase of social happiness: subsistence, abundance, and equality.[102] The argument is that in prosper societies, a natural tendency towards equality exists: prosperity is a result of hard work, which in its turn is motivated by security of property. "Property and law are born together, and die together. Before laws were made there was no property; take away laws and property ceases."[103] An excellent critique of Bentham's assumption of *homo economicus* is provided by Titmuss's study of blood donors, which shows that the American and Japanese blood supply system, which rests on economic inducement, is economically and administratively inefficient, more costly and qualitatively less secure than the British one, where blood supplies rest on altruism.[104] Arguably, history has proven Bentham wrong also on his assumption of prosperity leading to equality: without some system of redistribution, property necessitates growing inequality rather than equality. These arguments made some scholars to propose the debatable idea that utility seemingly provides more an argument against property rights, than an argument for them.[105]

Similarly to Bentham, John Stuart Mill wrote about the right to the disposal of the producer, too, and defined property as "the right to the exclusive disposal."[106] He focused more on income and income distribution, and argued that public ownership and public redistribution

---

[100] Munzer, *op. cit.*, p. 195.

[101] Jeremy Bentham, *Principles of the Civil Code*, reprinted in part as "Security and Equality of Property" in C.B. Macpherson (ed.), *Property: Mainstream and Critical Positions*, Basil Blackwell, 1978, p. 41; quoted by Carter, *op. cit.*, p. 60.

[102] Carter, *op. cit.*, pp. 52–3.

[103] Bentham; quoted by Carter, *op. cit.*, p. 51.

[104] Richard M. Titmuss, *The Gift Relationship: From Human Blood to Social Policy*, George Allen and Unwin, 1970, pp. 245–6; quoted also by Carter, *op. cit.*, p. 57, n. 15.

[105] Carter, *op. cit.*, p. 60.

[106] John Stuart Mill, *The Principles of Political Economy*, 2nd ed., p. 267; quoted also by Engerer, *op. cit.*, p. 38.

of the "fruits of labor" would be the best solution.[107] As to land ownership, Mill held that as long as land is cultivated properly, and serves the common wealth, it should be protected. However, if it is not the case, than the individual farmer should appropriate only the fruits of his work.[108] From a theoretical perspective—even if the income theory is inconsistent with private ownership of land—it follows that the state has the prevalent role in safeguarding property. Prevalent, though not exclusive, as Mill professed that a slight uncertainty concerning property rights will contribute to progress, while extensive state regulation would induce the individual to sluggishness.[109] He recognized, therefore, three different ways of protecting property: undertaken privately, it will constitute a private good; provided by the state, it will become a public good; and thirdly, it can be guaranteed by norms of behavior (following Hume's argument).

* * *

Thus far, I have provided a brief insight on the property theories formulated mainly in the late Middle Ages—after Reformation—up to the great thinkers of the Enlightenment and the whirl in the field that followed them, almost till the end of the nineteenth century. My purpose here was to put the focus on Locke, respectively the changes in thinking that preceded, were caused by, or followed him. Adding to what Macpherson described as "possessive individualism" (the theories spanning from the early English philosophers up to Locke),[110] also its subsequent critique and refinement (Rousseau, Hume, the utilitarians), I drafted an account of the more-or-less pre-political concept of property that—as I will argue—characterizes most of the restitution schemes of post-socialist Central and Eastern Europe. Feldmann even speaks about the commitment to extensive privatization as emphasizing the "natural right to private property [which] gains recognition and the incentive quality of private property [that] becomes effective" in the

[107] *Ibid.*, 4th ed., p. 255; also in Engerer, *op. cit.*, p. 39.
[108] *Ibid.*, 2nd ed., p. 280; also in Engerer, *op. cit.*, p. 38.
[109] Engerer, *op. cit.*, pp. 39–40.
[110] Crawford B. Macpherson, *The Political Theory of Possessive Individualism: Hobbes to Locke*, Oxford, 1962; quoted by Engerer, *op. cit.*, p. 40.

transition countries.[111] And although Engerer doubts whether one may speak about a natural requirement for privatization, she agrees that "possessive individualism" represents the "philosophical background of the kind of market economy taken as model by Central and Eastern European countries."[112]

Through the following subchapters, the journey into the world of property theories will continue with the neoclassical theory (Demsetz, Buchanan, North), Nozick (derivation from liberty), and Rawls (derivation from justice). The second part of the chapter is dedicated thus to those theories which no decent background on the philosophy of property could afford to ignore.

2. Neoclassical theories

What scholars call the neoclassical theory of property is a product of contemporary times: it was born in the second half of the twentieth century, under the influence of the Coase Theorem, published in 1960. Until then, neoclassical theory did not dedicate much attention to the origins of property rights. Mainstream economics usually took the existing system for granted and neglected institutional arrangements: they acknowledged the structure of the existing *status quo* as a prerequisite for analysis.[113] By demonstrating that in the absence of transaction costs, the initial distribution of property rights has no influence on the efficiency of production and the resource allocations for production, Coase turned the attention to the origin of property rights.

Perhaps the most influential neoclassical theorist of property rights is Harold Demsetz, who was the first to take up the challenge within economic theory through his analysis of ownership among the American Indians living on the Labrador Peninsula.[114] Similar to the classical theories, Demsetz also departs from an initial communal ownership:

---

[111] Horst Feldmann, *Die Eigentumstheorien Lockes und Humes und ihre Lehren für den Aufbau privatwirtschaftlicher Eigentumsordnungen in den Transformationsländern*, Tübingen, 1993, p. 15; quoted by Engerer, *op. cit.*, p. 41.

[112] Engerer, *op. cit.*, pp. 40–1.

[113] Engerer, *op. cit.*, p. 48; Sened, *op. cit.*, p. 33.

[114] Harold Demsetz, "Toward a Theory of Property Rights," *American Economic Review* 57 (1967), pp. 347–59.

the Indians shared the (beaver) hunting grounds, and used them to satisfy their individual needs for food and fur. To translate this into economic theory language: the goods were either not scarce enough to be valuable, or—if valuable—the marginal benefits from individualizing property rights were not high enough to offset the costs of such an individualization.[115] This initial setting changed, however, with the apparition of foreign traders and the increase of demand for fur. As fur became suddenly more valuable, and thus an incentive was created for increased hunting (beyond the individual need), the common hunting ground was divided. Demsetz explains this stating that "property rights develop to internalize externalities when the gains of internalization become larger than the cost of internalization."[116] He identifies exclusively external factors (new technologies, or, as in the above example, opening of new markets) behind the changes in the costs–benefits relationship. Essentially, the argument is that private property emerges under the influence of some external factors, due to which the costs of individualizing and enforcing individual property appear lesser than the marginal value of the right to producers and buyers.[117]

Critiques of Demsetz emphasize that he merely describes the change of property rights within a functioning community.[118] Sened adds to this the failure to "distinguish between the performance of the economy and the political structure that allows it to perform."[119] For property rights cannot be exchanged without a well-defined structure that protects them. Buchanan is hinting in the same direction when he argues that the Indians already must have had mutually accepted rights before they could negotiate their change.[120] In this respect, Sened notes that Demsetz's theory appears, interestingly, in a sense, like an "ultimate theory of natural rights," for he assumes that private property naturally emerges when goods become valuable. However, while Locke

[115] Sened, *op. cit.*, p. 34, referring to Anderson and Hill, "The Evolution of Property Rights: A Study of the American West," *Journal of Law and Economics* 18.1 (1975), pp. 163–79.

[116] Demsetz, *op. cit.*.

[117] Sened, *op. cit.*, p. 34.

[118] Engerer, *op. cit.*, pp. 56–7; Sened, *op. cit.*, p. 35.

[119] Sened, *op. cit.*, p. 35.

[120] James M. Buchanan, *The Limits of Liberty: Between Anarchy and Leviathan*, Chicago and London, 1975, p. 23; quoted by Engerer, *op. cit.*, p. 57.

assigned to the government the role of the guardian of rights, Demsetz fails to identify the importance of governments in the emergence and maintenance of property rights.[121] Therefore, one might say that while in Locke property appears as a pre-political institution, in Demsetz it becomes a truly apolitical one.

Needless to say, the post-communist transition took (takes) place in a markedly different context. Here the transition does not happen from lack of property to private property, but from an existing communal to an individual conception of ownership. Obviously, the state plays the paramount role in transition; in this sense it is instructive to point to the Hungarian Constitutional Court's theoretical construct of the "rule of law revolution,"[122] and the perceived necessity to ensure legal continuity between the "ancient" and the "nouvelle" regimes. However, at the same time the state should not be imagined as an autonomous subject separated from society. The power struggles inherent in the process of the formation of the new post-communist elite has had its effects also upon the faith of private property rights. Offe and Bönker, for instance, speak critically about the "arbitrary interests, privileges, and resentments" behind official preoccupations for justice and market economy.[123] Another kind of pressure upon the state was exerted not by more or less organized interest groups, but by the communities of villagers, especially in Romania. Here, exploiting the vacuum of administrative authority and normative regulation, many agricultural collectives were literally and instantaneously taken to pieces, in a manner somewhat resembling Demsetz's example (but out of different reasons), thus when legislation was finally enacted, not much remained to (re)distribute besides land.

Buchanan's version for the emergence of private property departs from the idea of contract, which could also be met amongst the classical theories. Criticizing Demsetz, Buchanan argues that the emergence of rights cannot be explained "independently of contractual agreement, whether this be explicit or implicit."[124] His theory maintains that in a pre-political community, without laws and government (what the

[121] Sened, *op. cit.*, pp. 34–5.
[122] HCC, AB 11/1992.
[123] Offe and Bönker, *op. cit.*.
[124] Buchanan, *op. cit.*, p. 23; quoted by Engerer, *op. cit.*, p. 57.

classical theorists usually called state of nature) individuals tend to increase their stock of scarce resources. As they both recognize the mutual threat (of theft) they represent for each other's stock, they both attempt to prevent this from happening by adopting precautionary measures. Thus, Buchanan argues, a natural equilibrium is reached, which, in economic theory language means that the benefit of protection equals the marginal cost of the respective precautionary measures. But this is only the prelude to an agreement: soon, the individuals will realize—if deterrence is successful—that the efforts spent on prevention are wasted, the marginal costs will exceed the benefit conferred. At that moment they will become interested in negotiating a mutual reduction of the resources invested in protection. Buchanan believes that the individuals will eventually internalize the negative externalities (just like in Demsetz); that is, they will impose behavioral restrictions upon themselves, without the necessity of creating equality.[125] This comes close to Hume's theory of coordinate behavior as the source of property's stability. Buchanan calls this "the first leap out of the anarchistic jungle."[126] But the state, as a guarantor of this—implicit or explicit—agreement does not exist yet. The main difference from Hume consists in the "large number dilemma": if the above-described model works perfectly for two, or a small number of persons, as the group grows, at a certain point the individual will lose sight of the connection between his and the others' behavior.[127] This situation, argues Buchanan, could lead to an overall agreement on an authority which will enforce the

[125] Engerer, *op. cit.*, p. 58.

[126] Buchanan, *op. cit.*, p. 59; quoted by Engerer, *op. cit.*, p. 59.

[127] Vanberg (quoted by Engerer, *op. cit.*, p. 60, n. 27) argues that there are two reasons why the individual will become tempted to breach the equilibrium: first, he assumes that as the group gets larger, his breach will not be sanctioned; second, he assumes that his behavior has no decisive influence on the social order. A more accurate explanation—at least for the first argument—is offered by Becker, who pointed out that increasing the probability of capture and punishment is the strongest deterrent for potential law-breakers (Becker, "Crime and Punishment: An Economic Approach," *Journal of Political Economy* 69 [1968], pp. 169–217). A similar conclusion is reached by Dnes, especially in the case of property crimes, where it appears that individuals engage in crime as a rational activity (Dnes, *The Economics of Law: Property, Contracts, and Obligations*, International Thomson Business Press, c2005, Chapter 7, "The Economics of Crime").

observance of the original contract.[128] The individual's advantage, of course, will be that everyone shall observe the law, and thus his property is respected (or, at least, he might expect reparations in case of breaches). For this, however, he will have to support a dual tax: the costs of the security of rights (which is expected to be less than the costs of private enforcement), plus a "freedom tax"[129] (consisting in the restrictions on his own actions). Buchanan considers that a Hobbesian state can be avoided by the self-commitment of the government to the rule of law.[130]

Interestingly, in a restitution context Buchanan's theory is partly confirmed and partly infirmed by reality. Remaining at the above-presented example of the Romanian agricultural collectives, the fact that in a vacuum of law and authority (which by no means qualified as a pre-political setting) individuals indeed attempted to increase their relatively scarce resources by appropriating assets from the collective goods, is in line with Buchanan's observations. However, this did not lead to a collective agreement upon an authority that would enforce the original *status quo*. Quite the opposite, the 2005 revision of the restitution scheme stipulated that those administrative decisions regarding the restitution of properties that were issued illegally are nullified, and property titles issued on their bases are revocable, unless legally transferred to third parties.[131] The Constitutional Court upheld this solution, arguing that the enforcement of rights obtained through ill will or by the abusive actions of the organs of public administration is not compatible with the constitutional guarantee of rights and liberties.[132]

In his critique of neoclassical economics, Sened argues that Buchanan is mistakenly assuming that his model of natural equilibrium works even on a small scale. According to Sened, it is unlikely that without an existing enforcement mechanism the players in a prisoner's dilemma game would prefer the optimal strategy combination: that is,

---

[128] I will leave aside the question of how this "constitutional" agreement can be reached, as it does not bear crucial importance for the purposes of my investigation.

[129] Buchanan, *op. cit.*, p. 112; quoted by Engerer, *op. cit.*, p. 63.

[130] *Ibid.*, p. 164; quoted by Engerer, *op. cit.*, p. 64.

[131] Law No. 247/2005, *Official Gazette*, No. 955, 27 October 2005.

[132] RCC, Decision No. 375 of 2005, published in the *Official Gazette*, No. 591, 8 July 2005, paras. 51–2.

they would cooperate and respect the right of the other player.[133] Furthermore, goes the reasoning, precisely the property rights' institutions are those who secure the binding character of private agreements, thus cooperative game theory, which presumes the pre-existence of such mechanisms, cannot explain the origin of property rights' institutions.

Douglass North maintains that property rights are "the rights individuals appropriate over their own labor and the goods and services they process."[134] "[A]s a first approximation"—adds North—"we can say that property rights will be developed [...] as a simple cost-benefit calculus of the cost of devising and enforcing such rights."[135] However, there are two different means of enforcement of property rights: informal (behavioral) and formal (normative and contractual) rules. North believes that the former characterizes relationships within small communities, and the development of trade[136] from small business to trading with large anonymous groups was the reason for the emergence of the state, and of the increasingly formal rules.[137] Albeit formal rules did not completely take over, and a mixture of the two exists, which cannot be readily explained through a cost-benefit calculation. Ultimately, North recognized that in the real world transaction costs are not zero, but positive, therefore bargaining power has a determinant role. The upshot of this consists in the fact that institutions (rules)[138] are not created to be socially efficient, but to serve the interests of those who have bargaining power.[139]

Thus, North, within the framework of transaction costs' theory, recognized the importance of political structures, though without for-

[133] Sened, *op. cit.*, pp. 40–3. He quotes Taylor (*The Possibility of Cooperation*, Cambridge University Press, 1987, p. 15), who argues that "[t]he prisoner's dilemma is defined to be non-cooperative. If it were not, there would be no 'dilemma'."

[134] Douglass C. North, *Institutions, Institutional Change and Economic Performance*, Cambridge University Press, 1990, p. 33; quoted by Engerer, *op. cit.*, p. 67.

[135] North, *op. cit.*, p. 51; quoted by Sened, *op. cit.*, p. 45.

[136] Just like Buchanan, North also assigns major importance to technological progress and trade.

[137] Engerer, *op. cit.*, p. 67.

[138] North mostly uses the terms "institution" and "rule" as synonyms.

[139] Engerer, *op. cit.*, p. 67.

mulating a theory of the state.[140] The rather disturbing meaning of this is that no guarantee can be provided for the establishment of a generally applicable and efficient system of ownership protection. An even bleaker vision is painted by Riker, who maintains that modern constitutions allow for individual preferences to play a role in institutional choice, and this leads to short-term, inefficient institutional arrangements, that easily fall pray to the inherent instability of human preferences over institutional outcomes.[141]

As it unfolds from the above discussed arguments, neoclassical theories of property did not come close enough to explaining the emergence of property rights. It is worth remembering Engerer's idea, mentioned in the introductory part of this chapter, according to which Western legal scholarship was concerned more with the functional aspect of property rights, as in the established democracies the existence of private ownership and the separation of private and public sectors is seen as a basic fact that requires no justification. This shortcoming is identified by Sened on one hand in the tendency to disregard structure in favor of performance,[142] and on the other hand in the failure to address the role of political actors.[143]

Apart from these theoretical objections, it is worth considering the experimental findings neatly summarized by Ulen, which show significant variations of human behavior relative to the presumptions of the Coase Theorem. For instance, experiments demonstrated that humans have a much stronger sense of what is equitable than what the rational choice theory predicts. Moreover, voluntary exchange may achieve efficient allocation in a broader range of circumstances than those of zero transaction costs.[144]

---

140 Sened, *op. cit.*, p. 47.

141 William H. Riker, "Implications from the Disequilibrium of Majority Rule for the Study of Institutions," *American Political Science Review* 74 (1980), pp. 432–6; quoted by Sened, *op. cit.*, p. 46.

142 Sened, *op. cit.*, p. 48, quoting also North (*Structure and Change in Economic History*, New York, 1981).

143 *Ibid.*, quoting Demsetz (*Economic, Legal, and Political Dimensions of Competition*, North-Holland, 1982).

144 Thomas S. Ulen, *Rational Choice Theory in Law and Economics*, 1999, pp. 790–818.

3. Nozick's theory of entitlement

If the aim of this book would be—if such a categorization could further the interests of knowledge—to stuff the existing multitude of property rights theories into conceptual boxes, which fortunately is not the case, Nozick could prove a hard nut to crack. For his theory, while it attempts to justify property from a libertarian point of view, represents at the same time a revised labor theory. In the seminal work, *Anarchy, State and Utopia*, Nozick develops his central thesis relating to property, according to which any attempt to artificially alter the existing *status quo* of justly acquired property rights (i.e., redistribution) upon egalitarian considerations will result in unacceptable restrictions on individual freedom.[145]

The concern of altering a *status quo* grounded on a—at least sometimes—legitimate appropriation was massively present in post-communist restitution contexts, although the arguments were seldom drawing on freedom, focusing rather on justice.[146] As it was already mentioned above, although the 2005 amendments to the Romanian restitution scheme provided for the annulment of the illegally obtained property titles, they maintained the validity of those which have already entered the civil circuit.[147] As a more detailed analysis will present later on, even the European Court of Human Rights demonstrated sensitivity towards this problem. It upheld restitution of property that was appropriated after confiscation in ways incompatible with the rules of the time, and it also upheld expropriation when property was appropriated illegally under the previous regime, even if afterwards the title was lawfully registered.[148]

---

[145] Robert Nozick, *Anarchy, State and Utopia*, New York: Basic Books, 1974.

[146] Hayashi Tadayuki, "Politics of the Agricultural Transformation in Czechoslovakia: 1990–1991," available online, at http://src-home.slav.hokudai.ac.jp/kaken/ieda2001/pdf/hayashi.pdf, p. 30; William R. Youngblood, "Poland's struggle for a restitution policy in the 1990s," *Emory International Law Review* (Fall 1995), p. 652.

[147] Law No. 247/2005, *op. cit.*.

[148] Pincová and Pinc v. The Czech Republic, ECHR, Application No. 36548/97, Judgment of 5 November 2002; Jahn and Others v. Germany, ECHR, Application nos. 46720/99, 72203/01, and 72552/01, Grand Chamber Judgment of 30 June 2005.

The problem with the original labor theory was that it ignored the question of scarcity: however, empirical reality has demonstrated beyond any doubt that while some resources are indeed—theoretically—unlimited (such as sunlight or radio frequencies), others are becoming scarcer and scarcer (land, oil, unpolluted air, etc.). Locke shook off this dilemma by stating that appropriation through labor is just, until there is "enough, and as good left in common for others."[149] Obviously, this cannot be a satisfactory solution anymore. Nozick, a "neo-Lockean,"[150] recognized the weakness of this theory: as most goods are scarce, there will come the point where no more appropriation would be possible if the Lockean imperative is to be preserved. The problem is that all those who managed to appropriate goods while there was "enough, and as good" left for the others, worsened the positions of every subsequent acquirer, plus of those who were barred from acquiring[151] any of the goods previously available for everyone. Thus, Locke's *proviso* is impossible to satisfy.[152] One needs not to presume that appropriation is taking place as a linear event; necessarily though, there can be distinguished different moments of appropriation along a time continuum. Therefore, any combination of prior appropriations could bar at a certain point the possibility of later acquisitions. Nozick came up with two solutions for amending Locke.

First, he suggested that prior acquisitions breach the imperative only if the later acquirers are barred from using what they previously could have. There are two problems with this: on the one hand, use is equated to a certain extent with ownership, which is not a valid proposal—one could perhaps remember the trinity of *utendi fruendi et abutendi*—; use is merely a stick in the conventional concept of property as a bundle. On the other hand, following also from the previous explanation, the "latecomers" would be similarly worse off as in the case of the original *proviso*, as ownership is a far more powerful and complete right than bare use. Munzer calls this solution "too anemic" to sub-

149 Locke, *op. cit.*, § 24.

150 Carter, *op. cit.*, p. 44.

151 "Appropriating" and "acquiring" are used in this section as synonyms, both designating the process through which goods that previously formed the object of common ownership become individually owned.

152 Munzer, *op. cit.*, pp. 269–70.

stantially improve Locke.[153] Nozick's second suggestion is to consider appropriations just until "the positions of others no longer at liberty to use the thing are thereby worsened."[154] Munzer considers this proposition "more plausible."[155]

To restate then Nozick's theory of entitlement: egalitarian (re)distribution of justly acquired property is wrong because it inadmissibly curtails individual freedom. Private property is acquired justly when it does not leave worse off those without the possibility of using them anymore. According to Munzer's critique, this theory fails to demonstrate that it is not worse than other property rights arrangements. In his turn, Carter takes a different line of attack against Nozick, which requires a brief explanation of the latter's critique of distributive justice.

Nozick divides theories of distributive justice into patterned and unpatterned—historical and unhistorical, respectively.[156] In patterned theories, some factor (or group of factors) determines the quantity of goods which the individual receives. For example, the 1856 Romanian land reform proposed to distribute secularized church land between liberated serfs in proportion with their households' working potential: thus, justice would have been satisfied if those with the most oxen and male children in the household could have received the most land. Unhistorical, non-patterned theories are based on "time-slice" or "end-result" principles. For instance, in the case of most post-communist restitution schemes, a citizenship clause was included, barring those who lost their former citizenship in the meantime from claiming their lands. A similar principle could arguably be detected also in the equally widespread limitations on the maximum amount of restorable property.[157] Equally representative are the cut-off dates (the points in time

---

153 *Ibid.*, p. 270.

154 Nozick, *op. cit.*, p. 178.

155 Munzer, *op. cit.*, pp. 271–80, argues that an acceptable property rights system need not be the best conceivable solution, but at least it must be established that it is not markedly inferior to other possible arrangements.

156 See also: Carter, *op. cit.*, pp. 40–1.

157 One might recall the quote in the Introduction from a former Romanian prime minister, who was speaking about the goal of "preserving [...] the authentic national spirit," instead of the individual claimants' relevant dimensions and the benefits which would flow to them.

until which the restitution norms reached back), or the various goals attached (beyond justice) to the programs.[158] As Nozick noted, one would hardly be satisfied if penal sanctions would be distributed in a similar manner: what is important for justice is not how many are in prison and how many are free, but that criminals are incarcerated while innocents stay free.[159] He includes the two (otherwise considered as prevailing) models in the concept of "redistributive theories of justice," as it is conceivable to happen that the end-result does not presently exist or that individuals do not own goods according to the relevant factor, and thus a redistribution must take place. This redistribution, however, interferes with individual freedom.

The example used to demonstrate how this interference actually works refers to a group of basketball fans who are willing to pay a certain amount of money to their favorite star for watching him play. Another example, more controversial and more actual in Central and Eastern Europe, could be the case of a patient who is willing to pay a certain amount of money to her doctor as a demonstration of gratitude. Nozick would argue in this latter case—just as he did in his own example—that it is unjust to prevent the patient (and similarly the fans) from giving the money to the doctor (or the star player). The doctor (player) would acquire the money in a just way—through the will and consent of those who gave it to him: thus, the freedom to present the loved (admired) ones is infringed by the patterned, or end-result theories of justice. As Carter notices, this critique is not based directly on property: rather, it emphasizes respect for individual liberty.[160] According to his own words, Nozick's "entitlement theory of justice in distribution is historical; whether a distribution is just depends upon how it came about."[161] This view could fit perfectly in the post-communist restitution schemes. The distribution effected during communist rule—politically motivated, aimed at the eradication of private property,[162] discrimination, or stigmatization of certain groups; or simply illegal (without any legal basis) or unconstitutional

[158] A detailed discussion of these will follow in the subsequent chapters.
[159] Carter, *op. cit.*, p. 40.
[160] *Ibid.*, p. 41.
[161] Nozick, *op. cit.*, p. 153.
[162] HCC, AB 27/1991, 91/E/1990.

(failure to provide the required compensation upon taking)—could hardly be perceived as just. Arguably, following this line of thought, redistribution of property appears as the objective necessity of undoing past injustice.

There are—at least—two lines of attack against Nozick's theory: first, against the liberties arguably infringed by redistributive theories; second, against the presumption holding that that which was justly acquired is justly owned, too. As to the first critique, it is worth noting Scanlon's argument.[163] He emphasized that the liberties involved in the basketball example—the liberty of the fans to pay extra for watching their star play, the player's liberty to decide whether to play or not for this fee, and subsequently, if yes, then to keep the money, and the liberty of his heirs to keep any amount of this money he wished to pass on to them—are not absolute. The second critique voiced by Carter links property with (political) power, maintaining that the power of the wealthy (mighty) to interfere with the freedom of the lesser is bought at the price of their freedom from interference. Property creates the power to restrict others, thus to limit other's freedom.[164] "[T]here must be more binding moral commitments than justice" argues Carter, and drafts a bleak picture not of one, but of two star players (presidents) sponsored freely by their fans to arm themselves up to their teeth with nuclear weapons, threatening to destroy—out of fear—each other and the entire planet.[165]

Taking them all together, the critics of Nozick can come up with two strong points: first, he fails to come out of the labor theory's scarcity dilemma. Second, he does not give sufficient arguments to show why his "entitlement theory" of strong individual ownership is better (or at least not worst) than other property rights arrangements.

[163] Thomas Scanlon, "Rights, Liberty and Property," in Jeffrey Paul (ed.), *Reading Nozick: Essays on Anarchy, State, and Utopia*, Basil Blackwell, 1981, pp. 110–1; also quoted by Carter, *op. cit.*, p. 41–2.

[164] Carter, *op. cit.*, p. 46.

[165] *Ibid.*, p. 43.

4. Derivation from justice: John Rawls's theory

Rawls is held to be one of the most influential scholars of the twentieth century, and his main work, *A Theory of Justice*,[166] is often seen both as a non-utilitarian and as a Kantian account.[167] He envisaged a moral community of mutual aid,[168] according to his own words "[i]n justice as fairness society is interpreted as a co-operative venture for mutual advantage."[169] In a quest for the principles of a "well-ordered" society—an idea that can be traced back to Plato's *Republic*—grounded on "fairness," Rawls proposed to change or to abolish all laws and institutions, no matter how efficient, if they are unjust.[170] Although he does not delineate an explicit theory of property, some basic ideas on property—that fit within his concept of justice—can be distinguished.[171]

In the Rawlsian model, justice is understood as a set of freely chosen principles guiding social arrangements. These principles are those that would have been chosen by rational, self-interested parties in the "original position," from behind "the veil of ignorance" (i.e., deprived from knowledge of their own desires, talents, status, and their country's level of development).[172] The veil bars them from subjecting the chosen principles to their own interests. This, however, entails that the parties behind the veil have no individual conception of the goods. To enable them to make a choice under these conditions, Rawls introduced the notion of "primary goods"—the things every rational person wants—a kind of baseline of human condition (rights and liberties, powers, opportunities, income and wealth, self-respect).[173] From behind the veil, thus, the parties have to chose those principles that govern the distribution of the primary goods.

According to Rawls, they will come up with the following two: 1) each person shall have an equal right to the most extensive total system

[166] John Rawls, *A Theory of Justice*, Harvard University Press, 1971.
[167] Munzer, *op. cit.*, p. 233.
[168] Carter, *op. cit.*, p. 58.
[169] Rawls, *op. cit.*, p. 84.
[170] *Ibid.*, p. 3.
[171] Munzer, *op. cit.*, p. 233.
[172] *Ibid.*.
[173] *Ibid.*, p. 234.

of equal basic liberties compatible with a similar system of liberty for all; 2) social and economical inequalities shall be arranged so that on one hand the greatest benefit is preserved for the least well-off (difference-principle), while on the other hand they are attached to offices and positions open to all under conditions of fair equality of opportunity.[174] Rawls also attaches priority rules to the two principles: liberty can be restricted only for the sake of another liberty, while equality of opportunity takes priority over the difference principle. The basic principles of justice so selected will be subsequently elaborated and implemented in later legislative and administrative stages.[175]

Property fits under both principles. Rawls does not make it particularly clear what he means by private property; he merely enounces that the first principle covers "some" kind of property, while the difference principle governs "other" kinds of property. Albeit, in a later article, he made it clear that the right to own certain kinds of property (as for example means of production) is not a basic one.[176] Further, as Munzer emphasized, it is not clear whether he believed that people have an equal right to property or that they have an equal amount of it. However, the first reading seems more plausible.[177] Turning back though to rights under the first principle, one may learn that this principle applies to "basic liberties," which include freedom of the person along with the right to hold personal property.[178] "Citizens of a just society"—argues Rawls—"are to have the same basic rights."[179] By contrast, the difference principle permits inequality of rights, but only to the extent to which unequal holdings maximally benefit the least well-off. However, property is only one factor among many others influencing social and economical position: hence, it should be distributed equally (unless inequality could maximally benefit the least advantaged). According to Munzer, the difference principle distributes—generally—life-time expectations with respect to social and economic advantages and the material bases of self-respect.[180] Later on, Rawls revised the difference

[174] Rawls, *op. cit.*, p. 302.
[175] Munzer, *op. cit.*, p. 233–4.
[176] *Ibid.*.
[177] Munzer, *op. cit.*, p. 235.
[178] Rawls, *op. cit.*, p. 61.
[179] *Ibid.*.
[180] Munzer, *op. cit.*, p. 236.

principle, assigning a more qualified, background role to it, with a less determinate effect on distribution (it holds for income and property taxation and fiscal and economical policy, but it does not apply for example to particular transactions).[181]

Rawls's theory received numerous critiques. On the property side, it was said that the scope of "personal property" is not defined; moreover, it is unclear, how property—as a basic liberty—is protected.[182] What Rawls says is only that it may not be restricted, only for the sake of another basic liberty, nothing else. Munzer considers this as being too rigid, arguing that conflicts between basic liberties often cannot be solved solely in terms of the extent (amount) of liberty.[183] Hart voiced his doubts to the validity of the holding that property under the first principle has always priority over rights under the second principle.[184] Daniels emphasized that if the difference principle allows for inequality, it will conflict with social stability; it will erode the effectiveness of civil and political rights and will undermine the equality of basic liberties.[185]

All this has made scholars claim that Rawls's theory "cannot treat satisfactorily the issue of distributive equity in property holdings,"[186] or, more critically, that "it ignores psychological, political, and economical realities, as well as the record of history and the findings of anthropology."[187] In the same line of argumentation, Sened refers to scholars arguing that Rawls's principles are inconsistent with intuitive notions of justice.[188] He also draws attention to the results of the

---

[181] John Rawls, "A Kantian Conception of Equality," in Virginia Held (ed.), *Property, Profits, and Economic Justice*, Wandsworth, 1980, p. 205; quoted by Munzer, *op. cit.*, p. 237.

[182] Munzer, *op. cit.*, pp. 237–8.

[183] *Ibid.*, p. 238.

[184] H.L. Harts, "Rawls on Liberty and Its Priority," in Norman Daniels (ed.), *Reading Rawls*, Basil Blackwell, 1975, pp. 230–52; quoted by Munzer, *op. cit.*, p. 238.

[185] Norman Daniels, "Equal Liberty and Unequal Worth of Liberty," in Daniels, *op. cit.*, pp. 253–81; quoted by Munzer, *op. cit.*.

[186] Munzer, *op. cit.*, p. 241.

[187] Pipes, *op. cit.*, p. 60, who even calls Rawls's work a "utopian treatise."

[188] Sened, *op. cit.*, p. 12, referring also to Partha Dasgupta, "On Some Problems Arising from Professor Rawls' Conception of Distributive Justice," *Theory and Decision* 4 (1974), pp. 325–44; Amartya K. Sen, "Rawls Versus Bentham," *Theory and Decision* 4 (1974), pp. 301–10; and *On Ethics and Economics*, Basil Blackwell, 1986.

experiments conducted by Frohlich *et al.*,[189] according to which "veil of ignorance" situations were modeled where the subjects did opt for Rawls's principles at an extremely low rate. This makes Sened state that Rawls's theory of justice is founded on "unwarranted, positive assertions about how humans act under given conditions."[190]

5. Practical applications

After briefly discussing the most significant theories of property in the history of thought, and signaling their connections with post-communist property reform practices, this subchapter is dedicated to a more collected description of the restitution schemes. It proposes to identify in the analyzed jurisdictions the governing theories and their materialization in the various phases of the programs.

5.1 The Lockean perception

As it has been already mentioned in the previous subchapters, in most of the studied cases, the schemes depart from a Lockean, pre-political view of property, which can readily explain why the dismantling of the state's wealth has to be done along pre-totalitarian baselines. This argument is upheld also by the formulations used: "restoration" or "renewal" of ownership rights.[191] The Lithuanian Constitutional Court went as far as literally stating that the right to property is "one of the most significant human natural rights."[192]

However, none of the governments managed to remain consequently, until the end, on the Lockean path. For a natural right view of property would demand complete restitution of all wrongfully taken goods, whereas such an attempt could have (arguably) created in-

[189] Norman Frochlich, Joe A. Oppenheimer, and Cheryl L. Eavey, "Choices of Principles of Distributive Justice in Experimental Groups," *American Journal of Political Science* 31 (1987), pp. 606–36; and "Laboratory Results on Rawls' Distributive Justice," *British Journal of Political Science* 17 (1987), pp. 1–21.

[190] Sened, *op. cit.*, p. 12.

[191] See: *supra*.

[192] LiCC, Ruling of 27 May 1994, *supra*.

surmountable social and financial barriers for the state. In the case of Lithuania, the Constitutional Court made it clear that "restoration" meant partial reparation.[193] "Partial" in this case had a rather radical meaning, as the scheme provided only for the "restoration of ownership rights" over immovable properties. The Hungarian Compensation Law itself speaks about partial reparation. The Constitutional Court made it clear that such a wording results from the legislator's intent to afford redress out of a moral rather than a legal obligation, having in mind the nation's economic possibilities, as well as a series of other considerations, too.[194] As already mentioned above, the revised Romanian scheme introduced the concept of full restitution (*restitutio in integrum*) in 2005, albeit it maintained the bulk of the previous restitution regulations which contained a number of clauses that ultimately limit restitution and lead to outcomes that fall far from being "complete."

Further examples could be mentioned to enumerate all the various conditions and limitations imposed by the reparation schemes—all of them to be discussed in detail in the following chapters of this book—, which essentially amount to a partial redress, as opposed to integral restitution.

5.2 A Hobbesian premise

The post-communist reapportionment of property, however, did take place neither in a state of nature, nor under a veil, but on the ruins of authoritarianism.[195] What was left of it—from a property perspective—was a Hobbesian, or perhaps Rousseauian state, as the (almost) exclusive owner that had to carry out extensive reform programs. Nevertheless, unlike in Hobbes or Rousseau, the legitimacy of the state's ownership was seriously disputed.

---

[193] LiCC, Ruling of 15 June 1994, "On the restoration of citizens' ownership rights to residential houses," and Ruling of 19 October 1994, "On the restoration of ownership rights to residential houses"; *infra* Chapter 2, Section 5.1 and Chapter 3, Section 2.2.

[194] HCC, AB 28/1991, 1160/A/1991, part I/A, para. 2.

[195] There was of course the above-described isolated example of the clandestine dismantling of some Romanian agricultural collective's movables (and sometimes buildings and other constructions); still, it was very far from constituting anything but a mere exception.

In the Baltic States, the blame for the transfer of private property in state hands was put on the Soviet occupation. The Lithuanian Constitutional Court held that property taken during the Soviet regime—in violation of the 1938 Constitution of Lithuania and of the "human natural right to private ownership"—can only be considered as having been "factually managed" by the state.[196] In former Czechoslovakia, the Constitutional Court adopted the astonishing "lawlessness of communism" decision, by which it announced that the communist regime cannot be regarded as a *Rechtsstaat*, and that the legal certainty of perpetrators may not be preferred to those of the victims.[197] The Romanian Constitutional Court also came to the conclusion that properties transferred to the state through unlawful means cannot be regarded as being passed into state ownership.[198] Finally, the Hungarian Constitutional Court managed to declare certain nationalization decrees unconstitutional for targeting the effective eradication of private property.[199]

In spite of this, instead of a "full restitution," which could have resulted logically from the two premises (Lockean view of property and unlawful/unconstitutional taking), the lawmakers and the courts ended up talking about the states' sovereign decision as to the extent and conditions of the redress. Thus, the Lithuanian Court insisted that the Supreme Council had the "unquestionable" right to choose a variant of the solution, and that the choice "was [...] predetermined by hard political and social conditions of that period"; therefore, it constitutes a "compromise solution."[200] In Hungary, the Constitutional Court did not find any obligation of the state to compensate former owners, victims of the unconstitutional takings. On the contrary, it emphasized that the partial compensation scheme put forward by the government

---

[196] LiCC, Ruling of 27 May 1994, "On the restoration of citizens' ownership rights to land."

[197] Decision quoted and commented by Radoslav Procházka, *Mission Accomplished: On Founding Constitutional Adjudication in Central Europe*, CEU Press, 2002, pp. 145–7.

[198] RCC, Decision No. 73 of 19 July 1995, published in the *Official Gazette*, No. 177, 8 August 1995; see also: *infra*, Chapter 2, Section 6.1.2.

[199] HCC, AB 27/1991, 91/E/1990, *infra*, Chapter 2, Section 6.1.2.

[200] LiCC, Ruling of 20 June 1995, "On the compliance of Article 2 of the Law of the Republic of Lithuania 'On the Procedure and Conditions of the Restoration of the Rights of Ownership to the Existing Real Property' with the Constitution of the Republic of Lithuania."

was an exclusive function of the state's sovereign will, based solely on its gratitude.[201]

5.3 Neoclassical cynicism

As it has already been explained above, Douglas North recognized the role bargaining power plays in the creation of institutions. According to this theory, in settings where transaction costs are above zero, rules are created to serve the interests of the players with the strongest bargaining positions. From what was argued under the previous point, it is also clear that decisions regarding the reparation schemes reflect political compromises, and according to North's theory, the strongest groups manage to make most out of these compromises on the expense of the weaker parties.

This observation gives an explanation as to why the group of former property owners enjoyed a privileged status among the victims of the past regimes.[202] The same argument applies in an indigenous claims context, too. Here, if one compares the relative success of American Indian, Aborigine, and Maori restitution claims, one will find that the New Zealand program was the most successful among them. One possible explanation is represented by the fact that the different proportion of the indigenous peoples in the population translates to different degrees of leverage. The Maoris count for approximately 13% of New Zealand's population, while the Native Americans or the Aborigines represent a much smaller minority.[203]

Moreover, it may constitute an explanation also for the various distinctions[204] induced (in spite of slogans of equality and justice) by the reparation norms within the pool of victims, through which—as it will be argued in the following chapters—winners and losers of restitution have been created.

---

[201] HCC, AB 21/1990, 1057/G/1990, part IV.

[202] See: Sajó, *op. cit.*.

[203] Elazar Barkan, *The Guilt of Nations: Restitution and Negotiating Historical Injustices*, Norton, 2000, p. 167.

[204] Between citizens/residents and non-citizens/residents, between members of the ethnical majority and members of various ethnical minorities, between various churches, between various types and categories of properties, etc..

This rather cynical view of property reparations may find fuel for example in the inability of the Polish legislature to come up with a comprehensive scheme,[205] as arguably no group can manage to impose its will upon the others, or in the rather frequent modifications of the Romanian program, which mostly occurred around the changes of government.[206]

5.4 Utilitarian aspects

A less cynical view of the post-communist property reparation schemes may resort to utilitarian explanations for the problems that were signaled in the previous paragraphs and which are discussed in detail in the following chapters. Namely, departing from the other goals attached to property reform—foremost the creation of the premises of market economy—it can be argued that the limitations imposed upon reparations were made in order to obtain the greatest benefit for the greatest number, with the consequence of excluding certain groups from the benefits of the program. This line of argument can be employed for justifying for example exclusion of non-citizens/residents or certain categories of properties from restitution.

An uncommon example from the post-communist restitution schemes is illustrative of this point. In Lithuania, the restitution law[207] stipulated that agricultural lands are returned (within certain limits) only if the beneficiaries are engaged in the tilling of land, or are returning to engage in farming. Albeit if the old-new owners do not begin to use the land according to its specific purpose within one year from its restitution, the respective plots are to be confiscated (with payment of compensation).[208]

The Hungarian Constitutional Court also employed a language which to a certain extent can be perceived as utilitarian, while explaining the limited character of compensations. The Court resorted to the general justifications presented by the authors of the Compensation

[205] On the Polish struggle for a restitution scheme, see: *infra*, Chapter 2, section 5.2.

[206] On the Romanian restitution scheme, see: *infra*, Chapter 2, section 5.4.

[207] Law "On procedures and conditions for the restoration of citizen's rights to the ownership of extant property," 18 June 1991.

[208] *Ibid.*, Art. 4.

Bill, who found reasons for a partial compensation—as already mentioned above—in the nation's limited financial possibilities, as well as in the fact that other types of material grievances have no chance for compensation. At the same time, the Court emphasized that compensations are merely a part of a longer process which involves the settling of property relations.[209]

Utilitarian justifications, however, are not able to explain a whole number of situations, in which the sacrificing of the "losers of restitution" did not bring any palpable advantage for the larger number of "winners."[210]

5.5 Rawls challenged

Taking it all together, Rawls's interpretation of property does give little support to the post-communist restitution attempts. Arguably, the Hungarian scheme was the one that came closest to Rawlsian ideals, in the sense that instead of restitution it preferred an original distribution of property (although the receivable amount was the function of past holdings), on the basis of vouchers usable during privatization. This way, both equal rights to own property, as well as an equal opportunity to appropriate (through participation in the privatization process) was theoretically created. Mihályi, whose work is referred in the subsequent chapters where the Hungarian scheme is discussed in detail, extensively presents the practical drawbacks of the voucher system.[211]

There are also other aspects of property reparations which can be explained from a Rawlsian perspective, such as the quantitative limitation imposed upon returnable property. According to Rawls's difference principle, inequality is permissible as long as it maximally benefits the least well off.[212] In the case of limited restitution of land for example, those former owners who had smaller plots may in certain situations obtain full restitution of the lost property, while owners of larger plots can receive only a fraction of their once lost lands. However,

209 HCC, AB 28/1991, 1160/A/1991, part I/A, paras. 2.1 and 3.

210 For example, it is unclear how the exclusion of non-citizens/residents does contribute to a more perfect social equality, or to a better development of market economy.

211 Péter Mihályi, *A kárpótlás*, Állami Privatizációs és Vagyonkezelő Rt., 1998.

212 Rawls, *op. cit.*, *supra*.

this theory could stand only if the presumption that (former) owners of larger estates are (still) better off than (former) small owners could be proven true.[213]

Finally, if the right to property is considered under Rawls's first principle, under which restrictions are possible only for the sake of another liberty, the various conditions attached to restitution by the reparation schemes are clearly challenging his conception of justice.[214]

6. Conclusions

There is quite a span from Thomas Aquinas to John Rawls, and this chapter could only highlight some of the multitude of property theories conceived of during the centuries that separate them. Albeit it was merely background drafting, what I proposed to achieve through these pages was to identify and point to the most significant and influential property theories, instead of offering a complete and detailed recapitulation of their history. Every scholar is, in a certain sense, the prisoner of his or her own epoch. The problems that demand resolution, their significance, the amount of knowledge assembled before and/or which are available are all functions of the times. This is also reflected in the gradual shift in the perceived dilemmas of property rights. One could identify with relative ease two major problems pertaining to property: justification (emergence) and operation (functionality). I believe that it could be safely argued that at the beginning of modernity, when the emerging middle class awoke to self-consciousness, its quest for social affirmation (power and wealth) made the question of justification more stringent. Classical theorists of property rights were all deeply concerned with the discovering of how the rights to private property emerged. They found answers in first occupancy, labor and desert, or free will. However, as property rights became more and more settled after the age of revolutions, the focus of property theory gradually shifted—already from the utilitarians—towards the second problem: func-

[213] However, more often than not, this might not be the case as those considered to be members of the former elite were systematically persecuted and subjected to unfavorable treatments by the communist authorities.

[214] For example, bans on transfer for a determined period or obligation to cultivate the land.

tionality. Contemporary theories are almost exclusively interested in how property rights function in society: they take the existence of ownership as granted. It is worth also recalling Engerer's argument, quoted in the introductory passages of this chapter, which calls attention to the fact that while contemporary Western legal theory emphasizes the functional aspect of property, the post-communist justifications for (re)distribution reach back almost to the beginnings and search for the theoretical foundations of ownership.

However, this shift of attention from emergence to functionality is not merely due to external evolutions. Within legal theory and philosophy, a certain skepticism can be detected towards the possibility of justifying private property. Carter, for instance, bluntly states that there is not and there never will be a valid derivation of individual rights to property from first principles.[215] He considers property to be a relationship between persons[216]—in contrast with a relationship to things, a conclusion to which individual liberalism is considered to lead[217]—a complexity characterized by claim right–duty, privilege–no right, power–liability, and immunity–disability dualities.[218] Contradicting Carter to a certain extent, Munzer identifies three main principles and their combinations as the justification of property: utility and efficiency, justice and equality, and desert based on labor.[219] Utility and efficiency means that property rights should be allocated so as to maximize utility and efficiency related to use, possession, transfer, etc., of things. In this reading, concerns about the social effects of property restitution (creation of the preconditions of market economy, stability of possessions, etc.) appear justified. Justice and equality conveys that unequal holdings are justifiable if everyone has a minimum amount of property and the inequalities do not undermine a fully human life in society.[220] This concern is at least partly reflected in the post-communist restitution context by the fear from causing new injustices and most importantly by the considerations that were at least rhetorically given to society's

[215] Carter, *op. cit.*, p. 126.

[216] Thus, he takes exclusion to be property rights' essential feature.

[217] According to him, since Hobbes most individualists perceive society as a mere sum of isolated individuals.

[218] Carter, *op. cit.*, pp. 127–9.

[219] Munzer, *op. cit.*, p. 3.

[220] The problem with these qualifications is that they are extremely vague.

financial capacities and sense of justice.[221] Finally, desert through labor would emphasize the differences in merit between persons, while the first two principles emphasize their equal worth (in the Kantian sense of worthiness due to being endowed with reason).[222] This scheme admittedly justifies some public property, but not unfettered private ownership. "At a practical level, the scheme emphasizes workers' rights within business corporations, favors substantial transfer taxes on large gifts and bequests, and supports sensible government regulation of private property."[223] This idea is more likely traceable in privatization than in a restitution context; therefore, its relevance to post-communist restitution or compensation policies is negligible.

Building in a sense on the above-depicted dichotomy, the emergence-focused view can be associated with a libertarian reading of historical entitlements, according to which the essential factor is the procedure by which the distribution of holdings came about. (Thus, it needs to build upon the past's moral significance.)[224] In turn, the functionality-based approach may be linked with liberal end-state theories, arguing that these derive the justice of property rights from the moral character of the pattern of holdings of which they are a part. (Thus, they have to explain why history does not matter.)[225]

Legislative and judicial history demonstrates though that lawmakers and judges were not necessarily interested in legal and political philosophy. The post-communist restitution schemes attempted—as it will be discussed in some length in the following chapter—to conceal a seemingly eternal and immutable right to property with ideals of social

---

221 Hungarian Compensation Law's (Law No. XXV of 1991) Preamble; debates over restitution bills in the Polish *Sejm* (Youngblood, *op. cit.*, pp. 668–9); German Constitutional Court Decision Gerechtigkeit and Sozialstaatlichkeit BverfGE 84, 90 (121, 130), quoted by the European Commission for Democracy Through Law, Opinion No. 277/2004, CDL-AD (2004) 009, comments by rapporteur László Sólyom, para. 7, available online, at http://www.venice.coe.int/docs/2004/CDL(2004)012-e.asp.

222 Munzer, *op. cit.*, pp. 4–5.

223 *Ibid.*, p. 7.

224 Patrick Macklem, *Indigenous Difference and the Constitution of Canada*, University of Toronto Press, 2001, pp. 83–4, referring to Waldron.

225 Macklem, *op. cit.*, quoting John A. Simmons, "Historical Rights and Fair Shares," *Law and Philosophy* 14 (1994), p. 149.

equality and economic security. Albeit the ideal of social equality is not so far off from property restitution: there are theories which, especially in an indigenous claims context, legitimate indigenous entitlements on grounds of just distributive outcomes that can make indigenous peoples better off. This idea gains special weight by pointing towards the significant disadvantage of indigenous people in comparison with the non-indigenous, a disadvantage that may be overturned through the recognition of the indigenous title.[226] The problem for post-communist property restitution schemes rests on the fact—as it will be shown in the following chapter—that former property owners cannot be considered to be found in such a fundamentally disadvantaged position within society (as the indigenous peoples are in post-colonial contexts).

An essentially different account of property is given by Sened, according to whom the origin of private property and the related rights are not derived from moral axioms or imperatives, and they are not more "natural" than any other creation of humans.[227] Sened believes that individual rights are established only after some central authority—that grants and enforces rights—establishes its monopoly of force. After this moment, rights are granted to gain political and economical support for maintaining control.[228] It may very well have been the case with post-communist restitution, as there are a number of authors that advance a similar argument.[229] However, even if such a utilitarian view of rights is taken seriously, one must note that in all cases the restitution programs heavily drew on the idea of past injustice, and that past holdings did always constitute the basis for the new redistribution. This lead to such curious (theoretically unexplainable) situations as the already mentioned Lithuanian case, where the Constitutional Court considered the right to property as a natural right, although the restitution

226 Macklem, *op. cit.*, p. 84, quoting also Will Kymlicka, *Liberalism, Community, and Culture*, Oxford University Press, 1989, pp. 158–61; and *Multicultural Citizenship: A Liberal Theory of Minority Rights*, Clarendon Press, 1995, p. 117.

227 Sened, *op. cit.*, p. 178.

228 *Ibid.*, p. 180.

229 Offe and Bönker, *op. cit.*; Verdery, *op. cit.*; John Elster, "A framework for the study of transitional justice," available online, at http://www.media.uio.no/forskning/prosjekter/1945/english/artikler/framework1.shtml.

law provided for the expropriation of those returned plots which were not tilled in a given time limit.[230]

A completely different approach to property rights is taken by Penner, who instead of looking for justification of functionality, asks why some things are objects of property and others are not.[231] Since Berle and Means published *The Modern Corporation and Private Property*,[232] the owners' (shareholders') right was seen as a right to a stream of income in an economic enterprise, and the notion of income rights as property started to haunt academics. Penner refers to Arendt, who argues that "very wealthy societies [are] essentially propertyless, because the wealth of every simple individual consists of his share in the annual income of a society as a whole."[233] Arendt distinguishes property from wealth, arguing that modernity has witnessed the dissolution of the former and the rise of the later.[234] Penner warns that—the predominantly economic—tendency of relying on a contract for shaping the concepts of income and interest, everything which serves an interest through a contract, could be regarded as property.[235] This (especially Arendt's) view is seriously countered by the post-communist preoccupation for tangible—usually landed—property. The quest for the once lost things goes against the post-modern tide and reaches back to the Enlightenment's concept of (property) rights, which are now seen (interpreted, presented) as cornerstones of the rule of law, of justice, and of democracy.[236]

230 Lithuanian Constitutional Court, Ruling of 27 May 1994, Law "On Procedures and conditions for restoration of citizen's rights to the ownership of extant property," 18 June 1991, Art. 4.

231 Penner, *op. cit.*, p. 5.

232 A.A. Berle and G.C. Means, *The Modern Corporation and Private Property*, Macmillan, 1933.

233 H. Arendt, *The Human Condition*, University of Chicago Press, 1958, p. 61; quoted by Penner, *op. cit.*, p. 215.

234 Penner, *op. cit.*, p. 217.

235 *Ibid.*, p. 218.

236 Verdery, *op. cit.*, p. 79; Vratislav Pechota, "Privatization and Foreign Investment in Czechoslovakia: The Legal Dimension," *Vanderbilt Journal of Transnational Law* 24 (1991), pp. 305, 308; Erik Mathijs, "Process and Politics of Agrarian Reform in Hungary," in Swinnen, *op. cit.*, p. 237.

As explained above, property theory has come a long way. Throughout this chapter my aim was to present examples of the colorful, controversial, but extremely thoughtful struggle to explain how property rights emerged, why it is good to have them, and how they influenced the social architecture. I did not intend to offer a thorough analysis of the theories presented, or to assess their scientific or social significance. All that I meant was to offer a background of the most significant conceptions of property, against which restitution claims and schemes from post-communist Central and Eastern Europe can be assessed.

CHAPTER 2

Justice and Reparation

This chapter explores the justice of post-communist reparation schemes. Starting from Raz's argument, according to which justice is an ideal distinct from the rule of law,[1] and also endorsing Radbruch's view of the relationship between these two ideals as an antinomy between two essential elements of legality,[2] the first part argues that this contrast is most difficult to deal with in regime change contexts. Section two is dedicated to the role of the rule of law in transitions, while section three explains the reasons and goals that transitional regimes attached to property redistribution. The following two sections are dedicated to a brief presentation of the forms of justice and, correspondingly, to the forms which restitution policies embraced in the various post-communist countries. Section six is dedicated to the two fundamental justice problems that transitional property reparation schemes have to answer: 1. why property injustices have to be mitigated; 2. and why former property owners enjoy a privileged status in comparison with other victims of past injustices. Answering the first question, the analysis concludes that neither international law, nor general principles of justice, not even domestic constitutions recognize a general right to restitution. Although in a number of cases that rather constitute the exception than the rule, in which the takings had an illegal character or the state failed to fulfill its obligation to afford compensation, a solid argument may be made for the existence of such a right. Therefore, while answering the second question, the inquiry identifies the possible arguments that may justify property restitution. However, the

---

[1] Joseph Raz, "Rule of Law and Its Virtue," in Cunningham (ed.), *Liberty and the Rule of Law*, Texas A&M University Press, 1979, p. 4.

[2] Gustav Radbruch, *Rechtsphilosophie*, ed. by Arthur Kaufmann and C.F. Müller, Juristischer Verlag Heidelberg, 1987.

three possible answers: recognition and protection of rights, past harm, and political persecution do not adequately explain why former property owners are preferred to other victims. In these conditions, section seven concludes that transitional compensation schemes have a pronounced distributive character, which, taking into consideration the fact that material justice is the arch enemy of formal rationality, constitutes a serious threat to the rule of law.

1. Justice and the rule of law

It is hard work to write about justice, for there is no single meaning of it which could have managed to impose itself as the reigning paradigm. Ranging from certain moral percepts and rules in Aristotle[3] to a peculiar ideal to which reality should be measured in Rawls,[4] the notion of justice is laden with a variety of meanings.[5] In spite of these theoretical difficulties, justice, along with the rule of law, constitutes one of the most important ideals that law is expected to achieve. Classically, justice is described as dynamic, capable of—sometimes—conflicting interpretations, while the rule of law is about regularity, generality, and prospectivity: values that inspire passivity and persistence.

According to Raz, the rule of law is a political ideal, one of the virtues that a legal system may possess—it shall not be confused with democracy, justice, equality, human rights, or dignity.[6] The rule of law cannot be expected to produce just outcomes such as human rights. These goals should be viewed as distinct from the rule of law.[7] Taken to an extreme, this line of thought may suggest that theoretically, an utterly unjust system may conform better to the requirements of the rule

[3] Aristotle, in *Politica* (Clarendon Press, 1957), identifies the law-abiding man as "just" and the lawbreaker as "unjust."

[4] Rawls, in *A Theory of Justice* (p. 3), proposed to change or to abolish all laws and institutions, no matter how efficient, if they are unjust.

[5] See also: P. Szigeti and P. Takács, *A jogállamiság jogelmélete*, Napvilág, 1998, pp. 259–60.

[6] Raz, *op. cit.*.

[7] Raz, *op. cit.*.

of law than an established democracy.[8] In communist practice, law was usually perceived as having a purely instrumental value,[9] and the Polish Supreme Court for instance, in the late 1950s, stated that the law must be observed even if it is unjust, as long as the legislator does not repeal it.[10] Justice Scalia of the U.S. Supreme Court, in a lecture delivered at Harvard, paraphrased the rule of law as the law of rules, professing that regularity and predictability count for more than what substantive justice does: in certain moments "even a bad rule is better than no rule at all."[11] Critical of Rawls and Raz, Neumann argues that they smuggle a seed of morality in their otherwise formal conception, consisting in reason (rationality) in Rawls and in correctness in interpretation (application) of norms in Raz, both envisaging a system that not only guides human conduct, but it does so in a legally good way.[12] Resembling to some extent Justice Scalia's approach, Neumann maintains that "[w]e know that life is not fair and we plan our lives accordingly... It matters not at all, whether this unfairness is found inside or outside the courtroom, so long as it is predictable."[13]

However, also a quite opposite approach exists in theory, and the conflict between them surfaced in the context of post-World War II trials, when the notorious Fuller–Hart debate on the nature of law mo-

[8] Raz, *op. cit.*, p. 4.

[9] It has to be noted though, that communist doctrine was not especially fond of the idea of the rule of law. For instance, the Soviet Juridical Dictionary gave the following definition of the concept: "Anti-scientific conception, established in bourgeois legal literature, picturing the bourgeois state as if in it there is no room for arbitrary executive power and where allegedly law and legality reign [...] the bourgeoisie of many countries utilize even in this age, by way of demagogic appeal, the doctrines of the Rule of Law in their class interests, by giving them a particularly reactionary meaning and by trying to inculcate with their help harmful illusions into the masses to mask the imperialist nature of the contemporary bourgeois state and law."

[10] Orz SN from 13.06.1959, OSPiKA 1960/45, quoted by Lech Morawski, "Positivist or Non-Positivist Rule of Law?" in Krygier and Czarnota (eds.), *The Rule of Law after Communism*, Ashgate, 1999, p. 44.

[11] Antonin Scalia, "'The Rule of Law as a Law of Rules,' Oliver Wendell Holmes Bicentennial Lecture, Harvard Law School," *University of Chicago Law Review* 56 (1989), pp. 1175–81.

[12] Neumann, *op. cit.*, pp. 8–9 and 10–11.

[13] Neumann, *op. cit.*, p. 45.

nopolized the attention of scholars.[14] Departing from a series of cases involving the prosecution of Nazi collaborators in post-war Germany, the two scholars reached fundamentally opposing conclusions. While Hart found that adherence to the rule of law also meant recognition of the former (Nazi) regime's laws as valid, Fuller read the rule of law as demanding a break with the prior legal regime.[15] The German judiciary solved the rule of law dilemma by stating that in "severe" cases, the moral right takes precedence over the formalist concept (procedural legal right), and accordingly adherence to prior law can be overridden.[16] Later, Fuller restated and developed his position arguing for the existence of an inner morality of law.[17] Joining to some extent this moralizing trend, Laurence Tribe warns that "to say that our idea of 'law' is to be constructed with straightedge and compass, without sympathy and compassion, is dead wrong."[18]

Fletcher identifies the two approaches described above as two versions of the rule of law: a "modest" one, corresponding to the formalist ideal, and a "more lofty ideal that incorporates criteria of justice."[19] A perhaps more accurate distinction is made by Gerald Neumann, who classifies the different visions of the rule of law in three categories: positivist (the rule of law means unconditioned compliance with the law—see the quote from the Polish court above), procedural or formal (the rule of law means rule in a legally good way), and substantive (the rule of law means the rule of good law).[20] According to his argument, the German *Rechtsstaat* as established by the *Grundgesetz* is reflecting a

---

[14] H.L.A. Hart, "Positivism and the Separation of Law and Morals," *Harvard Law Review* 71 (1958), p. 593; Lon L. Fuller, "Positivism and Fidelity to Law—A Reply to Professor Hart," *Harvard Law Review* 71 (1958), p. 630.

[15] See also: Teitel, *op. cit.*, pp. 12–3.

[16] *Ibid.*, p. 13.

[17] Lon L. Fuller, *The Morality of Law*, Yale University Press, 1969.

[18] Laurence H. Tribe, "Revisiting the Rule of Law," *New York University Law Review* 64 (1989), p. 726.

[19] George Fletcher, *Basic Concepts of Legal Thought*; quoted by Jonathan Rose, "The Rule of Law in the Western World: An Overview," *Journal of Social Philosophy* 35.4 (2004), pp. 457–70.

[20] Gerald L. Neumann, "The U.S. Constitutional Conception of the Rule of Law and the Rechtsstaatsprinzip of the Grundgesetz," Columbia Law School, Public Law and Legal Theory Working Paper Group, Paper No. 5, 1999, available online, at http://papers.ssrn.com/paper.taf?abstract_ud=195368.

substantive conception. This view is based on the provisions of Article 20 (3), which binds the executive and the judiciary by both law and justice (*Gesetz* and *Recht*).[21] A more moderate view of the *Rechtsstaat* is proposed by Rosenfeld, who stresses that all great rule of law traditions (the Anglo-American, the French, and the German) endorse a narrow (procedural, formal) vision of the rule of law, while at the same time betray significant differences.[22] The originality of the contemporary conception of the *Rechtsstaat* consists in the institutionalization of a legality that, beyond procedural or formal ideals, is also "contingent upon constitutional conformity and on the realization of constitutionally recognized substantive goals."[23]

Tremblay proposes one of the most radical theories on the relationship between justice and the rule of law, while attempting to conciliate two arch enemies: material justice and formal rationality, postulating a theory of the rule of law as justice. His construction is grounded on three main principles: the law is formally just, materially just, and equitable. The author claims that his theory allows for non-rational elements (intuition, emotion, etc., which also appear at Tribe, *supra*) to be taken into account in adjudication, while it demands that these elements to be rationally justified.[24]

Regardless which theory among the above-described one may prefer, the tension that exists between justice and the rule of law can be sensed in all of them. Gustav Radbruch[25] described the relationship between justice, the rule of law, and expediency as a chain of antinomies between the indispensable elements of legality. Albeit these conflicts are not left unsolved: various legal institutions are destined to alleviate the problem. The binding character of court decisions may also shield unjust outcomes, statutes of limitations may secure impunity for the authors of unjust (illegal) acts, and requirements of procedural fairness should be respected also in the cases of the most heinous criminals.[26]

---

21 *Ibid.*.

22 Rosenfeld, *op. cit.*, p. 19.

23 *Ibid.*, p. 35.

24 Luc B. Tremblay, *The Rule of Law, Justice, and Interpretation*, McGill-Queen's University Press, 1997, pp. 165–83.

25 Radbruch, *op. cit.*.

26 Szigeti and Takács, *op. cit.*, pp. 276–7.

There are peculiar situations, however, especially those characterizing regime changes, during which the contrasts described above can hardly be compromised. One attempt is represented by Teitel's argument, which maintains that in transitions, law's role itself is transitional and not foundational. Transitional jurisprudence's task is to bridge conventional legality and radical transformation. Which values prevail in this conflict—argues the author—are ultimately determined by particular historical and political legacies.[27] To these factors the—economical and political—interests of the emerging new elite can be added, even accepting the amendment that present interests are to some extent contingent upon the legacies of the past.

More importantly, however, it can be argued that while the above-enumerated elements determine the prevailing values of transition, the appropriateness of the choice is functional in the effectiveness of the chosen value in fulfilling the envisaged objectives. In other words: if radical transformation is the order of the day, and all this is done in the name of justice, the outcome of the process should be demonstrably just. Otherwise, lofty principles of justice will serve only as facades to arbitrariness. In the following, this chapter will argue that post-communist property restitution schemes fall short of this requirement in at least two respects. On the one hand, there is no evidence of a compelling argument which justifies the mitigation of past property deprivations at large. On the other hand, it cannot be satisfactorily demonstrated why property-related injustices enjoy a privileged status when it comes to reparations, in comparison to other types of losses.

Because property restitution schemes as retributive (reparative, corrective) justice cannot be unequivocally defended, plus the fact that in most states—as it will be shown below—reparations were deliberately linked with structural reform, restitution in Central and Eastern Europe features a mixed distributive-reparative character. In this context, the bad news for the rule of law, as formulated by Hayek, consists in the fact that "any policy aiming directly at a substantive ideal of distributive justice must lead to the destruction of the Rule of Law."[28]

---

[27] Teitel, *op. cit.*, p. 215.

[28] Hayek, *op. cit.*, p. 59.

2. The context

Writing on the agitated years of Central and East European transition to democracy, Preuss notes that "the principle of the rule of law was invoked time and time again during the revolutions of 1989, and in some cases was even declared the principal guide of all the political actions of the revolutionaries."[29] In this specific context, Preuss wonders what the true meaning of the notion of "rule of law" could be: the protection of legal rights, regardless of their moral, political, or economic justification? Prohibition of any kind of legal retroactivity, immunizing rights acquired in the past from takings (or at least from uncompensated takings)? Or does it simply require that any kind of change should be carried out legally?[30]

One radical answer is given by Elster, who notes that "transitional justice is often characterized by stark departures from the rule of law. The desire for thoroughness trumps the desire for justice. Although the actors often try to make them appear compatible with each other..."[31] Teitel takes a completely different approach, arguing that in periods of political upheaval, the rule of law serves to mediate the normative shift in justice.[32] For natural lawyers, continues Teitel, the predecessor regime's immorality determines the necessity for a "fresh start" for the rule of law to be grounded on something else than adherence to the preexisting law.[33] Accordingly, if law should be able to guide human conduct, prior arbitrariness that often resulted in unequal lawmaking and unjust outcomes must be overturned: rule of law regimes cannot be founded on immoral grounds. There was thus a perceived injustice characterizing society, an injustice reflected in many aspects of life: an injustice that had to be undone.[34]

---

[29] Ulrich K. Preuss, "A Forum on Restitution: Essays on the Efficiency and Justice of Returning Property to Its Former Owners," *East European Constitutional Review* 2 (1993), p. 39.

[30] *Ibid.*.

[31] Elster, *op. cit.*.

[32] Teitel, *op. cit.*, pp. 11–27.

[33] *Ibid.*.

[34] "What is deemed just is contingent and informed by prior injustice," notes Teitel, *op. cit.*, p. 6.

Restitution has also been thought of in terms of "national rebirth" and "moral purification,"[35] efficiency and historical justice,[36] or legitimation of the emerging order.[37]As Teitel puts it, "transitional reparatory justice [...] reconciles the apparent dilemma in the extraordinary context of balancing corrective aims with the forward-looking goals of the transformation."[38] However, not all theorists are content with this finding. Posner and Vermeule argue for instance that there is nothing extraordinary about transitions, and therefore they should not be treated as a self-contained (perhaps also self-justifying) subject.[39] Transitions should respect liberal norms, argue the authors, "at least to the extent necessary for and consistent with, the consolidation of liberal democratic institutions."[40]

These dilemmas are reflected also in constitutional adjudication. The constitutional courts of the transition countries were faced, in a restitution context, too, with the challenge to decide between or rather to conceal demands for justice with demands for legality. The Hungarian Constitutional Court quickly asserted its exclusive competence in explaining the constitution, and defined itself as the motor of transformation, envisaging its mission as perfecting the constitution (and legislation) by means of rational analysis.[41] The Court regarded the Constitution as "tainted" by political machinations,[42] thus it invented a cloudy construction, labeled "the invisible constitution," to take the profane text's place.[43] But its zeal did not stop here: it invented dur-

---

[35] Vratislav Pechota, "Privatization and Foreign Investment in Czechoslovakia: The Legal Dimension," *Vanderbilt Journal of Transatlantic Law* 24 (1991), pp. 305, 308.

[36] Erik Mathijs, "Process and politics of agrarian reform in Hungary," in Johann F.M. Swinnen (ed.), *Political Economy of Agrarian Reform in Central and Eastern Europe*, Ashgate, 1997, p. 237.

[37] Verdery, *op. cit., supra.*

[38] Teitel, *op. cit.*, p. 119.

[39] Posner and Vermeule, *op. cit.*.

[40] *Ibid.*, p. 769.

[41] Radoslav Procházka, *Mission Accomplished: On Founding Constitutional Adjudication in Central Europe*, CEU Press, 2002, pp. 222, 230–1.

[42] Unlike most of the post-communist countries, Hungary did not adopt a new constitution. Instead, it maintained the old, albeit comprehensively revised communist one from 1949.

[43] Procházka, *op. cit.*, p. 223.

ing its first decade of practice various comparable notions, including the so-called "novation" of property claims, which is of interest for the present inquiry and is presented *infra*. Interestingly, the Court—at least according to Chief Justice Sólyom—refused to consider its activity as a response to transition, but rather as a "normal development."[44] It was the idea of the continuity of the rule of law—"the rule of law revolution"—, another construction of the Court, which led to the conclusion that legal certainty is more important than necessarily partial and subjective justice.[45] Consequently, the Court could ban retroactive extension of the statute of limitations, as well as deny former owners' rights to claim the return of their properties taken during the previous regime(s).[46]

Such an approach was completely the opposite of the Czechoslovakian (subsequently) Czech vision of transitional justice. The Czech Court argued that precisely the notion of the state ruled by law is warranting retroactive justice.[47] Unlike their Hungarian colleagues, the Czech judges considered that if the role of constitution is limited to procedural guarantees, than all kinds of political content could be poured in it. The court refused to regard the communist regime as a *Rechtsstaat*, and maintained that preventing retroactive punishment (this reasoning applies *mutatis mutandis* to property restitution as well) would mean to prefer the legal certainty of perpetrators to the legal certainty of citizens (victims).[48] However, the rejection of a value-neutral reading of the constitution resulted also in negative outcomes from restitution perspective. Such an example is the case of the Beneš Decrees, which allowed for the mass expropriation of Sudeten Germans and Hungarians in the aftermath of World War II. The ruling, which is dis-

[44] Procházka, *op. cit.*, quoting Sólyom, p. 118.

[45] AB 11/1992.

[46] Procházka, *op. cit.*, p. 119.

[47] *Ibid.*, p. 118. It is worth comparing this view with the one worded by Sampford, who, taking a somewhat different line, considers that "[t]here may be reasons to allow an individual departure from the Rule of Law ideal within a system which displays a substantial degree of conformity to it; or it may be that other valuable goals override the normative force of the Rule of Law in particular cases" (Charles Sampford, *Retrospectivity and the Rule of Law*, Oxford University Press, 2006, pp. 63–4).

[48] Lawlessness of communism decision, quoted and commented by Procházka, *op. cit.*, pp. 145–7.

cussed in some detail *infra*, relied on the so-called democratic legitimacy that trumps the legitimacy of formal law, and upheld the validity of the post-war regime by relying on the continuity of values between the pre- and the post-Nazi governments.[49] In spite of this, commentators generally perceive the Czech Court's activity as producing fundamental changes not only in the constitutional system, but also in the domestic culture of legalism and judicial interpretation and application of law. In the case of the series of judgments on the restitution process—that are discussed *infra*—it is considered that the Court strengthened the principles of justice as fairness and equal treatment, according them precedence over formal law in certain cases.[50]

The Slovakian, and to a considerable degree the Romanian Constitutional Court represent a third approach to transition. Generally described as preservationist and deferential—in the case of Romania commentators also emphasize its relative lack of authority[51]—these courts did not manage to contribute to a significant extent to the development of the domestic legal system by way of restitution decisions. In Slovakia, the first abstract review petition on property restitution was filed only in 1998, and the Court fashioned an attitude labeled as "silly" by the scholars, as it found itself talking about the legislators' competence to decide when and in what form bills relating to restitution would be adopted.[52] The Court's reluctance to get involved in restitution matters is illustrated also by a 1994 decision in which it refused to hear an application on the grounds that it had no competence "to redress injustices committed through specific property wrongs."[53] Anchoring itself in

[49] US 14/94, quoted and commented by Procházka, *op. cit.*, p. 236.

[50] Jiří Přibáň, "Judicial Power vs. Democratic Representation: The Culture of Constitutionalism and Human Rights in the Czech Legal System," in Sadurski (ed.), *Constitutional Justice East and West*, Kluwer Law International, 2003, p. 393.

[51] Renate Weber, "The Romanian Constitutional Court: In Search of its Own Identity," in Sadurski, *op. cit.*, pp. 283–308.

[52] Slovakian Constitutional Court, US 23/98, quoted and commented by Procházka, *op. cit.*, p. 174. At stake were the statutory rules prohibiting restitution of plots from national cultural sites that precluded indefinitely certain former owners to apply for restitution. (Notably, the Czech Court ruled exactly in the opposite sense and struck down a similar provision as being unconstitutional.)

[53] Slovakian Constitutional Court, US 23/94, quoted by Procházka, *op. cit.*, p. 175.

the positivist tradition, the Slovak—and Romanian—Court was reluctant to adopt an activist attitude, and was happy to confine itself to the cases it was specifically asked to deal with, working solely with those rules and principles that had a concrete textual basis.[54] As what concerns the Romanian Court, the initial deferential attitude has started to gradually shift in the past years, albeit this could also be a consequence of political considerations, as commentators recognize that—at least occasionally—its decisions are politically motivated.[55] For instance, in a 2005 decision the Court ventured to talk about restitution in a rule of law context, arguing that the ambiguity of property titles affects the rule of law, and therefore, legalization of a historical injustice cannot be accepted in the name of legal stability.[56]

For most students of transition, the tension described above between the demand for justice and the necessity to comply with requirements of formal legality—the transitional dilemma—is represented by the question of retroactive justice: whether to prosecute communist political crimes, whether to "purge" ("lustrate") public life, and whether to restitute property.[57] Teitel, in the already quoted passages, gives a convincing answer to this question, arguing that the law's role is exactly to bridge conventional legality and radical reform. Even if certain measures "threaten the conventional rule of law, what supports their use [...] is that they are justified [...] by the future aim of constructing a more liberal state."[58] At present, more than fifteen years after the dramatic changes of regimes in Central and Eastern Europe, a suspicion arises that the "threat" about which Hayek spoke may very well have transformed into reality. The "illiberal" measures did not necessarily result in a "more liberal" outcome. While crossing from reform

[54] Procházka, *op. cit.*, p. 259.
[55] Weber, *op. cit.*, p. 284.
[56] Decision No. 375 of 6 July 2005.
[57] Csaba Varga, *Transition to the Rule of Law*, Eötvös Lóránd University and the Institute for Legal Studies of the Hungarian Academy of Sciences, 1995, pp. 119–156; Jiří Přibáň, *Dissidents of Law*, Ashgate, 2002, pp. 88–120; Adam Czarnota and Piotr Hofmański, "Can we do Justice to the Past?", Andrzej Kaniowski, "Lustration and Decommunisation: Ethical and Theoretical Debates," Jiřina Šiklová, "Lustration, or the Czech Way of Screening"—all three in Krygier and Czarnota (eds.), *op. cit.*; Preuss, *op. cit.*; Elster, *op. cit.*; Offe and Bönker, *op. cit.*.
[58] Teitel, *op. cit.*, pp. 187–8.

to legality, some may have fallen off the bridge. The retroactivity issue is just one—albeit fundamental—aspect of the puzzle. Analyzing the property restitution processes, one may encounter a fair number of small but painful details, which can hardly be considered as leading towards the "more liberal" outcome.[59]

3. Property (re)distribution

As Michael Heller describes it,[60] socialist property can be categorized according to the main type of actors (owners). On the top layer, we find the state and public goods, as belonging—in theory—to the people as a whole, or rather, to the working class. Socialist cooperatives and non-productive organizations can be found one layer below that. Close to the bottom are the individual households (personal property), while on the narrowest falls private property.[61] It goes almost without saying that the most important resources and means of production were state-owned. The hierarchy canvassed above entailed legal and practical consequences. One of the primordial consequences was that the degree of protection decreased from top to bottom, thus state property was the most protected, while private property the least.[62] Another consequence of the extensive state property was the murky relationship between the different layers of property. This was due to the immense structure which had to be administered, and administration entailed a mushrooming bureaucracy, with certain prerogatives of ownership being passed down to lower-level entities.[63] More bureaucracy, however, meant lesser control, and blurred the lines distinguishing the different types of property, especially those separating the lower layers, as socialist (state) property enjoyed strong protection.[64]

---

[59] Problems such as citizenship or residency requirements, quantitative limitations, or the establishment of cut-off dates will be the subject of a subsequent chapter.

[60] Michael Heller, "The Tragedy of Anticommons: Property in Transition from Marx to Markets," *Harvard Law Review* 111, p. 628.

[61] Verdery, *op. cit.*, pp. 49–50.

[62] *Ibid.*, p. 52.

[63] *Ibid.*, p. 57.

[64] *Ibid.*, p. 69.

Therefore, mitigation of past injustices was not the sole purpose of the restitution schemes, which were aiming, in a sense, to overturn a system that made "grand theft" possible.[65] Consequently, the burden was on the newborn post-communist governments to approach the question of property (re)distribution.[66] It must be emphasized that from the outset, two broad and distinct goals were usually entwined in most of the property redistribution schemes. On the one hand, to compensate individuals for the property losses they suffered as a consequence of unjust governmental actions. On the other, to resettle property relationships so as to achieve certainty in possessions, which was regarded as a precondition for the creation of an efficient market economy.[67] The processes were generally envisaged as being guided by the principles of the rule of law.[68] Such is the case of Hungary, where, as already mentioned above, property compensation had a declared social goal. Or, in Poland, the Constitutional Tribunal identified "a beneficial social aspect" of the compensation scheme dealing with the properties left beyond the Bug River.[69] A similar conclusion was reached by the Estonian Supreme Court,[70] arguing that "ownership reform was

[65] *Ibid.*, p. 76.

[66] The new governments were under serious popular pressure to undertake measures to this effect. For instance, The Proclamation of Timişoara (Romania) of 11 March 1990 claimed that "The economic foundation of totalitarianism is the all-powerful state property. We shall never have political pluralism without economic pluralism" (available online, at http://www.timisoara.com/timisoara/rev/proclamation.html).

[67] Preamble of the Hungarian Compensation Law, Law No. XXV of 1991 (available online, at http://www.complex.hu/kzldat/t9100025.htm/t9100025.html): "For the settling of ownership relationships, and the securing of enterprises in the terms of a market economy, guided by the principle of the rule of law and taking into consideration the society's sense of justice and financial capacities, for the redressing of property injustices caused by the state, the Parliament adopts the following law."

[68] The Preamble quoted above subjects the compensation scheme to the principles of the rule of law, the societies' perception of justice, and the limits of its tolerance towards bearing public burdens.

[69] K 2/04, Judgment of 15 December 2004, available online, at http://www.trybunal.gov.pl/eng/summaries/documents/K_2_04_GB.pdf, concerning the right to offset the value of property left in the former Eastern territories of Poland.

[70] Decision 3-4-1-10-2000 of 22 December 2000, available online, at http://www.nc.ee/english.

undertaken in public that is in general interests. Ownership reform is a specific task of the state in building up a rule of law state and a market economy."[71] The Lithuanian Constitutional Court has managed to find some social goals in restitution too, arguing that "[t]he restoration of the rights to land has actually meant process of agrarian reform. [...] The restoration of the rights of ownership and land reform are inseparable processes. The restoration of the rights to land was the basic means for implementing of land reform."[72]

Contrary views have been voiced, for example, by the Czech[73] and the Latvian[74] courts, which both held that the goal of restitution laws

[71] The Court identified the following goals of ownership reform: "to ensure the inviolability of property and free enterprise, to undo the injustices caused by violation of the right to ownership and to create the preconditions for the transfer to a market economy." And in the case of land: "based on the continuity of rights of former owners and the interests of current land users that are protected by law, [...] to establish preconditions for more effective use of land, to transfer relations based on state ownership of land into relations primarily based on private ownership of land." Decision 3-4-1-10-2000, *op. cit.*.

[72] On restoration of citizens' ownership rights to land, see: Decision of 8 March 1995, available online, at http://www.lrkt.lt/doc_links/main.htm. In another case, it was argued that the law on the restoration of citizen's rights of ownership is "a compromise solution aimed at elimination of consequences of the occupation in the sector of economic relations and stemming from the necessity to take into consideration the social-economic relations that have been formed in Lithuania. Besides, [it is an] attempt [...] to return to the economy based on the rights of private ownership and to reconstruct the system of former property relations which had existed before the occupation." Decision of 20 June 1995, available online, at http://www.lrkt.lt/doc_links/main.htm.

[73] I. US 38/02, Judgment of 24 March 2004: "The ratio legis of the restitution acts is to redress, at least to a certain degree, the consequences of the infringement of the fundamental rights of natural and legal persons in the totalitarian era." Available online, at http://test.concourt.cz/angl_verze/doc/1-38-02.html, p. 1.

[74] Case No. 04-01(99), Judgment of 20 April 1999: "The primary and the main objective of the law of any law-based and democratic state, consequently also of the Law 'On the Determination of the Status of Politically Repressed Persons Suffered During the Communist and Nazi Regimes' is justice and ensuring of it. In the above case, the initial objective of the legislator—restitution of equitable rights in accordance with the law to the persons, who have suffered repression during the communist and Nazi regimes—has remained unchanged." Available online, at http://www.satv.tiesa.gov.lv/Eng/Spriedumi/04-01(99).htm.

is (reparative) justice, that is, the rectification of past wrongs, without mentioning any related social aims. This statement of the Constitutional Court is especially interesting in the case of the Czech Republic, where commentators identified, at least at the moment of the adoption, additional purposes of restitution, those alike that were mentioned above. According to Cepl (a former member of the Czech Constitutional Court) for instance, the new political elite considered restitution as helpful means in speeding up privatization and developing market economy.[75] However, it seems that in 2004 the Court managed to find a narrower *ratio legis* behind the restitution scheme.

According to Stephen Holmes, the economic rationale could fail out of consideration of efficiency: record-keeping was poor under communist administration, the judiciary was undersized and undereducated, and promises to restore property in kind created serious uncertainty in possessions.[76] Fact is that, for example, the Romanian restitution process generated about 1 million lawsuits,[77] and as of 2007, the process has not been terminated. Albeit, argues Holmes, "even if restitution is both economically inefficient and morally unjust, it is good policy,"[78] because it helps legitimating the new property system by preventing the former communist elite from appropriating (all) state assets. "Good policy," however, does hardly further the case of the rule of law.

A more general criticism towards additional purposes of reparations is voiced by Pablo de Greiff, who pointed out that reparations should be thought of as a relationship between a set of benefits and a violation of fundamental rights—a fairly narrow perception, which he calls "purist"—with no additional aims involved. The task of reparation programs should be to establish the connection between wrongs

---

[75] Vojtech Cepl, "A note on the restitution of property in post-communist Czechoslovakia," *Journal of Communist Studies* 7 (1991), p. 367; also quoted by Richard W. Crowder, "Restitution in the Czech Republic: Problems and Prague-Nosis," *Indiana International & Comparative Law Review* 5, p. 237; also Vojtech Cepl, "The Transformation of Hearts and Minds in Eastern Europe," *CATO Journal* 17 (1997), pp. 229, 233.

[76] Stephen Holmes, "A Forum on Restitution: Essays on the Efficiency and Justice of Returning Property to Its Former Owners," *East European Constitutional Review* 2 (1993), p. 32.

[77] Verdery, *op. cit.*, p. 46.

[78] Holmes, *op. cit.*, p. 33.

and benefits, and nothing more. An interesting view is voiced by Allen, who parallels the communist treatment of the Holocaust with the transitional treatment of communist legacies. The argument states that in a rather ironic manner, in both cases the new economic order that was to be installed (socialism and market economy, respectively) was regarded as being able to solve individual claims to redress for injustices suffered under the previous regimes.[79]

Undoubtedly, by adding additional aims to property reparations as land reform and establishing the preconditions of a market economy, etc., a strong distributive aspect of reparations is created. Kutz notes, for instance, that because on the one hand communist takings of property generally maintained a semblance of legitimacy,[80] and on the other hand the communist regimes were "off the stage,"[81] post-communist reparations were pushed towards a more distributive approach to compensation.[82]

The UN Human Rights Committee has stressed in the case of Somers v. Hungary that objective compensation criteria of compensation have to be applied equally and without discrimination.[83] Patrick Macklem considers that this language is urging governments entertaining compensatory schemes to pay close attention to the demands of distributive justice.[84] The Hungarian Constitution Court recognized this a couple of years earlier, when it argued that the constitutionality of the compensation law has to be assessed on the basis of distributive justice, taking into consideration not merely the interests of the victims, but also the concurrent constitutional tasks.[85]

---

[79] Allen, *op. cit.*, p. 45.

[80] Remember that the Hungarian Constitutional Court's rulings, declaring the nationalization decrees unconstitutional, played a significant role in breaking the ground for the compensation legislation.

[81] Which arguably weakens the case for reparative justice.

[82] Kutz, *op. cit.*, p. 298.

[83] CCPR/C/57D/566/1993, Decision of 29 July 1996, para. 9.4.

[84] Patrick Macklem, "1 Rybná 9 Praha 1: Restitution and Memory in International Human Rights Law," *European Journal of International Law* 16.1 (2005), pp. 10–1.

[85] HCC, AB 15/1993, 1543/B/1991, p. 4: The constitutionality of the Compensation Law, however, according to the conceptions deductible from the legal text, has to be assessed by the Constitutional Court on the basis of the principle of distributive justice, examining the constitutionality of the scale

4. Aspects of justice

Classically, legal theory distinguishes three major conceptions of justice: formal, retributive, and distributive. To this, a fairly new theory has been added in the past decades, namely transitional justice. Formal justice essentially means that like cases shall be treated alike—Weber defined it as the formalization of just procedure.[86] Under this conception, justice and law are connected by two principles: a permanent one, according to which those pertaining to the same group shall be subject to the same rules, and a variable one, the criteria according to which the group is created.[87] Both principles can be the subject of criticism, as on the one hand those alike from one perspective could be radically different from another, while on the other hand, the criteria which distinguishing specific groups may be considered irrelevant or arbitrary.[88]

Retributive justice requires punitive reaction to the violation of a rule (norm). In a sense it combines a formal and a distributive feature, to the extent that it requires that everyone shall "get what one deserves" (as a consequence of breaking the norm), while the same punishment shall be applied in the same way to every offender (for the breach of the same norm).[89] Theorists also note that retributive justice is closely linked with corrective (reparative) justice, the difference being that the former is concerned with punishment, while the latter with compensation.[90]

Distributive justice attempts to explain the division of goods and burdens within society. Initially, it was concerned with the distribution of property, albeit after the emergence of the welfare state the focus shifted

of compensation, and taking into consideration not only the demands of the aggrieved parties, but also the concurrent constitutional tasks.

86 Max Weber, *Economy and Society*, ed. by Guenther Roth and Claus Wittich, Vol. 2, University of California Press, c1978, pp. 809–15; also quoted and commented by Ágnes Heller, *Beyond Justice*, Basil Blackwell, 1987, p. 1.

87 H.L.A. Hart, *The Concept of Law*, Clarendon Press, 1997, pp. 157–67.

88 Szigeti and Takács, *op. cit.*, p. 269.

89 *Ibid.*, p. 263.

90 Neil Vidmar, in Sanders and Hamilton (eds.), *Handbook of Justice Research in Law*, Kluwer Academic/Plenum Publishers, 2001, pp. 31–65; J.L. Coleman, *Risks and Wrongs*, Cambridge University Press, 1992, pp. 348–54; quoted by Sanders and Hamilton, *op. cit.*, p. 6.

to income.[91] Essentially, distributive justice aims to accomplish an ideal order of partition, which is justified upon various principles: merit, utility, need, or entitlement.[92] Frequently, the justness of distribution is assessed not on the basis of the above criteria, but according to fundamental (liberal) values like liberty or equality. Rawls's theory of justice attempts to find a way of combining both.[93] According to Heller, the arguments for initial equality ("equal amount of manna") are valid for redistribution amongst various forms of life. However, when it comes to distribution within each form of life concerned, no general pattern of justice can be established—it is up to the members of each community to elaborate their own perception of justness in distribution.[94]

The fourth, arguably peculiar conception, already mentioned above, is transitional justice. As Teitel notes, in periods of fundamental political change, law appears to represent "a pragmatic balancing of ideal justice with political realism that instantiates a symbolic rule of law capable of constructing liberalizing change."[95] John Elster laconically defines processes of transitional justice as "the legal treatment of former wrongdoers and victims after political transitions."[96] During transition periods, determinations of what is fair and just are products of what is perceived as previously endured injustices: transitional justice can be described through restorative and transformative features.[97] Albeit the already mentioned article of Posner and Vermeule maintains that "legal and political transitions lie on a continuum, of which regime transitions are merely an endpoint,"[98] the authors believe that there are no fundamental differences between regime and "intrasystem" transitions; what essentially differs is merely the scale of the process.[99] In their reading, transitional justice means a political and economic transition, consistent with liberal and democratic commitments.[100] Arguing

[91] Heller, Ágnes, *op. cit.*, p. 180.
[92] Szigeti and Takács, *op. cit.*, p. 260.
[93] *Ibid.*, p. 261.
[94] Heller, Ágnes, *op. cit.*, p. 205.
[95] Teitel, *op. cit.*, p. 213.
[96] Elster, "A framework."
[97] Teitel, *op. cit.*, p. 224.
[98] Posner and Vermeule, *op. cit.*, p. 763.
[99] *Ibid.*, p. 764.
[100] *Ibid.*, p. 768.

with this position, Wojciech Sadurski maintains that such a view—aiming to "normalize" transitional justice—distorts the "fundamentally different, sui generis problems that the system of constitutional justice in post-communist societies had to grapple with while handling the legacy of the immediate past…"[101]

5. Forms of reparations

There are three major forms which the actual reparations could take: in kind restitution, monetary equivalent, and vouchers. Out of these, the first two come closest to the ideals of corrective (reparative) justice, while the voucher system bears a more distributive character.[102] After all, victims are not given back what was wrongfully taken from them: instead they get the opportunity to participate in the reapportionment of the state property.

It could hardly be argued that there were "pure" systems, in the sense of embracing solely one of the above-enumerated options. Regularly, one of these prevailed, but out of objective necessities, the other forms of compensation occurred too, at least in the form of exceptions.

5.1 The Baltic States: military occupation

The Baltic States can be considered as a category in themselves while analyzing post communist restitution, because, unlike in the rest of the cases, the eradication of private property took place in the condition of Soviet military occupation. The conclusion of the 1939 Ribbentrop–Molotov agreement practically meant the division of Central and Eastern Europe between Nazi Germany and the Soviet Union. Thus, while Hitler attacked Poland, Soviet forces moved into the three Baltic States, and in August 1940, Estonia, Latvia, and Lithuania were in-

[101] Wojciech Sadurski, "'Decommunisation,' 'Lustration,' and Constitutional Continuity: Dilemmas of Transitional Justice in Central Europe," European University Institute, Florence, Working Paper Law No. 3003/15, available online, at http://cadmus.iue.it/dspace/retrieve/1758/law03-15.pdf, pp. 1–2.

[102] It must be stressed though that opting between in kind and voucher restitution significantly turns also on the reigning conceptions about which approach serves economic efficiency better (Elster, "A framework").

corporated into the Soviet Union. Briefly interrupted by the outbreak of World War II, Soviet rule resumed after the war, and gained stability with the 1949 collectivization and mass deportation.[103] The Latvian legislative, for instance, in a 1996 declaration, stressed that "during the whole period of occupation the USSR purposefully realized genocide against the Latvian nation [...] The occupation regime annihilated innocent people, repeatedly organized mass deportations, inflicted cruel penalties [...] illegally and without compensation expropriated property."[104]

The Estonian compensation scheme[105] envisaged the return or compensation for unlawfully expropriated property. The category of unlawful takings included also deprivations pursuant to repression (death penalty, imprisonment, exilement, or deportation).[106] As what concerns land, it was envisaged to be returned, as a rule, according to its former boundaries.[107] In case of property in form of shares, certificates, etc., or of property that was destroyed, compensation was to be paid. This compensation took the form of vouchers, which could be used in the privatization process.[108]

Latvia enacted a scheme which provided for the renewal of property rights.[109] When such renewal was not possible, compensation vouch-

---

103 Olaf Mertelsmann (ed.), *The Sovietization of the Baltic States, 1940–1956*, Kleio, 2003, pp. 11–4.

104 "Declaration on Occupation of Latvia," the *Saeima*, 22 August 1996; quoted in the Constitutional Court of Latvia, Decision of 20 April 1999 on Case No. 04-01(99), available online, at http://www.satv.tiesa.gov.lv/Eng/Spriedumi/04-01(99).htm.

105 Principles of Ownership Reform Act 1991, subject to considerable amendments, consolidated text published in the *State Gazette*, RT I 1997, 27, 391, available online, at http://www.legaltext.ee/en/andmebaas/ava.asp?m=022.

106 Unlawful expropriation was described as taken against the will of its owner or forced to give it up, taken on the basis of unlawful legislation or through arbitrary official actions. Repression was considered also unlawful, whether judiciary or extra-judiciary. *Ibid.*, para. 6.

107 Land Reform Act 1997, subject to several amendments, consolidated text published in the *State Gazette*, RT I 2001, 52, 304, para. 6.

108 Principles of Ownership Reform Act 1991, paras. 13 and 17. Entitled persons were given the possibility to opt between in kind return or compensation (para. 6.2).

109 Law "On Land Privatization in Rural Regions," 1992, Art. 1(2).

ers (certificates), alike in Estonia, were issued.[110] However, in this case, some categories of claimants—among them victims of political repression—have been granted the possibility to translate compensation certificates into cash. Those not falling into these categories were able to use their certificates in the privatization process.[111]

Lithuania, the third Baltic state, contemplated restoration of rights to properties nationalized or "otherwise unlawfully made public."[112] Restoration, as in the previous two cases, took two forms: in kind or through compensation (in case of lands either by other plots or financially).[113] As the Constitutional Court observed, the notion of restoration of property rights in the case of Lithuania essentially meant partial reparation, because the legislation took into account also the interests of private persons who subsequently gained lawful ownership over nationalized goods.[114]

5.2 Poland: the struggle for restitution

Poland has as yet not enacted a comprehensive norm for the regulation of nationalized properties,[115] albeit quite a number of bills were

---

[110] Law "On the Land Reform in the Republic of Latvia Rural Regions," 1990, Art. 12.

[111] Amendments to the Law "On Land Privatization in Rural Regions," 1994. Just like in the case of Estonia, here too, entitled persons had the possibility to opt between in kind return and compensation certificates (Constitutional Court of Latvia, Decision of 10 January 2003, on Case No. 2002–17–0103, available online, at http://www.satv.tiesa.gov.lv/Eng/spriedumi/17-0103(02).htm, also Decision of 20 April 1999, on Case No. 04-01(99), *supra*).

[112] Law No. I-1454 "On the Procedure and Conditions of the Restoration of the Rights of Ownership to the Existing Real Property," 1991, available online, at www.litlex.lt/Litlex/Eng/Frames/Laws/Documents/78.htm.

[113] Just like in the previous two cases, entitled persons could choose between the two options.

[114] LiCC, Ruling of 15 June 1994, "On the restoration of citizens' ownership rights to residential houses," and Ruling of 19 October 1994, "On the restoration of ownership rights to residential houses," both quoted in Jasiūnienė v. Lithuania, ECHR Judgment of 6 March 2003, Application No. 41510/98, para. 22.

[115] Marie-Benedicte Dembour and Magda Krzyzannowska-Mierzwska, "Ten Years On: The Voluminous and Interesting Polish Case Law," *European Human Rights Law Review* 5 (2004), pp. 517–43.

taken into consideration by the Parliament. The first of them, passed in 1990 by the Senate, provided for the return of small businesses, and was envisaged as the first step of a broader process. Restitution was perceived as historical justice, but the other reasons described above—preconditions of a new market, creation of a new elite—were also present.[116] A second bill followed soon, concerned with the returning of pharmacies nationalized by a specific communist enactment. However, both initiatives were blocked by the *Sejm*.[117] Further four rival bills were presented in 1992. They contemplated different approaches to restitution: ranging from return of property through compensation in kind to partial compensation for unlawful expropriation. Every proposal was turned down, however, by the *Sejm*, with the argument that neither of them meats the State's financial capacities to pay compensations. A new attempt was undertaken by the *Sejm* istelf, and resulted in a bill that provided for the return of property when possible, in kind compensation as alternative, and compensation in vouchers if the first two were not possible. The bill also included citizenship or residency requirements, and envisaged an upper limit on the returnable amount.[118] Unfortunately, before Parliament could have considered the proposal, a vote of no confidence was cast for the government. After the new election, further two initiatives failed to obtain the legislative approval.

According to commentators, the Polish situation was the result of a combination of factors that included an extraordinarily fragmented legislative with conflicting agendas, limited financial capacities and various private interests. Under these conditions, neither utilitarian, nor justice arguments could overcome concerns related to fiscal responsibilities and a return to a prewar social order.[119]

---

[116] There was a genuine concern that the "higher moral argument" of historical justice cannot gain sufficient popular support, thus pragmatic arguments—of more efficient business, stimulation of private entrepreneurship, and the creation of a new middle class—were also brought forward. See: Maria Los, "Property Rights, Market and Historical Justice: Legislative Discourse in Poland," *International Journal of Sociology and Law* 22 (1994), pp. 45–6; also quoted by William R. Youngblood, "Poland's Struggle for a Restitution Policy in the 1990s," *Emory International Law Review* 9 (1995), pp. 668–9.

[117] Youngblood, *op. cit.*

[118] *Ibid.*.

[119] *Ibid.*, pp. 676–7.

However, things have gradually changed towards the turn of the millennium. There is now a special act for the compensation of the properties left beyond the Bug River[120] (due to the exchange of population between Poland and the former Soviet republics, which was already mentioned above.) The compensation formula essentially consists of the right to offset (credit) the value of the abandoned properties against either the price of state property or the fee for perpetual use of such property.[121] The act initially envisaged a partial compensation, but this provision was found unconstitutional by the Constitutional Tribunal.[122] Moreover, pursuant to legislation providing for the restitution of religious properties, governmental commissions were established to hear restitution claims, and the solutions are mostly in favor of restitution.[123] The latest legislative attempt to deal with the restitution of private (individual) property was a bill adopted by the Parliament in 2001, only to be denied by presidential veto, allegedly out of budgetary concerns.[124]

5.3 Germany: fairness, justice, and the social state

The Federal Constitutional Court stated that compensation is not based on a right to property, instead on principles of fairness, justice, and the social state. Consequently, there was no obligation to afford full compensation. The main principle of compensation was declared to be equal treatment, but the financial situation of the state and other

---

[120] Offsetting the Value of Property Abandoned Beyond the Present Borders of the Polish State Against the Price of State Property or the Fee for the Right of Perpetual Usufruct Act, 2003.

[121] *Ibid.*, section 3 (quoted in Broniowski v. Poland, ECHR, Judgment of 22 June 2004, Application No. 31443/96, para. 116).

[122] K 2/04, Judgment of 15 December 2004, paras. I.5 and II.9, available online, at http://www.trybunal.gov.pl/eng/summaries/documents/K_2_04_GB.pdf.

[123] Paul Jaskaunas, Vilnius Lost, 2003-FEB Legal Aff. 63, pp. 65–6; U.S. Department of State, Summary of Property Restitution in Central and Eastern Europe, Submitted to the U.S. Commission on Security and Cooperation in Europe On the Occasion of a Briefing Presented to the Commission by Ambassador Randolph M. Bell, 10 September 2003, available online, at http://www.state.gov/p/eur/rls/or/2003/31415.htm.

[124] U.S. Department of State, Summary of Property Restitution in Central and Eastern Europe, *op. cit.*.

obligations arising from reunification (the change of system) were to be taken into consideration, too.[125] The Joint Statement[126] of the two German states regarding the solving of property issues—which subsequently was made part of the unification treaty—spoke about the necessity of "find[ing] a socially acceptable balance (sozial verträglicher Ausgleich) between the competing interests, while taking into account the need for legal certainty and clarity and to protect the right of property."[127]

Germany also opted for in kind reparations, when addressing the question of properties unlawfully expropriated by the former German Democratic Republic.[128] By way of exception, property that could not be returned[129] was compensated. The question of properties taken during the Soviet occupation was also solved through a scheme that allowed low-price (re)purchase by former owners, or provided for an indemnification.[130] The Federal Constitutional Court addressed this

---

125 Gerechtigkeit and Sozialstaatlichkeit BverfGE 84, 90 (121, 130), quoted by the European Commission for Democracy Through Law, Opinion No. 277/2004, CDL-AD (2004) 009, comments by Rapporteur László Sólyom, para. 7, available online, at http://www.venice.coe.int/docs/2004/CDL(2004)012-e.asp.

126 Joint Statement of the Federal Republic of Germany and the German Democratic Republic on the Resolution of Outstanding Property Issues (Gemeinsame Erklärung der Bundesrepublik Deutschland und der Deutschen Demokratischen Republik zur Regelung offener Vermögensfragen).

127 Wittek v. Germany, ECHR, Application No. 37290/97, Judgment of 12 December 2002, para. 27.

128 The rationale—the same as for Nazi takings—was that victims are entitled to as close an approximation as possible to the *status quo ante*. See: Kutz, *op. cit.*, p. 288.

The Resolution of Outstanding Property Issues Act of 23 September 1990 (Gesetz über Regelung offener Vermögensfragen)—enacted by the then still existing GDR—was also part of the German Unification Treaty (German Unification Case Study, in Lex Mundi World Reports, Supplement No. 15, 1992, available online, at http://www.foothill.fhda.edu/divisions/unification/restitution2.html).

129 Because it was "needed for urgent investment uses that would yield general economic benefits," or it was developed in such a way that it was impossible to be extracted for return, or it had been acquired by a good fate purchaser. Kutz, *op. cit.*, p. 289.

130 Wittek v. Germany, *op. cit.*, paras. 26–32; Maltzan and others v. Germany, ECHR, Application Nos. 71916/01, 71917/01, and 10260/02, Judgment of 2 March 2005, paras. 38–60.

issue in a number of judgments. The Court held that denial of restitution did not violate either any constitutional rights, or the principle of equal treatment.[131] This view was later confirmed when the Court argued that the government had a large margin of appreciation during the negotiations concerning reunification, and the government did not act outside its powers when it considered expropriations that occurred in the period in question as irreversible.[132] Finally, drawing on two judgments of the Federal Administrative Court, the Constitutional Court emphasized that the expropriations which took place under Soviet occupation were not a matter within the discretion of the two German States, and thus they should remain untouched.[133] Commentators praise this "exercise of judicial pragmatism," which recognized the necessity of compromise in order to achieve the higher goal of reunification.[134] However, the question of these properties was addressed by the Compensation Act, which provided state compensation (monetary or through the preferential acquisition of certain lands) for expropriations carried out during the occupation period.[135]

5.4 Former Czechoslovakia, Hungary, and Romania

The Czech and Slovak reparation laws were guided by the principle of restituting the original property to the entitled persons.[136] Financial

[131] Judgment of 23 April 1991.

[132] Judgment of 18 April 1996.

[133] Judgment of 4 July 2003 (all three judgments quoted by the ECHR in Maltzan and Others v. Germany, Decision of 2 March 2005, *op. cit.*, paras. 19 34).

[134] Donald P. Kommers, "The Basic Law under strain: constitutional dilemmas and challenges," in Anderson, Kartenthaler, and Luthardt (eds.), *The Domestic Politics of German Unification*, L. Rienner, 1993, p. 145, commenting on Federal Constitutional Court's Decision No. 84BverfGE 90.

[135] Gesetz über staatliche Ausgleichsleitungen für Enteignungen auf besatzungsrechtlicher oder besatzungshocheitlicher Grundlage, of 24 September 1994, quoted in Maltzan and Others v. Germany, *op. cit.*, paras. 46–55.

[136] Law "On extrajudicial rehabilitation," 21 February 1991, No. 87/1991 Coll. of Laws, Art. 3, and Law "On modifying ownership relationships with respect to land and another agricultural properties," 21 May 1991, No. 229/1991 Coll. of Laws (see also: CCC, I. US 754/01, Decision of 23 November 2003, available online, at http://test.concourt.cz/angl_verze/doc/1-754-01.htm).

compensation was to be granted in cases where restoration of property was not possible.[137]

The Hungarian Compensation Law[138] envisaged a different scheme, opting for compensation as a rule and restitution as exception (only church properties were restituted). Compensation embraced the form of vouchers, which could be used in the privatization process. The value of the vouchers was calculated according to a rather complicated scheme, which converted the value of various properties into a flat rate.[139] As it was already mentioned in the previous sub-section, Hungary dealt separately with the victims of political persecution whom were entitled—in function of the deprivations suffered—to receive the same vouchers, albeit in their case monetary compensation was also possible in the form of one-time payments or life annuities.[140] Similarly, as in the case of Germany, equal treatment was made a basic principle of compensation.[141]

In Romania, restitution was combined with original distribution of property (in the case of land).[142] Different laws dealt with different types of property: the restitution of buildings was regulated separately

---

137 Law "On extrajudicial rehabilitation," *op. cit.*, section 13. However, restitution was a rule only in case of real property. As para. 2 of the same section states, when the judicial decision affecting the taking was quashed under the Rehabilitation Act and the taking only concerned movables, the expropriated person is entitled only to compensation. The explanation given by the Supreme Court was that the purpose of the Act was to mitigate some, but not all, property and other injustices (Kopecký v. Slovakia, ECHR Judgment of 28 September 2004, Application No. 44912/98, para. 23). Even in the case of real property, if expropriated goods were transferred legally to private persons, the former owner could not claim restitution (Law "On modifying ownership relationships...", *op. cit.*, Art. 8).

138 Law No. XXV of 1991 (available online, at http://www.complex.hu/kzldat/t9100025.htm/t9100025.htm).

139 *Ibid.*, para. 3. The system employed a shifting scale, the value of the compensation being inversely proportionate with the value of the lost properties.

140 Law No. XXXII of 1992 ("On the compensation of those unjustly deprived of their life or liberty on political grounds").

141 Democracy Through Law, Opinion No. 277/2004, *ibid.*.

142 Law No. 18/1991, republished in the *Official Gazette*, No. 1, 5 January 1998. The law concerned the redistribution of collective lands and assets to their former owners, while those collective members who joined these type of communal agricultural production units had the right to participate in the distribution of these units' patrimony.

from agricultural properties.[143] Compensation was the rule in the case of properties which could not have been restituted. But while in the case of land the impossibility of the return of the original plot was compensated with other plots, in the case of buildings the law left to the interested parties to agree on the appropriate means of compensation. Accordingly, this could take the form of stock company shares, privatization vouchers, or money; even combinations of these were possible.[144]

6. Fundamental problems

As it was already hinted at above, two significant theoretical objections can be raised against post-communist property reparation schemes. Starting from the premise that at least one of the programs' goals was to do justice to the victims of the former regimes, the first objection shakes the justice-based arguments of reparations.

As it will be demonstrated below, there are no compelling arguments that may justify reparations at large. And cynically, in some of those peculiar cases, when such arguments appear to be most convincing, the courts managed somehow to neglect them.

Further, the second objection argues that the schemes do not appear to rest on normative values that may justify the preferential treatment of former property owners, in comparison with the former regime's other victims.

6.1 Do communist-era takings demand reparations?

The first fundamental question that needs to be answered is whether communist takings of property demand reparations or not. Undoubtedly, Article 8 of the Universal Declaration of Human Rights creates a right to effective remedy for acts violating fundamental rights guaranteed by constitution or by law.[145] A similar provision is reiterated by

143 Law No. 10/2001, published in the *Official Gazette*, No. 75, 14 February 2001.

144 *Ibid.*, Art. 1.

145 Universal Declaration of Human Rights, adopted and proclaimed by General Assembly Resolution 217 A (III) of 10 December 1948 (available online, at http://www.un.org/Overview/rights.html).

the International Covenant on Civil and Political Rights.[146] Commentators note, however, that the scope and content of the right to redress is fuzzy and unclear, and it does not necessarily create an obligation to compensate every type of violation.[147] Nevertheless, a right to compensation is consistently recognized for victims of serious violations (such as torture, forced disappearance, extra-legal executions, etc.)[148]

In addition, even if the major international documents, such as the Universal Declaration, Protocol to the European Convention on Human Rights, or the European Union's Charter of Fundamental Rights, mention the right to property, none of them recognizes a right to restitution.[149]

In the case of Somers v. Hungary, the UN Human Rights Committee held that the Covenant did not protect the right to property, and therefore "there is no right, as such, to have (expropriated or nationalized) property restituted."[150] On the other hand, the Committee also noted that the Covenant itself entered into force with respect to Hungary in 1976, and therefore the Hungarian state may not be held responsible under its provisions for facts that occurred before that date.[151]

---

[146] Art. 2(3) of the International Covenant on Civil and Political Rights, G.A. Res. 2200A (XXI), 21 U.N. GAOR Supp. (No. 16) at 52, U.N. Doc. A/6316 (1966), 999 U.N.T.S. 171, available online, at http://www1.umn.edu/humanrts/instree/b3ccpr.htm.

[147] Diane F. Orentlicher, "Addressing Gross Human Rights Abuses: Punishment and Victim Compensation," in Henkin and Hargrove (eds.), *Human Rights: An Agenda for the Next Century*, American Society of International Law, 1994, p. 449.

[148] *Ibid.*.

[149] Universal Declaration of Human Rights, *idem*, Art. 17; European Convention on Human Rights, Protocol 1, Enforcement of certain Rights and Freedoms not included in Section I of the Convention of 20 March 1952, Art. 1, available online at http://www.hri.org/docs/ECHR50.html; Charter of Fundamental Rights of the European Union, 2000/C 364/01, Art. 17, available online, at http://www.europarl.eu.int/charter/pdf/text_en.pdf.

[150] CCPR/C/57D/566/1993, Decision of 29 July 1996, para. 9.6.

[151] The issue was the failure to return property that was taken in the 1950s, *ibid.*, para. 6.3.

Moreover, in another case filed against Hungary (E.K and A.K. v. Hungary, CCPR/C/50/D/520/1992, Decision of 5 May 1992), the Committee held that failure to compensate does not amount to an affirmation of a prior violation—a precondition for the existence of a continuing violation, which, theoretically, could have been argued if it would have happened after the

A similar conclusion was reached by the European Court of Human Rights in the case of Jasiūnienė v. Lithuania, where the Strasbourg court refused to examine the nationalization of the claimant's land, on account of *ratione temporis* lack of competence.[152] At the same time, the Court stated that the Convention did not guarantee the right to restitution of property. This argument was repeated also in Rucińska[153] and refined in Broniowski.[154] Neither the hope that long extinguished property rights may be revived, nor a conditional claim which has lapsed as a result of failure to fulfill the condition, can be regarded as "possession," in the meaning of the Convention and its Protocol No. 1.[155] Albeit even if there is no clear-cut standard for property restitution in international law, the obligation of successor regimes to repair the wrong done by their predecessor is unequivocally formulated.[156] Moreover, it may also be invoked that general principles of international law also assert the

entry into force of the Optional Protocol (E.K and A.K. v. Hungary, *ibid.*, paras. 6.4 and 6.6).

On the issue of continuing violation, see also: the case of Vasilescu v. Romania, ECHR, Application No. 53/1997/837/1043, Judgment of 22 May 1998, para. 49.

152 Jasiūnienė v. Lithuania, *ibid.*, para. 38: the Court argued that this claim relates to events prior to the date of entry into force of the Convention and of Protocol 1 with regard to Lithuania. See also: Kopecký v. Slovakia, ECHR, Application No. 44912/98, Judgment of 28 September 2004 para. 35(d): "Article 1 of Protocol No. 1 cannot be interpreted as imposing any general obligation on the Contracting States to restore property which was transferred to them before they ratified the Convention."

153 Rucińska v. Poland, ECHR, Application No. 33752/96, Decision of 27 January 2000.

154 Broniowski v. Poland, *op. cit.*, para. 182: Article 1 of Protocol No. 1 "does not guarantee a right to full compensation in all circumstances."

155 Jasiūnienė v. Lithuania, *ibid.*, para. 40.

156 Theodor Meron, *Human Rights and Humanitarian Norms as Customary Law*, Clarendon Press, 1991, p. 171. However, the obligation of successor states to provide remedies to victims was removed from the draft: "Basic principles and guidelines on the right to a remedy and reparation for victims of violations of international human rights and humanitarian law" prepared under the aegis of the UN Commission on Human Rights in 2004, upon the Russian Federation's insistence. Materials of the Third Consultative Meeting, Geneva, 29 September to 1 October 2004, p. 3, available online, at http://www.ishr.ch/About%20UN/Reports%20and%20Analysis/CHRWG/Remedy/Remedy-3rdConsultation.pdf.

requirement of prompt, adequate, and effective compensation for the expropriation of property. But in James and others, the European Court of Human Rights pointed out that the principles in question apply exclusively to non-nationals, thus they do not govern the treatment accorded by the states to their own citizens.[157]

Symmetrically, most contemporary constitutions enumerate property among the protected rights, albeit merely takings, and not restitution, are constitutionally regulated. At a domestic level, however, things are even more complicated, and reparation efforts face serious dilemmas related to the retrospective/prospective or individual/collective dimensions of reparations.[158] "If we question acts of nationalization and land reform we will question the whole post-war legal structure of Poland," objected a former Polish minister of ownership transformation.[159] A somewhat similar concern was voiced by a former Czechoslovak minister of economy: "[w]e should not expose the society to the danger that insistence on one's rights will go with injustice to the other."[160]

Interestingly enough, a completely different approach characterized the Hungarian compensation scheme. The Constitutional Court in an early decision declared unconstitutional a number of laws and decrees pertaining to the nationalization of certain buildings and pharmacies. The Court held that the norms in question were targeting the property of certain social groups, and thereinafter aimed at the eradication of private property, both goals being in conflict with the requirement of public utility.[161] Astonishingly, even if the existence of a clear

---

157 James and Others v. United Kingdom, *ibid.*, paras. 58–65. Applicants were challenging the Leasehold Reform Act, on the basis of which they were deprived of a number of properties. They maintained, among others, that on the basis of the general principles of international law, they were entitled to adequate, prompt and effective compensation.

158 Teitel, *op. cit.*, p. 119.

159 Quoted by Youngblood, *op. cit.*, p. 652.

160 Tadayuki, *op. cit.*, p. 30.

161 HCC, AB 27/1991, 91/E/1990, p. 5: "Those acquisitions of property rights by the state that is resting on an encroachment upon or taking of the rights of the owners, on the stigmatization of individuals or groups, or on any kind of discrimination cannot be regarded as public utility not even by way of exception. Exceptions can be made neither in the case when the state acts *ex lege*, for the eradication of the bulk of private ownership."

breach has been demonstrated, this was seen as directly creating neither an obligation, nor a right to compensation. The Constitutional Court held that there is no constitutional requirement to restitute or compensate property losses. The compensation scheme depends solely on the sovereign will of the Hungarian State; thus is grounded on the idea of fairness.[162] An even more radical step was taken by the Czechoslovakian legislature, which declared null and void all judgments, convictions, and confiscation *ex tunc* (from the day of their pronouncement), thus the original owners' rights were considered as surviving without interruption.[163]

However, to make things more complicated, two different groups of communist-era property deprivations have to be distinguished. On the one hand we have takings resulting exclusively from the actions of the domestic governments, such as "common" nationalization of property as part of various—land and economical—reforms; and confiscation as a penal sanction (usually accompanying convictions for "political crimes"), as a consequence of absence (taking of vacant property) or of deprivations of citizenship (a measure illegal by itself). On the other hand there are losses of property endured as a consequence of international agreements regarding population exchanges along the redrafted boarders of post-war Central and Eastern Europe. On the top of all these, the very legitimacy of the post-war communist regimes which affected the takings is also debatable, as the regime changes commonly took place through elections which can hardly be characterized as fair and free.

6.1.1 Property loss as a consequence of population exchange

In these cases, subsequent bilateral treaties between the affected states attempted to solve the faith of the property left behind by those moved

[162] HCC, AB 21/1990, 1057/G/1990, p. 5: "The partial redress envisaged by the Government is resting solely on the idea of fairness [...] compensation [...] is a function of the state's sovereign decision."

[163] Law "On judicial rehabilitation," 23 April 1990, No. 119/1990 Coll. of Laws, as referred to by George E. Glos, "Restitution of Confiscated Property in the Czech Republic," Czechoslovak Society of Arts and Sciences, 2000, available online, at http://www.svu2000.org/issues/glos.htm.

from one country to the other.[164] Such treaties were sometimes characterized by a certain haste, which resulted in leaving the most important questions—namely those related to the payment of compensations—subject to further agreements.[165] The upshot of this was that the terms were susceptible to change from the original agreement until the later settling of accounts.

For instance, the Czechoslovakian–Hungarian agreement of 1946 provided that repatriates from Czechoslovakia would lose their immovable left behind, while the Czechoslovakian state pledged to pay compensation for these properties up to a 50 hectare limit; however, the details of the compensation were left subject to a subsequent agreement. The Paris Peace Treaty of 1947 made reference and enforced the provisions of this bilateral convention, but remained silent in the issue of the uncompensated immovable. The above-mentioned agreement—in the form of a minute—became reality only in 1964, and by that time the property rights systems changed in both countries. As a consequence, the minute only mentions immovable subject to personal property, for private property as such ceased to exist. To make things more complicated, the notion of personal immovable property is defined according to Czechoslovakian rules; consequently, it applies solely to family homes placed on plots not exceeding 2 hectares. The minute also provided for a lump sum[166] to be paid to the Hungarian government, through which all immovable-related Czechoslovakian debts towards persons of Hungarian citizenship were liquidated. Fi-

[164] Pursuant the Soviet-Polish agreements of 1944–5 (the Republican Agreements) 520,000 persons of Ukrainian, Russian, Byelorussian, and Lithuanian ethnicity have moved to Soviet territories, while 1.5 million persons of Polish origin were relocated to Poland.

The Czechoslovak–Hungarian Agreement of 1946 lead to the exchange of 73,000 Slovakians for 68,000 Hungarians. Ignác Romsics, "Az újraosztott Köztes-Európa," *Európai utas* 1 (2000), available online, at http://www.hhrf.org/europaiutas/20001/3.htm.

[165] In the case of the Republican Agreements, the mutual settlement of accounts was concluded in 1952 (see: Broniowski v. Poland, *op. cit.*, para. 41), while in the case of the Czechoslovak-Hungarian Agreement, the question of unsolved compensations was settled through a 1964 minute (joint communication of the Hungarian Ministry of Foreign Affairs and the Ministry of Finances No. 8004/1991).

[166] 20 million CZK.

nally, the Hungarian State assumed the obligation to compensate the above-mentioned Hungarian citizens. The subsequently issued Governmental and Ministerial decrees[167] contained dispositions for the compensation of persons repatriated from Czechoslovakia, but these regulations excluded from the scheme any immovable with agricultural utilization, thus the compensation did not even reach the 2 hectare ceiling.[168]

Romanian citizens have also lost their properties situated beyond the redrafted borders of the state. While in the case of persons living in the former Soviet Socialist Republic of Ukraine compensations for properties left behind were regulated by the Paris Peace Treaty, another treaty, concluded in 1940 with Bulgaria, regulated voluntary and forced migration due to a modification of the common borderline.

In the case of Poland, the Republican Agreements, concluded by the Polish Committee of the National Liberation in 1944 with the neighboring Soviet Socialist Republics of Ukraine, Belarus, and Lithuania, the Polish state assumed the obligation to compensate repatriated persons for the value of properties they had to abandon.[169] According to the Agreements (each drafted in a similar way), repatriated persons were allowed to take with them movable properties up to a total weight of 2 tons per family, plus cattle and poultry, and objects needed for the exercise of their profession. However, at the same time, a large number of goods—apart from immovable ones—had to be left behind: money exceeding 1,000 zloty or rubles, gold, works of art, jewelry, furniture, automobiles, and others.[170] The pact provided that the value of the properties left behind had to be calculated on the basis of their insurance valuation. In the absence of such a valuation, the representatives of the Parties should assess the value of the properties.[171] According

[167] Governmental Decree No. 17/1964, and Ministerial Order No. 9/1964.

[168] The passages on the history of the Czechoslovakian–Hungarian Agreement are drawing extensively on the decision of the HCC AB 45/2003, 960/B/1995, part II/A.

[169] The evacuation affected approximately 1,240,000 persons; for details, see: Broniowski v. Poland, *op. cit.*, paras. 11, 39, and following.

[170] Agreement between the Polish Committee of National Liberation and the Government of the Ukrainian Soviet Socialist Republic, of 9 September 1944, Art. 3; quoted in Broniowski v. Poland, *op. cit.*, para. 40.

[171] *Ibid.*.

to Polish domestic regulations in this matter, the repatriates had the right to have the value of their lost property offset against the fee for the right to perpetual use or against the price of immovable property purchased from the State Treasury. As a grotesque twist of faith, the repatriates from Soviet Union were accommodated on the real estate left behind by other repatriates—albeit this time from Poland to Germany—in the so-called "Regained Territories" (formerly under German authority) received by Poland as a kind of compensation for the territories lost to the USSR.[172] Thus, the Polish repatriates had had priority in purchasing these lands.[173] The offsetting of the value of the lost property, however, remained an open question, as it was repeatedly addressed by subsequent legislations.[174]

In these cases, the Hungarian Constitutional Court,[175] the Polish Constitutional Tribunal,[176] and the Romanian Constitutional Court[177] recognized the government's obligation to adequately compensate the repatriated citizens. However, stressed the Hungarian Court, the state had wide discretion to decide how it intended to fulfill its obligation.

172 This redrafting of borders, according to Polish estimations, resulted in a loss of territory of almost 20% (Broniowski v. Poland, *op. cit.*, para. 12).

173 Decree of 6 December 1946 on the transfer from the State of non-agricultural property in the Regained Territories and the former Free City of Gdańsk (Broniowski v. Poland, *op. cit.*, para. 43).

174 The Land Administration and Expropriation Act of 1985; Cabinet's Ordinance of 1985 "On the offsetting the value of real property abandoned abroad against the fees for perpetual use or against the price of a building plot and buildings situated thereon"; The Land Administration Act of 1997 and Cabinet's Ordinance of 1998 "On the procedure of offsetting the value of real property abandoned abroad..."; quoted in Broniowski v. Poland, *op. cit.*, para. 45 and following.

175 HCC, AB 45/2003, 960/B/1995: the government not only lacked a constitutional motive for failing to compensate for the lost agricultural properties of those resettled from Czechoslovakia, but it also had the obligation to provide such compensation.

176 PCT, K2/04, Judgment of 15 December 2004: "These agreements created an obligation for those authorities to adopt internal law measures. [...] The fulfillment of the promises [...] required therefore, the undertaking of appropriate legislative and administrative actions of an internal nature." Available online, at http://www.trybunal.gov.pl/eng/summaries/documents/K_2_04_GB.pdf, p. 4.

177 RCC, Decision No. 312/2002 of 19 November, 2002, published in the *Official Gazette*, No. 81, 7 February 2003.

In this context, the Court held that the state might disregard the original legal nature of the property losses suffered, and execute its obligation towards the aggrieved parties through compensation.[178] The Polish Tribunal arrived at a similar conclusion when it stated that it "does not, however, evaluate the appropriateness of the legislator's adoption of particular institutional [i.e., legal] solutions for compensating the loss of property interests [...] since this remains within the legislative autonomy."[179]

The Hungarian Court also stressed that the possibility of compensation may be contemplated only in those cases in which the state gave up its right to vindicate Hungarian citizens' property left abroad through international agreements. The argument explained that the Hungarian State had no obligations stemming from the damages caused to its citizens' property by other states, especially that the assets located abroad were not part of the Hungarian state's patrimony.[180]

The form of compensation was never challenged in Romania, where two distinct laws regulated this issue.[181] Similarly to the case of Hungary, the Romanian legislature imposed the same quantitative limits upon compensations as those applicable for similar properties under the "ordinary" restitution scheme. However, as what concerns the other details, the two laws contain significant differences. First and foremost, while Law No. 290/2003 provides for in kind compensation

---

178 HCC, AB 37/1996, 837/E/1995: "Accordingly, the state [...] fulfills its obligations towards the aggrieved parties through compensation, disregarding the original legal nature of the certain property grievances."

179 PCT, K33/02, Judgment of 19 December 2002, available online, at http://www.trybunal.gov.pl/eng/summaries/K_33_02_GB.pdf.

180 HCC, 1043/B/1992, section II.

The argument drew also on the Paris Peace Treaty of 1947, which provided that Hungary was obliged to restore only assets, legal rights, or interests which were located on its territory.

181 Law No. 9/1998 "On compensating Romanian citizens for their properties transferred to the Bulgarian state pursuant to the application of the treaty between Romania and Bulgaria," republished in the *Official Gazette*, No. 105, 7 February 2002; Law No. 290/2003 "On indemnifying or compensating Romanian citizens for their properties sequestrated, taken or left behind Basarabia, Northern Bucovina, and the Herta region, as a consequence of the state of war and the application of the Peace Treaty between Romania and The Allied Powers signed in Paris on 10 February," 1947, published in the *Official Gazette*, No. 505, 14 July 2003.

for agricultural lands and forestry (within the limits of available land), and monetary compensation for constructions and various (enumerated) unharvested crops,[182] Law No. 9/1998 provides only for monetary compensations for the same categories of property.[183] Second, while the restitution scheme for domestic takings contemplated only one personal limitation (the requirement of citizenship),[184] Law No. 290/2003 institutes a stricter regime, qualifying applications on condition of both citizenship and Romanian residence.[185] This strict requirement does not appear to be justified under the conditions in which neither the "ordinary" restitution scheme nor the other law regulating compensations for properties left abroad provides for Romanian residence as an exclusive condition. Third, both laws restrict the circle of beneficiaries to the former owners and their legal heirs: again, a limitation unknown in the scheme regulating domestic losses of property. Intriguingly, while in the case of Law No. 9/1998 this issue was successfully challenged before the Constitutional Court[186]—the Court found no reasonable justification for the distinction made between testamentary and legal successors—the similar provisions were re-enacted in Law No. 290/2003, only to be amended in 2006.[187]

Estonia represents a special case, as the law on ownership reform[188] provided that restitution or compensation of property belonging to persons who left Estonia on the basis of agreements entered into with the German State have to be resolved through an international agreement. Unlike in the cases presented above, where the population exchange took place after World War II, in the Estonian case the repatriation was effected before the outburst of the war. The German Reich and Estonia entered an agreement in 1939 concerning resettlement from Estonia to Germany, which provided that a German consul-

[182] Law No. 290/2003, arts. 1–4.

[183] Law No. 9/1998, arts. 1–3.

[184] Law No. 18/1991, Art. 48; Law No. 112/1995, published in the *Official Gazette*, No. 279, 29 November 1995, Art. 4.

[185] Law No. 290/2003, Art 1(2).

[186] RCC, Decision No. 312/2002, published in the *Official Gazette*, No. 81, 7 February 2003.

[187] Law No. 171/2006, published in the *Official Gazette*, No. 437, 19 May 2006, single article, para. 1.

[188] Law "On the Principles of Ownership Reform," June 1991.

ate in Tallinn would be set up to take under governance and liquidate the properties of the resettled persons. After the occupation and annexation of Estonia, a similar agreement had been concluded between the German Reich and the Soviet Union; however, in this case, lump sums were established to mutually and finally compensate for resettled persons' properties left on each other's territories.[189] The constitutionality of the Ownership Reform Act's above-mentioned provision was challenged on equality grounds, the argument being that the subsection became unconstitutional due to the fact that within more than ten years no international agreement had been entered into. Therefore, argued the petitioner, the resolution of the petitions for restitution or compensation in the case of resettled persons had been postponed into the indeterminate future, giving rise to uncertainty and ambiguity. In its decision, the Supreme Court held the challenged provision to be in conflict with the Constitution because the legislator failed to fulfill its duty to comprehensibly establish the rights of resettled persons, and of the users of the properties which belonged to them. For this, the Court called upon the legislator to bring the said provision into conformity with the principle of legal clarity.[190]

6.1.1.1 A footnote: the Sudeten Germans.

The Sudeten Germans represent quite a special case, as although their fate—just like the Hungarians'—turned upon the famous Beneš Decrees, no bilateral population exchange agreements were concluded: they were simply swept out of the country. In their case, lack of agreement meant lack of compensation. Although a 1992 act created the possibility to apply for restitution of properties taken under the presidential decrees, for individuals of German ethnicity this remained merely a theoretical possibility, as the eligibility criteria were set in such a way that they made application impossible.[191]

[189] ESC, Case No. 3-4-5-02, Decision of 28 October 2002, paras. 19–20.

[190] *Ibid.*, paras. 30–6.

[191] Law No. 243/1992 Coll. of Laws, as amended in 1996, required that applicants demonstrate their "loyalty" towards the (former) Czechoslovakian State, and have their citizenship granted by decree 33/1945, Act Nos. 245/1948, 194/1949, or 34/1953, and continuously retained until 1990. For more details, see: *infra*, Chapter 3.

The disinterested observer might sense a political motivation behind the restitution scheme,[192] but the present inquiry will focus only on the legal motivations given by the Czech Constitutional Court. Even if—as it will be shown in the following passages—the text of the decision creates the impression that the judiciary struggles to sustain an idea that can hardly be grounded on principles of justice and equality.[193]

The instant case questioned the validity of Presidential Decree No. 108/1945, contesting its compatibility both with the current constitutional rules, and those in effect in 1945. In rejecting the petition, the Constitutional Court engaged in a lengthy philosophizing argumentation about the necessity and justifications of the expropriation of Sudeten German holdings, a reasoning which beyond the not so well disguised ethnic bias[194] contains a number of contentious assertions that will be presented below.

First, justifying the Expropriation Decree, the Court resorts to the argument of specific historical situation, which legitimizes the measures that represent a reaction to the provocation represented by German occupation.[195] Employing arguments that evoke ideas of militant democracy, it is stated that democratic political systems have the duty to protect their foundations, and the decree was intended to "strengthen the fundamental democratic and legal principles."[196] Moreover, following this logic, it is made clear that "causes leading to the birth of to-

---

[192] A Czech MP had allegedly declared that "it would be politically impossible to give property back to those ethnic Germans because many controlled the economy and many also collaborated with the Nazis. The Germans in Czechoslovakia were kicked out after liberation in 1944 and their lands confiscated." Diane Francis, "Who owns what in Eastern Europe?" *Financial Post*, 8 September 1993, available in Westlaw, Int-News Database, p. 12.

[193] CCC, Pl. US 14-94, Judgment of 8 March 1995.

[194] *Op. cit.*, on p. 13 of the decision the Court speaks about the nation's "natural right to resist occupying aggressors," while "even (sic!) a minority is accorded the right to adopt its own political position." The two-tiered standard is obvious: the nation's right is "natural," the minorities' is "accorded." Even more outrageously, it is stated that German ethnics bear a particular responsibility "for the conflagration, which Nazism unleashed, was in large part the work of their nation and its leaders" (p. 16).

[195] *Ibid.*.

[196] *Ibid.*, pp. 13–4.

talitarianism" have to be eliminated, so as to bar the possibility of its recurrence,[197] alas it is not specified, what is exactly the relationship between nazism and Sudeten German private property rights? Finally, in some passages reminiscent of Louis de Saint-Just, the Court rhetorically asks, "can one demand the right to liberty [...] if he has himself destroyed it...?"[198] And gives the answer itself: of course, citizens of German nationality have such an extensive responsibility in the destruction of other citizens' rights, that their rights and freedoms should naturally be limited, provided the necessary balance between means and ends is preserved.[199] The conclusion, according to which expropriation was a sanction "aimed at ensuring the function and purpose of human rights and freedoms, their constructive contribution to society, and the deepening of the sense of responsibility,"[200] fits naturally into this twisted logic.

How far the theoretical construction falls from reality is illustrated by the tragicomic pattern of facts in the Fábryová v. Czech Republic case before the UN Human Rights Committee.[201] Here, the applicant's father, whose property was aryanized and who managed to survive the death camp, was declared "German as well as a traitor to the Czech Republic" by a district committee operating under Presidential Decree No. 12/1945, which based its findings on the fact that he had lived "in a German way."

Second, the required means-ends proportionality was found through an admirable exercise of creativity, by which the Court replaced the idea of guilt with the "much broader" concept of responsibility, and found the Sudeten Germans collectively "responsible" for all the wrongs of the occupying regime.[202] The decree created "merely" a presumption of "responsibility" of German (and Hungarian) ethnics, which could have been rebutted by demonstrating their "loyalty" towards the Czech or

[197] *Ibid.*, p. 17.
[198] *Ibid.*, p. 19.
[199] *Ibid.*, p. 20.
[200] *Ibid.*, p. 22.
[201] Fábryová v. Czech Republic (765/1997), ICCPR, A/57/40 Vol. II (30 October 2001) 103 (CCPR/C/73/D/765/1997).
[202] *Ibid.*, p. 15: "in a democracy"—so the Court—"all people bear common responsibility for the fate of the whole human society."

Slovak nation.[203] The Court inexplicably sees the refutable nature of this presumption as an indication of the nationality-blindness of the norm,[204] which creates the irrefutable presumption that all non-Germans and non-Hungarians have necessarily stood up and fought the Nazi and fascist regime. (Or, at least their indignation and repulsion towards it was so deep that they did not need to give any proof of their loyalty towards the nation.) Further, as the Court explained, the Germans' collective responsibility stemmed also from their resignation and lack of rejection of their political leaders. For, according to the argument, a society can be dominated by tyranny, only if "it does not possess the courage or the capability" to fight it.[205] It is more than admirable that this argument is valid for one, but it never occurred in relationship with the other totalitarian regime: as by applying this logic most former Czechoslovakian citizens should be held responsible and punished for their lack of resistance towards the communist governments.

Third, a further attempt to prove the neutrality of the Expropriation Decree is made by stating that the term "nationality" employed in the text meant "citizenship," but it was used because of the post-war context when the German State as such ceased to exist for a while.[206] And anyway, added the Court, the duty of loyalty towards the German Reich stemmed from citizenship, while in the case of Czechs and other nationalities their support for Nazi Germany was entirely based on their free will.[207] Although in the reasoning of the Court these two arguments were put next to each other, they can scarcely be held to follow from one another, at most they cast a shadow of doubt over the adequacy of the nationality-citizenship distinction.

Fourth (and final), reference is made to the Paris Agreement[208] and the Potsdam Agreement.[209] In the Court's reading, Article 6 of the

[203] *Ibid.*, p. 14: this meant that they had either to actively take part in the fight for liberation, or to suffer under Nazi or fascist terror.

[204] *Ibid.*, p. 15.

[205] *Ibid.*, pp. 16–7.

[206] *Ibid.*, p. 18.

[207] *Ibid.*.

[208] 21 December 1945 (on reparations to be paid by Germany, the establishment of a Reparations Authority and the return of gold currency).

[209] 2 August 1945 (which provided among others for the transfer of German population from Poland, Czechoslovakia, and Hungary to Germany).

Peace Agreement that authorized the signatory governments to retain German enemy property to be found under their jurisdiction (and deduct their value from the compensation to be received from Germany) constituted the international basis for the Expropriation Decree. The same article also stressed that properties that previously belonged to Allied governments or their citizens (and taken during Nazi occupation) were also to be retained but not deduced from the forthcoming compensation.[210] Rather strangely, the Court found in these provisions a justification for the taking also of minority (classified as "enemy") property, and not only of foreign property.

Finally, it has to be remarked that the Court discovered the same twin social and ethical goals in the taking of Sudeten Germans' property as were attributed in the post-communist context to many restitution programs, namely political and economical stabilization plus mitigating the damage caused (by the Nazi occupation).[211] But, it is argued throughout this chapter, that these two goals do not explain and justify each other in the post-communist context, and there is no reason to think differently in a post-World War II context either. The sanction argument operates with the foggy, faulty, and untenable notion of collective "responsibility," while the economic argument does not explain why only minority property was taken.

6.1.2 Property losses as consequence of various domestic takings

In the preceding paragraphs, I have emphasized the difference between losses of property that occurred as a consequence of international agreements (exchange of population), and losses endured as a consequence of takings. The latter case in its turn can be broken down into two subcategories: formally legal takings (land reform or criminal confiscation) and illegal takings. In the following, these two categories will be addressed.

Kutz, in his already cited article, argues that "expropriation on its own is not a categorical wrong like murder or political repression; it does not by its very nature vault to the head of the line for repair."[212]

---

[210] CCC, Pl. US 14-94, *op. cit.*, p. 20.
[211] *Ibid.*, pp. 19, 23.
[212] Kutz, *op. cit.*, p. 285.

Posner and Vermeule argue that property is always uncertain in domestic law, due to the government's freedom to regulate that property at any time.[213] (This line is sustained also by Justice Blackmun's remark: "property is fluid in time."[214]) However, the authors add, such unsettling of property rights is tolerated if it promotes a pressing social goal and its achievement does not significantly undermine the market.[215] Of course, this reasoning applies within the framework of a market economy. Still, a Hungarian Constitutional Court opinion cited in the foregoing paragraphs of this chapter managed to declare some of the nationalization decrees as unconstitutional, exactly because their goal could not be defended on the basis of social need, while their finality meant the liquidation of an entire property class.[216] (A quite contrary view was voiced by the Romanian Supreme Court,[217] which held that the manner in which nationalization decrees had been applied could not be reviewed by the courts.[218]) The Hungarian Court's arguments back Sadurski's critique[219] of Posner and Vermeule: communist takings were not promoting a pressing social goal, and they did significantly undermine the market (by basically terminating it), thus they fundamentally differ from "normal" takings; accordingly, the tasks for

---

[213] Posner and Vermeule, *op. cit.*, p. 68.

[214] Loretto v. Teleprompter Manhattan CATV Corp., 458 U.S. 419 (1982), available online, at http://caselaw.lp.findlaw.com/scripts/getcase.pl?court=US&vol=458&invol=419.

[215] Posner and Vermeule, *op. cit.*, p. 68.

[216] HCC, AB 27/1991, 91/E/1990, *supra*.

[217] Now High Court of Cassation and Justice.

[218] The Bucharest Court of First Instance found that the nationalization of the applicant's parents' house had been "a mistake," as they belonged to a category exempted from nationalization. For further details: Brumarescu v. Romania, ECHR, Application No. 28342/95, Judgment of 28 October 1999, paras. 15–20.

This line of thought was expressed also in an earlier decision in the same year, when the Court held that "legislation alone can bring the nationalization carried out under Decree No. 92/1950 into accord with the provisions of the present Constitution concerning the right of property." However, this approach did not last for long, as in 1998 the Court changed its position, and stated that "the courts have jurisdiction to entertain any action concerning an alleged infringement of the right of property or other rights *in rem* where such an infringement occurred between 1944 and 1989." *Ibid.*, paras. 37–8.

[219] Sadurski, *op. cit.*, *supra*.

the post-communist governments in handling past legacies were fundamentally different too.

If we think of law as a social experiment—in effect, the entire transition to communism can be described as a social experiment—then it follows that reparations for legally taken property are extremely difficult to justify, unless one wishes to address the question of the previous regime's morality. But the legality of communist takings is controversial, too. In many cases, nationalization and confiscation failed to comply with the then existing legal requirements. To formally demonstrate the criminality of legal takings, argues Kutz, one would have to adopt a Nozickean view according to which moral desert, following from the manner of the original acquisition and of the successive transfers justifies the *status quo*—and concomitantly limits state interference.[220] But, if this is the case, wonders Kutz, why can the *status quo ante* be entitled to a stronger normative deference? There is no reason to believe that in Central and Eastern Europe pre-communist "baselines" were morally unquestionable;[221] thus, the desert argument may not prove sufficient to condemn the transformation of the property system.[222]

And while legal takings are difficult to challenge, there is a much stronger case against illegal (or *de facto*) takings. One example of holding communist nationalization decrees unconstitutional is the above-cited example of the Hungarian Constitutional Court. Failure to comply with obligations assumed through international conventions is another example in this sense: the above described cases of the properties left over the Bug River and the Hungarian-Czechoslovakian population exchange agreement illustrate the problem. Another good example in this sense is Decree No. 52 of 1950 issued by the State Council of the People's Republic of Romania, which led to the nationalization

[220] Kutz, *op. cit.*, pp. 286–7.

[221] As Avineri argued, communist takings in many cases were "expropriations from (previous) expropriators": the first wave of mass expropriations in the 1940s being the purge of Jewish property during World War II. Thus there is no reason to believe that the pre-communist property status was the result of a legitimate appropriation. Shlomo Avineri, "A Forum on Restitution: Essays on the Efficiency and Justice of Returning Property to Its Former Owners," *East European Constitutional Review* 2 (1993), pp. 35–6.

[222] Kutz, *op. cit.*, p. 287.

of a large number of houses and apartments.[223] The decree disregarded constitutional guarantees, as it provided that the expropriated goods were transferred to the state without any compensation.[224] The Lithuanian Constitutional Court has found that the "nationalization and other unlawful socialization of property" was started by the occupation government (i.e., the Soviet Union).[225] Therefore, even if the post-communist government cannot be held responsible for the actions of the occupying forces, steps had to be taken towards the restoration of rights of people which had been violated.[226]

The Venice Commission, in its Opinion on the Albanian Draft Law on Recognition, Restitution, and Compensation of Property, considered that the "practicable solution" would be that instead of the recognition of original, pre-expropriation ownership, the compensation acts should create the title for regaining property.[227] In this regard, it is worth noting the arguments of the Romanian Constitutional Court as to the contrary. The Court emphasized that in the case of properties which were transferred into the state's possession through an unlawful act or without any legal basis, the individual's legal right has never been extinguished. This means that symmetrically, the state has no ownership rights, and therefore these properties cannot be covered by the same acts, which regulate the legal status of property that passed into state ownership. To hold otherwise would either confer a retroactive effect on such a norm, or create a form of taking unknown to the

223 The claim of the applicant in the above-cited case of Brumarescu v. Romania was also targeting Decree No. 92/1950.

224 The Constitution of 1948, Art. 10 provided that expropriations can be effected only for a public utility, through law and upon the payment of just compensation established by the judiciary ("Pot fi facute exproprieri pentru cauza de utilitate publica pe baza unei legi si cu o dreapta despagubire stabilita de justitie"). Available online, at http://www.constitutia.ro/const1948.htm. A similar provision was contained also by Art. 481 of the Civil Code.

225 LiCC, Ruling of 27 May 1994, states that property nationalized by Soviet authorities should be considered as being "under *de facto* control of the State." Available online, at http://www.lrkt.lt/doc_links/main.htm.

226 LiCC, Ruling of 20 June 1995, available online, at http://www.lrkt.lt/doc_links/main.htm. The fact of the occupation by itself delegitimizes the takings effected by the occupying forces.

227 European Commission for Democracy Through Law, Opinion No. 277/2004, *ibid.*, para. 9.

constitution.[228] Interestingly, in somewhat similar circumstances, the retroactive validation of the Crown's pastoral grants in Australia were never challenged. The National Native Title Act provided for such a possibility in cases of "inconsistent" grants, where the "inconsistency" stemmed from the existence of a native title over the same land.[229] As a consequence, notes Bartlett, State governments and industry demanded and got validation of all existing interests,[230] regardless of the fact that this practice in the end qualifies as an ex post confiscation, without any compensation being paid.

A peculiar case is formed by those who lost property as a consequence of their opposition to the regime, as an accessory punishment to criminal convictions. In many post-communist states, laws for the rehabilitation of those subjected to repression for political reasons were enacted. Rehabilitation also created the possibility to claim compensation for the property losses suffered.[231]

228 RCC, Decision No. 73 of 19 July 1995, *ibid.*: To provide through a legal norm that even the immovable taken without title form the object of state property would mean to attribute a constitutive effect to this norm, which would presume either a retroactive effect, or the application of a form of expropriation unknown to the 1991 Constitution, and thus unacceptable. It follows therefore that the objection of unconstitutionality raised against that part of Art. 1, para. 1, which refers to properties transferred into state ownership without title, is to be accepted.

229 Sean Brennan, "Native title in the High Court of Australia a decade after Mabo," available online, at http://www.gtcentre.unsw.edu.au/Public-Law-Review-native-title-as-published.doc+Native+Title+%22rule+of+law%22&hl=hu&start=3.

230 Bartlett, in Havemann (ed.), *Indigenous Peoples' Rights*, Oxford University Press, 1999, p. 419.

231 For example: in Czechoslovakia, The Extra-Judicial Rehabilitations Act No. 87 of 1991; in Germany, the Decree on registering property claims of 11 October 1990 applied for securing property which was taken away in connection with criminal proceedings for acting against the law-based state, if entitled persons applied for review of the criminal verdict under the Law on rehabilitation of 6 September 1990; in Latvia, Art. 9 of the Law "On the determination of the status of politically repressed persons suffered during the communist and Nazi regimes" determines that the state shall ensure restoration of politically repressed persons' rights (Constitutional Court of Latvia, Case No. 04-01(99), Judgment of 20 April 1999); in the other two Baltic states, similar measures were taken to compensate for injustices suffered through political repression (Institute of Economics, Estonian Academy of

However, it must be added with equal emphasis that under those circumstances in which the illegality of the takings can be demonstrated there are strong reasons to recognize the "survival" of former property rights,[232] even if the state withholds the discretion to decide upon the concrete form of the compensation which may be granted in these cases. A category of exceptional cases is represented by the situations in which the state assumed an obligation (to compensate property losses), which was never fulfilled. In these situations, the right to compensation should be recognized as flowing from the state's lack of compliance—as the Hungarian Constitutional Court put it: constitutional omission[233]—rather than made function of an *ex gratia* allotment.

The major problem with *ex gratia* restitution is that governmental benevolence does not equate with justice. Official magnanimity does neither presume (recognize) the existence of entitlement, nor of any governmental obligation towards their holders. Such compensation, like presidential pardon, is rather about those who exercise the discretion than those who benefit from it. This constitutes one of the main controversies of the Hungarian Compensation Law: the Preamble speaks about the principles of the rule of law and society's sense of justice,[234] but at the end of the day, the entire scheme is made a function of state generosity.[235]

Critiques of the *ex gratia* approach to reparations have pointed out that even acts of grace have to conform to constitutional requirements, and for instance should not affect the fulfillment of the state's constitutional, international, or previously assumed legal obligations. According to this view, even the sequential approach to restitution (the periodicity of regulation, as opposed to the periodicity of execution) may appear problematic.[236] Finally, it must be noted that magnanim-

Sciences: Review of Structural Reforms, 1995, available online, at www.ibs.ee/economics/esc/part-1.html).

232 In spite of the practical difficulties that it may generate because of the passage of time, in terms of proof, statutes of limitations, etc.

233 "Unconstitutionality by omission": HCC, AB 16/1993, 1378/E/1990; AB 37/1996, 837/E/1995; AB 45/2003, 960/B/19995.

234 Law No. XXV of 1991, *supra*.

235 HCC, AB 21/1990, 1057/G/1990, *supra*.

236 András Sajó, "A részleges kárpótlási törvény által felvetett alkotmányossági kérdések," *Állam és Jogtudomány* 1.4 (1992), pp. 200–1. The author points out that a serious differentiation is created between those entitled to com-

ity is classically regarded as a measure destined to attenuate the consequences of the application of harsh laws, and not as a lawmaking principle.[237]

The Constitutional Court has had a major role in turning justice into grace. This can be traced back to its unusual vision of the transition, labeled "rule of law revolution," and essentially entailing the maintenance of a certain degree of legal continuity between the formal regime and the current one. However, as it soon turned out, this perception was very difficult to conceal with demands for restitution. As the Court explained, settling of property relationships is a constitutional task because the preamble of the Constitution establishes, as a goal, social market economy. Albeit this settling of property relationships is a complex process which requires that the sealing of the past as well as the new redistribution to be done in conformity with the Constitution, from the point of view of past, current, and future owners.[238] Given this attitude, unlike, for example, in the case of Czechoslovakia, it was not possible to speak about the former owners' rights. However, as it was argued above, in many situations expropriations violated the then existing law, and in these cases compensation claims had a different legal basis. Still, the compensation laws provided for a single, common basis, as the entire scheme was envisaged only as part of the grand property resettling process. To explain this peculiar solution, the Court made use of the civil law institution of novation.[239] This—as the Court explained—meant that old obligations were renewed upon a new legal basis, to a new extent and in new terms.[240] Thus, the compensa-

pensation, and those who can merely hope for it, under the sanction of an un-enforceable decision of unconstitutional omission.

[237] *Ibid.*, p. 220.

[238] HCC, AB 28/1991, 1160/A/1991, para. I/2.2.

[239] The institution of "novation" in Hungarian law is covering those situations in which the contracting parties agree to modify an essential element of their contract, in such a way that it results in the termination of the original contract and the conclusion of a new contract. (Traditionally, it meant the alteration of the legal grounds of the obligations stipulated in the contract.) The biggest problem with the Court's analogy is that the past property takings—and the corresponding obligation to compensate—were not the result of a consensual agreement, and the unilateral "renewal" of the agreement is not known to civil law.

[240] *Ibid.*, para. I/2.1.

tion scheme could ignore the original legal nature of the claims, while taking into consideration the existing legal and economical context.[241] According to the Court's rationale, the application of this method was permissible because—as it was already mentioned above—the takings had an unusual character, as they were targeting the systematic eradication of private property.[242] It seems, however, that the justices had already forgotten what they said earlier on in the same judgment about certain "politically motivated" takings, mentioning as an example the case of dissidents.[243] At least in their cases, expropriation was about punitive retribution, rather than "systematic eradication of private property." Eventually, the principle of novation, which enabled the Court to justify the compensation scheme, was the means that led to the transformation of justice into governmental benevolence.[244]

A markedly different point of view has been voiced by the Romanian Constitutional Court, which, talking about the applicability of civil law norms to the restitution scheme, has stated that "it is unconceivable to apply private law norms in a domain belonging without any doubts in its entirety to the domain of public law." Consequently, "the state does no wise appear as a simple debtor of obligations," nor do "the former owners or their heirs have the status of creditors."[245]

6.2 Why only certain past wrongs deserve compensations?

The second fundamental question from justice perspective is why only certain wrongs committed under the preceding regime deserve compensation? In other words, what makes the difference between various past wrongs that justifies reparation? There are three possible justifications worthy of discussion: the recognition and protection of rights, the idea of past harm, and the principle of political persecution.[246]

---

[241] *Ibid.*, para. I/3.2.
[242] *Ibid.*, para. I/3.3.
[243] *Ibid.*, para. I/2.1.
[244] Procházka, *op. cit.*, pp. 124–5.
[245] RCC, Decision No. 73 of 19 July 1995, *ibid.*.
[246] Teitel, *op. cit.*, pp. 132–4.

The justification derived from rights departs from a breach of pre-existing rights. For instance, in post-colonial context,[247] the land claims of indigenous peoples were often founded on their special relationships with land, considered to be akin to the "Europeanized" concept of property. The existence of these "rights" were recognized either by treaties[248] or construed by the judiciary.[249]

In New Zealand, the debate concentrated around the 1840 Treaty of Waitangi by which the Crown acquired sovereignty, guaranteeing in exchange "full exclusive and undisturbed possession of [...] Lands and Estates Forests Fisheries and other properties."[250] The idea of Treaty rights has definitely penetrated legal discourse; however, its status in New Zealand law is still controversial. One view holds that where legislation makes no express reference to Treaty, Treaty rights are unenforceable. When such a reference exists, however, the current approach of the courts is to give effect to the reference. The other view holds that where relevant, Treaty principles should guide governmental conduct and permeate legislation without express incorporation.[251] As the Parliament has incorporated into domestic legislation the International Covenant on Civil and Political Rights, some of the Treaty rights have

[247] However, it has to be noted that indigenous claims essentially differ from post-communist restitution to the extent that the former represent group entitlements, while the latter are characterized primarily by individual claims.

[248] The 1840 Treaty of Waitangi concluded between Maori chiefs and the British Crown, or the various Indian treaties in North America.

[249] The case of the Aboriginal Native Title in Australia.

[250] Andrew Sharp, *Justice and the Maori: The Philosophy and Practice of Maori Claims in New Zealand since the 1970s*, Oxford University Press, 1997, p. 133.

[251] Sharp argues that in the Tribunal's interpretation, the Treaty did not so much specify rights, as suggesting a "continuing process of discovery and elaboration" of the principles of the Treaty; it made the Treaty "a basis for future-oriented policy": "[i]t was not intended to fossilize a *status quo*, but to provide a direction for future growth and development" (Sharp, *op. cit.*, p. 169, n. 15; quoting the Te Atiawa Report). This language stressing the importance of principles rather than of provisions can be associated with the rule of law concept according to which the rule of law provides procedural justice, rather than just outcomes. Consequently, it can be argued that inquiring whether the descendants of indigenous inhabitants of the land ought to enjoy a special status by virtue of original occupation, constitutes a blurring of the essential issue of the duty to keep promises and to repair breaches of contract (Sharp, *idem*, pp. 166, 177).

to be upheld as an international obligation. Furthermore, the right to equality before the law is now protected also under the newly enacted Bill of Rights (1990) and Human Rights Acts (1993).[252]

In the United States, it was held that Indian communities have retained "their original natural rights, as the undisputed possessors of the soil, from time immemorial."[253] Equally significantly though, the notion of "Indian property" was commonly understood as covering mere occupancy, which meant of course much less than fee title to land.[254] As early as 1890, the United States Supreme Court recognized that Indian lands could not be taken by the government "for such objects as are germane to the execution of the powers granted to it; provided only, that they are not taken without just compensation being made to the owner."[255] Almost 80 years later, the Court of Claims refined this position, distinguishing the two qualities in which Congress may exercise its authority over Indian land. On the one hand, Congress may exercise its plenary powers over such lands as trustee for the benefit of the Indians. If acting in this capacity, and making "a good faith effort

---

[252] "The New Zealand Legal System: A guide to the constitution, government and legislature of New Zealand," the homepage of the New Zealand Ministry of Justice, available online, at http://www.justice.govt.nz/pubs/other/pamphlets/2001/legal_system.html.

[253] Chief Justice Marshall in Worcester v. Georgia (31 U.S. 515 (1832)).

[254] In Oneida Indian Nation of N.Y. State v. Oneida County (414 U.S. 661 [1974]), the Court explained that while fee title to the lands occupied by Indians became vested in the colonial sovereign (and subsequently in the several states, than in the United States), Indian tribes' right to occupancy was nevertheless recognized. Initially, it was thought that "[Indians] occupy a territory to which we assert title independent of their will, which must take effect in point of possession when their right of possession ceases" (Cherokee Nation v. Georgia, 30 U.S. 1 [1831]). However, in United States v. Santa Fe Pacific R. Co. (314 U.S. 339, 345 [1941]) the Court stated that "Indian right of occupancy is considered as sacred as the fee simple of the whites" (referring to Mitchel v. United States). Justice Douglas in his dissenting opinion in Montgomery v. U.S. (414 U.S. 935 [1973]) argued that "the occupation of property by Indians' ancestors gives rise to Indian title, which, though not a property interest subject to Fifth Amendment protections, encompasses the right to occupancy and use—the right to fish, to hunt, and to cut timber sufficient for use on the land."

[255] Cherokee Nation v. Southern Kansas R. Co., 135 U.S. 641 (1890). This point of view was restated also in Shoshone Tribe v. United States, 299 U.S. 476 (1937).

to give the Indians the full value of the land," it merely "transmutes the property form land to money," and therefore no taking occurs. On the other hand, Congress may exercise its eminent domain power; in this case it must act in accordance with the Fifth Amendment.[256] However, this test covers merely those lands to which a recognized title exists, and "recognition" usually embraces the form of a treaty.

In Australia, where, unlike in the above-described cases, no treaties were concluded between colonists and the indigenous tribes, the High Court in the Mabo(2) case[257] offered a solution by arguing that a "subtle and elaborate system of rules in force amongst indigenous peoples of Australia [existed] prior to the acquisition of sovereignty by the Crown."[258] This meant that the doctrine of *terra nullius*[259] was rejected, and for the first time, the existence of an Aboriginal, traditional "legal system" comprising the title to land (in addition to or outside of the common law), in force prior to the claim of sovereignty by the Royal Crown, was recognized.[260] Following Mabo(2), the federal government passed the Native Title Act, defining the native title as the rights and interests of Aboriginal peoples observed both under traditional custom and common law. However the legal consequences of the fact of occupancy (at the time of the settlers' arrival) by Aborigines are less clear. Some argued that the basic presumptions of English land

---

256 Three Tribes of Fort Berthold Reservation v. United States, 182 Ct.Cl. 543, 390 F.2d 686 (1968).

257 Eddie Mabo and Others v. The State of Queensland 175 CLR 1, 1992.

258 Johnston, Hinton, and Rigney (ed.), *Indigenous Australians and the Law*, Cavending Publishing, 1997, pp. 133–49.

259 Prior to Mabo(2), Aboriginal people were denied land rights on the basis of two principles: the *terra nullius* and the of tenure doctrines. In a nutshell, the two principles held that on the one hand Australia is a settled territory (i.e., no recognizable legal system existed before colonization), and on the other, all land vests in the Crown, and all individual rights to interests in land derive from a grant of such an interest by the Crown, and involve a tenurial relationship between the grantee and the Crown (Anthony Moore, in Johnston, Hinton, and Rigney [eds.], *op. cit.*, pp. 133–5). This theory is echoed by a court decision such as Attorney-General v. Brown (1847) 1 Legge 312; Cooper v. Stuart (1889) 14 AC 286 (Privy Council Decision) or Milirrpum v. Nabalco Pty Ltd. and the Commonwealth (1971) 17 FLR 141, all quoted by Moore.

260 Barkan, *op. cit.*, p. 238; Moore, *op. cit.*, p. 134.

law suggest entitlement to a presumption of fee simple title.[261] Still, in Ward, the Federal Court[262] stated that mere occupancy does not identify the nature of rights and interests existent over the respective tracts. Occupancy therefore, is an insufficient basis for identifying any rights relating to the occupied lands.[263]

In a post-communist context, however, it is rather difficult to ground property restitution on the idea of rights. The communist regimes that affected the takings made use of their legal powers to do so, except for the cases where, as already mentioned above, takings took place under military occupation, in breach of the existing legal provisions governing expropriation or the state simply failed to fulfill its obligations regarding compensations. There was a much lesser degree of formal illegality involved than in the case of Native Americans or Maoris. Thus, as Teitel observes, "[p]roperty rights entitlements arising out of past wrongs are constructed ex post and are, simultaneously self-referential and justificatory of present property distributions."[264] But, the right to property is neither the sole, nor the paramount fundamental right recognized by post-communist constitutions. Allen notes in this respect that the claims are weaker when the blame cannot be attributed to the party required to compensate. A rather large part of the communist era takings might be regarded as the result of a bad economic policy which could hardly provide ground for reparation. Parallels can be made with victims of natural calamities, whose claims for redress have a distributive, rather than reparative justice character.[265] However, as it will be argued *infra*, this would amount to an oversimplification of the problem of communist era property deprivations.

---

[261] Kent McNeil; quoted with approval by Brennan, *op. cit.*.

[262] After the 1998 amendments to the Native Title Act, the Federal Court has become responsible for the management and determination of all applications relating to native title. Applications have to be filed with the Federal Court, which then refers them to the Tribunal. The Tribunal mediates claims under the direction of the Federal Court. If the claim is not resolved by agreement, the matter is referred back to the Federal Court for trial and determination (AIATSIS, http://www.aiatsis.gov.au/rsrch/ntru/research/resourceguide/national_overview/national02.html).

[263] Brennan, *op. cit.*.

[264] Teitel, *op. cit.*, p. 133.

[265] Allen, *op. cit.*, p. 42.

Thus, the fundamental question still remains unanswered: why losses of property are regularly compensated, while, for instance, former restrictions on the freedom of speech or conscience are not? One argument in favor of property restitution could be that the objects of property rights physically exist (or existed), thus they can be returned or compensated, while speech has only a potential existence. In other words: restrictions upon speech burdened or prohibited the exercise of this freedom, but the disappearance of the authoritarian regime automatically resulted in the disappearance of the restrictions. At the same time, however, the political change did not automatically entail repossession of taken property.[266] Another way out of this dilemma is offered by the already mentioned Hungarian Constitutional Court decision which declared unconstitutional a number of nationalization decrees, arguing that, through nationalization, the government attempted to eradicate the institution of private property without providing any compensation.[267] But note that the Hungarian Court is pointing towards a formal deficiency, and absent such a feature, the compensation scheme could hardly be justified on a rights-based approach.

The principle of past harm, as a normative value, does not offer enough guidance in justifying property reparations, at least in the post-communist context. And that is, because it simply sweeps too broad. As Elster remarked, "essentially everybody suffered under communism."[268] Some were imprisoned, placed under secret surveillance, had their books placed on index, were barred from leaving the country, or many simply lost career opportunities or suffered other losses. István Pogány noted that "the economic consequences of expelling Jews from certain sectors of employment [...] was at least as severe, for the individuals concerned and for their families, as the confis-

[266] This of course does not mean that for, e.g., the authors whose books, articles, etc., were censored or put on index by the communist authorities could not claim compensation.

[267] HCC, AB 27/1991, 91/E/1990: "It can be established then, that in effect, on the basis of the enumerated nationalization acts, until the end of the 1950s in Hungary [...] a liquidation of the institution of private property took place without compensation."

[268] John Elster, "On Doing What One Can: An Argument Against Post-Communist Restitution and Retribution," *East European Constitutional Review* 1.2 (1992), p. 16.

cation of property proved for others."[269] The suffering endured by the relatives and descendants of those Chilean and Argentine citizens who disappeared without a trace were probably no less severe.[270] The obvious result, to which the principle of past harm has to lead therefore, is universal and equivalent reparations.[271]

Therefore, the third justification, namely political persecution (discrimination) needs to be brought into play. The above-mentioned Hungarian Constitutional Court decision did also rely on the discriminating feature of past takings, while attempting to demonstrate their lack of compliance with constitutionally protected values. The argument of the Court maintained that the notion of public utility does not extend to takings that stigmatize or discriminate against individuals or groups.[272] The nationalization process initially was targeting the assets of a certain class, later properties of a certain size, and finally the near complete annihilation of the institution of private property.[273]

Discriminative taking, as a ground for restitution, appears perhaps most obvious in the case of Holocaust restitution. In the case of France, for instance, the Provisional Advisory Assembly (operating in exile) issued a decree on the re-establishment of the republican legality, which provided that "all [legal texts] which apply or enforce any sort of discrimination based upon the Jewish quality" shall become null and void.[274] Subsequently, another decree directed the judiciary to acknowl-

---

[269] István Pogány, *Righting Wrongs in Eastern Europe*, Manchester University Press, 1997, p. 171.

[270] Elster, "A framework...", *op. cit.*.

[271] As the charismatic former Czech president, Václav Havel asked: "[i]f everyone suffered, why should only some be redressed?" in Paul Wilson (ed.), *Open Letters: Selected Writings, 1965–1990*, Alfred A. Knopf, 1992.

[272] *Ibid.*.

[273] At the outset this was directed towards the assets of certain social groups, afterwards according to the defined seize of property, and in the end it finished with the near complete liquidation of private ownership.

[274] Decree of August 9, 1944, section 3: "Est expressément constatée la nullité des actes suivants: [...] Tous ceux qui établissent ou appliquent une discrimination quelconque fondée sur la qualité de juif." See also: Wouter Veraart, "'Reasonableness' or strict law? The postwar restitution rights in the Netherlands and in France (1945–1952)," Paper presented at Yad Vashem: The International Conference on Confronting History: The Historical Commissions of Inquiry, 2002, available online, at http://www1.yadvashem.org/about_yad/departments/institute/pdf/10.pdf, p. 8.

edge the nullity of any transaction of property performed after the respective property was taken from its original owner. Moreover, the norm went as far as to create a presumption according to which those possible victims of persecution that sold their property acted under duress, unless the buyer could prove the contrary.[275] Similar regulations were enacted in Hungary, after the fall of the right-wing regime, where an impressive number of decrees issued between 1945 and 1947 provided for the return of immovable and movable goods—especially those pertaining to small businesses—and regulating the fate of heirless properties.[276] In post-war Czechoslovakia, Decree No. 5 annulled all transactions that occurred on the basis of racial or political persecution under the German Reich beginning with 29 September 1938. This was soon reconfirmed by Law No. 128 of 1946.[277] Of course, Holocaust reparations took place in an entirely different context: confiscation of Jewish assets was part of a genocidal program, which makes these claims more compelling.[278]

A paradoxical counter-example is represented by the Czech Constitutional Court's decision upon the Beneš Decrees.[279] Concretely, the challenge was targeting the decree on the Confiscation of Enemy Property and the Funds of National Renewal.[280] The act in question identified as enemies of the nation persons of German and Hungarian nationality, with the scope of subjecting them to property confiscation. The presumption of enmity was refutable if these persons could demonstrate their loyalty to the Czechoslovak Republic.[281] As the Court

---

275 Decree of April 1945, sections 1 and 11; quoted by Veraart, *op. cit.*, pp. 9–10.

276 Prime Minister's Orders Nos. 7590/1945, 3630/1945, 10.480/1945, 300/1946, 12.530/1946, 6400/1947, 5280/1947, and Governmental Decree No. 13.160/1947.

277 Macklem, *op. cit.*, pp. 5, 11.

278 Kutz, *op. cit.*, p. 285.

279 CCC, Pl. US 14/94, *ibid.*. Edvard Beneš was the elected president of Czechoslovakia from 1935, his mandate having to expire in 1942. However, after the 1938 German occupation of the country he was forced to resign and flee. He formed an exile government, which in 1942 prolonged his term of office until an election was possible to hold. At the end of the war he returned, and retained his office until 1948 when, after the communist takeover, he resigned for the second time.

280 Decree No. 108/1945 Sb.

281 Proofs of loyalty were considered to be: abstention from wronging the Czech and Slovak nation (whatever this may mean); active participation in the fight

pointed out, the decree was based on a presumption of responsibility of the German and Hungarian minorities. However, the Court did not found any discriminatory feature in the decree under scrutiny, arguing that the presumption of responsibility is a "just sanction," a "proportionate response" to the Nazi aggression, and not a nationalistic revenge.[282] The question of the Beneš Decrees was raised at an international level in front of the UN Human Rights Committee by a complaint against Slovakia.[283] Here the applicant alleged that the restitution scheme was discriminatory because it left uncompensated the victims of the 1945 seizures. The Committee, however, found that the scheme did not appear *prima facie* discriminatory simply because it dealt with victims of communism, but because it ignored the victims of injustices committed by earlier regimes. For these reasons, the complaint was declared inadmissible.

In any case, the criterion of persecution does not give a satisfactory explanation that may justify property reparations. True enough, it helps drafting the pool of beneficiaries by distinguishing those persecuted—the confiscation of dissident's assets is the paradigm—from all the others who may also have suffered some property losses. Still, not only property owners were persecuted under communist regimes, and from a moral perspective, persecution that took the form of imprisonment for example, cannot be considered to be less worthy of compensation than confiscation.[284]

In this context, it is worth noting that the Hungarian legislature did design a scheme for the (monetary) compensation of those who were illegally deprived of their lives or liberty on political grounds.[285] A subsequent act extended the circle of beneficiaries to the heirs of those who lost their lives, and to those who suffer from bodily disabili-

for liberation; sufferings under Nazi or fascist terror (CCC, Pl. US 14/94, *ibid.*, p. 14).

282 CCC, Pl. US 14/94, *ibid.*, pp. 15–9.

283 Peter Drobek v. Slovakia, Communication No. 643/1995 (31 May 1994), CCPR/C/60/D/643/1995.

284 As Offe and Bönker, *op. cit.*, p. 31 argue, "it would be morally wrong to let the choice of rectificatory strategies be distorted by the morally irrelevant fact that property can be given back, while years lost in prison cannot."

285 Law No. XXXII of 1992 ("Az életüktől és szabadságuktól politikai okból jogtalanul megfosztottak kárpótlásáról"). The compensation could take the form of one-time payment, life annuity, or vouchers.

ties or severe degradation of their health as a consequence of an infringement of their fundamental human rights out of political, religious, or racial motives.[286] The justification for the scheme encompasses all the three grounds discussed above: harm (loss of life, bodily disability, severe degradation of health), breach of fundamental (human) rights, and discrimination.[287] This approach, however, does not do justice between victims, but merely widens the class of the privileged, and therefore cannot avoid the kind of criticism which is phrased by Elster: "as it would be absurd to indemnify everyone, it follows that one should not compensate anyone."[288] Whilst property, time (spent in detention), or lost working capacity is much easier to quantify than for instance lost opportunities, this still does not make the compensation of the former more compelling.

An essential distinction has to be made between the different kinds of takings that have been mentioned here, as the context of the takings exerts an essential influence on the reparations. As it was shown above, indigenous claims rest on the breach of an indigenous ownership established by treaties or constructed by the judiciary, while the plundering of Jewish property was part of a genocidal project. By contrast, except for the Soviet Union—where collectivization took place with terrible violence, famine, and massacres—the methods adopted in the rest of the communist countries were less extreme.[289] Roughly two main methods can be identified: taking through confiscation (especially in the case of those labeled "enemies of the regime," or of "the nation": those charged with war crimes, etc.) or through donations and exchanges. Even if the authorities "forgot" to provide for compensation, many formal requirements were still respected so as to uphold as much as possible the impression of legality. "Donations" were the usual method of forming the collectives—procedural requirements insisted on witnesses and signa-

[286] Law No. LII of 1992. This norm provides for a uniform monthly allowance called "national care" (*nemzeti gondozás*).

[287] Somewhat similar steps have been undertaken by Germany (2000), and Czechia (2005), for the compensation of political detainees, in the form of a monthly allowance in accordance with the time spent in detention. For details, see: http://www.amlaw.us/arauf_19.shtml and http://www.ujszo.com/clanok.asp?vyd=20041126&cl=109302.

[288] Elster, "On doing what one can," *op. cit.*.

[289] Verdery, *op. cit.*, p. 46.

tures to demonstrate free consent. Simultaneously, land exchanges had to be made between the newly constituted collectives and the neighboring non-members, so as to form compact plots. Cartwright notes—writing about Romania—that forcing through the exchange (despite the protests of the non-member landowner) was not decreed as lawful until 1951, even though the practice started much earlier.[290]

As a conclusion, it can be stated that the reasons underlying post-communist property compensation schemes do not satisfactorily justify the distinguished treatment enjoyed by former property owners in comparison with other categories who experienced some forms of injustice under communist regimes. Offe and Bönker note in this respect that

> underneath the proclamation of lofty principles of justice all kinds of arbitrary interests, privileges, and resentments have governed the actual practice of restitution. [...] The concentration on property losses primarily reflects the strategic importance attached to property reform and the greater political leverage of former property owners compared with other victims of the communist regime.[291]

Verdery observed that there was a strong political power-related feature of restitution (and privatization), as legislating majorities tried to use the restitution process so as to weaken their political opposition (by cutting them from economic sources), and at the same time to free some revenue-generating sources for themselves.[292]

7. The wolf, the goat, and the cabbage

According to the classical puzzle, a ferryman has to cross a wolf, a goat, and cabbage safely to the other side of the river, his problem being that only two of the three fit in his boat at the same time, and he is the only

---

[290] Cartwright, *op. cit.*, p. 83, n. 61.

[291] Offe and Bönker, *op. cit.*, p. 31.

[292] Verdery, *op. cit.* Elster makes the same argument, pointing out that the role of party interest in shaping transitional justice is highly significant, especially that in most Central and East European countries the former elite retains some support in the competition for votes in the free elections. This aspect appears more dramatically in the context of lustration. ("A Framework...," *idem*).

one who can row. The question then is how to pair up the passengers in a way that prevents them from harming the other. Post communist societies of Central and Eastern Europe faced a similar, although more complicated puzzle: they had, in a relatively short period, to solve competing, even conflicting problems. To deal with past injustice, to secure the preconditions of market economy, and to create and entrench a new elite.

To their misfortune, in the majority of the cases, the worst solution was chosen, namely to take on all the passengers at the same time, with the obvious risk of having the ferry sunk by the overload. Perhaps the river looked temptingly narrow, perhaps it was too enticing to talk about market economy in justice context. The mixture of reparative and distributive justice that resulted from this was not a consequence of some grand theory of property or justice. Rather, what currently is called transitional justice is explicable by external political values stemming from the political exigencies of the time.[293]

The conclusion that emerges from the above-presented is that it was wrong to link questions of reparation with questions of redistribution. Because they simply cannot justify each other. It is theoretically untenable for property restitution or compensation to target an even distribution because this would facilitate better the emergence of a market economy. It is equally untenable to compensate property-related injustices of the previous regime because market economy is contingent upon privately owned property.

When reparative concerns are linked with structural reform, the whole scheme—including reparations—can only be upheld on distributive justice grounds. The conclusion to which the Hungarian Constitutional Court has arrived in the above-cited decision, according to which the concept underlying a partial compensation is of distributive character because the compensation scheme pursues property reform goals, is inevitable.[294] But the problem with distributive justice is that it can easily turn against the rule of law, if it is interpreted in terms of substantive equality.[295] I could not agree more with Ágnes Heller: "what

[293] Teitel, *op. cit.*, p. 147.

[294] HCC, AB 15/1993, 1543/B/1991: "The Constitutional Court [...] examines the Compensation Law not in itself, but in the context of the regime change."

[295] Hayek, *op. cit.*, p. 59.

form of distribution is just or unjust is something that only members of each community are qualified to decide."[296] However, in the post-communist context it is difficult to talk about "a community": in the case of heirless properties there was no community at all, while ethnical and/or religious minorities, the emerging elite, the old nomenclature, all constituted interest groups with diverging, often conflicting aims, and necessarily some found themselves on the losing end of restitution. I do not argue that it was wrong to try to tackle more problems at once, but that it was wrong to link issues that did not support each other. As a consequence of such an approach, the majority of Central and East European restitution programs presented some problematic components which questioned the justice of restitution.

First, it appears that there is no compelling justice argument for the mitigation of past expropriations at large. It is indeed up to the government whether it wishes to link redistribution of property to pre-existing holdings or not. Nevertheless, in a number of significant, albeit less numerous exceptions, it is possible to point to an actual past injustice (illegal takings) or failure of the government to fulfill its promises (international obligations, omissions of compensation) towards the claimants. In these cases, it appears unjust to derive the right to claim and the corresponding obligation to compensate from governmental gratitude.

Second, the distinction made between former property owners and the rest of the society (whose members have undoubtedly suffered a number of injustices) with respect to compensations can be defended only by reference to the social dimension of the property reforms. The analyzed normative values (past harm, breach of fundamental rights, and political persecution) used to define the circle of beneficiaries do not adequately explain why other victims are excluded from this scheme.

The principle of past harm sweeps too broad, because, as I have just mentioned, virtually everyone experienced some kind of loss under the authoritarian regimes. The principles of violation of fundamental rights or of political discrimination may work in case of ancient claims (where indeed one may talk about violation of rights) or Holocaust restitution (discriminative takings as part of the genocidal project), but

296 Heller, *op. cit.*, p. 205.

are difficult to sustain in a post-communist context. Most of the takings maintained a formal legality, and while political persecution may be a legitimate ground to claim reparations, it does not essentially distinguish itself from other forms of political persecution, unless the market economy reasons are brought into play. It is worth also noting that a way out of this trap was to extend the compensation scheme as to encompass also other types of persecution; however, this was done only with respect to fairly easily quantifiable losses (as life, physical integrity, or time).[297]

In this context, the Hayekian statement, according to which "any policy aiming directly at a substantive ideal of distributive justice must lead to the destruction of the Rule of Law [...] It cannot be denied that the Rule of Law produces economic inequality,"[298] constitutes a very serious objection that post-communist restitution programs must face. What Hayek means by inequality is the requirement that different people should be treated differently—so as to allow for, but not deliberately produce inequality. "To give different people the same objective opportunities is not to give them the same subjective chance."[299]

[297] Perhaps one of the reasons was to limit the number of potential beneficiaries.

[298] Hayek, *op. cit.*, p. 59.

[299] "[A]ll that can be claimed for is that this inequality is not designed to affect particular people in a particular way," *ibid.*. Ronald Dworkin is making the same point when arguing that equal moral worth of persons requires not equal treatment, but treatment as equals (*Taking Rights Seriously*, Harvard University Press, 1978, p. 227).

CHAPTER 3

Rule of Law, Equality, and Limited Restitution

The previous chapter argued that restitution programs have a definite distributive character, and emphasized that a distributive approach represents a serious threat to the rule of law. Building on this argument, the present chapter is dedicated to the analysis of the effects of a distributive concept of justice on the pool of victims of past property losses, the persons whose grievances the restitution schemes attempt to mitigate.

I concluded the previous chapter with some quotes from Hayek, reflecting his concerns about distributive justice, peculiarly with regard to inequality. Hayek contrasted "subjective chance" with "objective opportunities," claiming that equal treatment entails preference of the latter to the former.[1] Therefore, the fundamental question from an equality perspective is whether post-communist restitution schemes manage to draft the pool of beneficiaries in such a way so as to create objectively equal opportunities at least for those placed in an equal situation. At this stage it is worth noting that for instance both the German and the Hungarian constitutional courts referred to equal treatment as the main principle of compensation.[2] Of course, distributive justice *per se* is not objectionable, as long as it fulfills the Hayekian requirement of treating different people differently. However, there are at least four aspects of post-communist reparations (regardless of the form they may take) that are questionable from this perspective.

Here I take a closer look at the pool of victims of property losses, arguing that even those in an equal situation—that is, former owners—were denied in some instances equal opportunities to repara-

[1] Hayek, *op. cit.*.

[2] European Commission for Democracy Through Law, Opinion No. 277/2004, *op. cit.*, para. 7.

tions. This was achieved by the limitations imposed through the restitution laws. These limitations pursued two broad aims: exclusion and approximately leveled outcomes of the process. Under the first category of aims fall person-related limitations (citizenship or residency requirements), temporal limitations (cut-off dates), and property-based limitations (excluding of certain categories of property). The schemes attempted to achieve the second goal through quantitative restrictions (caps based on the returnable amount of property or receivable compensation). However, as it will be shown in this chapter, substantive equality turns into an objective inequality: everyone is entitled to the same scale of restitution (compensation), while everyone experienced different amounts of loss. Hence, grievances are redressed to unequal extents.

In the following, each subchapter is dedicated to a different limitation on property restitution. Thus, the first subchapter addresses the issue of citizenship and residency, which in one or another form was a widespread requirement—at least in the incipient phase—of the various restitution schemes. The second subchapter deals with quantitative, while the third with temporal limitations, both to be found directly or indirectly in each restitution program.[3] Finally, the fourth subchapter explores property-based limitations. It is divided into four sections, each dedicated to a problematic distinction: movable and immovable, various types of immovable, economic, and religious and communal properties. The outcome of the analysis is that the various property objects are treated differently by the restitution schemes, but this distinction is mostly arbitrary, and in certain cases complicates, rather than settles property relationships.[4] Taking all this into consideration, this chapter concludes that in certain respect restitution schemes fulfill the

---

[3] Express limitations took the form of a general ceiling or an explicit cut-off date. Indirect quantitative limitations are for instance the measures providing for the incorporation of the value of movable assets found within the expropriated building in the compensation to be received for the immovable. Indirect temporal limitations are represented by the situations in which although there is no expressly stated general cut-off date, the law states that restitution or compensation can be claimed only for those properties that were taken on the basis of specific acts.

[4] This is the case of Germany or Latvia for example, where it was not uncommon for a plot to be awarded to an owner, while the house built upon the respective plot stayed with another owner.

Hayekian predictions, and by producing unjustifiable inequalities between the former property owners, they conflict with the tenets of the rule of law.

1. Personal limitations: the citizenship and/or residency requirement

The most common person-related limitation on restitution is the one that requires for the victims to possess the citizenship and/or to be resident of the state against which they are willing to vindicate their claim to restitution. These requirements were set in order to exclude certain "undesirable" individuals, who left the country during or even prior to the communist takeover. This is the case of the former, pre-communist elite and of the dissidents, and in many cases also of certain ethnic groups, like Sudeten Germans and Hungarians (expelled from post-war Czechoslovakia), Russians in the Baltic States, and Jews in several cases.[5]

Such personal limitations can be met in other, non-European settings too. For instance, in the case of Australian Aborigines, to prove the native title, there must be an established entitlement to occupy or use particular lands. A special relationship needs to be demonstrated between users and land,[6] but it does not need to amount to possession as known to common law, neither does it require the exploitation of the lands in question.[7] The test of continuous traditional connection and the usage of the particular land turned out to be extremely demanding and only less than 10% of the Aborigine population became eligible for restitution.[8] In this case, however, the aim of the requirement is not to distinguish and exclude certain sub-groups from the pool of beneficiaries, but instead to simply limit the size of the pool as such.

Many restitution laws were drafted in such a way so as to bar non-

---

[5] Avineri, *op. cit.*.

[6] The question of whether this relationship must be a physical one gives rise to contradictory positions. In this sense, see: Coe v. Commonwealth (1993) 118 ALR 193 and Mason v. Triton (1994) 34 NSWLR 572; both referred to by Moore, *op. cit.*, p. 141 (footnote 17).

[7] *Ibid.*, p. 140.

[8] *Ibid.*, p. 244.

citizens or non-residents—either *ex lege* or *de facto*[9]—from participating in the process.

1.1 Strict regimes: citizenship and residence

In such cases, both of the conditions were—at least originally—contemplated by the restitution or compensation schemes; in certain cases a subsequent easement was brought by the courts. Lithuania, Czechoslovakia, and subsequently Slovakia managed to stick to the harsh rule, while in the case of Czechia and Poland the residence condition was considered as unconstitutional and eliminated by the constitutional courts.

Out of the three Baltic States, Lithuania adopted the most restrictive rules from the perspective of residence and citizenship requirements. The law on property restitution requires claimants to concomitantly possess "certified Lithuanian citizenship" and be permanent residents of the republic.[10] The same conditions have to be fulfilled also by successors of the entitled persons. The single exception from this rule is the case of deportees (under the communist regime, for participating in movements resisting Soviet occupation) and their heirs.[11]

Czechoslovakia opted for a similarly restrictive approach to restitution, setting a double requirement of permanent residence and citizenship for eligibility.[12] The Czech Constitutional Court acknowledged

[9] *De facto* obstructions can be considered for instance the short deadlines within which compensation claims had to be filed initially. These significantly reduced the chances of those potential claimants residing outside the respective state (especially that filing the claim also entailed the introduction of required evidence), who were not barred by the citizenship requirement, but had extremely short period available to take notice and act. This is also demonstrated by the fact that these deadlines were commonly extended, as it proved difficult even for claimants residing within the territory of the respective state to file their requests on time.

[10] Law "On the Procedure and Conditions of the Restoration of the Rights of Ownership to the Existing Real Property," *op. cit.*, Art. 2.

[11] Institute of Economics, Estonian Academy of Sciences, Review of structural reforms, *op. cit.*.

[12] Federal Act No. 87/1991 "On the extra-judicial rehabilitations" and Federal Act No. 229/1991 "On regulation of property in land and other agricultural property."

that the United Nations Human Rights Committee found the citizenship requirement as contrary to the ICCPR's clause on the prohibition of discrimination.[13] However, it stated that this provision allows for unequal treatment, if sufficient reasons for discrimination exist. Consequently, the Court held that differentiation on the account of citizenship was compatible with the ICCPR clause.[14] In the case of those persons whose claims for restitution were grounded on the Act on Judicial Rehabilitation[15] (property lost as a consequence of criminal condemnations), the Court repeated that unequal treatment is compatible with reigning international agreements, to the extent that it is based on reasonable and objective criteria. It was held, again, that "the aims of the restitution legislation and the legal regulation of citizenship fulfil these requirements."[16] The oddity of this highly restrictive approach is best demonstrated by the case of a former Czechoslovakian citizen, who was denied restitution by a Czech land office after the dissolution of the Federal Republic, on the grounds that after the dissolution she became a Slovakian citizen, and therefore lost her entitlement to restitution. The Czech Constitutional Court has set aside the contested decisions, arguing that the claim for restitution was filed within the legal limits, and therefore the requirement of legal certainty and of equal treatment were infringed.[17]

Slovakia "inherited" its property restitution laws from the dismantled federal republic; therefore, the same regulations applied as in Czechia. There was one significant difference though: unlike in Czechia, where the Constitutional Court declared it in violation of the Constitution, in Slovakia the permanent residency requirement was

---

[13] Šimůnek, 19.7.1995, No 516/1992; Adam, 23.7.1996, No 586/1994.

[14] CCC, Pl. ÚS 24/98, Coll. of the decisions 15(1999 – Part III), 211 and the following.

[15] Act No 119/199.

[16] CCC, Pl. ÚS 9/99, Coll. of decisions 16(1999 – Part IV), 9 and the following.

For the foregoing two decisions, see also: Hofmann, "Impact of the views of the UN Human Rights Committee in the national legal order of some Eastern and Central European countries," available online, at http://www.abo.fi/instut/imr/ILA-files/Hofmann.doc, pp. 3–4.

[17] CCC, IV. US 215/94, available online, at http://test.concourt.cz/angl_verze/doc/4-215-94.html.

maintained as a precondition of restitution claims.[18] The European Court of Human Rights, touching upon the residence requirement, held that the applicant could not have legitimately expected that his claim would be determined in his favor, because he failed to establish a permanent residence according to applicable regulations. Moreover, stressed the Court, Article 1 of Protocol No. 1 neither guarantees the right to acquire property, nor imposes "any restrictions on the Contracting States' freedom to choose conditions under which they accept to restore property that was transferred to them before they ratified the Convention." As to the applicant's claim of Article 14's prohibition of discrimination, the Court briefly dismissed it, holding that this article only complements the other substantive provisions, without having an independent existence. Thus, as no violation of a protected right was found, there was no possibility of invoking Article 14 either.[19]

However, after the dissolution of the federation, the Czech Constitutional Court declared the residence requirement as unconstitutional. The argument was that the residence requirement conflicted with the principle of the state governed by the rule of law, the guarantee of equal rights, the prohibition of discrimination, the provisions on statutory limitations on fundamental rights, and with Art. 1 of the Additional Protocol to the European Convention for the Protection of Human Rights.[20]

The Polish law regulating compensation for properties left beyond the Bug River also provided for a double constraint on claimants. Entitled persons had to possess Polish citizenship and reside, following relocation, within Poland's present borders; moreover, permanent residence on Polish territory after the entry into force of the act in question (30 January 2004) was required, too.[21] The Constitutional Tribunal, however, found these requirements too harsh. While residency after relocation and citizenship were considered as being in rational conjunc-

[18] This requirement was not challenged in court as of 2002 (Procházka, *op. cit.*, p. 174).

[19] Janter v. Slovakia, ECHR, Judgment of 4 March 2003, Application No. 39050/97, paras. 29–42.

[20] CCC, Pl. US 3/94, pp. 8–9.

[21] Offsetting the Value of Property Abandoned Beyond the Present Borders of the Polish State Against the Price of State Property or the Fee for the Right of Perpetual Usufruct Act, 2003, *op. cit.*, Article 2(1), points 2 and 3.

tion with "the compensating-beneficial nature" of the state's obligation, the requirement of residence after the entry into force of the act was found as unconstitutional. The Tribunal reasoned that this date is "arbitrarily specified and accidental," while lacking any substantive justification, thus creating an excessive differentiation in protection of property rights.[22]

1.2 Milder regimes: citizenship or residence

Those schemes fit this category that established only one—or, both, but alternatively—of the two criteria. Accordingly, further distinctions may be made depending whether a policy fashioned exclusively the citizenship condition, obviously harsher, as it excludes those who lost their citizenship in the meantime, or accepted also residence as an alternative, which is obviously milder, as it accommodates also returning expatriates. In this section fall the two other Baltic States, and Hungary and Romania.

In Estonia, both the citizenship and residence principles were invoked, albeit in different contexts. In order to qualify for reparations, claimants had to either reside on the territory of Estonia, at the date of entry into force of the restitution act, or had to have Estonian citizenship at the cut-off point (16 July 1940) established by the same act as the baseline for compensation.[23] By way of exception, with regard to unlawfully expropriated property which was in the ownership of citizens of foreign states and stateless persons, successors of the entitled persons had to fulfill either the residence, or the citizenship requirement, but this time both at the time of entry into force of the pertaining legislation.[24] Another exception was created for the treatment of property expropriated from foreign actors. Finally, similar treatment was envisaged for those persons who left Estonia on the basis of agreements with the German State; in both cases compensation was left to be dealt with through international agreements.[25] As such agreements have yet to be concluded, this latter provision was successfully chal-

[22] K 2/04, Judgment of 15 December 2004, *op. cit.*, paras. II/7 and II/8.
[23] The Principles of Ownership Reform Act, 1991, *op. cit.*, para. 7.
[24] *Ibid.*.
[25] *Ibid.*, paras. 7(2) and (3).

lenged before the Supreme Court, which found that the respective provision is not in conformity with the principle of legal clarity and violates the fundamental rights of persons to organization and procedure (Art. 13(2) and 14 of the Constitution).[26]

Latvia adopted a largely similar approach, granting the right to restitution to current citizens and to those who had been citizens at the cut-off date (21 July 1940). The same rules applied also in the case of successors, without any residency requirement.[27] Interestingly, in the case of deportees (for opposing the Soviet occupation) the residence principle is used: former deportees may claim compensation only if they reside on the territory of Latvia.[28]

The Hungarian Compensation Law restricted the circle of possible claimants to persons of Hungarian citizenship: persons who held Hungarian citizenship at the date when the loss was suffered and non-citizens who had established permanent residence in Hungary before 31 December 1990.[29] The constitutionality of these requirements was never directly challenged. However, the Constitutional Court did touch upon the question of discrimination between former property-owners. Its conclusions in this question, albeit focusing on the problem of distinguishing properties apt for and excluded from restitution, may, *mutatis mutandis*, cast some light on the Court's conception of discrimination. To comply with the constitutional prohibition of discrimination, any differentiation between former owners has to fulfill the requirements of positive discrimination. According to the Court, this mainly consists in procedural guarantees, which ensure that all interests were

[26] ESC, Case No. 3-4-1-5-02, *op. cit.*, para. 35.

[27] Institute of Economics, Estonian Academy of Sciences, Review of structural reforms, *op. cit.*

[28] Cabinet of Ministers' Resolution No. 148 "On the Procedure by which The Property is Restituted or its Value is Compensated to Persons, whose Administrative Deportation from the Latvian SSR is Recognized Unfounded," 1997, section 2 (as subsequently amended); quoted by the Constitutional Court in case No. 04-03 (98), Judgment of 10 June 1998.

[29] Law XXV/1991, *op. cit.*, para. 2(1).

With respect to the residence requirement, the original text reads: "that non-Hungarian citizen, who had his regular residence in Hungary as of 31 December 1990."

weighed with impartiality and equal circumspection.[30] Even in these conditions, discrimination can be considered constitutional only if it serves as a precondition of a more perfect social equality.[31] In another decision, the Court stated that the *in personam* effects of the compensation law have to be evaluated together with its effects in time. Concretely, the constitutionality of the differentiation between the former owners can be appropriately assessed only after the conclusion of the compensation process. Theoretically, said the Court, a distinct norm of the body of laws dealing with compensation could be held unconstitutional if it introduces an unalterable discrimination. However, in the case of the compensation law, no such risk was present.[32]

According to the Romanian restitution laws, only claimants possessing Romanian citizenship (at the date of filing the request) were entitled to restitution, regardless of their residency status.[33]

1.3 The exception: Germany

The German solution—under this aspect, as under some others too, as it can be seen in other sections of this book—constitutes an exception, because the Property Act[34] did not envisage any residence or citizenship related restriction on the potential circle of beneficiaries. The

[30] HCC, AB 21/1990, 1057/G/1990, section V.

This reasoning follows also from the conception according to which compensation is not done on the basis of constitutional rights and obligations, but as an *ex gratia* allotment. Therefore, former owners may only have a right to a fair procedure that treats their interests with equal concern. "Thus they are not entitled to receive a share from state property, but to be treated as equals at the regulation of such an opportunity, and to have each and every one's point of view assessed with similar attention and fairness. Without this, the discrimination is unconstitutional."

[31] *Ibid.*.

[32] HCC, AB 28/1991, 1160/A/1991, section B 1.4: "Elvileg alkotmányellenes lehet, ha egy részszabály később ki nem egyenlíthető megkülönböztetést vezet be..."

The Court explained that due to the limited amount of disponible resources, the limitations imposed on the pool of beneficiaries cannot be considered arbitrary (*idem*, section B 1.1).

[33] Law No. 18/1991, *op.cit.*, Art. 48; Law No.112/1995, *op.cit.*, Art. 4.

[34] The Resolution of Outstanding Property Issues Act of 23 September 1990 (Gesetz über Regelung offener Vermögensfragen), *ibid.*.

initial approach excluded, however, restitution properties taken during the Soviet occupation.

As it was explained in the previous chapter, property restitution schemes had, almost in every case, a dual objective: the mitigation of past injustice and the resettlement of property relationships and structures. Therefore, the evaluation of citizenship and residence requirements has to take note of this duality of aims. Under the first objective—rectification of past injustices—there is little justification for the imposition of such conditions. The decisions of the Czech Constitutional Court and the Polish Constitutional Tribunal upon the unconstitutionality of the residence requirement emphasize the arbitrariness of this restriction. Interestingly, all courts found the citizenship condition unproblematic; unfortunately none of the relevant rulings offered an explanation for this. Under the second objective—restructuring of property relationships, with a view to the transition to market economy—arguments could, *prima facie*, be brought in favor of the citizenship/residency requirements, especially on economic grounds.[35] Taking, however, a closer look will reveal that certain categories of potential beneficiaries were excluded from the system mainly on grounds of scarcity, rather than political economy. True enough, as the Hungarian Constitutional Court emphasized in most of its above-quoted decisions, if compensation is delivered not on constitutional basis, but only as matter of governmental benevolence, there is a much wider discretion in defining the pool of beneficiaries. This wide scope of discretion was recognized also by the European Court of Human Rights, when it spoke about the margin of appreciation enjoyed by the states in drafting their restitution policy.[36] However, when the Hungarian Constitutional Court ventured into analyzing the permissible grounds of discriminating between former property owners, it laid down very strict

[35] Essentially it could be an efficiency-based argument, according to which property handed over to residents/citizens will contribute more efficiently to the development of market economy than property handed over to foreigners/non-citizens. This could be argued either in the sense that these properties would be somehow kept out of the countries productive resources (in case of in kind restitution or vouchers), or that capital falling in "foreign" hands will result in profits travelling also abroad. However, the accuracy of these arguments is more than doubtful.

[36] Janter v. Slovakia, *op. cit.*.

limitations on such a practice. Eventually, it arrived to the conclusion that positive discrimination can be accepted in a finite period of time, and unalterable differences should not be created.[37]

The Hungarian Court resorted to utilitarian arguments in justifying the discriminations created, considering that present inequalities are acceptable if they lead to a more perfect social equality in the future.[38] It is unclear, however, how could the preclusion of non-citizens and non-residents from the compensation scheme enhance future equality. Another explanation may draw on Rawl's difference principle—which is not a utilitarian account—social and economical inequalities shall be arranged so that the greatest benefit is preserved for the least well off.[39] Still, it is more than arguable whether this holds true for, and can be applied at all in, a resident/non-resident or citizen/non-citizen comparison.

2. Quantitative limitations

Restitution and compensation programs differed significantly under the quantitative aspect. In the case of Hungary and Poland, original properties were not returned—except for certain religious assets—, only a partial compensation in form of vouchers or the possibility to offset the value of the taken property against new acquisitions was offered instead. In the other analyzed countries actual restitution—of the originally taken or in kind—was contemplated, but to different extent: almost all programs included an upper limit on the reparations that could have been received by individual claimants.

2.1 Partial compensation

The Polish scheme in the Bug River case provided a double limitation on the right to offset, which could exceed neither 15% of the value of real estate left beyond the Bug River, nor 50,000 PLN.[40] Interestingly, in its first judgment on the properties left beyond the Bug River,

[37] HCC, AB 21/1990, 1057/G/1990, *op. cit.*.
[38] *Ibid.*.
[39] Rawls, *A Theory...*, p. 302.
[40] PCT, K 2/04, *op. cit.*, para. I/5.

the Constitutional Tribunal emphasized the necessity of taking into consideration the difficult financial situation of the State, and of the citizens other than the victims of property injustices (the Court in the specific case was talking about citizens other than Bug River evacuees). In these circumstances, argued the Court, partial compensation, subject to time limits, and embracing a specific form is not *eo ipso* contradicting principles of justice.[41] However, while reviewing the Bug River compensation scheme, the Constitutional Tribunal declared itself rather unhappy with the caps placed on the right to offset. In the already quoted judgment, the Tribunal held that a uniform upper limit leads to unequal treatment consisting in unequal protection of entitled persons' property rights.[42] The Tribunal emphasized that quantitative restrictions are at odds with the principles of protecting acquired rights and citizens' trust in the State and with the principle of social justice.[43] Full restitution is also the rule for the Catholic Church and Jewish religious properties. Arguably, the relative economic efficiency of the small farm lots is one of the reasons for refraining from altering the existing system of distribution. Even if it were to be done in the name of reparatory justice, redistribution might not have increased efficiency but only transaction costs.[44] True enough, in the case of Poland,[45] the land reform undertaken after World War II did not lead to large-scale collectivization, instead former estates were converted into small individual plots.[46]

---

[41] PCT, K 33/02, *op. cit.*; quoted in Broniowski v. Poland, *op. cit.*, para. 81. This language strongly resembles the Hungarian Compensation Law's Preamble, which speaks about the necessity of taking into consideration the society's financial possibilities and its sense of justice (Law No. XXV/1991, *idem*).

[42] *Ibid.*, para. II/9. (The right to offset is construed by the Tribunal as being a property right of peculiar character, para. II/4.)

[43] *Ibid.*.

[44] Kutz, *op. cit.*, p. 290.

[45] 50% of all agricultural land was redistributed through the post-war reform, affecting 57% of the population (employed in agriculture). Collectivization was slow (3.5 % in 1952, compared with 8.1% in Hungary, 19% in Czechoslovakia or 51% in Bulgaria in the same year), and it was given up early. As a consequence only about 4% of the lands were collectivized, the majority—approx. 78%—remained in private property (Verdery, *op. cit.*, pp. 43–6, 86).

[46] While the explanations above may hold true for agricultural lands, the faith of other types of properties was substantially different. Nationalization was at least as speedy as in the rest of the region, being largely completed by the

The Hungarian legislator made it clear from the outset that their scheme envisaged only a partial compensation. The law on compensation provides a rather complicated formula for calculating a flat rate for compensating all kinds of property losses.[47] This system resembles the German one presented above, to the extent that the same gliding scale is employed. However, the Hungarian system makes it more complicated in so far as it sets different, climbing thresholds, above which only a fraction of the value of the lost property is compensated. At the extreme, this represents only 10%. Moreover, even a general upper ceiling was added to all this, which limited the maximum amount of receivable compensation at 5,000,000 HUF.[48] In sustaining this scheme, the Constitutional Court has stressed that while claims to full restitution/compensation can be made in the name of reparative justice, the concept of justice underlying the compensation law is one of distributive justice.[49] Compensation is done out of a moral obligation; therefore, the state has wide latitude to chose the appropriate mode and its extent. Partial compensation is justified by the nation's limited financial possibilities, which render impossible the compensation of all those who had suffered some kind of prejudice in the past. A further argument rests on the other aim of compensation, namely the formation of such property relationships, which correspond to the requirements of market economy.[50]

Initially, the Hungarian compensation system also distinguished land claims from claims relating to other kinds of property, in the sense that the upper limit up to which full compensation was possible was set to a value five times higher for land than for everything else.[51] The justification of this measure rested upon the comparatively lesser increment of land, the higher expenses incurred by the beneficiaries during

end of the 1950s (Kutz, *op. cit.*, p. 290). In these latter cases, efficiency and transaction costs-related arguments would be more difficult to make.

[47] Law No. XXV of 1991, *op. cit.*, para. 4.

[48] *Ibid.*.

[49] HCC, AB 15/1993, 1543/B/1991 "Claims for restitution or for full compensation are [...] made [...] in the name of reparative justice [...] the constitutionality of the compensation law however [...] has to be determined [...] on the basis of distributive justice."

[50] HCC, AB 28/1991, 1160/A/1991.

[51] 1,000,000 HUF and 200,000 HUF respectively; paras. 3, 4, 13, and Annex 2 of the original bill.

the process of compensation, the larger volume of investment needed (compared, for example, with shares).[52] These motives were deemed as unconvincing by the Constitutional Court, which found that the difference between the two ceilings is ostentatious, arbitrary, and unconstitutional. The Court stressed that the differentiated ceiling benefited only 1.5% of the lands, while for at least 94% this difference is irrelevant. Thus, because for the overwhelming majority the higher ceiling cannot compensate for the enumerated extra burdens, a more favorable treatment is not constitutionally justified.[53]

2.2 Partial restitution

Some of the schemes provided for restitution of lost properties if possible within the original boundaries, but subject to certain (uneven) limitations (caps). This was the case of Lithuania, the former Czechoslovakia, and Romania.

In Lithuania land was restituted within the original boundaries, albeit to a maximum extent of 150 hectares.[54] The Constitutional Court explained that restitution essentially denoted partial reparations. This was explained on the one hand with the lack of responsibility of the post-communist authorities for the acts done under the Soviet occupation and the consequences thereof, while on the other hand with the necessity of taking also into account the interests of the current lawful possessors.[55]

In the cases of Czechia and Slovakia, the Law "On extra-judicial rehabilitation" provided for an "at least partial" alleviation of past property injustices. Restitution was to be done in kind; compensation (in form of vouchers) was to be the exception. In case of agricultural properties, the maximum size of claimable landed property was es-

[52] HCC, AB 28/1991, 1160/A/1991, part C, para. 3.1.

[53] *Ibid.*, the said provisions of the bill were considered as breaching para. 70/A of the Constitution, concerning equality. The concurring opinion of Justice Vörös noted that neither the objectively limited quantity of available land, nor the specific characteristics of agricultural property—in comparison with other types of goods—do justify such a differentiation that the bill proposed (concurring opinion, para. 3.1.1).

[54] Bronislovas Mikuta, "Land Privatization in Lithuania," 1999, available online, at http://www.ies.wisc.edu/ltc/live/baseur991115.pdf.

[55] Užkurėlienė and Others v. Lithuania, ECHR, Application No. 62988/00, Judgment of 7 April 2005, para. 27.

tablished at 150 hectares.[56] In this context, the Czech Constitutional Court stressed that this "alleviation" cannot be seen in cases where another plot or financial compensation is awarded. Preference must be given—argued the Court—to restituting the original parcel(s) of land.[57] However, if the state expropriated the entire movable property of a citizen, only monetary compensation was foreseen, within uniform limits (60,000 CZK).[58] Moreover, the Slovakian Supreme Court, while interpreting the provisions of the same act, found that only movables which can be individually identified are liable to restitution.[59]

Romania offers one of the most unstable restitution systems, with frequent and significant changes across the years. (The latest bill amending the restitution scheme was adopted in June 2005.) The first norm regulating restitution provided for restitution of agricultural land within its original boundaries, but only to a maximum extent of 10 hectares per family.[60] In the case of forests, this limit was set to 1 hectare. In 1997 the law was amended to allow for the restitution of the difference between 10 hectares and the claimant's contribution to the collective farms.[61] The ceilings were lifted again to 50 hectares and 10 hectares respectively in 2000.[62] The latest modification envisaged also a 50 hectare limit, which was calculated not per family, but per expropriated owner. For forests the law provides for full restitution.[63]

2.3 Restitution and compensation

Under this section come Estonia, Latvia, and Germany. In all three cases, restitution of the originally taken property was the rule, com-

---

[56] Law "On modifying ownership relationships with respect to land and another agricultural property," *op. cit.*.

[57] CCC, I US 754/01, Judgment of 23 November 2003, available online, at http://test.concourt.cz/angl_verze/doc/1-754-01.html.

[58] Kopecký v. Slovakia, ECHR, *op. cit.*, para. 23.

[59] *Ibid.*, para. 24.

[60] Law No. 18/1991, *op. cit.*, para. 8. ("Family" is used here in the sense of household.)

[61] Law No. 169/1997, published in the *Official Gazette*, No. 299, 4 November 1997, Art. 3 (amending Law No. 18/1991).

[62] Law No. 1/2000, published in the *Official Gazette*, No. 8, 12 January 2000, Art. 3 and 24.

[63] Law No. 247/2005, *op. cit.*, Art. 1, section 3 and 22.

bined with compensation in those cases where restitution was not considered possible. As it will be seen below, the case of German properties lost during the Soviet occupation represent an exception, as in their case compensation was restricted to certain limits. In Estonia[64] and Latvia,[65] a largely similar approach was adopted. Law regulating restitution provided for the return of property within its original boundaries. In the case of properties which were destroyed, were impossible to restitute, or were made of shares, certificates, etc., compensation was provided. Commonly, there was no limitation to the extent in which property was returned or compensated.

In Germany, the only problematic question with respect to limitations on restituted property came up in the context of the compensations for the properties taken during the Soviet occupation. For in the case of these properties, compensation was the sole possible remedy. (As it was mentioned *supra*, former owners had the possibility to (re)purchase lands at a low price.) The Federal Constitutional Court found that this program did neither infringe the principles of the rule of law, nor the prohibition of arbitrariness. The legislature was pursuing a dual goal: to enable those whose lands were taken to redevelop them, on preferential conditions, and to support the agricultural industry in the former DDR.[66] The scheme, through which the compensation was calculated, aimed to achieve a relative equality without setting a uniform ceiling. Full compensation was provided for properties whose unit value did not exceed 10,000 DM, while above this threshold, a gliding scale was applied reducing the amount of indemnification in function of the size of the unit value.[67]

The question of ceilings is problematic because instead of giving each individual an equal objective opportunity, it gives an equal subjective possibility to receive compensation within general and equal limits.[68] This treatment goes categorically against the rule of law, according

---

[64] Principles of Ownership Reform Act, *op. cit.*.

[65] Law "On the Land Reform in the Republic of Latvia Rural Regions," Law "On the Return of Buildings to their Legal Owners," Law "On Land Reform in Cities."

[66] Maltzan and Others v. Germany, *op. cit.*, para. 32.

[67] *Ibid.*, paras. 48–55.

[68] This critique is well founded, even if the very pragmatic reason of limited resources is invoked. Limited funds may justify partial compensation, but even

to the above-cited passages from Hayek, as they deliberately produce inequality.[69] What is problematic here is the fact that these schemes under the guise of equality result in fact in exactly their opposite.

3. Temporal limitations

The third type of limitations that were imposed by all restitution programs were related to the cut-off date, that is, the point in the past which marks the beginning of the period of time that the scheme was meant to cover. As these programs were—at least partially—intended to rectify past injustices, they naturally had to have some definition of this "past." However, even if seemingly objective in its character, the cut-off dates could have been manipulated in such a way so as to discriminate between the victims, and to favor certain groups over another. Setting the cut-off date proved problematic not only in Central and Eastern Europe. In New Zealand, for instance, the Waitangi Tribunal was initially instituted to investigate only contemporary violations of the Waitangi Treaty—through which the British Crown obtained sovereignty over the Maori islands in exchange for the promise of respecting their possessions, a promise that was never honored.[70] Although

in this case they do not justify the degree of difference in treatment presented here. For equality entails objective equality of opportunities, and exactly this requirement is breached by the fact that small holders did have an opportunity to full compensation, whilst those claiming large plots did not.

[69] In this respect it is edifying to quote the Prime Minister of Romania, whom at a parliamentary debate in 1990, found himself talking about the necessity to "prevent the concentration of land in the hands of one proprietor, for that would discourage the formation or preservation of village communities as spaces of the authentic national spirit" (quoted by Verdery, *op. cit.*, *supra*). Although this statement sounds funny, it is actually voicing a Kantian concern to treat persons as equal in moral worth (see: Munzer, *op. cit.*, pp. 247–8). This is, however, a bootstrap: equal moral worth demands equal distribution, and this leads right back to the initial question, namely why former property owners should be treated differently than everybody else.

On the other hand, this approach has also a lot to do with the political substrate of restitution—related to the struggle between the old, the new, and the prospective elite for the reapportionment of economic/politic resources—already mentioned above.

[70] Treaty of Waitangi Act, 1975; referred to by Barkan, *op. cit.*, pp. 269–70.

some commentators ironically noted that the Tribunal was created to act as a buffer for Maori land claims,[71] after ten years of operation it was reformed and its jurisdiction was extended to all acts committed after 1840—the year when the treaty was signed.[72]

In post-communist context the various restitution schemes came up with different solutions as to the setting of a cut-off date. The policies fancy diverging cut-off dates: ranging from the Polish case, in which, due to its exceptional character of compensating only a rather small category of victims, the cut-off date problem does not exist as such,[73] to the German approach, which logically and unequivocally rolled back the baseline so as to cover both Nazi and communist era takings.

3.1 Straightforward baselines

The Baltic States and Germany represent a fairly unproblematic category from this perspective, as their restitution programs were drafted in such a way so as to include from the outset both Nazi and communist era takings. In the case of the Baltic States, as it was already mentioned in the previous chapter, they fell under Soviet occupation already in 1940, and from this fact it naturally followed that the baseline

[71] Sharp, *op. cit.*, p. 74. Bisharat made a similar argument, albeit in a different context, with regard to Israel's use of litigation as a buffer for Palestine land claims: George E. Bisharat, "Land, Law and Legitimacy in Israel and the Occupied Territories," *American University Law Review* (Winter 1994), p. 7.

[72] Barkan, *op. cit.*; Sharp, *op. cit.*, p. 74. Sharp also notes that the reforming of the Tribunal's operation, which included beside the extension of its temporal jurisdiction also the enhancement of its staff and research capacity and the dropping of court-like proceedings, resulted in a large number of claims being filed: by the end of 1998 more than 700 claims were presented, and their review was expected by 2005. All this made it possible for the Tribunal to compile a history of wrongs done to the Maori, and this, according to Sharp, was an essential element in its reparative jurisprudence.

[73] As already shown in the previous chapter, Poland's restitution legislation thus far only covers religious properties and the case of the properties left beyond the Bug River. Catholic Church property lost at any time in history can be subject to full restitution, as well as Jewish religious property taken after the German invasion and during the communist rule (Kutz, *op. cit.*, p. 290). Therefore, rather unfortunately, due to the extremely limited character of the program, the question of the cut-off date does not represent an issue.

of restitution will be set at the date of the occupation. Consequently, in each case the period covered by the programs was defined as lasting from 1940 until 1991.[74] Thus, the scheme managed to include from the outset also the wrongs done under Nazi occupation during World War II—exclusion was achieved through other means (e.g., by personal and quantitative limitations).

The German Property Act too, as amended in 1991, reaches back until 1933 (the year in which Hitler was appointed chancellor), so as to cover both Nazi and communist expropriations.[75]

3.2 Unequivocal baselines: Romania

The Romanian restitution process is characterized by mushrooming legislation with multiple amendments. Resembling to some extent the Czech approach, different types of properties were made subject of separate laws. The first piece of legislation concerned land, and the issue of restitution formed a part of a more comprehensive regulation concerning landed property. At this stage, restitution lacked reparatory features: it was merely a means of agricultural reform. Consequently, no specific cut-off date has been set either. As the section regulating the establishment of the right to private property in lands speaks about the dismantling of the collectives, and the distribution of its landed property primarily amongst its members, one may conclude that the implied cut-off date is the beginning of collectivization.[76] Another provision, however, mentions persons of German origin, deportees and displaced persons, who lost their properties after 1944.[77] No mention is made however of property losses that occurred prior to this date. The law was substantially modified in 1997,[78] but the only change affecting the cut-off dates was the introduction of a reference to the 1945 law on

[74] Institute of Economics, Estonian Academy of Sciences, Review of structural reforms, *op. cit.*.

[75] German Unification Case Study, *op. cit.*.

[76] *Ibid.*, Art. 8.

[77] *Ibid.*, Art. 16. (On 23 August 1944, following a *coup d'état*, the Nazi government was overthrown and Romania declared war against Germany.)

[78] Law No. 169/1997, *op. cit.*. The modified Law No. 18 was republished in the *Official* Gazette, No. 1, 1998.

agrarian reform,[79] which effected the first post-war expropriation. Further amendments were made in 2000, but without affecting the cut-off date.[80] The first norm regulating the legal status of other real estate properties (with housing destination) was enacted in 1995,[81] and set the cut-off date to 6 March 1945, but included, just like the law agricultural properties, no reference to grievances dating from earlier years. In 2001, a new law was adopted, which addressed the question of arbitrarily taken properties (excluding those covered by the 'land laws'), and for the first time, the cut-off date was pushed back beyond the end of WWII, as the law was intended to cover also goods taken through a 1940 requisition law.[82] For the return of religious properties (other than churches)—not regulated yet—a governmental ordinance (later approved by Parliament) was provided that established the relevant time limits as 6 March 1945 and 22 December 1989.[83] To make things more complicated another ordinance was issued to regulate the status of immovable properties taken from organizations of national minorities (juridical persons); in this case the cut-off date was set to 6 September 1940.[84] Finally, the last and newest piece of legislation in this field dates from 2005, when a comprehensive law has been enacted, for reform in the fields of property and justice.[85] This, however, has not brought any changes to the baselines of restitution. Accordingly, three different baselines may be distinguished: properties taken during the war can be restituted, if the takings were based on the requisition law of 1940, or, in the case of minority organizations' properties, the baseline is 6 September 1940, while for all other properties the baseline is 6 March 1945.

[79] Law No. 187/1945, *Official Gazette*, No. 68, 1945.

[80] Law No. 1/2000, *Official Gazette*, No. 8, 2000.

[81] Law No. 112/1995, *Official Gazette*, No. 279, 1995.

[82] Law No. 10/2001, *op. cit.*, Art. 2(1); goods taken on the basis of the requisition law were to be returned if they were not restituted or no compensation was paid yet.

[83] Governmental Emergency Ordinance No. 94/2000, *Official Gazette*, No. 308, 2000, Art. 1, approved by Law No. 501/2002.

[84] Governmental Emergency Ordinance No. 83/1999, *Official Gazette*, No. 266, 1999, approved by Law No. 66/2004.

[85] Law No. 247/2005, *op. cit.*.

3.3 Problematic dates: Hungary and Czechoslovakia

Out of the two countries grouped in this category, Hungary represents the less problematic one. Its inclusion, however, is justified by two considerations. First, the legislature failed to address at the same time the question of communist and Nazi era takings. The First Compensation Law, dealing with takings that occurred after 1949, was adopted already in 1991, while the one addressing Nazi era takings came about only one year later, in 1992. And, while sequential implementation of compensation measures can be regarded as constitutionally justified by the exceptional context of the transition period, similar constitutional arguments can hardly be brought for the justification of the fractionated legislation.[86] Second, as what concerns religious properties, the law indicated as baseline takings any that occurred after 1948.[87] The Czechoslovakian scheme is more problematic, as it clearly intended to exclude certain groups from the pool of beneficiaries—notably Sudeten Germans, Hungarians, and churches—by setting the baselines in such a way as to avoid the period between 1945 and 1948.

In former Czechoslovakia, four different laws set three different timeframes. First, the possibility for returning some small properties (stores, workshops, and apartments), confiscated between 1955 and 1961 was created.[88] Second, two separate laws addressed the issue of industrial and agricultural properties, both covering the period between 25 February 1948 and 1 January 1990.[89] It goes almost without saying that these baselines were established in such a way so as to cover solely communist-era takings. Nazi and other, post-war confiscations (especially the Beneš Decrees, presented in the previous chapter), were left untouched. Thus, Jews, Sudeten Germans, and Hungarians were excluded from the scheme. In 1992 a new piece of legislation was enacted especially to address this problem, and it was the first norm that

[86] See also Sajó, "A részleges."

[87] Law No. XXXII of 1992, para. 1(1).

[88] Law "On mitigation of some property injustices," 2 October 1990, No. 403/1990 Coll. of Laws.

[89] Law "On extrajudicial rehabilitation," *op. cit.*; and Law "On modifying ownership relationships with respect to land and another agricultural properties," *op. cit.*.

reached back beyond the 1948 barrier.[90] Targeting the contested Presidential Decrees Nos. 12/1945 and 108/1945, the new regulation provided for the restitution of properties to those individuals who were loyal to the Czechoslovak state,[91] plus retained their Czechoslovakian residence and citizenship.[92] The decrees themselves were not declared unconstitutional or void, but merely opened the door for claims in specific cases (e.g., where the takings contravened the provisions of the decrees themselves).[93] After the dissolution of Czechoslovakia, the Czech legislature amended the law on extrajudicial rehabilitation, so as to become applicable also to those individuals who suffered property losses during the Nazi regime if they qualified for restitution or compensation under the Beneš Decrees.[94] Thus, the amended restitution scheme managed to include former individual property owners whose estates were taken by the Nazi government, but still excluded communal (e.g., Jewish religious) properties, as well as those former owners whose properties were nationalized after the war in the 1945–8 period. Although the Constitutional Court's decision in the permanent residence case (mentioned *supra*) held that to restrict the pool of potential beneficiaries by additional subjective criteria (as the residency requirement) is unconstitutional, subsequent claims dwelling on the discriminative

[90] Law No. 243/1992 Coll. of Laws.

[91] On the Constitutional Court's interpretation of the idea of "loyalty," see: comments on the Judgment of 8 March 1994, Pl. US 14/94, *supra*, Chapter 2.

[92] In fact, the initial version construed citizenship as being granted by Decree no. 33/1945, Act No. 245/1948, 194/1949, or 34/1953. Later, there was an attempt to expand its application also to those who regained citizenship after 1953, but a 1996 amendment added the requirement of continuous citizenship until 1990, thus excluding Sudeten Germans and emigrants who lost citizenship during the communist rule.

[93] European Commission, "The Czechoslovakian Presidential Decrees in the light of the Acquis Communautaire," Summary Findings of the Commission Services, Brussels, 2002, available online, at http://www.mzv.cz/servis/soubor.asp?id=3138, p. 7; Cheryl W. Gray, "The Legal Framework for private sector activity in the Czech and Slovak Federal Republic," World Bank, Working Paper Series, 1992, available online, at http://www-wds.worldbank.org/servlet/WDSContentServer/WDSP/IB/1992/11/01/000009265_3961003211939/Rendered/PDF/multi_page.pdf, p. 5; Crowder, *op. cit.*, p. 246.

[94] Law of 29 April 1994, No. 116/1994 Coll. of Laws, amending the Law on extrajudicial rehabilitation.

feature of certain criteria did not enjoy the same degree of success. The Court had problems neither with the above-described baselines, nor with the restriction of compensation to a particular category of wrongs, those subject to racial discrimination.[95] Interestingly enough, a presumably unexpected critique came from the United Nations Human Rights Committee, which in Brokova v. Czech Republic found that the Czech legislation denies equal protection of the law. The argument was building on the arbitrary distinction between former owners (whose properties were taken by the Nazi regime and afterwards nationalized, and whose properties were also taken by the Nazi, but were spared by the post-war nationalization decrees.)[96] In the other sister country, Slovakia, the temporal limitations were kept unaltered and—much like most of the other restitution-related problems—remained unchallenged.

The Hungarian Compensation Law determined the cut-off date as starting with 8 July 1949, while providing that property-related injustices caused by the state earlier to this date will be compensated, according to the same principles, through a separate norm.[97] This provision had to face constitutional challenge—on preliminary review—together with other provisions of the compensation scheme, and the Hungarian Constitutional Court managed to declare this baseline unconstitutional.[98] The reasoning explained that as the entire compensation process rests on political grounds,[99] and the circle of rectifiable wrongs is blurred, claims resting on such past damages can be restricted through a symbolic cut-off date. This argument is a good illustration of what may happen if justice is transformed into magnanimity: baselines do not have to be justified in any peculiar way, as they have merely a symbolic character. The state cannot be compelled in its benevolence to indemnify all victims. However, the Court went on, somewhat curiously,

---

[95] CCC, Pl. US 45/97, 16/94; referred to by Procházka, *op. cit.*, pp. 149–50.

[96] Dagmar Brokova v. The Czech Republic, Communication No. 774/1997, UN Doc. CCPR/C/73/D/774/1997 (15 January 2002); also quoted by Macklem, *op. cit.*. As the dissenting opinion of Committee member Ms. Christine Chanet pointed out, in the Czech courts only the question of the right to property was raised, the discrimination claim was first (and successfully) asserted in front of the Commission.

[97] Law No. XXV of 1991, para. 25, *op. cit.*.

[98] HCC, AB 28/1991, 1160/A/1991, sec. D.

[99] "[T]he entire process is politically motivated," *ibid.*.

and completed the above *tour de force*, with the amendment that this cut-off date cannot be set arbitrarily with regard to the certain case-types of reparations. This "objective symbolism" was justified by the facts that on the one hand the takings to be compensated (of private property for the benefit of state and co-operative property) had already begun before the envisaged baseline, while, on the other hand, before the said date other property injustice had also taken place, the compensation of which may also become the moral obligation of the contemporary state.[100] It seems that the Court could not firmly separate the criteria of justice from the criteria of governmental grace. As the separate opinion of Justice Vörös demonstrates, the law under scrutiny refers to the period of time, which it is intended to cover as "past regime"[101] (a legally unconceivable term), and only the cut-off date set at 1949 hints towards the communist regime. The use of such an undetermined terminology—argues the dissent—leads to an unconstitutional discrimination between victims, as it provides for the indemnification of those who suffered property losses after the cut-off date, but it leaves uncompensated those who lost their property before this baseline, but already as part and consequence of the communist social experiment.[102]

Arguably, the Hungarian Court trapped itself in the paradox between the "rule of law revolution"—a concept largely of its own making—and an uncompromising equality principle. The first required continuity between the previous and the current legal regime, which led to the refusal of recognition of any rights of the former owners to their expropriated properties (making compensation a function of grace), while the second barred discrimination between individuals, expecting governmental grace to respect criteria of justice.[103] As it was explained in the previous chapter, the appeal to the institution of novation was enabling the shift from justice to *ex gratia*, but the Court

[100] "the rectification of which [...] can be also a 'moral obligation' of the present-day state."

[101] HCC, AB 28/1991, 1160/A/1991, separate opinion of Justice Vörös, para. 2.2 (*múlt rendszer*).

[102] *Ibid.*, para 2.5.

[103] See: Gábor Halmai, "The Hungarian Approach to Constitutional Review: The End of Activism? The First Decade of the Hungarian Constitutional Court," in Sadurski, *op. cit.*, pp. 189–213; Procházka, *op. cit.*, pp. 119–25.

warned that novation cannot breach constitutional rights or principles; hence none of the concerned shall be disadvantaged by the scheme.[104] Probably aware of the trap which it had walked into, the Court tried later to back out—Procházka argues that there was also a shift in the Court's opinion on compensation which was extremely difficult to hide under a legalistic disguise[105]—and flatly stated that the term novation is not used by the Court in its original civil law understanding. Instead, it is only a succinct indication of how the legislature may take into account the specific circumstances of transition during the statutory resolution of property prejudices.[106]

Setting a timeframe for restitution law's applicability was an objective necessity: the legislators had to decide how far they intend to reach back into the past for rectifying former property injustices. Obviously, the history of property injustices cannot be restricted to Nazi and communist takings. Rectification programs may attempt to deal with wrongs older than a century: the post-colonial examples of Native Indian, Aborigine, and Maori claims constitute the relevant paradigm. Of course, to design such a scheme it does not take merely a willing government, but also a significant popular demand in this respect. The relative success of the above-enumerated examples is largely due to the existence of well-organized and goal-oriented organization of former owners, with a significant enough political weight to exert sufficient pressure on the government.[107] For example, Verdery notes about post-communist Russia that restitution is impossible because collectivization took place much earlier than in the rest of the communist countries, while the pre-existing private ownership structures were extremely unstable.[108] Accordingly, the absence of a comprehensive restitution scheme is partly due to the lack of surviving victims. This lack of such survivors can be covered by organizations, as in the case of the indigenous claims, or, more closer to Europe, the various Jewish organizations (arguably the most successful of them being the Claims Conference) that sustained

[104] HCC, AB 28/1991, 1160/A/1991, part I/4.

[105] Procházka, *op. cit.*, p. 125.

[106] HCC, AB 15/1993, 1543B/1993, part (e).

[107] For instance, while writing about Maori restitution, Barkan notes that the Maoris count for about 13% of the population; Barkan, *op. cit.*, p. 167.

[108] Verdery, *op. cit.*, pp. 91–2; quoting Caroline Humphrey, *Marx Went Away but Karl Stayed Behind*, University of Michigan Press, 1998.

with relative success claims for heirless properties.[109] Being an essential element of any restitution program, the cut-off date is, at the same time, a handy tool of exclusion. As it was shown in this subsection, through the setting of such baselines certain groups of victims can be distinguished and excluded from the benefits of the scheme.

4. Property-based limitations

In the previous sections it was already mentioned that in most cases the various types of properties were treated separately, sometimes also by separate norms. The most common distinction made by the legislators was the one between agricultural properties (and forestry) and buildings, thus between different kinds of real property. As it will be shown in this section, this separation usually meant also a difference in treatment, and in certain situations this resulted in unequal outcomes for the former owners. Another type of—perhaps less artificial—distinction was the one between movable and immovable properties, and this was quite important, too, as post-communist restitution schemes mostly avoided addressing the issue of movables—a question which, in turn, was more present in Holocaust restitution claims. Finally, a third type of problematic property-based distinction was made on the basis of ownership: some of the programs discern between communal (and various forms of communal) and individual types of holdings, while in every case distinction is also made between commercial and non-commercial properties.

4.1 Movable and immovable property

As it was mentioned above, post-communist restitution programs commonly distinguish movable and immovable properties and subject them to different treatment from a restitution perspective. While immovable estates are extensively regulated, no special enactment deals

[109] See, for example: Avi Beker (ed.), *The Plunder of Jewish Property during the Holocaust: Confronting European History*, Palgrave, 2001; Ronald W. Zweig, *German Reparations and the Jewish World: A History of the Claims Conference*, Frank Cass, 2001.

with movables. The reasons for this are manifold. First, due to the additional goals attached to restitution—ownership reform and market economy—redistribution of landed property required more normative attention than movable goods, in the case of which redistribution is a lot less feasible. Second, again partly due to the reformative character of the program, restitution of immovable property concerned arguably a significantly larger pool of possible beneficiaries than the restitution of movables.[110] Third, usually a higher degree of material and spiritual value is attached to landed property, than to movables.[111] Fourth, movable properties are more difficult to identify and in many cases ownership can be very difficult to demonstrate.

However, if one departs from the idea of reparation, differentiation on the basis of the lost property's nature is theoretically just as unsound as differentiation between various types of losses suffered. The arguments that immovable property plays a more significant role in economic reform, or that hence it concerns more people, are of fundamentally distributive character, which cannot justify restrictions on reparative measures. Movable properties of course may take various forms, and may be formed of goods of different values, ranging from simple furniture (for example, in the case of the repatriates) to precious metal, jewelry, cash, accounts, bonds, shares, insurance policies, artwork, etc. Some of the latter may very well surpass in their value certain landed properties. But, regardless of its economic or moral worth, according to the principle of reparative justice, for that which was wrongfully taken, compensation is due. The fact that in some situations restitution or compensation will prove practically impossible should not rule out the theoretical possibility of relief.

Claims for movable property were raised also in indigenous restitution contexts: these claims chiefly targeted works of art and human remnants[112] which fell pray to art collectors, treasure hunters, or

[110] This can be translated in stronger popular pressure and higher number of possible voters.

[111] See: Verdery, *op. cit.*, pp. 20–5. This is especially the case with indigenous lands, where the relationship with land bears also strong religious characteristics.

[112] Under the common law, human remains represent "quasi-property," in which relatives or descendants have a limited property interest for the sole purpose of proper burial. See: Margaret B. Bowman, "The Reburial of Na-

scientists, and were to be found usually in museums or various collections.[113] In 1990, the United States Congress enacted the Native American Graves Protection and Repatriation Act, to protect Indian remains and cultural items[114] from continued desecration.[115] Beyond regulating the exploration of burial sites and cultural properties, the act criminalizes the trafficking of these objects, and above all, provides for a mechanism to ensure the proper disposition or repatriation of Indian remains and cultural items.[116] Commentators note, however, that while focusing on human remnants and funerary objects, the act did not manage to significantly further the case of other cultural items.[117]

---

tive American Skeletal Remains: Approaches to the Resolution of a Conflict," *Harvard Environmental Law Review* 13 (1989), pp. 167–74.

[113] Racism, curiosity, and desire for profit were the forces that drove many to acquire, sell, and exhibit Indian remains. According to estimates, almost 2 million Indian graves have been exhumed without authorization. In 1868, exhumation of Indian graves was done pursuant to a Surgeon General's Order directing Army personnel to procure Native American remains for the Army Medical Museum. Moreover, in 1906 Congress adopted the Antiquities Act, which classified Indian burial sites as "archeological resources" and the exhumed remnants as federal property. See: Ritchie Lucus, "Indian Burial Sites Unearthed: The Misapplication of the Native American Graves Protection and Repatriation Act," *Public Land & Resources Law Review* 26 (2005), p. 74.

[114] When speaking of "cultural property," one has to be aware of the fact that—according to Greenfield's seminal work—the term has different interpretations. In its Anglo-Saxon use it has a narrow, ethnological and/or artistic sense. In the Third World—and arguably also in post-communist Central and Eastern Europe—a more political meaning is attached to it, considering that it heightens national consciousness and/or identity, but overall the term is used more generally and less precisely (Jennifer Greenfield, *The Return of Cultural treasures*, Cambridge University Press, 1996, p. 253).

[115] Jack F. Trope and Walter R. Echo-Hawk, "The Native American Graves Protection and Repatriation Act: Background and Legislative History," *Arizona State Law Journal* 24 (1992).

[116] *Ibid.*.

[117] Museums and agencies have published 2,713 Federal Register repatriation notices for "human remains" and 122,948 notices for "funerary objects," but only 212 notices for "sacred objects" and 16 for "cultural patrimony." See: Isaac Moriwake, "Critical Excavations: Law, Narrative, and the Debate on Native American and Hawaiian 'Cultural Property' Repatriation," *University of Hawaii Law Review* 20 (1998), p. 261, n. 33; Steven Platzman, "Objects of Controversy: The Native American Right to Repatriation," *American University Law Review* 41 (1992), pp. 549–51.

Moreover, the faith of goods that do not fit under the act's definition of funerary or cultural objects remains uncertain. In Australia, the return of Aborigine cultural properties (human remains, "secret and/or sacred objects") is effected on the basis of a federal program, which aims to repatriate all such objects from the museums involved to their communities of origin.[118] However, the program is limited to eight museums, and to the above-mentioned objects. Movables of other sort, or held by other actors, are left adrift.[119]

Movable properties also form a major part of Jewish restitution claims, and concern all types of valuables, from precious metals to bank accounts. The fact that even wedding rings, watches, or golden teeth (from the deceased) were "harvested" is typical for the unimaginable perversity of Holocaust. Obviously, a large part of these are impossible to restitute in nature, either because they were altered in form (e.g., melted) or destroyed, or because they could not have been traced down after the war. Still, Jewish organizations and even individual claimants have managed to obtain at least significant compensations in the form of settlements. The contemporary Holocaust restitution movement was born—a good 50 years after the end of World War II—in the United States.[120] The U.S. courts turned out

---

[118] Return of Indigenous Cultural Property (RICP) Program, available on the homepage of the Australian Cultural Ministers' Council, at http://www.dcita.gov.au/arts/councils/return_of_indigenous_cultural_property_(ricp)_program.

[119] According to certain estimates, the indigenous arts and craft market—including, but not limited to wrongfully taken properties—is worth about $200 million per year, and half of the sales are related to the tourism market (ATSIC, available online, at http://svc003.wic001g.server-web.com/issues/Indigenous_Rights/intellectual_property/Default.asp).

[120] By "contemporary Holocaust restitution movement" I understand the recent attempt originating from the United States to obtain financial restitution from European and American corporations for their involvement in the wartime activities, which is considered to begin with the class action law suit filed against Credit Suisse, the Union Bank of Switzerland, and the Swiss Bank Corporation in a federal district court in Brooklyn, New York in October 1996. See: Michael J. Bazyler, "The Holocaust Restitution Movement in Comparative Perspective," *Berkeley Journal of International Law* 20 (2002), p. 11; Bazyler and Amber L. Fitzgerald, "Trading with the Enemy: Holocaust Restitution, The United States Government, And American Industry," *Brooklyn Journal of International Law* (2003), p. 683; Burt Neu-

to be very welcoming venues for reparation claims after the seminal Filartiga v. Peña-Irala decision had been passed, creating the possibility for human rights victims to bring suits in the United States against foreign perpetrators, if found in the United States.[121] Among the procedural factors that explain this leading role of the North American judiciary, commentators enumerate the issue of jurisdiction (clarified in the Filartiga judgment) and the style of judicial fact-finding (quite different from continental Europe, which requires all evidence to be presented at the outset of the trial).[122] In property matters, restitution claims were targeting dormant bank accounts (un-returned deposits of Holocaust victims) in Swiss, French, and Israeli banks (in this latter case the respondent was the successor of the Anglo-Palestine Bank), insurance policies and annuities in about dozen European insurance companies, and artworks. As a consequence, many countries undertook novel investigations of wartime conduct; in many cases this led to the establishment of specialized commissions.[123] Claims were, however, filed not only against European corporations, but also against the United States, concerning Nazi looted art and books that ended up in the United States,[124] jewelry, gold, and other precious metals. Al-

borne, "Preliminary Reflections on Aspects of Holocaust-Era Litigation in American Courts," *Washington University Law Quarterly* 80 (2002), p. 795; Stuart Eizenstat, "Imperfect Justice: Looted Assets, Slave Labor, and the Unfinished Business of World War II (Speech)," *Vanderbilt Journal of Transnational Law* 37 (2004), p. 333.

121 Filartiga v. Peña-Irala, 630 F.2d 876 (2nd Cir. 1980). The decision relied on the 1789 Alien Torts Claims Act (28 U.S.C. § 1350). In 1990 the Congress confirmed foreign torture victims' right to sue in U.S. courts through the Torture Victims Protection Act (Publ. L. No. 102-256, 106 Stat. 173 (1992)). Prior to this decision, only about dozen Holocaust restitution lawsuits have been filed in American courts, most of them being summarily dismissed (Bazyler, *op. cit.*, pp. 12–4).

122 *Ibid.*. Additionally other factors, concerning more the legal culture than procedural rules, as the relative easiness with which juries award huge compensations, the risk-oriented attorneys, whose fee is paid only if they win the case, and only by the party which they represent are considered also relevant. The recent Holocaust-era settlement payoffs were estimated to be over $8 billion, as of 2002.

123 Bazyler and Fitzgerald, *op. cit.*, pp. 712–25.

124 Estimates talk about several million copies of books; a centralized database of artworks in American museums has not yet been functional as of 2002, *ibid.*.

though the U.S. government was reluctant to admit that it retained any of the gold collected during the war,[125] and claimed that it contributed only out of "moral leadership" to the Nazi Persecutee Relief Fund,[126] recently it was forced to settle with claimants in the case which became notorious as the "Gold Train Case."

In 2001, Hungarian Holocaust survivors filed a class-action suit against the United States, claiming that their personal property—mainly made up of gold, jewelry, art, religious objects, and silverware—which was looted by the Nazi government was subsequently seized and unlawfully appropriated by the U.S. Army.[127] The litigation concluded in the fall of 2005 in a 25.5 million USD settlement, the money being used for the provision of "social services and humanitarian relief" to eligible victims of Nazi persecution.[128] At the initial admissibility ruling, the U.S. District Court in Miami rejected a governmental motion for the dismissal of the case. The Court's argument pointed out that claims targeting the return of property are not restricted by sovereign immunity; moreover, vital information necessary for timely filing of charges were withheld, thus the statute of limitations does not apply, either.[129]

Generally it can be stated about the restitution of movables in the above-presented cases that they were treated separately, and to some extent differently from immovable properties, and this is especially true in the case of indigenous claims. Effective restitution of indigenous lands is a solution neither in Australia, nor in the United States. In the former, the Native Title Acts[130] recognizes rights and interests of Aboriginal peoples or Torres Strait Islanders, as observed under tra-

---

[125] Estimated to 300 tons (*ibid.*, p. 738).

[126] *Ibid.*.

[127] Rosner v. United States, 231 F. Supp. 2d 1202 (S.D. Fla. 2002).

[128] *Ibid.*, final order and judgment part IV/A, available online, at http://www.hbsslaw.com/files/Final_Judgment1128719666357.pdf.

[129] For detailed information, see: Hungarian Gold Train—Complete Background Information and Documents, available online, at http://www.hagens-berman.com/hgt.

[130] See: Australian Institute of Aboriginal and Torres Strait Islanders Studies (AIATSIS), available online, at http://www.aiatsis.gov.au/rsrch/ntru/research/resourceguide/national_overview/national02.html; Anthony Moore in Johnston, Hinton, and Rigney, *op. cit.*, pp. 142–3.

ditional custom and as recognized by the common law.[131] However, there is a considerable uncertainty as to the precise legal nature of the native title. The High Court of Australia in a number of cases[132] has had the opportunity to clarify this question, but it chose to emphasize its spiritual character, at the expense of its economic and pragmatic aspects.[133] Therefore, the native title is generally considered to entail fishing, hunting, and gathering rights, and taking into consideration that it can be considered at least as partially extinguished by governmental pastoral leases, it clearly cannot be interpreted as akin to ownership.[134] In the United States, the Claims Commission Act of 1946 attempted to settle with finality, through monetary payments, all Indian claims to territories that had been illegally taken from them. The act contemplated only the possibility of monetary compensation, excluding physical restoration. Moreover, amounts of aid and assistance paid by the United States to the claimants were to be deduced from the compensation.[135] Still, the ideal of "wiping the state clean" of Indian claims was never achieved, and some authors argue that the limited amount of awards created new dissatisfactions.[136]

The post-communist restitution schemes' approach to movables differed significantly. In certain cases—notably the Baltic States—there were no special regulations addressing restitution of movables, although restitution of certain goods was unproblematic, while especially in the case of artworks, return was expressly denied. Another approach, fancied by Poland and Hungary, considered that the value of the lost movables is included in the calculation for the loss of the im-

---

131 Frank Brennan in Johnston, Hinton, and Rigney, *op. cit.*, p. 170 notes that "[c]ommon law native title is a very fragile form of title when compared with Crown grants made under legislation of a state parliament."

132 Western Australia v. Ward (2002) 76 ALJR 1098; [2002] HCA 28; Wilson v. Anderson (2002) 76 ALJR 1306; [2002] HCA 29; and Members of the Yorta Yorta Aboriginal Community v. Victoria (2002) 77 ALJR 356; [2002] HCA 58.

133 Brennan, *op. cit.*.

134 *Ibid.*

135 Bradley Reed Howard, *Indigenous Peoples and the State*, Northern Illinois University Press, 2003, p. 62.

136 A total amount of $818 million was distributed (as awards), largely in per capita payments. See: Francis Paul Prucha, *American Indian Treaties*, University of California Press, 1997, pp. 383–5.

movable (with certain exceptions, notably compensation for precious metals and jewelry confiscated in Hungary during the Nazi regime). A third way was chosen by Germany and Czechoslovakia, which enumerated a relatively wide array of movables for which compensation could have been demanded. Finally, in Romania neither the legislation, nor the case law on restitution recognized a right to claim restitution of lost movables.

4.1.1 The Baltic States: exclusion of artworks

Estonia constitutes an exception as what concerns the distinction between movable and immovable properties. The law on ownership[137] regulates together the restitution of immovable, as well as of various movable properties, such as ships, agricultural inventory, factory fittings, stakes, and shares.[138] However, unlike the post-colonial and Holocaust cases presented above, the Estonian legislator created the possibility of refusing restitution of "cultural community objects," upon the decision of the Supreme Council.[139] Compensation was envisaged also for the case of bonds and shares, but otherwise the law did not create significant differences between movable and immovable property.

Lithuania, on its turn, represents a radical example in the sense that no normative provision has been adopted for the restoration of movable property. In exchange, the law on museums declares that all museum valuables, comprising the fund of state museums, shall be state property and the laws on archives and on libraries contain basically similar provisions. On top of all these, the Law on the Basics of National Security enumerates cultural heritage amongst the main objects of national security.[140] These provisions practically exclude the possibility of restitution in the case of artworks. A claim submitted to the Constitutional Court of Lithuania challenged the relevant provisions of the Law on Museums, emphasizing that they deny the constitutional guarantees given to private ownership. Representatives of the

[137] Law "On the Fundamentals of Ownership Reform," June 1991.

[138] *Ibid.*, Art. 11.

[139] *Ibid.*, Art. 13, if return of such properties would damage the interest of the Estonian State.

[140] LiCC Ruling of 16 March 1999, available online, at http://www.lrkt.lt/dokumentai/1999/n9a0316a.htm, part III, para. 2.

other party concerned (Vilnius State Art Museum) argued that there is no legal disposition concerning the restitution of movable properties; the existing regulation of the return of real property does not provide for unconditional in kind return of properties either. Therefore, an eventual return of museum valuables would give rise to equality concerns between owners of real and movable properties.[141] The Court in its ruling explained that the decision to restitute nationalized property is of a political nature, and is the prerogative of the legislator; consequently, until no relevant norm is adopted, persons whose properties were taken do not enjoy subjective rights of ownership. While not troubled at all by the inequality created between former owners of real and movable properties, the Court recognized the legislator's determination to effect restitution only by special laws, and taking into consideration the needs of the society and its economical possibilities.[142]

Latvia took the middle course between the two rather distinct approaches of the other Baltic States. Besides the usual categories of immovable, land and buildings, the restitution scheme comprises also certain religious properties, enterprises, and related movable properties.[143] The question of other categories of movables, however, has not yet been addressed.[144]

4.1.2 Poland and Hungary: immovable and movable together

In Poland, the restitution scheme as of 2005 covers only the question of repatriates' property and certain religious properties. As it was already discussed in the previous chapter, when post-war Poland's borders were redrafted, it lost some territories in the favor of the Soviet Union. Moving the borders involved also the moving of people, thus a large number of persons were repatriated. This necessarily meant that a significant part of their property—both movable and immovable—re-

[141] *Ibid.*, parts III and V.
[142] *Ibid.*, holding of the Court, para. 4.
[143] Law "On the Renewal of Property Rights in Enterprises and other Property Objects," March 1993.
[144] For a more generous discussion of the restitution process in the Baltic States, see: Frances H. Foster, "Restitution of Expropriated Property: Post-Soviet Lessons For Cuba," *Columbia Journal of Transnational Law* 34 (1996), p. 621.

mained with the new sovereign of the land.[145] The bilateral agreements that accompanied the population exchange provided for the receiving state's obligation to compensate these property losses. Interestingly, the acts addressing the issue of compensation initially talked about compensating losses of real property, although as already mentioned, repatriation involved also serious losses of movable property.[146] Albeit the latest, 2003 act does not explicitly talk anymore about compensating real property left beyond the Bug River, still, from the reasoning of the Constitutional Tribunal in the second Bug River case it appears that the judges have had real property on their mind. The argument in question mentioned that former owners (Polish citizens) were "in no way compensated for the loss of property (also in form of real estate)," while former owners of real estate taken during the implementation of the land reform did not receive equivalent compensation. A similar fate has been experienced by those who lost their property during the "nationalization of the basic branches of the economy," and former owners of the "grounds lying within the borders of Warsaw," who received very limited, or no compensation at all.[147] The analogy drawn by the Tribunal compares repatriates' losses to the uncompensated takings of various real properties targeting resident citizens.

Hungary has chosen to regulate the restitution of movables together with immovable property, and the first comprehensive norm on compensation subordinated movables to real estate. As it was already explained in the previous chapter, a rather complicated formula was employed to convert the value of taken properties into a flat rate. According to Article 3 of the Compensation Law, this flat rate comprised also the value of movable properties. The oddity of the formula consists in the fact that it takes into account only two variables: in the case of buildings (including apartments, houses, shops, and empty building plots), their size expressed in square meters, while in the case of enter-

[145] For more details, see: *supra*.

[146] Land Administration and Expropriation Act of 29 April, 1985 section 81: "Persons, who in connection with the war that began in 1939 abandoned real property in territories which at present do not belong to the Polish State [...] shall have the value of real property that has been abandoned offset [...]." The Land Administration Act of 1997, section 212 essentially used the same wording. Both quoted in Broniowski v. Poland, *op. cit.*, paras. 46–8.

[147] PCT, K2/04, Judgment of 15 December 2004, *op. cit.*, part II, para. 6.

prises, the number of their employees.[148] A different formula is used in the case of agricultural properties. The law is silent about situations in which the takings targeted only movables. This treatment of movables was never discussed by the Constitutional Court, which merely stated *en passant* that the formulas used for determining the value of lost properties contain rational distinctions that take into consideration the need for simplifying the process of compensation, as well as the differences in the nature of the various property objects.[149]

A controversial conclusion may be found in a relatively recent Constitutional Court judgment regarding various securities.[150] According to the compensation laws,[151] property losses caused by Decree No. 1600/1944, concerning the declaration and sequestration of Jewish assets, are covered by the compensation scheme. However, the relevant provisions pertaining to the calculation of the receivable amount of compensation mention only precious metals and jewelry, as a reference,[152] while the above-mentioned decree regarded other movable properties as well, for instance securities. The complainant before the Constitutional Court alleged the legislator's unconstitutional omission consisting in the failure to dispose of the compensation for such sequestrated securities. The Court found that sequestration of securities did not amount to a taking (although securities had to be deposited at the Central Bank's unites, at the disposal of the financial authorities),[153] and that all securities—regardless of their former owner—were cast off

[148] Law No. XXV of 1991, *op. cit.*, Annex No. 3.

[149] HCC, AB 28/1991, 1160/A/1991, part I(C), para. 3. See also: AB 411/E/1996, part II/2, para. 4: "taken into consideration the fact that the funds available for compensation are limited, the economical situation of the country does not make it possible for the state to take into consideration—while defining the groups of entitled persons—each and every grievance."

[150] *Államadóssági kötvény* and *kamatozó állami nyereménykölcsön kötvény.*

[151] Law No. XXV of 1991, *op. cit.*, Art. 1(1), as well as Appendix 1, point 6; and Law No. XXIV of 1992, *op. cit.*, Art. 1(1).

[152] Law No. XXIV of 1992, *op. cit.*, Art. 3, and Appendix No. 3 The compensation is made function of the weight and fineness of the precious metals and jewelry items.

[153] For a detailed discussion, see: Krisztián Ungvári, "Nagy jelentőségű szociálpolitikai akció—adalékok a zsidó vagyon begyűjtéséhez és elosztásához Magyarországon 1944-ben," available online, at www.rev.hu/html/hu/kiadvanyok/evkonyv02/ungvary.html.

in 1949, when a new currency was introduced and claims in the old currency were considered as valueless.[154] For these reasons, it was held that grievances stemming from the sequestration of securities are not, and need not to be, covered by the compensation scheme.[155]

---

[154] HCC, AB 411/E/1996, part III, paras. 4–8.

[155] The fact that all similar securities were cast-off was not perceived as a problem, although there was a clear loss experienced by their owners. Although according to the *ex gratia* nature of the compensation scheme, lack of compensation would not constitute a problem, it is interesting that the loss itself was not acknowledged. A theoretically comparable situation arose in Romania, where special bank deposits—opened with the scope of purchasing a Dacia automobile—were arguably lost soon after the regime change. The system of car purchasing which existed in Romania prior to the regime change required the opening of such an account with the state-owned Savings Bank (CEC), and when the equivalent value of the car was deposited, an ordinal number was given to the prospective buyer, who, when his turn came, could conclude the sales contract with the car dealer company. In 1990, however, this system of acquisition was abolished, the price of the car doubled, and after a while it was left up to the regular market mechanisms to determine its scale (Governmental Decree No. 1109/1990). Romanian sources offer diverging data, but on average it can be said that roughly 90% of the deponents withdrew their deposits immediately, while the rest maintained them, and arguably soon found themselves in the impossibility of withdrawing their money (http://www.realitatearomaneasca.ro/content.php?c=articole&id_categorie=6&articol_id=4630&p=; http://www.jurnalul.ro/modules.php?op=modload&name=News&file=article&sid=14439; http://stiri.rol.ro/stiri/2004/10/154459.htm; http://news.softpedia.com/news/1/2004/October/9831.shtml).

Currently (as of July 2006), the situation of the former deponents is extremely controversial. The legal successor of the Savings Bank (CEC SA.) maintains that according to their statute any deposited sums (including those to be found in the special car purchasing accounts) can be withdrawn at any time (*idem*). Still, statements to the contrary were made in the justifications of the bills attempting to address the situation of former deponents (http://www.cdep.ro). A number of complaints were filed with various domestic courts; however, all of them failed, and an application with the European Court of Human Rights was rejected on procedural grounds, the Court considering that the association of the deponents does not have standing to sue on behalf of its members. Addressing at the same time also the merits of the complaint, the Court found that Article 1 of Protocol No. 1 cannot be interpreted in such a way as to require states to maintain the purchasing power of deposited sums. Further, the Court emphasized that Article 1 of Protocol No. 1 does not create the right to become the owner of a good. Ultimately, the complaints were considered as ill founded (L'As-

The Hungarian Supreme Court has also had the chance to pronounce its view on the question of movables. The Supreme Court recalled the relevant provisions of the Compensation Law,[156] and of two governmental decrees for the application of the compensation laws,[157] arguing that the value of movables are comprised in the flat rate calculated for the immovable properties. This, taken together with the fact that neither of the decrees mentions movable properties, and that the form which has to be completed at the filing of the compensation claim does not contain a head for movable industrial property, lead towards the conclusion that takings of movable property are not compensated.[158] Interestingly, the Constitutional Court went on explaining in detail that differentiation according to the nature of the property objects in certain cases leads to impermissible discrimination between the owners.[159] This argument was used to declare unconstitutional those provisions of the Compensation Law, which made possible in kind restitution of land. Apparently, the difference in treatment between movable and immovable property is not seen as creating problematic discriminations between former owners.

4.1.3 Germany and Czechoslovakia: compensation for some movables

The German Property Act[160] made possible a wide array of claims, targeting immovable as well as movables and commercial properties.

sociation et la Ligue Pour la Protection des Acheteurs d'Automobiles, Ana Abid et 646 Autres c. La Roumanie, CEDH, Requête No. 34746/97, Décision de 10 juillet 2001).

156 Law No. XXV of 1991, *op. cit.*, Art. 3.

157 Art. 5 of Decree No. 104/1991 for the implementation of Law No. XXV/1991, and Art. 7 of Decree No. 92/1992 for the implementation of Law No. XXIV/1992.

158 Supreme Court of Hungary, Kfv. II, 28.205/1996, BH1997.507. In the instant case the applicant was claiming compensation for the taking of his father's distillery. Besides the presented argument, the Court also considered that the applicant did not produce convincing evidence about the taking itself.

159 HCC, AB 4/1996, 1482/B/1992, part II/1.

160 The Resolution of Outstanding Property Issues Act of 23 September 1990 (Gesetz über Regelung offener Vermögensfragen), *op. cit.*.

The most important condition to be met was the illegal character of the communist-era takings. Thus, as Barkan argues, the legality of the old system was upheld because restitution was envisaged only in the cases of takings that were effected in violation of the then applicable East German laws.[161] The scheme was addressing properties left behind by refugees between 1945–53 which were confiscated without compensation,[162] properties of refugees who left after 1953,[163] properties previously owned by West Germans (before 1953),[164] properties inherited by West Germans (after 1953),[165] and finally some 12,000 small firms nationalized in 1972.[166] A further condition for restitution for the properties in question was for it to be state owned at the date of reunification—*bona fide* private owners were shielded from restitution claims.[167] This was especially the case with plots of single-family houses, where the good-faith current user retained the undisturbed right to the building. Typically, the former owner got the property rights restored over the land, and received compensation for the house, which remained in the current user's hands. Thus, instead of clarifying, property relationships became more obscured.[168] In spite of the generosity of the scheme, commentators note that the most extensive takings took place during the exempted period (of the Soviet occupation), which concerned all large enterprises and many medium-sized ones, all financial institutions, mines, all agricultural properties over 100 hectares,

---

161 Barkan, *op. cit.*, p. 118.

162 Some 31,000 real estate properties and 3,000 enterprises.

163 About 80,000 real estate items.

164 About 100,000 real estate and 2,000 commercial items.

165 Approx. 70,000 items of real estate.

166 Dissident and heirless properties were placed under trusteeship, and transferred to the state when over indebted (this was induced artificially, by the means of exorbitant fees charged). All data provided in Gerlinde Sinn and Hans-Werner Sinn, *Jumpstart: the economic unification of Germany*, MIT Press, 1992, pp. 87–90.

167 Good faith purchasing was not protected, however, in the case of properties taken on racial, religious, or ideological grounds during the Nazi regime. In these cases compensation is granted only if the properties cannot be restituted (lost, destroyed, etc.). Settlement of Property Claims Act (Vermögensgesetz), Official Notice of 2 December 1994, and Compensation for Persons subjected to Nazi Persecution Act (NS-VEntschG), Official Notice of 27 September 1994.

168 *Ibid.*, p. 89.

and other, Nazi-owned properties.[169] The last category could have been a most problematic one, as these properties obviously included many items from previous expropriations. As Avineri points out, communist takings in many cases were "expropriations from (previous) expropriators": the first wave of mass expropriations in the 1940s (and 1930s in Germany) being the purge of Jewish property before and during World War II.[170] The dilemma of Soviet-era takings was finally solved through the adoption of the Compensation Act in 1994, which provided for some compensation for these properties.[171]

In Czechoslovakia, the act on extra-judicial rehabilitations created the possibility for submitting claims resulting from the quashing of confiscation sentences.[172] The relevant provisions set restitution of confiscated properties as the rule, while compensations were granted solely for real property, except for the case when the state acquired the entire property of a citizen (made up only from movables). In this latter case a uniform amount of monetary compensation was envisaged.[173] Regarding the restitution of movables, only those properties are liable for restitution that "can be individually identified by specific features which mean that it cannot be confused with other objects."[174] Furthermore, the claimants had the obligation to demonstrate where the property in question can be found, at the filing of their request.[175] The Law "On modifying ownership relations with respect to land and

[169] *Ibid.*, pp. 89–90; Soviet-era takings are estimated to amount to approximately 70% of the industrial output of the DDR and almost 42% of the privately owned land.

[170] Avineri, *op. cit.*, pp. 35–6.

To this might also be added, for example, the case of 3.5 million Germans and of the Hungarians expelled from post-war Czechoslovakia before the communist takeover.

[171] See also the comments in the previous chapter, section 5.3.

[172] Federal Act No. 87/1991 "On the extra-judicial rehabilitations," *idem*, part 1, section 1, para. 2; part 2, sections 3–5 and 13; and part 3, sections 19–20.

[173] *Ibid.*, section 13; the total amount of compensation was established at 60,000 CZK.

[174] Supreme Court of Slovakia, Judgment No. 1 Cdo 27/94, 25 May 1994; quoted in Kopecký v. Slovakia, *op. cit.*, para. 24.

[175] Federal Act No. 87/1991 "On the extra-judicial rehabilitations," part 2, section 5.

other agricultural properties,"[176] while providing for the restitution of real estate, fashioned a similar stance towards movables, stating that compensation is available for original livestock and supplies taken at collectivization. Compensation was to take the form of in kind payment of goods of comparable type, quality, and quantity, services designed to support agricultural production, or shares in the legal entity that took over matters as a legal successor. The legislator seems to be very undecided about this issue, and the last form of compensation enshrined in the quoted section (namely any "other form") does enforce this suspicion. Finally, the Law "On mitigation of the consequences of certain property losses" also mentions movables "used in conducting activities inside the restituted property" (presumably industrial or commercial properties: fittings and accessories).[177] However, their treatment represents a stark departure from the compensations outlined above: instead of payment in one or another way, merely a right to preemption of the former owner of the real property in question is assured, claimants having the right of first buyer at a "depreciated rate."[178]

4.1.4 Romania: no grounds for restitution of movables

In the case of Romania, no specific legal enactment deals with the question of movables.[179] Restitution claims, thus, have to conform to the "ordinary" legislation, that is, the Code of Criminal Procedure, which creates the possibility to lodge complaints against measures and decisions taken during criminal investigation. However, this obviously covers merely those takings that were part of criminal proceedings. The Romanian Supreme Court[180] has confirmed this view when it refused to afford compensations for confiscated movables on the basis

[176] Law "On modifying ownership relations with respect to land and other agricultural properties," *op. cit.*, section 20.

[177] Law "On mitigation of the consequences of certain property losses," *op. cit.*, section 13(1).

[178] *Ibid.*, para 2.

[179] A special case is the one of communal movable properties, which is discussed *infra*.

[180] Today known as High Court of Justice and Cassation.

of one of the restitution laws,[181] arguing that compensations for such goods have to be claimed according to ordinary legislation.[182] The route recommended by the Supreme Court, however, may easily turn into a dead end for claimants, as the case of Vasilescu v. Romania has demonstrated.[183] The claimant followed the ordinary way, as provided in the Code of Criminal Procedure,[184] and lodged her claims with the competent state council's (prosecutor's) office, and subsequently with the Procurator-General of Romania. Both offices refused to entertain her claims, arguing that there is no evidence in their records pertaining to the alleged confiscation of the gold coins in question. However, there was evidence from the Ministry of the Interior, confirming that indeed investigations were ordered with respect of the claimed property, and that charges against her husband were later on dropped. In this situation, the claimant turned to the courts, and secured in two instances an order for returning the claimed coins. In the end, however, the Prosecutor-General made a special application to the Supreme Court (under the Code of Civil Procedure that allowed the office to apply for the quashing of any final court decision on a number of grounds). The Prosecutor-General argued—and the Supreme Court agreed with this argument—that the lower courts have exceeded their *ratione materiae* jurisdiction, and encroached upon the state counsel's competence.[185] The European Court found in this case—amongst others—also a violation of the right to property, emphasizing that the Supreme Court decision deprived the applicant from any procedural means of protecting her right to property. The loss of ability to dispose of the property in issue, together with the failure of the attempts to have the situation remedied by the national authorities, amounts to a *de facto* confiscation, incompatible with Article 1, Protocol No. 1 provisions.[186]

---

[181] Law No. 10/2001, *op. cit.*.

[182] Supreme Court of Romania, Civil Section, Decision No. 2276 of 30 May 2003.

[183] Vasilescu v. Romania, ECHR, Application No. 27053/1995, Judgment of 22 May 1998.

[184] Art. 169 according to the Code in force at the date of filing the complaint.

[185] Vasilescu v. Romania, *op. cit.*, paras. 7–23.

[186] *Ibid.*, paras. 44–53.

4.2 Different kinds of immovable property

The most reasonable explanations for the distinction made by most restitution schemes between agricultural and other landed property lies in the different faith of these properties after expropriation. As a rule, most of the properties were taken within the framework of the economic reform. However, agricultural property was massed into collectives—a form of co-operative organization[187]—which, from ownership perspective, were lying between state and individual property. Former landowners became members of the collectives, and also owners of the new entity, as co-operative property belonged only to those who pooled it.[188] Of course, their autonomy was seriously limited by the state, and made the members' ownership only a theoretical one. In practice, co-operatives were treated as part of the state property. Some of the expropriated lands were not pooled into collectives (especially woodland), but instead they were transferred into the state's property. However, except for Poland (where most of the land was farmed privately)[189] and the former Soviet Union (where the state owned the largest part of farmland),[190] in the rest of the analyzed countries collective farming was the rule.[191] This made the dismantling of collective farms and the restitution of lands a lot easier: no third persons were involved in the process. Contrarily, most of the taken buildings—and this is especially the case of dwelling units—while transferred to the state, were subsequently leased to different individuals, assigned to state-owned or co-operative units, or to various public organs. The

[187] Not only private agricultural property was transformed into co-operative type of ownership, but other non-agricultural enterprises, too, typically small craftsman shops: barbers, tailors, potters, etc. Following Verdery's distinction, I use the term "collective" to designate agricultural enterprises, and the term "co-operative" when referring to both, i.e., agricultural and non-agricultural enterprises (Verdery, *op. cit.*, p. 50).

[188] Verdery, *op. cit.*, pp. 50–2.

[189] 78% in 1987.

[190] 68% in 1986–7.

[191] 64% in former Czechoslovakia (1986–7), 61% in Romania (1985–7), 71% in Hungary (1987), and 82% in East Germany (1987) (Verdery, *op. cit.*, p. 86, Table 2.2).

problem represented by these third parties was an obvious obstacle in the path of restitution.

From the perspective of the treatment of various forms of immovable properties, the post-communist restitution schemes, the various schemes appear surprisingly unitary, at least to the extent that the majority of them betray a biased attitude towards former landowners. Thus, in most cases (except for Poland, Germany, and later Hungary), farmers (or their heirs) were entitled to receive other plots if the originally taken could not have been restituted, while former owners of unrestituted buildings could hope only for compensations, usually in form of bonds or vouchers. Lithuania appears as an interesting exception, as it created the possibility for former owners of unrestituted buildings to claim apartments from the state funds instead. Lithuania is also the sole case where severe conditions were imposed upon farmers with regard to the use of the restituted lands. Finally, the Romanian scheme distinguishes itself through its unclearness: up until the 2005 revision of the restitution laws, it was unclear whether restitution or compensation was the guiding principle in the case of buildings.

4.2.1 In kind compensation only for unrestituted lands

In Estonia, the Law "On the fundamentals of property reform"[192] addressed both the returns of lands and buildings; however, in the same year a separate law was enacted on land reform, dealing exclusively with restitution of land, within the framework of a more comprehensive transformation.[193] The Fundamentals dealt with buildings and collectivized property, while the Land Law addressed other types of land, too. As to what concerns buildings, the Fundamentals laconically provides for their restitution or compensation. The only serious condition is that in case of residential property which is rented to natural persons, the former owner has to take upon himself all the rights and duties resulting from the rental agreement.[194] Collectivized property, according to the law, is also restituted, but if this is not possible, farmers have pri-

[192] Law "On the fundamentals of property reform," *op. cit.*.
[193] Law "On land reform," 17 October 1991.
[194] Law "On the fundamentals of property reform," Art. 12(4).

ority to receive compensation in kind (i.e., other plots),[195] while former owners of buildings can receive only bonds (which are exchangeable for stocks in the privatization process) as compensation.[196] Another difference is represented by the fact that collectivized property could be returned earlier than other types of immovable, as the law provided that before restitution a register of previous owners and property has to be compiled.[197] It is worth noting that the Hungarian Constitutional Court found a similar provision—which provided for restitution of agricultural properties and only compensation of all others—unconstitutional, for discriminating between entitled persons, and therefore conflicting with the Constitution's equality clause.[198] The Land Law provided for the restitution of lands in their original boundaries,[199] but entitled persons had the possibility to opt for compensation instead of restitution if certain conditions were fulfilled. In the case of lands occupied by buildings, it was left up to the two owners to settle the problem (through instituting a right to superficies, usufruct, lease, etc.), but in certain conditions partial restitution was also a possibility.[200]

The Latvian restitution scheme is made up of several pieces, separate acts being dedicated to the regulation of agricultural and other landed properties.[201] The scheme regarding restitution of lands resem-

---

195 *Ibid.*, Art. 14(5).

196 *Ibid.*, Art. 17.

197 *Ibid.*, Art. 14(6) and 17(2).

198 See: *supra* for details.

199 Representative for the Estonian meticulosity is the fact that the law established an 8% margin of tolerable error (but not more than 5 hectares) in re-establishing the old boundaries, a margin for which no additional compensation was due. Law "On land reform," *op. cit.*, section 6(1).

200 Law "On land reform," *op. cit.*, sections 6(2), 6(4), 8, 9(1), 9(1-1), and 10. The scheme generally gives evidence of great flexibility for settling possible problems.

201 Law "On land reform in rural regions," December 1990; Law "On the return of buildings to their legal owners," October 1991; Law "On denationalization of buildings," October 1991; Law "On land reform in cities," November 1991; Law "On land privatization in rural regions," July 1992; Law "On the rights to receive compensation," and Law "On completion of the land reform in rural regions," October 1997. This mushrooming legislation was further complicated with subsequent amendments, which resulted—according to commentators—in incoherence and a slowing down of the entire process (see: Review of structural reforms, *op. cit.*).

bles the Estonian one, to the extent that it envisaged restitution within the original boundaries in equivalent land or compensation in the form of property certificates (these, in turn, were translatable into cash or securities).[202] Beneficiaries of the scheme had the possibility to opt between restitution and compensation, but cash was paid only to a certain category of claimants in the exchange for their property certificates. Others had the opportunity to use them in the privatization process, to acquire shares and apartments and lands (from the state fund) or to establish individual farms.[203] Somewhat resembling the Lithuanian solution, the Latvian scheme excluded a variety of lands from restitution: lands affected to public utility or containing individual homes, or used by certain public institutions.[204] In the case of buildings, the same route is followed as for agricultural properties: beneficiaries may choose between restitution and compensation, and certain categories may receive cash for their privatization certificates. Similarly, if the buildings are affected to certain public needs, restitution claims cannot be satisfied. An additional element again resembles the Lithuanian scheme: if the claimed object was subject to improvements which exceed 65% of the original building, the former owners may not be granted restitution.[205] Landowners enjoyed absolute priority, in the sense that claims were accepted even for plots containing industrial constructions. Thus, in certain cases the result was that the land belonged to one owner, and the structure on it to the other (a situation resembling the German

202 Law "On land privatization in rural regions," *op. cit.*, Art. 12 and Art. 14, amended in 1994, October and December 1995; Cabinet of Ministers' Regulation No. 187 "On the procedure for the repayment in cash to persons who were granted compensation certificates for the former landed property in rural regions," May 1997.

203 The main argument for this was the limited financial capacity of the Latvian economy. For more details, see: Constitutional Court of Latvia (hereinafter: LaCC), Case No. 1999-04-01, Judgment of 20 April 1999 and Case No. 2002-17-0103, Judgment of 10 January 2003, available online, at http://www.satv.tiesa.gov.lv/ENG/spriedum.htm; Marja Nissinen, *Latvia's Transition to a Market Economy: Political Determinants of Economic Reform Policy*, St. Martin's Press, 1999, p. 106.

204 World Bank report, "Latvia, the transition to a market economy," 1993, p. 93; quoted by Foster, *op. cit.*, p. 634.

205 Viktor Kvetkovskis and Edvins Kapostnis, "The legal ways of privatization in Latvia, the State Land Service of Latvia," 1999, available online, at http://www.ies.wisc.edu/ltc/live/baseur991124.pdf.

restitution).[206] The obvious outcome was an avalanche of lawsuits between the different owners who could not agree on the usufruct.[207]

In former Czechoslovakia, the restitution laws[208] seemingly do not provide for a difference in treatment for various forms of real properties. The general rules in all cases envisage restitution of the originally taken property or compensation, or the combination of these two. However, a closer look at the details of the Land Law[209] reveals some considerable differences in compensation matters. While section 14(1) of the Land Law and section 7 of the Law "On extra-judicial rehabilitation" both enunciate the principle of compensation for non-returnable properties, the Land Law fine-tunes compensation for non-returnable lands, enriching the claimants' options. The Law "On extra-judicial rehabilitation" provided for compensations in form of cash payments and securities (the latter especially for the cases where the former owner has passed away and heirs lodged the claim).[210] Similar means of compensation were envisaged by the Land Law, too; albeit former landowners had the extra option of claiming a plot of similar size and quality, if possible in the same community where the original plot was located, when this was not restituted.[211] Cash or securities could be claimed only if another plot was not made available in return for the taken property.[212]

In Romania the variety of restitution laws also meant a variety in approach to diverse forms of real property. The first relevant norm, the

---

206 One of the most obvious differences between restitution of land and buildings was the disproportionate deadline for filing claims. initially established at 10 and 3 years respectively, but subsequently repeatedly extended (Nissinen, *op. cit.*, pp. 107–8).

207 Nissinen, *op. cit.*, p. 107; the author argues that in certain cases the old–new landowners attempted to milk the companies which were situated on their lands.

208 Law "On the mitigation of the consequences of certain property losses," 1990, *op. cit.*; Law "On extra-judicial rehabilitation," 1991, *op. cit.*; and Law "On modifying ownership relations with respect to land and other agricultural property," 1991, *op. cit.*.

209 Law "On modifying ownership relations with respect to land and other agricultural property," 1991, *op. cit.*.

210 Law "On extra-judicial rehabilitation," *op. cit.*, section 13.

211 Law "On modifying ownership relations with respect to land and other agricultural property," *op. cit.*, sections 11(2)–(3).

212 *Ibid.*, section 14(1).

Land Law of 1991[213] contained numerous property-based distinctions. First, it distinguished privately used building or other plots within the building perimeter of settlements from all other plots. In the case of the former restitution was not possible, the current possessions being preserved. Former owners of such plots had only the right to claim compensation in kind through other plots situated, if possible, in the same building perimeter, and if not, outside of the boundaries of the settlements.[214] Second, the law subjected to different treatment claims related to forestry and all other types of lands. While former owners of forests could claim the return of maximum 1 hectare of their expropriated property,[215] former owners of other types of land were restituted within a 10 hectare ceiling.[216] To make things more complicated, the two types of returnable properties were counted together, and had to fit into the general 10 hectare limit.[217] Later amendments of this act modified the ceilings and renounced the common general cap, but still maintained the difference in the returnable quantity.[218]

While the laws regulating the restitution of lands distinguished between the different types of lands, the laws pertaining to the fate of other immovable property created further differentiation between former real property owners. The first norm to address the issue of buildings was passed only in 1995, and provided for the restitution of apartments (i.e., dwellings that constituted a single unit at the time of the taking) which were legally taken.[219] However, restitution was envisaged only for those dwellings which were either empty or were rented by their former owners. Otherwise only compensation was made available,

---

213 Law No. 18/1991, *op. cit.*.

214 *Ibid.*, Art. 23.

215 *Ibid.*, Art. 41.

216 *Ibid.*, Art. 8.

217 *Ibid.*, Art. 41, para. 3.

218 Law No. 18/1991 republished in the *Official Gazette*, No. 1, 5 January 1998; Art. 9 and 45 established the maximum amount of returnable land to 50 hectares for agricultural lands and 30 hectares for forestry. Later on, Law No. 1/2000, *op. cit.*, Art. 24 modified again the ceilings for forestry, reducing it to 10 hectares, but this does not affect the imbalance created between former owners.

219 Law No. 112/1995, *op. cit.*, Art. 1 and 3. The law uses the wording "transferred into the state's or other legal persons' property [...] on the basis of a title."

in form of cash, and calculated according to a complicated scheme which was made up of elements scattered in various earlier regulations. In any event, the compensations payable in cash could not pass the arithmetical sum of the medium wages per economy, calculated for the past 20 years, beginning with the date when the calculation was made.[220]

This arrangement was seriously criticized by the European Court of Human Rights, which stressed the lack of clarity of both legislation and case law, regarding the cases in which the lost property has passed in from the state to third parties acting in good faith.[221] The Court found an inconsistency in the application (by the authorities, which in certain cases prohibited the sale of disputed flats, while in others made exceptions), and in the interpretation of the law (by the courts, which declared the taking unlawful, while sustained the sale as lawful). Such inconsistencies that produce uncertainty in the law are relevant, according to the Court, when assessing the fairness of the balance established between general interests and individual rights.[222] In the end, the lack of clarity makes the applicants' chances of obtaining any compensation improbable, and therefore an excessive burden is placed upon them, which amounts to a violation of Article 1, Protocol No. 1.[223]

A different piece of legislation was enacted to solve the question of real property abusively taken during the communist rule, or through the Requisition Law of 1940. In their case, the law elusively talks about restitution as the rule, while also mentions compensations which can take a multitude of forms,[224] resembling in its generosity the above-presented Lithuanian approach to restitution of buildings. However, the Romanian scheme under this law is not restricted merely to buildings, but includes also lands (mainly building plots) and certain movables (which either became immovable through incorporation into constructions, or were fittings and installations—presumably in the case of industrial or commercial properties). Generally, the law contains a large

---

[220] *Ibid.*, Art. 2, 12, and 13.

[221] Strain and Others v. Romania, ECHR, Application No. 57001/00, Judgment of 21 July 2005, para. 46.

[222] *Ibid.*, paras. 48–9.

[223] *Ibid.*, paras. 55–9.

[224] Law No. 10/2001, *op. cit.*, Art. 1.

number of vaguely defined exceptions from restitution: for instance, if the building has been transformed in such a way that it became a new one in comparison with the originally expropriated one, only compensation can be afforded if the parties did not convene otherwise.[225] The law manages also to differentiate between compensation for lands and constructions: the value of constructions is calculated according to the existing norms at the date of the expropriation (taking into attention also the inflation rate); while the value of the land is calculated according to the existing norms at the entry into force of the present law.[226] Compensations could take the form of vouchers that can be used during privatization, shares, other goods and services offered by the current possessor (legal person).[227] Obviously, this generous formulation does not exclude cash or in kind compensation for non-returnable immovable; however, these possibilities are expressly mentioned only in the case of dwellings.[228] A very strong limitation on the right to claim restitution was contained by the procedural regulations, which basically left the question of restitution up to the administrative institution or the legal entity that possessed the property in question. Accordingly, restitution was a function of the approval of the current possessor, which had the discretion to decide whether to restitute or offer compensation.[229]

Law No. 10/2001 was also analyzed by the Strasbourg court, which, beyond the above-mentioned inconsistencies in adjudication,[230] criticized also the unclear provisions of the new enactment, emphasizing that some of its provisions gave birth to at least five different,

[225] *Ibid.*, Art. 18, para. (c).

[226] *Ibid.*, Art. 11, paras. 5 and 6.

[227] *Ibid.*, Art. 9(2).

[228] *Ibid.*, Art. 24, also 36–40. The modality and maximum amount of cash compensation was left subject to later regulation; the law only mentioned that such compensations might be limited.

[229] *Ibid.*, Art. 20–33.

[230] Paduraru c. Roumanie, CEDH, Requête No. 63252/00, Arrêt de 1 decembre 2005, paras. 34–7. The Court pointed to inconsistencies in the (then) Supreme Court's approach to certain expropriation decrees, which were sometimes considered as constitutional, but sometimes regarded as unconstitutional. This inconsistency is reflected also by the lower courts, which have chosen to follow either one or the other decision of the highest court.

even contradicting interpretations.[231] The Court has restated its view already expressed in the above-cited Strain Case, according to which a once adopted (normative) solution has to be implemented with reasonable clarity and coherence in order to avoid legal uncertainty and insecurity.[232]

This law had been modified during 2005, as the legislator attempted to eliminate the ambiguity of the regulation. Thus, restitution became the only solution envisaged for the undoing of past injustices, while compensations are afforded only if restitution is effectively impossible.[233] Similarly, the differences between lands and buildings in establishing their value were erased,[234] as well as all the other problematic points mentioned in the forgoing analysis. The law is intended to represent a comprehensive reform of property restitution legislation, and accordingly contains amendment of all previous statutes in this field. Interestingly, the difference between former owners is still maintained with regard to the upper limit of restitution. This time the legislator tilts the balance once again in the favor of former owners of forestry, as in their case it makes full restitution possible, while owners of agricultural land are still kept within a 50 hectare limit.[235]

This final revision could not, on its turn, escape the European Court of Human Rights' scrutiny. In a very recent decision, the Court recognized that the latest modifications to the restitution scheme (especially those with regard to Law No. 10/2001) create "at least a theoretical possibility" of receiving a market value compensation for the immovable that is not returned. Alas, in the concrete case there were no signs of the authorities' intention to give effect to the legal provisions and to actually pay the compensation.[236]

---

[231] *Ibid.*, para. 43.

[232] *Ibid.*, para. 92.

[233] Law No. 247/2005, *op. cit.*, Art. 1.

[234] *Ibid.*, Art. 1, sections 28 and 29; the new common modality of calculation is based on current market value according to international standards of evaluation.

[235] See also: *supra*, section 4.

[236] Porteanu c. Roumanie, CEDH, Requête No. 4596/03, Arrêt de 16 février 2006, para. 34; the Court also noted that the new law does not take into account the length of the deprivation endured by the entitled persons until its entry into force.

4.2.2 No distinction between former owners of lands and buildings

Hungary's Compensation Law initially provided for a clear-cut distinction between the treatment of agricultural lands and other real property.[237] The difference—as it was already explained above[238]—consisted in the calculation formula employed for the conversion of the value of the taken properties into a flat rate that ultimately resulted in a five time higher limit up until which full compensation was possible in the case of lands. This scheme was, however, found unconstitutional as, according to the Constitutional Court, none of the presented evidences justified a more favorable treatment of former owners of agricultural lands.[239]

Finally, as it was already stated above, Poland and Germany remain the genuine exceptions, where one may not speak about a genuine differentiation between the claimants of various types of landed properties.

4.2.3 Strict conditions upon restituted land

The Lithuanian Law "On procedures and conditions for restoration of citizen's rights to the ownership of extant real property" addresses the question of both lands and buildings.[240] The law covers lands, forests, structures of economical and commercial nature (i.e., enterprises), and their accessories and residential buildings.[241] As what concerns the restitution of lands, severe conditions have to be fulfilled by the claimants. First, they have to be engaged in the tilling of land, or have to demonstrate their commitment to engage in farming. Second, if they do not begin to use the restituted lands according to their destination within one year's time from the restitution, the land is to be confiscated (with payment of compensation).[242] These requirements convincingly demonstrate that the Lithuanian scheme gives a far greater

[237] Law No. XXV of 1991, *op. cit.*, Art. 3 and 13.
[238] See: *supra*, section 4.
[239] HCC, AB 28/1991, 1160/A/1991, part (c), para. 3(1); see also: *supra, ibid.*.
[240] Law "On procedures and conditions for restoration of citizen's rights to the ownership of existent real property," 18 June 1991.
[241] *Ibid.*, Art. 4.
[242] *Ibid.*.

importance to agricultural reform than to the mitigation of past injustices. A similar conclusion is upheld by the regulation of plots situated within city boundaries. In these cases, a different parcel will be granted to the claimants in the same city, but the dimensions of this plot will be determined by governmental regulation. Moreover, if claimants have a residential building on, and have exercised a *de facto* ownership of their former plot, their right is restored, but only up to a 0.2–0.3 hectare limit.[243] A seemingly more flexible approach is taken towards buildings, where the claimants have multiple options: they may choose restitution or compensation in equivalent (i.e., instead of their former dwelling they can opt for the one they currently rent from the state, or, if this is not applicable, another apartment from the state fund); even partial restitution is possible. In this latter situation, if the property offered in compensation is not equivalent in value with the original one, lump sum compensation for the difference in value is available.[244] The Lithuanian scheme also knows a procedure called "state re-purchase," which essentially is a form of compensation for non-restorable properties. In this category fall lands affected to public utilities (but if certain conditions are met, partial restitution of these plots is also possible), and buildings turned over to medical, educational, cultural, and alike institutions, or fundamentally improved, or increased in surface.[245] "Re-purchase" takes place through equivalent property, lump-sum payments or stocks, or cancellation of the former owner's debts towards the state that have arisen since the alienation of the property. Through the severe conditions set for land restitution, the Lithuanian scheme subjects former owners of agricultural properties to a much less favorable treatment than the former owners of residential buildings.

4.3 Commercial property

Enterprises arguably were the primary target of the communist economic reforms all over Central and Eastern Europe. The broad and comprehensive nationalization waves resulted in the seizure of the bulk of the economic output, reaching from small shops to entire industries.

[243] *Ibid.*, Art. 5.
[244] *Ibid.*, Art. 8.
[245] *Ibid.*, Art. 12 and 14.

Nazi-era takings targeting Jewish enterprises swept equally broad, albeit the "aryanization" of the economy was pursuing the goals of a genocidal project, rather than those of an economic transformation.[246] Enterprises, of course, are abstract entities; however, their assets (land, buildings, bank accounts, shops, inventory, etc.) are tangible, quantifiable, and measurable objects, and seizure meant, besides the end of the legal person's existence in its original form, also the transfer of its assets into state (or co-operative) property. (In the case of "aryanization," the enterprises were often transferred into "Aryan" private ownership.) Under these conditions, any program that aims at the rectification of past property injustices, according to the principle of equality, has to address, somehow, the question of nationalized commercial properties, too.

The issue, however, is complicated by two important factors. On the one hand, during the decades that have passed since the seizures, the assets of the enterprises have undergone serious transformations. As Nissinen notes, in many cases it is almost impossible to separate the expropriated property from the units added since the takeover.[247] On the other hand, due to their economic value, the web of interests surrounding them is much denser than in the case of other properties. This of course also means that even if restitution is not possible, in the eventuality that compensations are afforded, they are likely to be a lot higher than in the case of farms or houses. Under these conditions, the post-communist restitution schemes addressed the issue of commercial properties in various ways, but the focus in most cases was on small shops and individual entrepreneurs' properties, rather than heavy industry or financial institutions.

Generally, it can be observed that in the case of commercial properties distinction is made between small firms and larger corporations.

---

[246] Robert Hochstein, "Jewish property restitution in the Czech Republic," *Boston College International & Comparative Law Review* 19 (1996), pp. 426–7 notes that in spite of the proliferation of such legislation and other anti-Semitic laws, in 1938 some 40,000 Jewish firms were still functioning in Germany. A complete elimination of Jewish businesses was avoided as certain large Jewish-owned corporations got involved into producing indispensable military supplies for the German remilitarization. After Kristallnacht, however, the expropriation of Jewish property speeded up and extended to most of the remaining assets.

[247] Nissinen, *op. cit.*, p. 106.

Those schemes that provided also for the possibility of returning the taken commercial properties contemplated restitution for small shops and businesses. This was the case of Germany, Czechoslovakia, and Romania. The problem of commercial properties did not arise in Poland, while in Hungary merely compensation was offered, and only to natural persons, for the stocks representing their participation in the companies. Compensation was the preferred form of rectification also in Latvia, while Estonia and Lithuania included various items of commercial property in the case of which restitution or compensation was offered.[248]

4.3.1 Restitution of small businesses

The German restitution scheme features some interesting solutions with respect to the restitution of commercial properties. As commentators argue, the Resolution of Outstanding Property Issues Act provided for wide commercial property-related claims.[249] Accordingly, entire enterprises could have been claimed back, with all subsequent investments. Interestingly, if an approximately constant debt–equity ratio was present, no compensation had to be paid for eventual improvement or deterioration. Due to the specificity of the German scheme which initially had to ignore takings that occurred during the Soviet occupation (and later only afforded a limited monetary compensation for these properties), restitution only concerned small firms taken in the early 70s.[250] Hence, the government could more easily afford this relative generous approach. However, this scheme turned out to be obstructive of privatization, in the sense that former owners through the submis-

[248] The Estonian law enumerated ships, factory fittings, stocks, and shares between the objects of property reform (Law "On the fundamentals of property reform," *op. cit.*, Art. 11.). In the case of the latter, compensation is to be paid in the form of bonds (*idem*; also Art. 17(2)). The Latvian scheme provided mainly for monetary compensations in the case of industrial properties (Nissinen, *op. cit.*, p. 106.). Similarly, the Lithuanian Restitution Law included "structures of economic-commercial nature" and their accessories in its scope, providing for their return or compensation (Law "On the procedures and conditions for restoration of citizen's rights to the ownership of extant real property," *op. cit.*, Art. 3.).

[249] Sinn and Sinn, *op. cit.*, p. 87.

[250] See also: *supra*.

sion of their claims had the possibility to delay or block privatization.[251] Consequently, the legislator reacted by enacting the Obstacle-removal Law, which gave preference to investors over former owners in certain of situations, and thereby managed to do away with the reparatory character of commercial properties' restitution. According to the modified scheme, former owners were granted restitution if they promised to keep the enterprise functioning, and, in case there were interested investors, the former owner had to guarantee to undertake an equal amount of investment. Furthermore, if former owners did not manage to live up to their promises, they could have been forced to give up the restituted property (under the condition of due compensation being paid).[252]

In former Czechoslovakia, the first restitution law, "On the mitigation of the consequences of certain property losses," addressed the issue of commercial and residential properties nationalized during the late 50s, mostly small shops and businesses, including movables "used in conducting activities inside restituted property."[253] The law provided for restitution, while compensation was an option where restitution was not possible. Commentators note that the law concerned only a small portion of the expropriated properties.[254] The subsequently enacted Law "On extra-judicial rehabilitation," although a lot broader in its scope, excluded most commercial property related claims by restraining the circle of beneficiaries to natural persons. Therefore, under this second norm, former owners of an expropriated private company could not have a valid claim to the assets of their firm.[255] This differentiation

[251] Sinn and Sinn, *op. cit.*, pp. 94–5; Berhnard Seliger in "Ten Years After German Unification," *Central Europe Review* (2001), available online, at http://www.ce-review.org/01/4/seliger4.html explains that restitution was preferred to compensation out of fiscal concerns, and emphasizes that the long-time blocking of investments was also due to the fact that in almost 90% of the cases restitution was contested.

[252] Sinn and Sinn, *op. cit.*. However, the authors note that even after these amendments, former owners were left with plenty of room to delay privatization.

[253] Law "On mitigation of the consequences of certain property losses," *op. cit.*, Art. 13(2).

[254] Hochstein, *op. cit.*, pp. 440–1.

[255] Valová, Slezák, and Slezák v. Slovakia, ECHR, Application No. 44925/98, Judgment of 1 June 2004, paras. 8–18.

between owners of small commercial properties and larger corporations is obviously unjust, for there is no plausible legal argument that can explain why, for example, pharmacies were restituted, while corporate owners were excluded from the scheme. The Czech approach to commercial property, while generous in appearance, proves narrow and restrictive in practice. Illustrative of its limits is the story of the Brok family's three times nationalized property, whose heirs were unable to obtain restitution under the reigning scheme.[256] The Brok family's business was confiscated by the Nazi regime and was transferred to a Slovak company involved in the Axis war effort. After the war, the new government nationalized all possessions of "persons unreliable to the state," among them being, of course, the holdings of the company that was administering the former Brok assets. Finally, after the communist takeover, the already nationalized company remained in state possession and part of its assets—including those belonging to the Brok family—were transferred to another state-owned enterprise. The lawsuits filed by the heirs failed one by one at each level of jurisdiction, as the courts invariably found that the post-war nationalization decree prevented restitution. Therefore, the assets legally remained in the state's hands, and thus became state property before the cut-off date established by the restitution scheme. In the end, the Constitutional Court argued that the Fundamental Law protects only existing rights, and, as the claimed property did not belong to the Brok's anymore, denial of restitution did not violate the heirs' right to property.[257] The case ended up before the U.N. Human Rights Committee, which considered that the Czech restitution laws deny equal protection of the laws by arbitrarily distinguishing between former owners.[258]

In Romania, the Law "On abusively taken real property" provided for the return of commercial property (including also movable assets) to the natural persons, shareholders of the former, expropriated legal entity.[259] However, in case of former shareholders, only equivalent compensation was envisaged, with the exception of firms with a single shareholder, or if all shareholders were members of the same family.[260]

[256] For the detailed case-study, see: Macklem, *op. cit.*.

[257] CCC, III. US 132/96.

[258] Brok v. Czech Republic, *op. cit.*; all data based upon Macklem, *op. cit.*.

[259] Law No. 10/2001, *op. cit.*, Art. 3.

[260] *Ibid.*, Art. 18(a), without specifying the notion of "family."

Compensations in the above case were to be afforded in the form of shares, preferably of the company, which took over the expropriated property, or of other enterprises. However, the law also vaguely mentions that during privatization the entitled persons have the possibility to negotiate with the privatizing authority other forms of compensation, too.[261] The amount of the compensation was to be determined according to the actualized value of the former shares.

4.3.2 Compensation for lost commercial property

The Hungarian Restitution Law[262] did not expressly provide for the restitution of commercial property, and, although the law defined the circle of beneficiaries as consisting only of natural persons, from the interpretation of its certain provisions means that losses resulting from the seizure of enterprises are eligible for compensation. Namely, Annex No. 3 of the Restitution Law, which contains the variables for the calculation of the flat rate for compensation, mentions stores and shops in the section dealing with immovable property, while an entire section is dedicated to the variables for enterprises (dealing with immovable property). Similarly, the governmental decree for the implementation of the Restitution Law makes references to compensations for commercial properties.[263] However, in cases of seized enterprises, all assets used for its activity—movable and immovable—have to be considered as a single property item.[264] These provisions were also quoted by the Hungarian Constitutional Court when rejecting a complaint that challenged the alleged discrimination made by the Compensation Law against shareholders of former corporate entities.[265] However, it needs to be emphasized that the above-mentioned provisions do not create a universal claim to the seized enterprises' assets, but merely to stocks or other properties representing the members' participation in the corporation.

A further point argued by the above-mentioned constitutional complaint related to the discrimination made by the Compensation

[261] *Ibid.*, Art. 32(1) and 32(8).
[262] Law No. XXV of 1991, *op. cit.*.
[263] Governmental Decree No. 104/1991, *op. cit.*, Art. 3 and 5.
[264] *Ibid.*, Art. 3 and 5.
[265] HCC, AB 707/B/1997, part III/2.

Law between various types of co-operatives. The complaint maintained that there are no constitutional bases for excluding from the compensation scheme members of various former co-operatives, while members of the former milk co-operatives are granted the right to claim compensation.[266] The Court in its analysis compared the provisions of two governmental decrees regulating the incorporation of diverse existing co-operatives in the newly formed agricultural co-operatives. According to the rationality test applied by the Court, if a normative enactment contained explicit provisions on taking of property which could give rise to grievances, the legislator had the constitutional obligation to include the act in question in the scope of the restitution scheme. However, while the act regulating the incorporation of the milk co-operatives was found as representing a veritable expropriation, the act on the other forms of co-operatives did not contain such express provisions for the taking of members' property. Thence, the Court was able to conclude that there was no constitutional requirement to include the latter decree—and thereby the former co-operative members—in the compensation program.[267]

Finally, it has to be stressed that the Compensation Law created the possibility of redress only for individuals (former shareholders, members of cooperatives, etc.), and not for legal entities. The Constitutional Court's interpretation of the compensation laws in this respect demonstrates a relative inconsistency. While in a somewhat early decision[268] it considered that the laws' focus on the individual grievances does not constitute an *ab ovo* exclusion of legal persons from the possibility of—at least partial—compensation, four years later it was flatly stated that there is no legal basis for the compensation of legal entities.[269]

An entirely different set of problems was raised by the compensation mechanism with regard to the translation of vouchers into agricul-

[266] The Compensation Law in its annexes specifically enumerated those normative acts which were considered—due also to their normative content—as giving rise to property grievances. Those property prejudices that were not a consequence of the application of the enumerated norms fell outside of the restitution scheme.

[267] HCC, AB 707/B/1997, part III/3, para. 2.

[268] HCC, AB 16/1993, 1378/E/1990, part IV(b).

[269] HCC, AB 707/B/1997 part II/2, para. 3.

tural land. The Compensation Law created a so-called "right to purchase" for former property owners, which essentially meant that they were entitled to acquire—by participating in a competitive bid—lands from the agricultural cooperatives' patrimony.[270] The fundamental problem, which was raised by these rules, is whether the "right to purchase" represents a taking or not. The Constitutional Court dealt with the question of trading vouchers for agricultural lands, but it essentially upheld the idea of the "right to purchase," as representing merely a lien on property, rather than a taking.[271]

"The right to purchase," just like the theory of "novation"[272] was transplanted from civil law—albeit this time by the legislator, rather than the Court—and differed likewise, significantly, from its civilian counterpart. According to the Compensation Law, the "right to purchase" means that the entitled person can acquire property at a price established by the law, upon his unilateral manifestation of will. On the other hand, "the right to purchase," as known in civil law, stands for the entitled person's possibility to acquire the good upon a unilateral declaration. The essential difference is that in civil law, the "right to purchase" is a special form of sales contract, which presupposes the parties' previous agreement. Under the Compensation Law, however, "the right to purchase" does not bear any of the above characteristics. There is no previous agreement between the parties, their will does not meet, they establish neither the price, nor the plot, which forms the object of the contract.[273] Therefore, commentators argue, the "right to purchase" as defined by the Compensation Law, can be construed only as a form of taking. Such an extensive legal right—unknown to the major legal traditions—hardly compatible with the idea of the rule of law, is regarded as a characteristic product of authoritarian legal systems.[274] But, the intriguing "right to purchase" cannot be construed as a legal form of taking. For—as the legislative intent was clearly contrary to the creation of a new form of taking—the law does not confer upon it those

[270] Law No. XXV of 1991, *op. cit.*, Art. 15 and the following.

[271] HCC, AB 21/1990, 1057/G/1990; AB 16/1991, 952/A/1991; AB 28/1991, 1160/A/1991; AB 15/1993, 1543/B/1991.

[272] See: *supra*, Chapter 2.

[273] Sajó, "A részleges...," pp. 192–3.

[274] *Ibid.*, p. 194.

guarantees that necessarily have to accompany takings. Especially the requirements of public interest and fair compensation are missing.[275]

4.4 Religious and communal property

This section is dedicated to two important, non-commercial types of property, which formed a significant and controversial part of restitution programs in post-communist countries. Restitution of church properties was controversial for a number of reasons, among which the following can be mentioned. The size and value of the once dominant—mostly Catholic, but also Orthodox—churches' assets. In the case of certain religious communities—especially the Jewish—the size of the community shrunk to almost symbolic numbers, while claims were targeting a wide array of valuable property. Finally, the assets of certain churches were transferred during the communist regimes to other, preferred religious organizations. For instance, the Greco-Catholic Church in Romania lost all of its properties mostly in favor of the Orthodox Church. The other category—communal property—is employed to cover properties such as pastures and forestry owned (and exploited) in common by villagers, and assets[276] of profit organizations, which are problematic because the specific form of ownership and/or the associations themselves (the entire community, too, in many cases) have since disappeared.

4.4.1 Distinctions between religious and other communal properties

From the perspective of communal and religious properties, except for Germany, all restitution programs present certain problematic features. Most programs—with the notable exception of Romania—distinguish religious and communal properties, and give a clear preference to the former (it is especially the case of Lithuania and Hungary). In Roma-

[275] Transferring property from one owner to another might be regarded as fulfilling a public interest, if it pursues the constitutional aim of establishing preconditions of market economy. However, it is arguable, whether this requires taking of cooperative properties. The compensation vouchers received in exchange for the lands cannot be regarded as compensation, as their value and subsequent utilization was unclear at the time (Sajó, *op. cit.*, pp. 195–7).

[276] E.g., hospitals, schools, libraries, baths, etc.

nia, the 1998 amendments to the Land Law enabled also the return of communally owned forestry, a traditional form of undivided, joint ownership. However, the rather foggy wording provides that former members of these communities have to apply individually, upon proof of past membership. The provisions on the claimable amount are also unclear: paragraph 1 enounces that the individual members can claim the amount of forestry indicated in the document that certifies their former membership, while paragraph 5 subjects these claims to the general requirements—quantitative limits—that apply for individual claims.[277] The Land Restitution Law of 2000[278] made it clear that one property title will be issued for all former members' claims; thus, although the applications are filed individually, restitution is done to the former association, while mentions are be made about each member's stake. Subsequent articles of the law[279] attempt to bring these traditional models of communal ownership in line with the current legal system; therefore, they provide for the organization of these entities with the scope of acquiring legal personality.[280]

A third category of properties whose restitution is regulated by the Romanian scheme is made up of communal properties belonging to national minorities' organizations. The relevant provisions are comprised yet again in an emergency ordinance, as amended by the above-mentioned 2005 law.[281] The act covers abusively taken immov-

277 Law No. 18/1991 as amended and republished in 1998, *op. cit.*, Art. 46 provided for the return of maximum 30 hectares of former church forests to each entitled parish or monastery.

278 Law No. 1/2000, *op. cit.*.

279 *Ibid.*, Art. 28.

280 This approach resembles the New Zealand attempts to accommodate tribal conceptions of property within the reigning legal system. In New Zealand, this was achieved through the constitution of a corporate body for the beneficiary tribe as the legal representative and property-holding entity. The corporation (made up of a charitable trust and various companies) is constituted under the general legislation—thus the relevant norms are indirectly determining also the social and political organization of the tribe. Within these structures, the authority of individuals is not established, and the impression of a collective exercise of ownership is created (John Dawson, "A Constitutional Property Settlement Between Ngai Tahu and the New Zealand Crown," in Mclean, *op. cit.*, pp. 219–21).

281 Governmental Emergency Ordinance No. 83/1999, as amended and republished in the *Official Gazette*, No. 797, 1 September 2005.

able properties beginning with 1940, regardless of their destination. In order to qualify as a claimant, an organization has to be organized as a private law legal entity according to Romanian legislation, representing the interests of a minority community affected by past abusive takings. Moreover, the applicant has to prove that it is the recognized successor of the legal entity from which the claimed properties were taken—such recognitions are issued by the courts of law.[282] The norm, which could cover also Holocaust takings (although Jewish organizations define themselves as religious, rather than national minorities), subjects restitution to the same conditions as for the return of religious properties.

In Lithuania, the Restitution Law, while providing for the return of religious properties, neither addresses non-religious communal property, nor does it permit the restitution of agricultural land. Allegedly, the term "religious" is used as broadly as possible and thus communal buildings not strictly "religious" in nature returned can be returned, too.[283] However, the Jewish community formed in 1991 faced serious difficulties in obtaining official recognition of its succession to the dozens of pre-war Jewish organizations, as such a status for re-registered organizations was dependent—unlike in the other Baltic States—on the recognition by the religion's "supreme authority," an entity that does not exist in Judaism.[284] A special problem is represented by cultural properties, especially the collection of Yiddish and Hebrew manuscripts, which managed to escape Nazi confiscation only to be subsequently taken by the Soviets and finally ending up in the Lithuanian government's hands.[285] The government invoked a special claim to its cultural patrimony, which justifies retention of the valuable collection, while the Jewish community emphasized the communal (and religious) property character of the manuscripts, claiming their restitution.[286] As both the communal and the religious character of the collection is

[282] *Ibid.*, Art. 1.

[283] Stuart Eizenstat, "Justice after confiscation: Restitution of Communal and Private Property in Central and Eastern Europe," *East European Constitutional Review* 6.2–3 (1997).

[284] Jaskaunas, *op. cit.*, p. 64.

[285] For more details, see: Pamela Bruzzese, "Distributing the Past, Jewish Cultural Property in Lithuania," *New York University Journal of International Law & Politics* 31 (1998), p. 145.

[286] *Ibid.*, pp. 152–60.

disputed, and conflicts have arisen even within the Jewish community (mostly between Lithuanians and emigrants) over selecting the most entitled organization to claim restitution, the situation of the manuscripts remains unsolved.[287]

The relevant provisions of the Czechoslovakian restitution scheme were amended after the secession by the Czech government so as to extend its effects also to Nazi-era takings, and made possible the return of communally-owned Jewish properties (synagogues, cemeteries, schools), which were taken by the Nazi regime and were still in the state's hands.[288] As the amendment ties the right to restitution to the racial reasons present behind the takings, some commentators criticized this racial exclusivity clause to be in violation of the major international human rights agreements.[289] Another problematic feature of the amendment is represented by the fact that the Law "On extra-judicial rehabilitation" originally provided only for individual claims, thus a special exception has been created for Jewish communal properties, *vis-á-vis* every other type of communal or corporate holding.

The Hungarian legislators dedicated a separate law to the settlement of former ecclesiastical real properties,[290] which entered into force in the same year as the Compensation Law. The regulation of former church immovables was also based both on ideas of justice and reform, aiming at the rectification of grave injustices and also at securing the appropriate material conditions for the continuation of the churches' social and cultural activities.[291]

However, no similar provision has been introduced as regards other non-governmental organizations (foundations, associations, etc.). This situation was challenged as unconstitutional by a complaint invoking the legislator's unconstitutional omission. In its decision, the Constitutional Court explained that the question of unconstitutional

[287] At the same time, the case is a perfect illustration of the identity problems, which are so obvious in the context of indigenous claims, but which can be detected also behind post-communist restitution claims.

[288] Hochstein, *op. cit.*, p. 423.

[289] *Ibid.*, pp. 443–6.

[290] Law No. XXXII of 1991.

[291] The Preamble emphasizes the historical role played by churches in the country's cultural life, as well as their significant activity in education, healthcare, and other social and cultural matters—in one word, their social function.

discrimination could be raised only with respect to comparable parties, and therefore the application is raising a false question. Religious organizations—so the Court opines—cannot be compared to other (non commercial) legal persons, but only to entities with similar function, role, size, and autonomy, whose right to property is similarly strongly, even compellingly tied to the insurance of certain fundamental constitutional right. The motivations behind the restitution of religious property significantly differ from the goals of the compensation laws. Fundamentally, restitution of religious assets targeted not the mitigation of property grievances, but rather the damages caused to the free exercise of religion. Hence, the restitution of church property is grounded on the principle of functionality, justified by the peculiarities of religious organizations and the necessity to insure the fundamental right to the free exercise of religion.[292] Further, in its earlier decision on the constitutionality of certain provisions of the Law "On the restitution of church property," the Court also emphasized that because restitution is limited to those properties that were originally affected to the exercise of religion, claimed solely for this purpose and only to the extent necessary, the exclusion of those religious organizations that were not[293] operating in the normative period, or did not suffer property losses, is reasonable.

Interestingly, when faced with a challenge alleging the unconstitutional discrimination made by the law on the restitution of religious property between various churches and between churches and not for profit organizations, the Constitutional Court found a provision relating to the payment of annuities problematic. Annuities were to be paid as compensation for those properties that cannot be restituted under the law, with the condition that the funds have to be spent for socially useful purposes.[294] According to the reasoning of the Court, if the article in question is regarded as providing for governmental support for ensuring the financial independence of churches, the differentiation made between organizations on the basis of the cut-off date lacks any constitutional motive. Conversely, if the provision is considered as

[292] HCC, AB 1395/E/1996, part II/3, para. 2; also AB 4/1993, 1651/B/1991, part C III/1–2, paras. 1–3.

[293] HCC, 4/1993, 1651/B/1991, part C III/2, para. 7.

[294] *Ibid.*, Art. 15.

a restitution rule, the distinction between churches and other not for profit organizations that encountered similar property losses appears again to lack a well-grounded reason. Curiously, the Court satisfied itself with merely noting the absence of constitutional justifications.[295]

4.4.2 Priority for "historical churches"

Another common feature of the Central and East European restitution programs is the relative delay with which Jewish properties were included in the schemes, especially in Poland, Czechoslovakia, and Hungary. In Poland for instance, the law on the restitution of Jewish property was enacted several years after the restitution of the other (notably the Catholic Church's) property, only in 1997. The law allows only for local community's claims; however, these are extremely reduced in numbers, as almost the entire Polish Jewry has fallen prey to the Holocaust.[296] In these conditions, the restitution scheme allegedly comprises roughly one tenth of the claimable properties and it is restricted to state-owned religious properties, excluding land and communal property.[297]

In the former Czechoslovakia, the Restitution Law set the cut-off date to 1948, thus from the outset excluded Jewish property taken during the Nazi regime,[298] as well as other church properties taken in the aftermath of World War II, before the communist takeover, although churches were on the losing end of the nationalization that took place between 1945 and 1948. Even if a later amendment managed to modify the baselines so as to include also the period of the Nazi government, it still managed to maintain the original distinction between citizens and non-citizens and different kinds of landed property in the case of Jewish assets, too, as non-citizens and former owners of agricultural

---

[295] HCC, 4/1993, 1651/B/1991, part C III/3, paras. 2–4. The Court explained that such reparative payments can be made only after a system of state subsidies for churches and other autonomous organizations had been worked out, and if reparations can be fitted into this system in such a way which does not amount to discrimination.

[296] *Ibid.*; Eizenstat, *op. cit.*; Annual Report…, *op. cit.*; available online, at http://www.state.gov/g/drl/rls/irf/2005/51573.htm.

[297] Barkan, *op. cit.*, p. 147.

[298] Law "On extra-judicial rehabilitation," *op. cit.*.

lands were unable to benefit from its provisions. This odd situation was perpetuated for several years, when finally non-citizens' claims were accepted to looted art being held in state possession, as well as individual claims to agricultural property.[299]

The restitution of church properties in general was not satisfactorily resolved as of 2006. Although various proposals existed—including the payment of an annual rent for the non-restituted church properties—, no concrete measures have been taken. The situation is complicated by the fact that according to national law, the government cannot compel local governments to restitute properties, even in the case of Jewish religious properties which have been restituted in the central government's or the city of Prague's hands.[300]

The Hungarian legislator has also set the cut-off date to 1948—excluding, thus, pre-communist era takings—and targeted those properties which served spiritual, cultural, and social purposes, and were taken without compensation, if, at the date of the entry into force of the law, they were in the central or local authorities' possession.[301] However, not even the so-called "historical" churches were entirely satisfied with this deadline, arguing that a part of their properties was seized already beginning from 1945. Similar dissatisfaction was expressed with regard to the fact that the law limited restitution to immovable property.[302]

This normative exclusion of pre-communist era takings appears problematic from the perspective of Jewish properties. Although immediately after the war nazi-era expropriation decrees were annulled, and promises were made about solving property grievances, significant gaps remained. In 1946, a law was enacted to address the material consequences of the Holocaust, but the executive orders issued for its implementation remained silent on various aspects concerning—especially—

299 Tomas Kraus, Executive Director of the Federation of Jewish Communities in the Czech Republic, presentation given at the AJC Conference in Bucharest, March 2002, "Anti-Semitism, Holocaust Memory, Property Restitution and Related Issues Confronting the Jewish Communities of Central and Eastern Europe"; U.S. Department of State, Under Secretary of Political Affairs, Bureau of European and Eurasian Affairs, "Summary of Property Restitution in Central and Eastern Europe, 2003" (Updated as of 12 April 2006), available online, at http://www.state.gov/p/eur/rls/or/64425.htm.

300 Summary of Property Restitution in Central and Eastern Europe, *op. cit.*.

301 Law No. XXXII, *op. cit.*, Art. 1 and 2.

302 Mihályi, *op. cit.*, p. 16.

heirless properties. For instance, it did not address those affected by a 1944 decree, which obliged persons of Jewish origin to declare and deposit their precious metals, jewelry, cash, stocks, bonds, or shares. At the same time, it did not specify who could be regarded as an heir, in the absence of whom the property items in question were transferred to a fund created for the compensation of the Holocaust victims.[303] In the meanwhile, however, already in 1946 (before the baseline created by the compensation scheme) an ordinance was issued, which provided for the mandatory surrender of precious metals and foreign currencies, without regard to the owner's identity.[304]

Consequently, arguments to the incompatibility of the compensation laws[305] with the provisions of the Paris Peace Treaty of 1947 were raised. Under Article 27(1) of the Treaty, Hungary pledged to restitute—or, if this is not possible, to adequately compensate for—those goods, rights, and interests which were seized, confiscated, or placed under trusteeship after 1 September 1939, upon consideration of race or religion. The second paragraph of the same article provided that all unclaimed goods, rights, and interests of persons, organizations, or communities subjected to fascist, persecuting legislation out of religious, racial, or other considerations will be transferred to domestic organizations representing these persons, organizations, or communities.[306] Although individual claims were rejected as inadmissible, the Court went on to examine *ex officio* the compatibility of the compensation scheme with the cited provisions of the Treaty.[307] The Court's analysis led to the conclusion that no normative enactment ever attempted to implement the above provisions of Article 27(2), hence this omission resulted in an unconstitutional situation because Hungary did not fulfill its obligations assumed through an international treaty. The

303 For a more detailed description, see: HCC, AB 16/1993, 1378/E/1990, part II.

304 Prime Minister's Ordinance No. 4800/1946, quoted by the HCC, *op. cit.*.

305 Law No. XV/1991, *op. cit.*; Law No. XIV/1992, *op. cit.*.

306 Quoted in HCC, AB 15/1993, 1543/B/1991 and AB 16/1993, 1378/E/1990.

307 According to Art. 21(3) of Law No. XXXII of 1989 on the Constitutional Court, such complaints cannot be filed by individuals, but only by the Parliament or any of its members, the President, the Cabinet or any of its members, the President of the Supreme Court or of the Court of Auditors, or the Chief-Prosecutor.

Court interpreted Article 7 of the Constitution providing for the concordance of domestic law with international legal obligations, as not merely precluding contradictions between these two categories, but also as requiring the enactment of those norms necessary for the implementation of international obligations.[308]

However, as to what concerns the compensation of individuals persecuted out of racial or religious motive, the Court considered that the compensation scheme is capable of awarding satisfactory relief.[309] Although the quoted passages of the Treaty provided for restitution as the rule and compensation as the exception, for the cases when restitution is not possible, the Court reasoned that "due to the changed historical circumstances," the Treaty provisions cannot be implemented in the envisaged way.[310] Thus, the Court could lightly state that "appropriate" does not necessarily mean "full" compensation because depending on the economic possibilities of the country, a partial compensation can also be considered as "appropriate" if victims can benefit from it without discrimination.[311] Moreover, wrapping up this argumentation, the Court—while calling upon the Parliament to act for the elimination of the unconstitutional situation—emphasized that what has been said about "appropriate" partial compensation in the case of natural persons is also authoritative for organizations. Thus, it is not unconstitutional if the compensation of such organizations is effected in the same manner and to the same extent as provided in the compensation laws.[312]

An attempt to redress the above-described unconstitutional situation was represented by a 1997 law, on the basis of which funds were transferred to a public endowment founded by the government.[313] The endowment received a relatively large sum in compensation vouchers, plus several items of landed property and looted artwork. The vouchers could have been translated only in annuities paid in the favor of entitled

[308] HCC, AB 16/1993, part IV.

[309] Law No. XXIV of 1992, *op. cit.*, rolled back the cut-off date to 1939, so as to cover also the Nazi-era takings.

[310] HCC, AB 16/1993, *op. cit.*.

[311] HCC, AB 15/1993, *op. cit.*.

[312] HCC, AB 16/1993, *op. cit.*.

[313] Law No. X/1997 for the execution of the provisions contained in Art. 27, para. 2 of Law No. XVIII on the Paris Peace Treaty.

Holocaust survivors. Further vouchers were granted as a compensation for a number of confiscated Jewish properties; these had to be used in the benefit of the Jewish community.[314] This normative regulation was kept in line with the Constitutional Court's opinion discussed in the precedent paragraph, and, therefore, even if the original law from 1946 was contemplating the transfer of heirless properties to several Jewish organizations, the new solution was mostly confined to voucher compensation. The relevant paragraphs of the old law were even deleted, by stating that those heirless properties which will devolve to the state after the entry into force of the new regulation, will be transferred to the public endowment according to separate legal regulations.[315]

Romania distinguishes itself again by the lack of a clear and unitary normative approach to church property: relevant provisions are scattered through various laws and ordinances. On the one hand, provisions on the return of some church lands[316] were already included in the first Land Law, while on the other hand, buildings taken from religious organizations and other communal properties were initially exempted from the scheme. Although the initial scheme in their case was rather about original distribution than restitution (the article spoke about "attribution"), religious bodies were gradually included in the restitution scheme, and the pool of beneficiaries and the amount of returnable land were gradually increased.[317] Finally, forestry was included into the pool of claimable church property, too, within the same quantitative limits as in the case of individual claims.[318] The outcome

[314] See also: Claims Conference, Compensation/Restitution in Hungary, available online, at http://www.claimscon.org/?url=hungary.

[315] Law No. X/1997, *op. cit.*, para. 4(2).

[316] Law No. 18/1991, *op. cit.*, Art. 21. provided for the allocation of 5 hectares of agricultural plots to each local religious community in rural regions.

[317] The amended version of Law No. 18 republished in 1998, *op. cit.*, through its Art. 22 extended the pool of claimants also to monasteries, which were entitled to receive 10 hectares of agricultural land. Moreover, the new regulation already mentions restitution of previously taken lands, within the general limits of 10 hectares of agricultural lands for parishes and 50 for monasteries. The amount of claimable land was growing along the hierarchical structure, thus the patriarchal center could already demand the restoration of 200 hectares. For the first time, plots within urban areas were also included into the scheme, within similar limits.

[318] *Ibid.*, Art. 47.

was a complicated and arguably inconsistent system in which different claimants were entitled to the restoration of their former property rights to various amounts of lands and forestry.[319]

As to what concerns buildings belonging to religious organizations, mushrooming governmental regular and emergency ordinances complicated their situation. Things were clarified to some extent by the enactment of a law for the parliamentary approval of the last emergency ordinance in this field, in 2002.[320] According to the ordinance, immovable church property abusively taken after 1945, other than houses of worship, and in state possession at the entry into force of the ordinance, can be restituted.[321] The ceiling was set to 10 items for each religious center—which is, according to the vague language of the enactment, a central or regional institution of co-ordination.[322] The law for the approval of this ordinance largely maintained its provisions, and specified that if the claimed building is affected to use by public interest institutions (education and healthcare), or by socio-cultural establishments (whatever this may mean), political party headquarters, diplomatic missions, or intergovernmental organizations, the claimant may opt between restitution or compensation. If the claimants opt for restitution, merely the *nudum ius* is restituted, that is, for five years the current affectation will be maintained, while the restituted church will be exempted for taxes related to the building and will receive a rent established by the government. If the option is for compensation, this can be done under many forms, according to the provisions of Law No. 10/2001: goods and services offered by the current user, shares, privatization vouchers, or cash.[323] In the latter case, an inter-ministerial commission was to establish the amount of money to be received.[324]

[319] For instance, parishes and monasteries were entitled to receive different quantities of agricultural land, but they could only claim the same amount of forestry.

[320] Law No. 501/2002 for the approval of Governmental Emergency Ordinance No. 94/2000, *Official Gazette*, No 561, 31 July 2002.

[321] The exclusion of the houses of worship and the requirement that claimed items to be in state possession are preventing the Greek Catholic Church from demanding restitution of its churches and other immovables which were taken by the communist government and transferred to the Orthodox Church.

[322] Governmental Emergency Ordinance No. 94/2000, *op. cit.*, Art. 1.

[323] Law no 501/2002, *op. cit.*, Title I, Art. 1, para. 3.

[324] Law no 10/2001, *op. cit.*, Art. 36–40.

The comprehensive 2005 law for the reform of property did modify the above-presented emergency ordinance. The amendments did not alter the cut-off date, but erased the cap on the returnable properties, and provided that compensations would be calculated according to international standards, and be paid according to a special law to be enacted for this purpose.[325]

Somewhat resembling the Romanian situation, the faith of heirless Jewish properties in Slovakia is subject to no principled normative regulation. Rather, it is dealt with through negotiations with the representatives of various Jewish organizations. Recent legislation made it possible for registered churches and religious communities to file claims for the return of agricultural lands and forests and any buildings on these sites if taken after 1945 (and 1938, in the case of the Jewish community). As most of the eligible church properties had already been restituted, a normative date for the end of the church property restitution process had been set at 30 April 2006.[326] As what concerns heirless Jewish properties, the solution consisting in monetary compensation[327] paid to the Union of Jewish Religious Communities in the Slovak Republic came about as a consequence of negotiations between the government and the representatives of the Jewish community.[328]

4.4.3 Privileged status of churches

From certain perspectives, religious communities sometimes also enjoy a distinguished status within the restitution schemes. This is clearly the case in Poland and Hungary, where the churches were the only entities that benefited from actual restitution of their former assets. Poland, for instance, gave clear preference in treatment to the Catholic Church, which was the beneficiary of the first large-scale property restitution, even before legislation regulating private property was enacted.[329] It

---

325 Law no 501/2002, *op. cit.*, Title II, Art. 1, para. 3.

326 *Ibid.*.

327 Amounting to 10% of the estimated value of the identified heirless Jewish property.

328 Summary of Property Restitution in Central and Eastern Europe, *op. cit.*.

329 Law "On Relations between the State and the Catholic Church," 17 May 1989, quoted in Zwiazek Nauczycielesta Polskiego v. Poland, ECHR, Application No. 42049/89, Judgment of 21 September 2004, para. 18; see also:

provided for restitution, or alternatively, compensation through the grant of alternative property or cash payments.[330] Religious property was subsequently restituted to other churches, too.

In Hungary, the most obvious difference made by the legislator between religious and other types of property is that immovable church property can be restituted in nature, while no other type of property can. Church immovable, as defined by the legislator, is considered to cover also the foundations established in the benefit of the religious organization, plots of land belonging to the constructions that are still unoccupied, to the extent that they serve the envisaged use of the building (or are used as cemeteries). Upon agreement with the claimant, restitution could be replaced with compensation under the form of other publicly owned constructions or construction plots, cash for acquisition or construction of other buildings, or rent. If the claimant specifically demands compensation instead of restitution or the claimed property cannot be restituted, or the above forms of compensation are not agreed upon, the claim can be offset in the form of annuities.[331]

4.4.4 Less privileged communities

While churches enjoyed a special, mostly preferential treatment within the restitution schemes, it is also true that from certain perspectives, some communities are less privileged than others. It is the case of all other churches but the Catholic in Poland, which was the first one to profit from the restitution scheme. It is also the case of Jewish communities in Lithuania, hindered by a strange recognition requirement, and the case of the Orthodox Church subordinated to the Moscow Patriarch[332] in Estonia and Latvia. Finally, in Romania, a very special problem is represented by the properties of the Uniate (Greek Catholic) Church.

Beker, *op. cit.*, pp. 101–3. On the role of Catholicism and the position of the Church in Polish society, see: Barkan, *op. cit.*, pp. 122–4.

[330] Zwiazek Nauczycielesta Polskiego v. Poland, *op. cit.*.

[331] *Ibid.*, Art. 2(4).

[332] Annual Report to Congress on International Religious Freedom, released by the Bureau of Democracy, Human Rights, and Labor, U.S. Department of State (from herein Report), 2005, available online, at http://www.state.gov/g/drl/rls/irf/2005/51550.htm.

In Estonia and Latvia, restitution was contemplated only to those organizations which operated before the cut-off date, and whose statutory activity has not been terminated. Their status as subjects of the property reform was to be determined upon request by the courts of law.[333] As church properties were state-owned during the communist period, the preferred church (subordinated to the Moscow Patriarch) being only their lesser, these requirements managed to prevent it from obtaining ownership rights over these assets. In Hungary, the cut-off date set to 1948 affected not only Jewish, but also some "historical churches," which maintain that part of their properties were already seized beginning from 1945.[334]

The assets of the Uniate Church of Romania (Greek Catholic Church) represent a constant source of conflict between Church and State, but also between various churches. The Uniate Church of Romania, which came into being during the 17th Century, was dissolved by decree in 1948, and believers were forced to affiliate to the Orthodox Church.[335] The properties of the dissolved church followed its former members, as according to another decree, in situations when members of a sect leave their religion and embrace another one, the goods belonging to the abandoned sect have to be transferred to the receiving church.[336] The dissolving decree was set aside very soon after the fall of the communist regime in Romania by the Decree/Law No. 9 of 1989. The Uniate Church was recognized officially the next year, and the norm provided that the legal status of the re-established church's properties would be sorted out by mixed commissions constituted according to the will of each local community, and made up by representatives of the Orthodox and Uniate churches.[337] As the act did not contain any further provisions on this issue, in most of the cases the mixed commission could either not have been formed, or eventually could not reach an agreement (especially where Orthodox believers outnumbered the Uniate ones).[338]

---

[333] Law "On the fundamentals of property reform," *op. cit.*, Art. 9.

[334] Mihályi, *op. cit.*, p. 16.

[335] Decree No. 358/1948.

[336] Decree No. 177/1948.

[337] Decree/Law No. 126/1990.

[338] According to the participants of a round-table discussion organized by the Group for Social Dialogue, as of 2005, not more than 0.1% of the proper-

A number of the Uniate communities turned to the courts of law. In some cases their complaints were accepted by the courts, and, on the grounds of the very same 1948 decree which constituted the basis for transferring Uniate property to the Orthodox Church, they found that the re-converted believers were entitled to a proportionate share of their former (Orthodox) church's property. Consequently, curious situations arose where two sects became co-owners of the same building, and were required to use it on the basis of an alternative schedule. Alas, in some cases complaints were rejected on the ground that such issues fall exclusively within the jurisdiction of the special commissions provided for by Decree/Law No. 126/1990.[339] The Romanian Constitutional Court has emphasized that provisions of the Decree/Law No. 126/1990 do not impair the parties' right to turn to the courts of law, but only require that the procedure before the mixed commissions be exhausted before, and, therefore, are completely in line with the Constitution.[340] (This latter finding is especially interesting, as the Constitution was adopted one year after the challenged decree/law came into force.) The Romanian Supreme Court in its turn adopted contradictory positions in this matter. First, in a 1996 decision, it ruled that the courts of law did not have jurisdiction to decide upon the utilization of a religious building. Second, three years later, it found that even failure to constitute the mixed commission required by the 1990 act might not constitute a ground to deny jurisdiction. Its argumentation was built on the fundamental character of the right to access to court, and on the fact that this right is provided for also in international conventions (notably the European Convention for Human Rights) to which Romania is a party. Consequently, the Supreme Court considered that the lower courts did not act outside their com-

ties claimed by the Uniate Church have been restituted, while according to the same source, the Orthodox and Catholic Churches' return rate was over 10%. For more details, see: 22, No. 789, 22–9 April 2005, available online, at http://www.revista22.ro/html/index.php?nr=2005-04-21&art=1676.

339 La Paroisse Gréco-Catholique Sâmbăta Bihor c. Roumanie, CEDH, Requête No. 48107/99, Décision sur la recevabilité de 25 mai 2004, part A. The complaint was found admissible under Art. 6, 9, 13, and Art. 1 of Protocol No. 1, and is currently pending trial.

340 RCC, Decision No. 127 of 16 November1994, published in the *Official Gazette*, No. 66, 11 April 1995; and Decision No. 49 of 19 May 1995, published in the *Official Gazette*, No. 224, 29 September 1995.

petence when passing judgments on the claims filed under Decree/Law No. 126/1990.[341]

5. Winners and losers of restitution

Some of the features of restitution as presented above are unfortunately hinting towards concerns of substantive equality, while in practice the examples analyzed create unacceptable inequalities. The rule of law, as Hayek remarked, produces economic inequality—and the only safeguard against this inequality is the requirement that it shall not be designed to have particular effects on particular people.[342] The citizenship/residence requirement denies equality of opportunity to persons placed in same situation. This can hardly be upheld either by justice, or by economic arguments. It is unclear how denying non-citizens/residents the possibility of redress will contribute to a more perfect social equality. The ceilings on the extent of compensation lead towards the idea of substantive equality (especially in the case of lump sum compensations for movables). But in practice they deny equality of opportunity, as small holders may achieve full compensation, while those who lost larger estates have to settle for a merely partial one. Paradoxically, the scheme seems to presume that those who lost larger estates are somehow still better off than those from whom smaller assets were taken.

The cut-off dates, again, discriminate between victims of past property injustices. In a post-communist context, distinction between takings according to their occurrence in time results in the exclusion of certain groups, such as Jews, Sudeten Germans or Hungarians, from the pool of victims. Obviously, no society could feasibly attempt to redress all past injustices: economic constraints, evidence-related problems, and the question of standing (who could be considered as rightful claimant) all represent objective hurdles in the way of such at-

[341] La Paroisse Gréco-Catholique Sâmbăta Bihor c. Roumanie, *op. cit.*, quoting Romanian Supreme Court judgments of 22 March 1996 and 17 February, 1999, *op. cit.*, part B.

[342] Hayek, *op. cit.*, p. 59.

tempts.[343] However, when the different injustices were perpetrated in a relative short period of time, it is much more difficult to build a convincing argument upholding legislative preference for selective redress. Distinctions made according to the certain property objects produce exclusion—the loss of certain objects is simply not compensated, while other objects lost in similar circumstances are—or, attempt to equalize the outcome of the process, by including different categories of property under a broader ceiling.[344]

These inequalities created winners and losers of restitution. In the Baltic States, the citizenship requirements were drafted to exclude ethnic Russians from participating in the restitution scheme. As Nissinen points out, this policy backfired in Latvia, as for example most of Riga's ethnic Latvians lived in the old city center's premises, in houses subject to restitution, while ethnic Russians lived mainly in the new districts, in blocks of flats which had no previous owners.[345] In the case of Germany, a generous program made available for restitution a wide array of goods, under two conditions: the claimed properties must have been taken without compensation, and must be found in the state's hands at unification. However, as Ragnitz argues, this scheme in fact favored claimants from West Germany.[346] Under the original Czechoslovakian restitution laws, Jews, Sudeten Germans, and Hungarians who lost their properties either during the Nazi rule or under the short-lived regime of Eduard Beneš, were all excluded from the benefits of restitution. In Hungary and also in Romania, Jewish, church, and vari-

---

343 However, as the cases of indigenous restitution demonstrate, if there are well-organized identifiable and sizeable group of victims (descendants of victims) who could muster enough political leverage, restitution claims could be pursued with relative success even from a more than one hundred-year distance. On the contrary, if the victims (their successors) have left the country, or they have diminished in numbers, their bargaining power is a lot more reduced.

344 For example, the amount of agricultural lands counted together with that of forestry, movables with the building in which they were to be found, etc.

345 *Ibid.*, p. 108.

346 Joachim Ragnitz, "German Unification: Restitution of Nationalized Properties," presentation at the Goethe Center, Nicosia, Cyprus, 2004, available online, at http://projusticia.net/i_009.php. See also: Sinn and Sinn, *op. cit.*, p. 88.

ous communal properties were—and to some extent still are—placed on the losing end of transition.

Thus, post-communist restitution or compensation schemes, due to their distributive character, contain at least some features that result in theoretically unjustifiable distinctions between their beneficiaries (i.e., the pool of former owners), producing arbitrary outcomes. Such a breach of the criteria of formal equality before the law is in conflict with the idea of the rule of law.[347] Whatever role the rule of law is considered to have during transition, the consequences of these restitution policies reach far beyond the transition period, as at the same time they perpetuate old, and create and entrench novel property injustices.

[347] See: Hayek, *op. cit.*, p. 59.

CHAPTER 4

The Rule of Law as the Law of (Restitution) Rules

As Jowitt remarked already at the dawn of post-communist transition, Leninist regimes promoted a worldview which regarded political life as suspect, dangerous, and distasteful—thus their legacy was more favorable for an authoritarian than a liberal democratic regime. Accordingly, the most difficult question for transitional governments was not how to create the preconditions of market economy, but rather how to institutionalize public virtues.[1] Law under communism, argues Krygier, was conceived mostly in instrumental terms: of social control and accomplishing centrally determined goals. It was a flexible, lofty statement of ideals, easily moldable by executive decrees, which lead to government through administrative decisions, rather than government through laws.[2]

This tradition was carried over to the post-communist legal culture (in making) to some extent, and its reflections can be detected also in a property restitution context. It is edifying to point to the Romanian tradition of legislating through emergency ordinances, or to the Lithuanian case that will be described in the third section,[3] in which various administrative and judicial bodies managed to disregard each other's decisions, putting the individual in an impossible situation.

Under these conditions laws and institutions may have an enhanced significance in the defense of rights and in the engendering of the rule of law.[4] However, to be able to perform these tasks, laws

---

[1] K. Jowitt, *New World Disorder: The Leninist Extinction*, University of California Press, 1992; quoted by Martin Krygier, in Krygier and Czarnota (eds.), *op. cit., supra*, p. 93.

[2] Krygier, *op. cit.*, p. 93.

[3] Jasiūnienė v. Lithuania, *op. cit.*.

[4] For a critique of the institutionalist approach to transition, see also: Krygier, *op. cit.*, pp. 79–86.

and institutions have to satisfy at least a minimalist reading of the rule of law, namely rule in a legally good way.[5] As Neumann put it in the phrase already quoted in the first chapter, there is a certain degree of unfairness in life—and this was especially true in transitional contexts—that, while it cannot be eliminated, it has to be predictable.[6] Justice Antonin Scalia of the U.S. Supreme Court shares the same view, stating—in a much-quoted phrase—that regularity and predictability count for more than substantive justice does.[7]

The European Court of Human Rights, in the already quoted Paduraru judgment, has explained in some detail the legal uncertainty that may be engendered by lack of clarity and coherence of norms.[8] It has also noted that the great number of complaints filed with the Romanian courts for the return of properties or for the annulment of purchase contracts is exactly the product of this uncertainty, while the judges required to decide these cases lack a sufficiently predictable and coherent legal ground.[9] The Court has also noted that diverging outcomes are inherent in adjudication, but the role of the supreme judicial body would be exactly to solve such contradictions in the case law (and pointed to Romanian highest instance's indecision on controversial questions of law). Absent of a mechanism that ensures coherence in adjudication, persistent and profound divergences in questions of great social interest can lead to the engendering of a permanent uncertainty and a loss of confidence in the judiciary, a fundamental component of *l'État de droit.*[10]

Accordingly, even at its most minimalist interpretation, the rule of law must mean the rule of regular and foreseeable law, which, in a perhaps overoptimistic reading, may eventually amount to procedural fairness. This chapter will focus on several procedural aspects of the post-communist restitution laws, arguing that to certain extent the legislators seriously tested this minimal requirement. The present chapter will examine the challenges posed to the rule of law by three different procedural aspects of property restitution schemes. The first subchapter is dedicated to the various quantification methods, while establish-

---

[5] See: Neumann, *op. cit., supra.*

[6] Neumann, *op. cit.*, p. 45

[7] Antonin, *op. cit., supra.*

[8] Paduraru c. Roumanie, CEDH, *op. cit.*, paras. 94–9.

[9] *Ibid.*, para. 96.

[10] *Ibid.,* para. 98.

ing the amount and nature of compensation that was to be received by the former owners. The second subchapter deals with the deadlines envisaged for filing the claims—and for the relevant authorities to solve those claims. The third subchapter analyzes the evidence required by the restitution schemes for proving the applicants' entitlement to restitution or compensation.

As what concerns the question of valuation, the analyzed restitution schemes contain a large number of examples where the exercise of the right to restitution or compensation was hindered by the very norms regulating the process. In some cases it was made impossible for the entitled persons to exercise their rights, in others subsequent enactment altered the previously established entitlement or the concrete decision upon the form and amount of compensation was left to future executive decisions. Finally, there were cases in which provisions of international treaties regarding compensations were disregarded. The compensation voucher solution fashioned in many cases, as an exception as the sole, and regularly as a complementary form of compensation, demonstrated incoherence in practice as, besides, due to its distributory, rather than compensatory character, it represented only a theoretical possibility of compensation.

In the case of the time limits, it soon became obvious that the ambitious (or perhaps ill-considered) submission deadlines were impossible to respect both for the claimants and the decision-making authorities. In most cases these deadlines had to be subsequently prolonged, sometimes several times. Interestingly, in certain states the constitutional courts found the excessively short deadlines as unconstitutional for barring the entitled persons from exercising their rights, while in others they sustained the special procedural rules established for special situations. Finally, as what concerns the length of proceedings, the domestic courts either found a breach of the right to remedy, or spoke about a constitutional omission to fulfill certain obligations. The Strasbourg court, especially in the context of the Croatian apartment cases, stated that even if the state enjoys a certain margin of appreciation while enacting necessary regulations in cases involving a large number of significant pecuniary claims, it still has to respect Article 6 requirements.

As for the requirements pertaining to evidence, a large number of documents, usually obtainable from various administrative authorities, had to be submitted together with the restitution claim. This, combined with the short deadlines, decreased chances of exercising the right to claim. In certain cases it was possible to complete the already submitted application even after the expiry of the deadlines, in others it was held that failure to comply for whatever reason in the given period amounts to the lapse of the right to claim. Further, in certain cases the conditions attached to the use of certain evidence made their employment impossible in practice. For example, in the case of movables detailed description had to be made of each item and its current place indicated, whereas claimants were simply denied access to certain institutions. Or, in the case of witness testimonies, in some cases most of the qualifying witnesses were already dead. Finally, in the case of commercial property, for establishing the value of the former property a list of the former employees had to be submitted to the relevant authority, which—on the basis of the list—would than certify the number of persons employed at the date of the taking.

1. Quantifying reparations

In the previous chapters considerable attention was dedicated to the presentation of the various approaches to undoing past property injustices, ranging from the actual restitution of the once lost goods to diverse forms (in kind, voucher, or monetary) of reparations. The present subchapter is dedicated to the analysis of the latter, arguing that the very way of establishing the value of reparations raises certain rule of law problems, questioning fundamental values such as clarity, certainty, security, and protection of legitimate expectations.

1.1 The just compensation dilemma

While discussing the justness of the post-communist restitution schemes, some hints were already made towards the lack—in both international and national context—of a clear-cut obligation to restitute previously lost properties.[11] Here, the issue is analyzed in more detail,

[11] No convincing analogy can be made, therefore, between the nationalization of foreign citizens' properties and the takings targeting domestic owners' estate. See: *supra*.

and at a more abstract level. The question to be answered is whether expropriated owners should be entitled to receive "just compensation" for their losses.

Classically, social welfare theory offers two answers. The Pareto theorem of efficiency requires that social change should leave no one worse off. Consequently, takings may not produce losers, regardless how much benefit they could generate to the rest of the society. On the contrary, the Kaldor-Hicks theorem postulates that social change is desirable and justified, if winners can—in principle—compensate losers, while still remaining better off. Thus, the "just compensation" requirement does not necessarily have to be satisfied.

The compensation requirement is held to respond to "distributional concerns of fairness," albeit theorists note that "its allocative consequences [...] dominate the distributional concerns."[12] According to Epstein, the "just compensation" requirement is set out to foster the individual endowments from government excesses.[13] This is ensured by the requirement that private property should pass into state hands, only if it is worth more to the society (represented by the state) than its market value in private hands. The market value standard is used because it is a lot more easily determinable than the subjective value that owners attach to their properties.[14] In a restitution context this approach may lead to serious problems, especially when religious properties are at stake. For instance, in the case of indigenous land claims, arguments are frequently focusing on the various holy or sacred site's spiritual role in preserving the tribe members' identity. This was for instance the situation in the notorious Black Hills case in the United States, in which the Supreme Court awarded a historic 122 million USD compensation, but the Sioux tribe refused to collect the money,[15] and this rejection of monetary settlements was not a singular event. Barkan argues that money settlements in such cases do end the mourning, but they do not offer a new identity.[16] An interesting view was voiced also by Waldron, who postulated that due to the length of the deprivation,

[12] Richard A. Epstein, *Bargaining with the State*, Princeton University Press, 1993, p. 85.

[13] *Ibid.*, pp. 75–105.

[14] *Ibid.*, p. 182.

[15] Barkan, *op. cit.*, pp. 182–3.

[16] *Ibid.*, p. 187.

claimants could not reasonably maintain that the respective asset still formed a significant part of their life and identity.[17]

The case of religious properties is of course only on aspect of the problem. More important than this are the consequences of the passage of time, of the gap between the moment of the takings and the moment of compensation. The fact that several decades have elapsed between these two moments in time means that all the relevant factors have changed: there is a different government in place, society (with all its needs, possibilities, and sense of (in)justice) has itself changed, and of course the entire economy is in a different status, which all make the question of compensation and valuation very difficult. In the previous chapters it was shown how the post-communist governments attempted to deal with these problems. In some cases, restitution (and consequently compensation, too) was limited to unlawfully taken properties,[18] or it was made function of the society's "sense of justice and financial capacities,"[19] and various schemes were deployed for determining the once taken property's current value.[20]

To make things even more complicated, the passage of private property into state hands was effected through many ways, of which what properly can be called "taking" was only one. The reforms were—except for certain special situations—not unconstitutional by themselves, and arguably tried to address the pressing social problem of disproportionate and dysfunctional land distribution, but the solution they fancied led to social injustice, represented by uncompensated takings, that is, throwing a disproportionate and excessive burden on the dispossessed owners. The Hungarian Constitutional Court, for instance, argued that the nationalization project was essentially aiming at the eradication of the institution of private property.[21] It was not about

[17] J. Waldron, "Historic Injustice: Its Remembrance and Supersession," in Oddie, G., and R. Perrett (eds.), *Justice, Ethics, and New Zealand Society*, Oxford University Press, 1992, p. 158; also referred to by Gregory S. Alexander, "The Limits of Property Reparations," Cornell Legal Studies Research Paper No. 05-004, 2002, available online, at http://papers.ssrn.com/sol3/papers.cfm?abstract_id=404940, p. 13.

[18] Which led to all sorts of problems in demonstrating the "illegality/unconstitutionality" of the former expropriations.

[19] Hungarian Law No. XXV of 1991, Preamble.

[20] E.g.: the German and Hungarian formulas.

[21] HCC, AB 27/1991, 91/E/1990, *supra*.

sacrificing a private interest for a greater public good, but about the destruction of any private property interest as such. Interestingly, most of the post-communist restitution schemes betray a similar disproportionate treatment of land and former landowners, as agricultural property enjoyed a privileged status in comparison with other types of property losses. Unquestionably, the status of landowners in restitution policies can be linked also to identity concerns.[22] Neither can the other ways—the seizure of Nazi or "enemy" properties after the war, the losses occurring after the population exchanges, the confiscation or expropriation of the dissidents and other opponents' properties—be fitted under the notion of takings. The question that arises then is what would be the adequate standard of compensation?

1.1.1 To compensate or not to compensate?

Firstly, a short look has to be taken at the two extremes. On the one hand, it can hardly be argued in a convincing manner that the state should never compensate for property losses. Such an argument was advanced in the midst of the Australian Aboriginal land litigation, when in the Mabo[23] and the State of Western Australia v. Commonwealth[24] decisions the High Court conceded that the Crown—although it has not done so—could have extinguished all (native) titles[25] at the assertion of its sovereignty. Commenting on this, Frank Brennan voiced the view that the sovereign could appropriate any person's property without compensation, and the fact that it usually paid does not create a legal requirement to do so, or a fetter on its sovereign discretion. Thus, extinction of the native title without compensation was lawful.[26] Such an argument, however—as it was pointed out *supra*—, undermines the

[22] E.g.: Pechota, *op. cit.* (see also *supra*, Chapter 2), mentioned the "national rebirth" function attached to restitution by certain commentators; or a former Romanian prime minister spoke about the goal of "preserving [...] the authentic national spirit" besides property redistribution.

[23] 175 CLR 1, 1992.

[24] 183 CLR 373.

[25] It must be noted though that indigenous restitution claims represent a peculiar case due to the difficulties in describing and picturing the relationship between them and the objects claimed as property rights in the traditional sense.

[26] Brennan, *op. cit.*, p. 169.

very existence of property. As Munzer emphasized, even from a utilitarian perspective such an approach could prove suboptimal, as the dissatisfaction experienced by those who lost their holdings may outweigh the public gains.[27] On the other hand, it could be equally implausible to hold that the state should always compensate all property losses. As Munzer argues, in some cases the encroachment upon individual property rights causes such a minor loss that it would be suboptimal to compensate each and every case (the transaction costs of compensation may make the entire process too expensive).[28] To give a concrete example: in Romania, from the mid-80s, the circulation of private automobiles[29] was restricted in such a way, that only automobiles with even license numbers were permitted to circulate on one weekend, while automobiles with uneven numbers on the next weekend. To compensate every former car owner for this limitation on the use of their automobiles would necessarily produce sub-optimal results.

This line of thought is not entirely alien to the European Court of Human Rights either, although the Strasbourg forum employs a different argumentation. The Court has stated on several occasions that if the interference with the property right in other respects satisfies the condition of lawfulness and it is not arbitrary, the lack of compensation "does not by itself and always" make the taking unlawful. Non-compensation, according to the Court, may result in a breach of the Convention if the expropriated owners have to bear a disproportionate and excessive burden.[30] However, added the Court, total lack of compensation may be justified only in exceptional circumstances. The context of political and economical regime changes was considered to

---

[27] Stephen R. Munzer, "Compensation and Government Takings of Private Property," in John W. Chapman (ed.), *Compensatory Justice*, New York University Press, 1991, p. 204.

[28] *Ibid.*.

[29] Automobiles fell under the category of "personal property"; thus, they could have been privately owned, but any commercial use was forbidden.

[30] Jahn and Others v. Germany, ECHR, Application Nos. 46720/99, 72203/01, and 72552/01, Grand Chamber Judgment of 30 June 2005, para. 95; The Former King of Greece v. Greece, ECHR, Application No. 25701/94, Judgment of 23 November 2000, para. 90; Zvolský and Zvolská v. the Czech Republic, ECHR, Application No. 46129/99, Judgment of 12 November 2002, para. 71.

represent such exceptional circumstances, which confer a wide margin of appreciation upon the states.[31]

Accordingly, Munzer—in the footsteps of Michelman—concludes that if certain conditions are met, losses of private property should be mitigated. The conditions, which are determined on a utilitarian basis, are that the gains achieved through the taking should exceed the costs, while compensating for the losses should be cheaper than not doing so.[32] In other words, if the disappointment of those expropriated can be contained through other means with lower expenses than operating a compensation scheme, the state should choose the cheaper option.[33]

---

[31] Jahn and Others, *op. cit.*, paras. 111–3; Kopecký v. Slovakia, Application No. 44912/98, Judgment of 28 September 2004, para. 35; Zvolský and Zvolská, *op. cit.*, paras. 67–8 and 72; Maltzan and Others v. Germany, *op. cit.*, paras. 77 and 111–2.

[32] Munzer, *op. cit.*, pp. 205–19. The notion of "cost" covers both the disappointment and possible unrest caused by an uncompensated taking ("demoralization cost") and the administrative expenses of operating a program that must be undertaken to avoid demoralization ("settlement cost").

[33] An illustration of this theory is the Zimbabwean "fast-track" land reform undertaken in the year 2000. As on the losing side of the land-redistribution scheme were a handful of farmers, and the economy was heavily underperforming anyway, the government chose to sacrifice the rule of law, rather to look for coins in an empty purse. Thus, the takings clause of the constitution was altered so as to exclude any obligation to compensate expropriated farmers. The Constitution of Zimbabwe Amendment (No. 16) Act of 2000 provided: "(i) [T]he former colonial power has an obligation to pay compensation for agricultural land compulsorily acquired for resettlement, through a fund established for the purpose; (ii) [I]f the former colonial power fails to pay compensation through such a fund, the Government of Zimbabwe has no obligation to pay compensation for agricultural land compulsorily acquired for resettlement" (quoted by Nading, *op. cit.*, p. 773, n. 170).

Furthermore, the President himself, under an emergency clause permitting him to temporarily legislate—The Presidential Powers (Temporary Measures) Act, referred to by Cass, *op. cit.*, p. 12—, amended the Land Acquisition Act to permit uncompensated takings and later on the Parliament adopted legislation to the same effect (Cass, *op. cit.*, p. 11). Under the new scheme, apart from shifting the responsibility for compensations to the British, farmers' rights to compensations were reduced to the improvements to the land, excluding the value of the land itself. Moreover, compensation was set off if governmental subsidies were previously received by the expropriated landowner (Shirley, *op. cit.*, p. 164). Under these circumstances, it was an admirable judicial exercise on the behalf of the Supreme Court to undertake a

Post-communist governments, too, found it difficult to resist the temptation of the cheapest solution when such an alternative arose. The previous chapter is laden with examples of victims, or groups of victims, of former property injustices that were excluded from the benefits of the restitution schemes. Those who were small in number and—consequently—underrepresented found themselves quickly on the losing end of restitution and property reforms. Although the governments in question seemingly managed to avoid the transaction costs that would have been incurred by including these groups in the pool of the compensated, in the long run the outcome resembles the Zimbabwean one, to the extent that they ultimately endangered the very value that everyone was pledging to stand for: the rule of law. Further, in certain cases it turned out that the government's ability to contain those disappointed was over-optimistically assessed and occasionally backfired, and settlements with the initially excluded victims had to be concluded at a cost by far exceeding that which would have been incurred at the outset. A good example in this respect is the Romanian case of

scrutiny of these acts. The Court invalidated the law permitting the President to exercise temporary legislative powers as an unconstitutional delegation, and, subsequently, found the land acquisitions carried out without compensation and without possibility of review to be contrary to the Constitution and to the Land Acquisition Act's provisions (Commercial Farmers Union v. Minister of Lands, Agriculture, & Resettlement, Zimbabwe Supreme Court Judgment No. SC-132/2000, 21 December 2000; quoted by Cass, *op. cit.*, p. 12, n. 37).

The Court also placed a moratorium on land seizures, until a "workable program of land reform" would be drafted (Nick Dancaescu, "Land Reform in Zimbabwe," *Florida Journal of International Law* 15 [2003], p. 622). The fact that the government did nothing to protect farmers and their workers from acts of violence and intimidation coming from the armed mobs which begun to move by force onto various lands was considered as a failure to uphold constitutional rights. Unfortunately, such brave undertakings are usually honored solely in working democracies. In Zimbabwe, the Chief Justice was quickly replaced after the Commercial Farmers Union decision, and three new judges were appointed. The new court reconsidered the case, and unsurprisingly, found the resettlement scheme unobjectionable under constitutional and statutory standards and lifted the moratorium (Cass, *op. cit.*, p. 13; Jonathan Shirley, "The Role of International Human Rights and The Law of Diplomatic Protection on Resolving Zimbabwe's Land Crisis," *Boston College International Comparative Law Review* 27 [2004], pp. 164–5; Dancaescu, *op. cit.*, p. 622).

the extraordinary annulment procedure initiated by the Procurator-General "in the interest of the law," permitted by the procedural rules in force at the time, through which many final and irreversible court rulings holding the government liable for restitution or compensation were set aside. As already mentioned in the previous chapters, Romanian courts were finding it relatively easy to rule in favor of the former owners, by scrutinizing the nationalization decrees. In the above-mentioned Brumărescu case, the court of first instance amazingly found that the property taken was not covered by the decree which formed the basis of the nationalization, and consequently concluded that the property was taken by duress; therefore, the state could not even invoke the acquisitive prescription. More importantly, the court (of first instance) also stated that the subsequent nationalization decrees were contrary to the then in force constitutions. As an upshot of all this, the court ordered the relevant authorities to return the claimed property.[34] As no appeals were lodged, the decision became final and irreversible, and the property was returned. However, on an unknown date, the Procurator-General lodged an extraordinary appeal[35] with the Supreme Court for the annulment of the above judgment. The Supreme Court quashed the lower court's judgment, arguing that the courts cannot review the manner in which the nationalization decree was applied. Thus, explained the Supreme Court, the lower court encroached upon the powers reserved to the legislature, which has the exclusive competence to decide upon the redress for wrongful seizures. Consequently, the property in question shifted back to the state.[36]

Interestingly, the Supreme Court's case law demonstrates a rather undecided grasp of the matter: up to its ruling in the Brumărescu case, the Court's Civil Division upheld lower courts' powers to decide on nationalization matters. But the Brumărescu precedent did not survive for long either, as only three years later the full Court decided that courts have jurisdiction to entertain any action related to property infringements that took place during the communist rule.[37] These frequent changes of mind create suspicions about the courts' indepen-

[34] Brumărescu v. Romania, ECHR, Application No. 28342/95, Judgment of 28 October 1999, para. 15.

[35] "Recurs în anulare."

[36] Brumărescu v. Romania, *op. cit.*, paras. 24–5.

[37] *Ibid.*, paras. 36–8.

dence and question the transitional rule of law's ability to mediate the normative shift in justice. The Constitutional Court—in the year of the Supreme Court's decision in the Brumărescu case—voiced a slightly different view, claiming that wrongfully taken properties could have never passed to the state, and therefore recognized the former owners' right to bring suits for recovery of possession. However, rather inconsequently, it also stated that it is up to the Parliament to afford or not restitution or compensation through legislative means in these cases.[38]

The European Court of Human Rights, not surprisingly, found the broad powers conferred upon the Procurator-General (who in spite of the fact that it was not party to the proceedings, could apply for a final—and executed—judgment to be quashed within an indefinite period of time) as infringing the principle of legal certainty, and the exclusion of courts to decide on this and similar claims as contrary to the right of access to court.[39] Moreover, the Court also found that because the first instance judgment was executed, the applicant became the owner of the property in question; thus, the Supreme Court judgment that quashed the first instance decision amounted to a *de facto* taking. As neither compensation was afforded for the deprivation, nor the existence of any public interest has been demonstrated, a breach of Protocol I, Article 1 was also considered to exist.

Like Brumărescu, most of those claimants that adventured to take their case to the Strasbourg court had the satisfaction of being awarded the claimed compensation, and had such a success rate[40] that the government, in despair, was contemplating the possibilities of barring their citizen's from reaching the European forum.[41]

[38] *Ibid.*, para. 39.

[39] *Ibid.*, paras. 56–65.

[40] Paduraru v. Romania, CEDH, *op. cit.*; Basacopol v. Romania, ECHR, Application No. 34992/97, Judgment of 9 July 2002; Paulescu v. Romania, ECHR, Application No. 34644/97, Judgment of 10 June 2003; Tandreau v. Romania, ECHR, Application No. 39184/98, Judgment of 25 November 2003; Sofletea v. Romania, ECHR, Application No. 48179/99, Judgment of 25 November 2003.

[41] The projected bill, "Law of Compensations," was intended to provide for "equitable compensations" for those properties that could not have been restituted in nature, and the initiators hoped that due to its effects, complaints to the Strasbourg court would be rejected as inadmissible. However, the project never got past the lower chamber's juridical committee. Details are avail-

The European Court itself had to answer the question whether an obligation to pay compensations upon takings exists under Protocol I, Article 1. In Lithgow, the Court concluded that although the relevant article is silent on this issue, it can be read as impliedly requiring the payment of compensation as a necessary condition.[42] The protection afforded by Article 1—reasoned the Court—would necessarily become illusory in the absence of this principle.

1.1.2 The limits of "justness"

As it was already mentioned above, the usual standard of compensation for takings is market value, that is, the price a willing seller would receive from a willing buyer. This standard is questionable to the extent that it takes as reference a voluntary transaction. However, even in the case of takings—not to speak about communist nationalization—often, perhaps more often than not, the expropriated owner was not willing to renounce his property. Thus, the market value standard overlooks the emotional value, which—although highly subjective and difficult to quantify—commonly exceeds the exchange value. Epstein employs the term "use value" for this argument.[43] Emblematic for such a situation is the case of religious properties, also mentioned above, at the beginning of this section.

However, regardless what standard is used for determining the lost property's value, constitutions, while mentioning "just compensation" (in takings context), do not define the form it shall take. Consequently, compensations may embrace various forms. Obviously, the most common modalities are in kind (i.e., replacement of the taken good with another one of the same nature, type, etc.) and monetary, but theoretically no other options are excluded. Within the reparation schemes, different weight and significance was attached to compensations. While in Hungary and Poland (except for church properties) compensation was the sole means of reparation, in the other cases presented in this study, compensation appeared as an alternative or a

able online, at http://www.ziua.ro/archive/2002/07/19/docs/26089.html.

[42] Lithgow and Others v. United Kingdom, ECHR, Application No. 2/1984/74/112-118, Judgment of 7 August 1996, para. 120.

[43] Epstein, *op. cit.*, pp. 182–3.

substitute for restitution. Accordingly, while in Holocaust and indigenous claims context monetary settlement was the widespread solution, accompanied by restitution in certain cases, post-communist governments proved to be rather creative in inventing alternative forms of compensation.[44] Some programs provided for in kind compensation especially for land (Estonia, Lithuania, Poland, Hungary—only for religious properties—, Czechoslovakia, and Romania). Some schemes included the possibility of compensation in form of vouchers (Estonia, Latvia, Hungary—if it was almost the only form of compensation—, and Romania for the abusively taken real properties), which could have been translated into shares (stocks) during the privatization process. As a unique solution amongst the analyzed, the Latvian law created the possibility for certain categories of beneficiaries to translate their vouchers into cash or securities. Another variation of this scheme was employed in Lithuania, where claimants could receive directly stocks as compensation, without the "mediation" of compensation vouchers, and Czechoslovakia, where the entitled persons could receive securities directly (especially when these were the heirs of the expropriated owner). Exceptionally, the Latvian and the Hungarian schemes included the possibility for the vouchers distributed as compensation to be used to purchase agricultural land (in both cases), apartments, or to establish an individual farm (only in Latvia). A further solution was of course cash payment, contemplated in Latvia (for industrial properties), Lithuania (for plots and for the difference between the value of the original building and the one received as compensation), Germany (uniform, up to a general ceiling, above which a gliding scale was applied), Czechoslovakia (subject to a uniform ceiling in the case of movables), and Romania (employing various schemes). More original approaches could have been met in Lithuania, where the procedure called "state re-purchase" for properties affected to public utilities, consisting, apart from the above-mentioned solutions, also in the cancellation of the former owner's debts towards the state, which have arisen since the taking of the property in question. Resembling this to a certain degree, the Polish solution

[44] To be fair, it has to be noted that this creativity was largely induced by the reduced financial possibilities of the transitional economies, combined with the massive amounts of claims that needed to be satisfied.

in the Bug River case consists in the offsetting of the value of the lost property against either the price of state property or the fee for the perpetual use of such property. Germany also created a peculiar form of compensation, through offering the possibility of preferential acquisition of land for those former owners who lost their properties during the Soviet occupation. The Hungarian scheme, which, similarly to the Polish, afforded a separate, more favorable treatment to churches, included the opportunity for religious organizations to receive cash for acquisition of land or construction, but also to rent real estate or to offset their claims in the form of annuities. Interestingly, the Czechoslovakian program in the case of movable agricultural properties left the door wide open for negotiations—presumably between the former owner and the legal successor of the former agricultural enterprise which had the seized property in its patrimony—by enshrining the expression "any other form" in the text of the relevant norm.

Similar freedom was left by one of the Romanian laws[45] for the interested parties to decide upon the form of compensation, but they only could have opted for one of the following: shares, vouchers, cash, goods, and services, or a combination of these.

The above-enumerated forms of reparations practiced by the post-communist governments can be divided in two large groups: cash and non-cash compensation. Writing on the compensation design alternatives, Posner and Vermeule[46] note that one of the essential distinctions between cash and non-cash compensations is that in the latter case, beneficiaries have significantly reduced options in enjoying their award, or, viewed from the other perspective, the state has significantly increased possibilities to steer the beneficiaries behavior.[47] In case non-cash solutions are preferred because of the possibility they offer

[45] Law No. 10/2001, published in the *Official Gazette*, No. 75, 14 February 2001, Art. I.

[46] Eric A. Posner and Adrian Vermeule, "Reparations for Slavery and Other Historical Injustices," *Columbia Law Review* 103 (2003), pp. 725–6.

[47] This is not to say that in the case of actual restitution the beneficiaries necessarily enjoyed an entirely free hand to do what they wished with the received properties. Indeed, as some restitution solutions demonstrate, at times quite harsh constrains were imposed—especially in the case of agricultural lands—, ranging from a blanket ban on sale (e.g., Romanian Law No. 18/1991) to the possibility of having the property "taken back" by the state (e.g., Lithuania) if the restituted owners did not comply to the required conduct.

for steering the beneficiaries' behavior, the option has to overcome the following criticism. Although a paternalistic approach—that is, the government knows better what makes the individual recipient better off—may in certain cases seem *prima facie* reasonable, both in ordinary civil and takings cases, the usual or presumptive form of remedy is cash. And it is granted irrespective whether the receiver of the compensation can be trusted to spend it wisely or not.[48] As it was already mentioned in this subchapter, another reasonable justification for granting non-cash compensation could be the precarious financial status of the post-communist economies. However, if due to the extraordinary circumstances the budget could not bear the burden of affording cash compensation for all entitled persons, a possible solution could have been to acknowledge these former owners' right to compensation and postpone its actual payment until the necessary funds are collected. In this respect, a recent judgment of the Lithuanian Constitutional Court found that the legal provisions which granted the executive the competence to decide upon the procedure, conditions, and the periodicity of the payments, without providing any criteria for the establishment of the terms of the payment, is in conflict with the Constitution, the principle of the separation of powers and the rule of law.[49] Notably, the Court—*inter alia*—spoke about the state's duty to allot the necessary funds and to pay the monetary compensation within the terms provided by law, while these terms must fulfill the requirements of clarity, certainty, security, and protection of legitimate expectations. Similarly, the Hungarian Constitutional Court found that the breaking down of the compensations in separate phases is *eo ipso* unobjectionable as long as the length and content of the entire process is previously established.[50] A third objection, which applies in the case of both arguments, is that it sends the wrong message, according to which the state may condemn a property and offer in exchange for instance tax exemption for another property (as in the case of Lithuania). The Nollan v. California Coastal Commission case, in which the issuance of a building permit

[48] Posner and Vermeule, *op. cit.*, pp. 726–7.

[49] LiCC, Case No. 19/02, Ruling of 23 August 2005; as quoted in Toma Birmontiene, "The Perspectives of Introducing the Constitutional Complaint in the Republic of Lithuania," available online, at http://www.venice.coe.int/docs/2005/CDL-JU(2005)067-e.asp.

[50] HCC, AB 16/1991, 952/A/1991.

was conditioned upon an easement to pass across the appellant's land, brought a somewhat similar problem before the U.S. Supreme Court.[51] The Court held that such a condition could lawfully be imposed only if it serves public purposes related to the permit requirement. *Mutatis mutandis*, the argument sounds in the following way: tax exemptions may be considered as compensating for a taking only if the exempted taxes served the same public purpose as the taking did. It is more likely than not that such a link between taking and taxes cannot convincingly be established.

This is not to say that stocks, bonds, or securities represent an inadequate means of compensation. For instance, in Lithgow the European Court of Human Rights sustained a compensation formula taking the form of government stock ("Compensation Stock"), where the conditions as to repayment, redemption, and other matters, including the rate of interest which was to accrue thereon, were determined by the Treasury.[52] What is more problematic is the case of the so-called privatization vouchers, which were not directly translatable into cash, but merely created an opportunity to participate in the privatization process, and thus did not have a truly compensatory character. The Hungarian scheme constituted an exception, in the sense that the compensation vouchers, just like securities, had inherent value and were marketable, although technically they did not have the status of securities. Critiques note that the market price of the vouchers almost never reached their nominal value, and could have been sold only with a significant discount;[53] moreover, the privatization process has in most cases started before all entitled persons received their vouchers.[54] Further, it is argued that recipients of compensation vouchers preferred to obtain cash for their vouchers, rather than stocks, and even where opportunities were created for a voucher–stock exchange, holders usually opted for those enterprises where the majority owner was willing to repurchase the stocks at their nominal price.[55] Vouchers could be used

[51] 483 U.S. 825 (1987).

[52] The Aircraft and Shipbuilding Industries Act 1977, nationalizing the aircraft and shipbuilding industry, as quoted in Lithgow and Others v. United Kingdom, *op. cit.*, para. 21.

[53] Mihályi, *op. cit.*, p. 39.

[54] *Ibid.*.

[55] What actually happened, according to Mihályi, was that the mostly state

to purchase stocks from state-owned companies during the privatization process, and in the case of each company, at least ten (in certain cases twenty) per cent of the stocks had to be traded for compensation vouchers. However, although there was never any concrete regulation in this sense, regularly no enterprise could have been purchased solely for compensation vouchers. (Original recipients of compensation vouchers were anyway unable to acquire an entire enterprise, due to the relatively low general ceiling and the even lower average value of vouchers received per compensated persons.) Another awkward situation was created through the participation of employees in the privatization of their company. Employers were granted the possibility to buy shares at a significantly reduced (usually around 50%) price; moreover, compensation vouchers were accepted in exchange for the shares. As it became a practice of the majority owners to repurchase these preferentially sold shares at their nominal value, speculation with vouchers bought at prices below their nominal value on the secondary market became a profitable enterprise in this aspect, too.[56]

What follows from all these is the conclusion that unless the subsequent use of the vouchers is meticulously regulated, the process of their marketing may engender an entire network of speculators, and thus the original scope of the scheme (at least the compensatory feature) is hijacked towards unworthy recipients. Even in those cases in which the original holders successfully translate their vouchers into shares or bonds, the process as such presents no guarantees of possible future gains: these are function of the performances of the company, upon which minority holders can hardly exert any meaningful influence.

In former Czechoslovakia, compensation was essentially afforded in those cases where restitution was not possible. It took the form of in kind (land of comparable size and quality, preferably in the same community where the original plot was situated,[57] goods of comparable quantity and quality, services designed to support agricultural

owned companies repurchased their own stocks at the expense of their profit (and the taxpayers' money), while those compensated—and the speculants engaged in voucher-trading—received an indirect cash award.

[56] For more details, see: Mihályi, *op. cit.*.

[57] Law "On modifying ownership relations with respect to land and other agricultural property," *op. cit.*, section 11(2)–(3).

production),[58] cash, and securities payments.[59] Compensation was envisaged as the sole form of remedy only in those cases in which the entire movable patrimony of the claimant was expropriated. In this case it took the form of monetary payments within uniform limits.[60] The Czech Constitutional Court has pointed out that the guiding principle of the restitution scheme was to at least partially alleviate the consequences of past property injustices, and the Restitution Law[61] itself enunciated the aim that entitled persons should be given back their original properties. Accordingly, these principles cannot be considered to be met when, although the restitution claim is well founded, claimants merely receive in kind or financial compensation.[62] Commentators note that the Czech Court's case law reflects a considerable deferential attitude towards the legislative, often invoking the exclusive policy-making competence of the Parliament and its inability to substitute political will with judicial rulings.[63] Illustrative of this attitude is the ruling which upheld—in spite of the above-enunciated guiding principles—a legislative solution that provided merely financial compensation in those cases where the claimed property was already privatized. The Court grounded its arguments on the principles of legal certainty and vested rights.[64] Interestingly, the very same ideas were invoked for striking down a statute that attempted to replace the former owners' previously granted entitlement to their full property shares in collective farms with bonds or vouchers.[65] Procházka found this as illustrative of the Court's "ideological commitment" towards restitution, although a more cynical reading may put the blame on the influences exerted by the politics upon the judiciary.[66]

---

58 *Ibid.*, section 20.

59 Law "On extra-judicial rehabilitation," *op. cit.*, section 13.

60 60,000 CZK, Kopecký v. Slovakia, *op. cit.*, para. 23.

61 Law "On modifying ownership relations with respect to land and other agricultural property."

62 CCC, Pl. US 754/01, Decision of 23 November 2003.

63 Procházka, *op. cit.*, pp. 149–50.

64 CCC, Pl. US 1/98, Coll. Vol. 12, 71–9; quoted and commented in Procházka, *op. cit.*, p. 151.

65 CCC, Pl. US 17/99, Coll. Vol. 16, 267–76; quoted and commented in Procházka, *op. cit.*.

66 It has to be noted that the latter decision was issued shortly after the 1998 parliamentary elections. Procházka himself admits that the Court's approach

While in the case of the Czech Court merely a doubt of some political determination exists, in the case of its sister, the Slovakian Constitutional Court, this becomes almost a factual reality.[67] The restitution-related decisions of the Court start with a categorical refusal to deal with these problems within concrete review. It held that it is incompetent to rule on the mitigation of past injustices, as the competence to make decisions in this respect was vested into the "State authorities" by the restitution laws.[68] In the sole abstract–review petition directly related to restitution issues filed in the 90s, the Court emphasized that claimants do not qualify as owners, but only as applicants for the renewal of their property rights. Consequently, the Parliament has a wide margin of appreciation in attaching conditions to restitution.[69] Therefore, the Court could easily state that "[i]n case of extensive and complex special-purpose laws that give rise to certain legal entitlements of eligible persons [...] no objections may be raised against the decision of the legislator to introduce certain restricting rules that are not in conflict with the original object and concept of the law and that had not been initially foreseen or fully appreciated [...], even if such changes are disadvantageous for persons for whom the initial wording of the law was more favorable."[70] Under these conditions it is no wonder that the Constitutional Court has issued an unusually small number of restitution-related decisions, and is yet to be found in favor of the petitioner.[71]

to the issue of legal certainty and vested rights was "at times rather selective." For a contrary view, see: Přibáň, "Judicial Power vs. Democratic Representation: The Culture of Constitutionalism and Human Rights in the Czech Legal System," in Sadurski (ed.), *op. cit.*, p. 397: "It is obvious that the Court's decision-making cannot be simplified in the language of the political parties interests or governmental policy."

[67] Procházka, *op. cit.*, pp. 172–3; for a different view, see: Darina Malová, "The Role and Experience of the Slovakian Constitutional Court," in Sadurski (ed.), *op. cit.*, p. 371: "the Justices usually act as a single and coherent body, proving their commitment to the idea of independent judicial review."

[68] Slovakian Constitutional Court (hereinafter SCC), Pl. US 23/94 of 12 April 1994, available online, at http://www.concourt.sk/A/a_index.htm.

[69] SCC, Pl. US 23/98, Coll. 1999, 462–70; quoted and commented in Procházka, *op. cit.*, pp. 173–4.

[70] SCC, Pl. US 3/00 of 24 April, 2001, available online, at http://www.concourt.sk/A/a_index.htm.

[71] According to Procházka, *op. cit.*, p. 175, as well as the Court's online case law, at http://www.concourt.sk.

The Polish solution of offsetting (crediting) the value of the formerly lost property against the value of new properties acquired from the state, or of the fee for the perpetual use of such state properties, also came before the European Court of Human Rights. While the modality of compensation as such was not challenged, the applicant complained about the state's refusal to satisfy his entitlement to compensation. The Court found that the restrictions placed upon the right to offset resulted in the paradoxical situation that the right could not be realized in practice, "so it ha[d] become illusory and a mere sham."[72] Discussing the state's alleged discharge of all obligations arisen in relation to the applicant's right to offset, due to the fact that his family has received partial compensation in the past, the Court argued that (although there is no requirement of full compensation),[73] compensations have to respect the requisite fair balance.[74] Fair balance, in the Court's reading, means that "an individual and excessive burden" shall not be imposed,[75] that is, the compensation for taken property has to be of an amount reasonably related to its value.[76] The Court has also indicated that by "value" it understands "market value, as determined at the time of the expropriation."[77]

Although the Court generally refrains from questioning the basis on which domestic courts assess the amount of payable compensation, in the Pincová and Pinc case it found that a compensation amounting to one-fifth of the "market value" of the taken property is unreasonable. Further, the Court also noted that the compensation failed to take into account the applicant's "personal and social situation," the non-pecuniary damage of being deprived of their sole property, as well as the costs "incurred for the upkeep of the house" during the time elapsed from the day when the judgment on the transfer of title be-

[72] Broniowski v. Poland, *op. cit.*, para. 173, quoting the Polish Constitutional Tribunal's judgment of 19 December 2002.

[73] James and Others v. UK, *op. cit.*, para. 54; Broniowski v. Poland, *op. cit.*, para. 182.

[74] Lithgow, *op. cit.*, para. 120; Former King of Greece and Others v. Greece, *op. cit.*, para. 89.

[75] Sporrong and Lönnroth v. Sweden, ECHR, Appliction No. 7151/75, 7152/75, Judgment of 23 September 1982, para. 73.

[76] Broniowski v. Poland, *op. cit.*, para. 176.

[77] Pincová and Pinc v. The Czech Republic, *op. cit.*, para. 53.

came final.[78] Interestingly, the Court demonstrated a more relaxed attitude towards the British nationalization scheme discussed in Lithgow, where it found no unreasonableness in disregarding for instance the value of works undertaken from after the "notice to treat" and until the effective hand-over.[79] Equally interestingly, the Court also approved the valuation period chosen by the British scheme, noting that although in most international cases the date of the nationalization announcement and the date of taking were, in fact, one and the same,[80] in those cases where these dates differ, the distortion in the property's value caused by the threat of impending nationalization may reasonably be taken into account.[81] Accordingly, in Pincová and Pinc, the Czech authorities could have reasonably chosen a valuation period that preceded the day of the final judgment on the title transfer; however, the purchase price paid thirty years earlier—which was returned as compensation—cannot be considered as reasonably related to the value of the property.[82]

It seems, however, that even the experienced Strasbourg court can lose its way every now and then in the murky waters of post-communist transition. In this sense it is edifying to compare the Court's findings in Pincová and Pinc with those argued in Jahn. Although the fact pattern is different, the underlying problem is ultimately the same in both cases. In Pincová and Pinc, the applicants lost their property in favor of the heirs of the original owner, on the ground that they acquired it from a state enterprise for a price established through a valuation procedure that did not comply with the rules in force at the time.[83] In Jahn, the applicants lost their properties in favor of the state (various Lands), on the ground that they have acquired (inherited) them in a way incompatible with the rules in force at the time, their possession being made possible only by the indifference of the former GDR authorities.[84] Strangely

[78] *Ibid.*, paras. 60–2. Other cases, in which the Court found the amount of compensation as unreasonable was Scordino v. Italy, Application No. 36813/97, Judgment of 29 July 2004, paras. 98–103 (the compensation was set at roughly 50% of the market value and subsequently taxed at a rate of 20%).

[79] Lithgow, *op. cit.*, para. 101.

[80] *Ibid.*, para. 134.

[81] *Ibid.*, para. 135 and following.

[82] Pincová and Pinc, *op. cit.*, para. 61.

[83] *Ibid.*, para. 18.

[84] Jahn and Others, *op. cit.*, paras. 101–4.

enough, while in the first case the Court found that the amount of compensation paid was unreasonable, and thus in violation of Article 1 of Protocol I, in the latter case it held that regime changes can be regarded as exceptional circumstances, justifying the lack of any compensation. In Jahn, overturning its Third Section's judgment, the Court argued that "the right of the new farmers in the GDR cannot be classified as a property right such as existed at the time under democratic, market-economy regimes."[85] This odd statement was employed in order to demonstrate the applicants' lack of good faith possession, albeit there is no reason to believe that in former Czechoslovakia, or indeed, in any other former communist state, a genuine Western-type of private property existed. Further, reasoned the Court, the applicants were able to retain the possession of the lands in question only because the state failed to effect the necessary transfers. Although, it had to be noted, as for that matter the Court itself did in the same paragraph,[86] that these lands were generally managed by agricultural co-operatives. (In any event, it was the authorities' duty to effect the transfers, not the applicants'; the latter had no legal obligations in this respect.) On the contrary, in Pincová and Pinc the Court reasoned that the applicants did not need to know that the property they were buying was confiscated, and also accepted that they had neither influence on the terms of the transaction, nor knowledge about the unfairness of the acquisition price. In Jahn, the Court considered that the "upheavals and uncertainties" of the transitional period question the applicants' certainty (hinting towards legitimate expectations) in their possessions.[87] Intriguingly, no such finding was made in Pincová and Pinc. Fundamentally, in both cases the relevant norms attempted to level the consequences of an unlawful advantage obtained in the past, the major difference being that in Jahn the Court saw this as a decisive factor justifying the lack of compensation. Taking it all together, no convincing argument can be found which may explain the difference

[85] *Ibid.*, para. 100.

[86] *Ibid.*, para. 103.

[87] *Ibid.*, para. 116(i). It was also argued that the law, on the basis of which the applicants' acquired their formal title, was not adopted by a democratically elected parliament, although, as one of the dissenters mentions, none of the GDR parliaments were democratically elected. Conclusively, if the democratically elected standard is a valid argument, all previous regulations are questionable (partly dissenting opinion of Judge Pavlovschi).

in outcome between the two cases. A similar conclusion is voiced by one of the dissenting judges in Jahn, who also emphasized that in the Former King of Greece judgment, which also dealt with transitional takings, the Court was able to find a violation of Protocol I, Article 1 due to the lack of compensations for deprivation of property.[88]

From the above it follows that there are no theoretical impediments in the case of dealing with past property injustices which would bar the government from resorting to a variety of compensations besides cash payments. However, in doing so, it has to observe certain constraints. Most of the problems featured by the post-communist compensation schemes pertain to the practical workability of the chosen solutions. As it was shown above in the Polish case, for example, crediting the value of the once lost property against various state properties (purchased or in use) was made impossible by the subsequent regulations. Or, the Hungarian compensation vouchers could hardly be marketed at their nominal value, and even in those cases in which they were employed to purchase land or shares, the process was tainted by the massive involvement of speculators who acquired vouchers on the secondary market. Further, in the case of all schemes including vouchers, shares or the like, these means of compensations—unlike cash payments—represented only a virtual compensation, a function of future circumstances beyond the control of the recipients, and to a fair extent of the state too, presenting no guarantee of an eventual relief. This, however, does not mean that money is the ultimate solution and that—as it will be argued in the next section—in those cases where transitional reparation schemes resorted to this form of compensation, the outcome was significantly better.

1.2 Questions of valuation

In the previous sections a lot of space was dedicated to the idea of just or fair compensation. It has to be noted, however, that these theories were predominantly discussed in takings, and not communist expro-

[88] Jahn, *op. cit.*, dissenting opinion of Judge Barreto, part II, paras. 7–8. The dissent questions whether there is any such difference between the two regime changes which qualifies one as "an exceptional circumstance," but is indifferent from the perspective of the other. The same point is raised by the joint dissenting opinions of Judges Costa, Borrego, Ress, and Botoucharova.

priation contexts, where the scope and the goal of the seizures, as well as the number of affected individuals was significantly different. Moreover, the compensating government was mostly identical with the expropriating one, while both events always took place under the same regime.

As the above-mentioned arguments and court decisions demonstrate, a fairly clearly articulated theory of compensation exists in takings context, according to which governmental takings of private property regularly need to be compensated. Further, the value of the compensation has to be reasonably related to the value of the expropriated property, which is usually assessed in "fair market value" terms, however no requirement of full compensation is set forward.

Therefore, it is a difficult exercise to make a *mutatis mutandis*-type of argument and claim that whatever solution is practiced for takings, it may apply in a restitution context, too. The above analyzed judgments of the European Court of Human Rights in Pincová and Pinc[89] and Jahn[90] demonstrate how difficult is to construe the fair compensation theory in transitional contexts, even if in these two cases the Court had to decide upon what may be called "common" takings. Still, the case of compensation is stronger than that of restitution in the sense that while there are no international or national (constitutional) provisions demanding restitution of expropriated properties, the requirement of compensation is clearly formulated at both levels.

The most significant restitution case, in which the Strasbourg court had pronounced its views upon the compensation standards applied in transitional restitution context, was Broniowski. Here, the Court has spoken about the necessity to respect the "requisite fair balance,"[91] however, the circumstances of the case significantly differed from other restitution cases in which the Court declined its competence *ratione temporis* or *ratione materiae*.[92] In this case, as the argument unfolded, the applicant was not complaining of being deprived of his family's original property left beyond the Bug River. Instead, he alleged the failure of the authorities to afford him satisfaction according to an

[89] Pincová and Pinc, *op. cit.*.

[90] Jahn, *op. cit.*.

[91] Broniowski v. Poland, *op. cit.*, para. 176.

[92] E.g., Janter v. Slovakia, ECHR, Application No. 39050/97, Judgment of 4 March 2003.

entitlement which was vested in him by law before Poland's accession to Protocol I, but which continued to exist up to the date of the hearing. Luckily for the applicant, his entitlement, which was recognized between 1946 and 1994[93] by several legislative acts, was also reaffirmed through a 1997 law on land administration.[94] Thus, for the foregoing reasons the Court was able to assert its *ratione temporis* jurisdiction over the case. However, it was cautious enough to emphasize that it considered only those acts and omissions of the Polish State which might have violated the applicant's entitlement to compensation as vested in him on the date of the Protocol's entry into force.[95] As the right to offset (credit) was considered to be a possession, in the meaning of Article 1 of Protocol I—the view of the Polish Supreme Court on the matter, which considered that the right to offset was "a particular proprietary right" of a "pecuniary value" was endorsed by the Strasbourg court[96]—the "fair balance" standard was easily brought into action. Conclusively, according to the lesson that can be drawn from the Broniowski judgment, whenever an individual entitlement to receive compensation for a past property injustice exists, the European Court of Human Rights' "fair balance" standard has to be respected in establishing the value of the compensation. Thus, the forthcoming passages investigate to what extent did post-communist restitution schemes recognize and live up to this requirement.

1.2.1 Partial compensation: the reasonable percentage

As it is demonstrated by the above-quoted Pincová and Pinc judgment of the Strasbourg court, while there is no established requirement to afford full market value compensation, a "reasonable" relationship has to be established between the value of compensation and the value of the

[93] The date of entry into force of Protocol I with respect to Poland.

[94] Broniowski v. Poland, ECHR, Application No. 31443/96, Grand Chamber Decision as to the admissibility of the application of 19 December 2002, paras. 74–7; Broniowski v. Poland, ECHR, Application No. 31443/96, Judgment of 22 June 2004, paras. 122–5.

[95] Broniowski v. Poland, ECHR, Application No. 31443/96, Judgment of 22 June 2004, para. 125.

[96] *Ibid.*, paras. 129–33; also Grand Chamber Decision, paras. 97–101.

taken property.[97] In that specific case the Court found compensation amounting to one-fifth of the taken property's value as unreasonable. In the light of this finding, the compensation rules of several restitution schemes appear questionable.

In Estonia, the Principles of Ownership Reform Act[98] enounced the principle of state compensation for those unlawfully expropriated lands which were not returned. The actual problems of valuation were left to be dealt with through subsequent normative acts: The Land Valuation Act[99] and the Unlawfully Expropriated Property Valuation and Compensation Act.[100] In the case of lands, the value of the expropriated land was determined on the basis of the total area of the land at the time of the expropriation. Distinction was made between properties situated in low density and high-density areas. Accordingly, in low density areas, the value of the property "was determined on the basis of the weighted average assessed value of one hectare of the total area of the rural municipality, without considering tax incentives which decrease the assessed value of land."[101] In high-density areas, however, the value of properties not exceeding half hectare was established "on the basis of the assessed value of land per square meter of residential land in the value zone, without considering tax incentives which decrease the assessed value of land." The portion exceeding the half hectare limit had to be multiplied by 0.1 to determine its value. The method of valuation has to be considered in the light of the provisions of the Land Reform Law, which, while defining the objectives of the reform, departed from the idea of "continuity of rights of former owners."[102] Although the subsequent normative acts concerned with restitution did not touch upon this question, this does not make the cited formulation less compelling. Therefore, so long as the continuity of former owners' right is contemplated, and restitution (also compensation) is not based upon official grace, the Broniowski example can be considered as authoritative in the sense that whenever restitution of the taken property is refused, compensation should conform to the "fair balance" standard. On the basis

[97] Pincová and Pinc, *op. cit.*, *supra*.
[98] Act of 2 June 2003, *op. cit.*, section 13(1).
[99] Act of 9 February 1994, consolidated version in July 2002.
[100] Act of 1993, consolidated version in 2002.
[101] Land Valuation Act, *op. cit.*, Art. 9(4).
[102] Act of 17 October 1991 (as amended), section 2, para. 1.

of this, taking into account also the position of the Strasbourg court in Pincová and Pinc, the reasonableness of the compensation in the case of high-density areas is more than arguable. A compensation that secures only a reward amounting to one-tenth of the value for those (fractions of) properties that exceed half hectare can hardly be considered as being reasonably related to the value of the lost property.

The narrow Polish scheme provided only for compensation, as it was already mentioned above, in the form of offsetting (crediting) the value of the lost properties against the value of new properties acquired from the state, or of the fee for the perpetual use of such state properties. While confronted with the first constitutional challenge against this scheme, the Constitutional Tribunal has stated that it does not have the competence to decide upon the appropriateness of the solution, as this remains within the sphere of the legislature.[103] The scheme—irrespective of the value of the lost property—provided that only 15% of this value may be offset and a uniform upper ceiling was also established.[104] The European Court of Human Rights, while examining this scheme, did not have to pronounce on the extent of the compensation offered,[105] but it signaled that denial of compensation to those who have received in the past a much lower percentage amounts to an unequal treatment. While noting that it is not for the Court to indicate what would constitute a "reasonable" compensation, it nevertheless stated that the 2% received by the applicant are not a convincing reason for depriving him of the possibility of obtaining at least a fraction of his entitlement.[106] After the Broniowski ruling, the Polish Constitutional Tribunal had the chance to a second scrutiny of the compensation scheme, which, at this time, was laid down in a special act.[107] The Tribunal found the limitations "excessive," and contrary to the principles of "protecting acquired

[103] PCT, K 33/02, Judgment of 19 December 2002, "Right to offset the value of property left in the former Eastern Territories of Poland (I)," para. 10.

[104] Of 50,000 PLN.

[105] It has to be noted though that the Polish law afforded a lower level of compensation (under one-sixth) than the Czech one (one-fifth) found unreasonable in Pincová and Pinc, *supra*.

[106] Broniowski v. Poland, *op. cit.*, para. 186.

[107] Offsetting the Value of Property Abandoned Beyond the Present Boarders of the Polish State Against the Price of State Property or the Fee for the Right of Perpetual Usufruct Act, 2003.

rights and citizens' trust in the State as stemming from the constitutional clause of the rule of law" and the principle of social justice. According to the Tribunal's view, the uniform cap results in unequal treatment of the former owners and unequal protection of their property rights.[108] Furthermore, after the above-cited Strasbourg ruling, the Tribunal had little problem in pointing towards the unconstitutionality of the exclusion of those previously compensated under other statutes from the reach of the new scheme. The reasons invoked—equal treatment, equal protection, social justice, and the citizens' trust in the State—were identical to those employed under the analysis of the quantitative restrictions.[109] Finally, in the summer of 2005, Polish legislature passed a new law on the issue.[110] The law, which entered into force in October 2005, provides for a 20% ceiling.[111]

Hungary represents a peculiar case amongst the analyzed restitution programs, as it envisaged only compensations—except for church properties—for the properties taken under the previous regimes. These compensations—again, unlike in the other countries presented in this study—took only the form of vouchers. A somewhat similar situation can be met in Poland, where the only available form of reparation was also compensation (the right to offset the value of the lost properties), although with two important qualifications. First, in Poland the restitution of the actually lost properties was a physical impossibility: the former owners were repatriated from the territories falling beyond the current borders of the country. Second, the right to offset (credit) was ultimately considered as falling under the protection of Article 1 of Protocol I to the European Convention. In Hungary, however, the choice of policy was defended by the Constitutional Court, through invoking the distributive character of the Compensation Law (as opposed to reparative justice) and the moral obligation of the state to compensate (as opposed to the former owners' right to receive compensation).[112] Thus,

[108] PCT, K2/04, Judgment of 15 December 2004, "Right to offset the value of property left in the former Eastern territories of Poland (II)," para. 9.

[109] *Ibid.*, para. 11.

[110] "On the realization of the right to compensation for property left beyond the present borders of the Polish State," 21 July 2005.

[111] Broniowski v. Poland, ECHR, Application No. 31443/96, Judgment (Friendly settlement) of 28 September 2005, para. 13.

[112] HCC, AB 28/1991, 1160/A/1991; AB 15/1993, 1543/B/1991.

for these reasons, the legislator was considered to enjoy wide latitude in establishing the mode and extent of compensations. Still, because the compensation scheme attempted to address all past property grievances through a unitary approach, a common theoretical ground needed to be found for the similar treatment of various claims (nationalization and collectivization, confiscation of dissident properties, repatriations, obligations arising from the Paris Peace Treaty). The Court found the common denominator in the civil law institution of novation, which, according to the Court, meant that old obligations received new legal basis, extent, and terms.[113] Consequently, the compensation scheme was able to ignore the original legal nature of the claims.[114] The Court invoked, in the reasoning justifying its solution, the unusual character of the takings, which were targeting the systematic eradication of private property.[115] This argument was made in the context of the novation of obligations arising from nationalization, albeit the Court did not give any explanations as to why the institution of novation was justified in the case of obligations having other legal basis. It is obvious at least that confiscation of dissident properties was not targeting any grand scheme of property reform, but had a merely punitive nature. Equally doubtful is the case of obligations arising from the Paris Peace Treaty (providing for restitution), which was solved by the Court through the volatile argument of "changed historical circumstances"[116] justifying, in its reading, the applicability of the compensation law's terms.

Regarding this latter case, it is worth remembering what the European Court of Human Rights had to say in the Broniowski decision. The legislative history of the two cases is by and large similar: in both cases the state acknowledged by means of international agreements its obligation to offer compensation for the lost properties (the Republican Agreements in the case of Poland and the Paris Peace Treaty in the case of Hungary). In both cases, domestic norms restated this obligation.[117] Again, in both cases, the right was created in an imper-

[113] HCC, AB 28/1991, 1160/A/1991, para. I/2.1.

[114] *Ibid.*, para. I/3.2.

[115] *Ibid.*, para. I/3.3.

[116] HCC, AB 16/1993, part IV.

[117] In Poland: Decree of 6 December 1946 "On the transfer from the State of non-agricultural property in the Regained Territories and the former City of Gdańsk"; The Land Administration and Expropriation Act of 29 April

fect form, as its materialization depended on subsequent administrative decisions, which the two states mostly failed to enact.[118] Finally, in both cases the government's obligation to afford compensation was recognized to exist at the date when the claims were filed. The most significant difference is that while in Poland the domestic courts had no problem in qualifying the former owners' right to offset as a property right, the Hungarian Constitutional Court did not even bother to define the character of the entitlement, contenting itself with the above-described novation doctrine.[119] Of course, the state may take property—also compensatory entitlements granted by law—and may significantly reduce the levels of compensations, argues the Strasbourg court, especially when the compensations are mitigating takings which are not attributable to the compensating state.[120] Arguably, through "novation" the former owners' entitlement to compensation was taken (transformed into something else)[121] and taking demands compensation. Compensation, according to the Strasbourg court, has to be reasonably related to the taken property's value.[122] It has to be noted that in the light of the Court's judgment in Pincová and Pinc,[123] where the compensation amounting to one-fifth of the taken property's market value was found unacceptable, the Hungarian scheme's near one-tenth offer at the top end of the scale can hardly be taken as reasonable.

Nevertheless, the above-presented compensation conception, besides the wide margin of appreciation it conferred upon the Parliament, also meant that no successful Protocol I, Article 1 claims could have been launched against Hungary in Strasbourg. All such applications had been declared inadmissible like, for example, the case of Széché-

1985; The Land Administration Act of 1997, etc. (Broniowski v. Poland, *idem*, para. 42 and the following). In Hungary: Order of the Prime Minister No. 1600/1944; Law No. XXV of 1946; Law No. XVIII of 1947 (HCC, AB 16/1993, 1378/E/1990).

[118] See: Broniowski v. Poland, *op. cit.*, paras. 137–9; and AB 16/1993, *op. cit.*, parts II/4 and IV.

[119] Broniowski v. Poland, *op. cit.*, paras. 129–33; and AB 16/1993, *op. cit.*, part III.

[120] Broniowski v. Poland, *op. cit.*, para. 186.

[121] See: the comments on the institution of novation, *supra*, in *Justice and Restitution*.

[122] Broniowski v. Poland, *op. cit.*, para. 186.

[123] Pincová and Pinc, *op. cit.*.

nyi v. Hungary, which, among others, complained of the lack of any relationship between the nominal value of the compensation and the market value of the former property.[124]

As the previous chapters already hinted, the Hungarian compensation scheme employed a shifting scale for calculating the value of the vouchers to be received. The value of the former properties was converted into a flat rate, which took account of two variables in the case of immovable (location and size), and one in the case of commercial (number of employees) properties.[125] Once the value of the former property was established, a gliding scale was used to determine the actual value of the compensation. This means that the law provided for four different thresholds, up to which a determined sum plus decreasing fractions of the value of the lost property exceeding that threshold were paid. The relationship between the two was inversely proportional; thus, at the bottom of the scale, full compensation was possible, while at the top only one-tenth of the taken property's value—exceeding the threshold sum—was compensated.[126] Furthermore, a general uniform cap was also placed on the maximum amount of receivable compensation.[127]

A different valuation formula was originally projected for agricultural land and forestry. The value of the lost lands was calculated based upon the net cadastral return of the land, called "golden corona." The Compensation Law established that the value of one "golden corona" amounts to 1,000 HUF for agricultural lands, and 4,000 HUF for forestry.[128] (Comparatively, the Estonian scheme provided only for a thirty per cent difference in value between forestry and agricultural lands.) Reliance on this peculiar proxy was reasonable, as the "golden corona" was the standard means of land valuation at the time of nationalization and collectivization, too.[129] Finally, in this case full compensation was possible up to a threshold of 1,000 "golden corona."

---

124 ECHR, Application No. 21344/93, Decision of the European Commission of Human Rights (Second Chamber), 30 June 1993.

125 Law No. XXV of 1991, *op. cit.*, Annex No. 3.

126 *Ibid.*, para. 4(1).

127 5,000,000 million HUF, *Ibid.*, para. 4(3).

128 Law No. XXV of 1991, *op. cit.*, para. 13(1).

129 The "golden crown" was introduced as a standard means of land valuation in 1875, to ensure the proportional taxation of estates. The original law

As it was already shown in the previous chapter,[130] the Constitutional Court has invalidated the valuation system envisaged for agricultural properties. According to the Court's reasoning, the fact that non-agricultural lands were subject to general limitations,[131] while in the case of agricultural lands the above "golden corona"-based system was used as standard valuation, constituted an ostentatious, arbitrary, and ultimately unconstitutional differentiation in treatment.[132] At the same time, however, the Court upheld the constitutionality of the valuation scheme as what regards the employment of flat rates, the gliding scale, and the general cap on the amount of receivable compensation, invoking the large margin of appreciation conferred by the general character of the scheme.[133] A flat rate conversion was employed also for the calculation of the value of properties lost in the period between 1939 and 1949 (second Compensation Law).[134] Although the relevant provisions of the first Compensation Law as what concerns the calculation of the amount of compensation were applicable also in the case of the victims determined under this second law, a special conversion scheme was also set forward. Accordingly, in the case of precious metals and jewelry which had to be placed under mandatory deposit (during the Holocaust), their value was established in function of their standard (carat). If their carat could not be determined, the sixteen-carat value was employed. Moreover, the law also provided an average weight for

(No. VIII of 1875) distinguished seven different categories of cultivation, registered along other data on the cadastral sheets. On the basis of these, the net cadastral return of each plot was established, and a certain percentage of this income constituted the rate of the land tax (see: József Rajczi, "Földminősítés történeti áttekintése," available online, at http://www.magyaringatlanklub.hu/?page=tudastar_foldminosit).

130 *Supra*, in *The Rule of Law, Equality and Limited Restitution.*

131 Which, according to para. 3 of Law No. XXV of 1991, *op. cit.*, ensured full compensation only up to a value of 200,000 HUF, whilst, according to the "golden corona" currency conversion, this value was 1,000,000 HUF for agricultural properties.

132 HCC, AB 28/1991, *op. cit.*, part C, para 3(1).

133 *Ibid.*, para. 1: the Court invoked the new legal basis of compensation, which, due to the novation doctrine, is different from the former owners' original entitlement, and related to this, the fact that compensation is afforded on grounds of gratitude, instead of justice.

134 Law No. XXIV of 1992.

various jewelry objects for those cases in which the weight of the deposited items could not have been determined anymore.[135]

Finally, it is worth mentioning a German Federal Constitutional Court decision upon the reasonable amount of compensation. The Joint Declaration of the two German states on the Resolution of Outstanding Property Issues mentioned the possibility of monetary or in kind (substitute real estate), "socially acceptable indemnification" for those properties that cannot be restituted.[136] The same principles were restated by the Resolution of Outstanding Property Issues Act (Indemnification Act),[137] the Act Governing State Compensation for Expropriations Carried Out on the Basis of the Laws or Other Powers of the Occupying Force (Compensation Act),[138] and the Property Act.[139] The Federal Constitutional Court has had the chance to pronounce several judgments upon the restitution scheme. The Court managed to exhibit a firm and consequent approach towards the issue, recalling in each case the same principles. Accordingly, it was held from the outset that "there is no constitutional obligation to provide reparation to the same value as restitution." Further, as the Court explained, the Parliament enjoyed a "particularly wide" margin of appreciation in calculating the compensation and could take into consideration also its financial limitations and the other duties incumbent on the state.[140] As the property injustices that the above-enumerated acts attempted to mitigate were perpetrated by another State, the guarantees of Article 14 of the Basic Law regarding the right of property find no application in this case. Therefore, even if the generally prescribed amounts of reparation were less than the current marked value of the respective properties, these differences were justified in the light of the State's financial means and its other expenditures,

---

[135] *Ibid.*, Art. 3 and Annex No. 3.

[136] Maltzan and Others v. Germany, *op. cit.*, para. 38.

[137] Gesetz über die Entschädigung nach dem Gesetz zur Regelung offener Vermögensfragen/ Entschädigungsgesetzt, 27 September 1994.

[138] Gesetz über staatliche Ausgleichsleistungen für Enteignungen auf besatzungsrechtlicher oder besatzungshoheitlicher Grundlage, 27 September 1994.

[139] Of 1990, as amended in 1994 and 1997, section 9, but repealed in 2000.

[140] Judgment of 23 April 1991; quoted in Maltzan and Others v. Germany, *op. cit.*, para. 18.

as the reimbursement of full market value was not financially feasible.[141] However, the gliding scale applied for calculating the concrete amount of the indemnification split the Court in two, resulting in a four to four judgment, which—according to the rules of the Court—meant that no violation of the Basic Law was found.[142]

The calculation scheme employed essentially consisted in a progressive reduction of the indemnification according to the value of the property. Half of the judges held that the legislature—for the reasons explained above—did not have to take into consideration the real value of the property when determining the amount of compensation. The other (dissenting) half of the judges considered that the compensation had to reflect the real value of the property, and it could not be less than 50% of this value. According to their reasoning, the scheme applied could be considered justified for extreme cases (the smallest and largest estates), but not for the middle category (mostly individual houses or other small buildings).[143] Still, the case for such a heightened protection is considerably weakened by the findings of the Court in the same case, according to which the restoration-related legislation (as cited above) did not create any concrete property rights for former property owners that could fall under the protection of Article 14 of the Basic Law.[144] The European Court of Human Rights on its turn accepted the reasoning of the Federal Constitutional Court, and stated that the applicants did not have a legitimate expectation going beyond the compensation scheme laid down in the above-cited acts. Thus, the existence of any sufficiently established (enforceable) claim was not demonstrated; therefore, they did not have "possessions" within the meaning of Article 1 of Protocol I.[145]

[141] BverfG 1 BvR 2307/94 vom 22.11.2000, Absatz-Nr. (1–376), available online, at http://www.bverfg.de; also quoted in Maltzan and Others v. Germany, *op. cit.*, paras. 21–5.
[142] Bundesverfassungsgerichtsgesetz, section 15(4).
[143] Maltzan and Others v. Germany, *op. cit.*, paras. 26–8.
[144] *Ibid.*, para. 23.
[145] *Ibid.*, paras. 65–114.

1.2.2 Past taking, present compensation: establishing the value of property

It was again the Pincová and Pinc judgment of the European Court of Human Rights in which the Court stated that using a thirty-year-old record to calculate the value of the taken property constitutes a breach of Article 1 of Protocol I. However, designers of post-communist restitution or compensation schemes did not find it always necessary to rely on current market value. In the context of the enormous financial hardships of (economic) transition, with steadily devolving currencies and skyrocketing real estate prices, it is understandable that governments were not especially eager to pay out huge compensations. Still, by proposing to afford less than what was due, all that these schemes achieved was perpetuating an existing injustice.

The Lithuanian Constitutional Court, for instance, explained that compensation must be based not only on the market value of the property, but has to take into account also its value at the moment of taking, as well as the subsequent changes in its quality and value. Consequently, just compensation for unlawfully taken property may not be identified with just compensation for takings under the present Constitution, which requires an equal value award.[146] Moreover, it was held that "actual and fair compensation" must be secured, but this has no bearing on how the compensation is established.[147] The Court has also held that "rightful compensation shall also guarantee the restoration of the rights of ownership."[148] While discussing the meaning of justness, the Court departed from the fundamental idea which influenced the entire restitution scheme in all three Baltic States, namely, the thesis of foreign occu-

---

[146] *Ibid.*.

[147] Accordingly, although the town where the property is situated and the fact whether it was attributed to the respective territory until or after its unlawful nationalization determine the discretion of the legislator to establish different ways of evaluation, this does not mean that the law would not compensate fairly. LiCC, Ruling of 2 April 2001, "On the restoration of the rights of ownership of citizens to land," available online, at http://www.lrkt.lt/dokumentai/2001/r010402.htm.

[148] LiCC, Ruling of 8 March 1995, "On restoration of citizens' ownership rights to land," available online, at http://www.lrkt.lt/dokumentai/1995/n5a0308a.htm.

pation.[149] This, in the opinion of the Court, justifies partial restitution. According to the Court, the former owners' property rights date from the moment when the relevant authorities return property or compensate for it.[150] To make things more complicated, the Court also spoke about the "broader concept" of the constitutional guarantee of property protection, including the "lawful interests" of former owners.[151]

The Restitution of Property Act[152] envisaged compensation in kind (alternative plots of land), lump sum, stock, or cancellation of debts, citizens having the possibility of choosing between land and money.[153] The nature of the former owners' right was, however, rather unclear: the Constitutional Court spoke about the State's *de facto* control of the nationalized property, albeit also stated that the Restitution Act did not provide any rights by itself.

The Latvian scheme, instead of speaking about the continuity of rights, as it was the case of Estonia, talked about the "renewal" of ownership rights,[154] something akin to the "novation" theory of the Hungarian Constitutional Court.[155] This approach could have led the Latvian Constitutional Court to conclusions similar to those formulated by its Hungarian correspondent, in what concerns the amount of the com-

149 "[O]ne has to take account of the fact that it was not the State of Lithuania that unlawfully nationalized or disseized in other unlawful ways the property of the owners." LiCC, Ruling of 4 March 2003, "On restoration of the rights of ownership," available online, at http://www.lrkt.lt/dokumentai/2003/r030304.htm.

150 *Ibid.*.

151 LiCC, Ruling of 27 October, 1998, "On restoration of citizens' ownership rights to land and houses," available online, at http://www.lrkt.lt/dokumentai/1998/n8a1027a.htm.

152 Law "On procedures and conditions for restitution of citizens' rights to the ownership of existent real property," 18 June 1991 (as amended).

153 The possibility of opting—contained in the original version of the act—was concretized, ironically, in the written permission of the person concerned for the authorities to proceed with the decision. After the act's 1999 amendment, the authorities can decide upon the question of compensation without any preliminary approval. The decision can be appealed in the court of law (Jasiūnienė v. Lithuania, *op. cit.*, para. 22).

154 Law "On land reform in rural regions," 21 November 1990; Law "On land reform in the cities of the Republic of Latvia," 20 November 1991; Law "On land privatization in rural regions," 9 July 1992.

155 HCC, AB 28/1991, 1160/A/1991, para. I/2.1.

pensations.[156] The Latvian Court, however, took a completely different and intriguing approach. In a complaint filed in 1998,[157] the applicants were challenging the compatibility of the compensation scheme with Article 1 of Protocol I.[158] Essentially, they complained about the fact that in those cases where the restitution of the former property (land) was denied for public purposes, the compensation offered could not exceed the value of the object as defined in land books or other cadastral documents drawn up before 22 July 1940. According to the case law of the Strasbourg court, as it was already quoted in the foregoing passages from the Pincová and Pinc judgment, to define the amount of compensation according to the value of the property as recorded some thirty years earlier was violating the Convention. In the Latvian case, the gap was even larger—over fifty years—and the difference in value was considerable, too. Also, it has to be noted that due to the fact that the property rights of the applicants were "renewed" under new terms, and not considered as continuously existing, the European Court of Human Rights—if petitioned—would arguably find little difficulty in rejecting this case as unfounded (making an abstraction of the fact that Latvia had entered a reservation against Protocol I when ratifying the

---

[156] According to the Hungarian Court, due to the novation principle, the compensation scheme could ignore the original legal nature of the claims; thus, the state was able to determine the quantity of compensations at will.

[157] Latvia ratified the European Convention for the Protection of Human Rights and Fundamental Freedoms and its Protocols in 1997, albeit with reservations—among others—to Protocol I. Thus the demands of Article 1 Protocol I were not applicable in the case of restitution or compensation of those properties taken during the period of annexation by the USSR (LaCC, Case No. 2002-17-0103, *op. cit.*).

[158] LaCC, Case No. 09-02 (98), Judgment of 30 April 1998, "On Conformity of Paragraph 2 of the Supreme Council September 15, 1992, Resolution on the procedure by which the Republic of Latvia Law 'On Eminent Domain Takes Effect'" (wording of the Amendment of 19 December 1996) with Article 1 of the First Protocol of the European Convention of Human Rights and Fundamental Freedoms; quoted and commented by Aivars Endziņš, "Practice of the Constitutional Court of the Republic of Latvia in the sector of economic rights," paper presented at Commission for Democracy Through Law (Venice Commission) seminar on Economic transition: property rights, restitution, pensions and other issues concerning the constitutional protection of economic rights of citizens, Bishkek, 27–8 April 2001, available online, at http://www.venice.coe.int/docs/2001/CDL-JU(2001)026-e.asp#_ftn12.

European Convention). In spite of this, the Latvian Court engaged in an analysis of the provisions of Protocol I, Article 1, and held that Article 1 did not demand full compensation. Accordingly, combining this finding with the fundamental principle of Latvian restitution—"to renew social fairness and to fairly balance public and individual interests in the context of the consequences of annexation of Latvia by the USSR" (i.e., denationalization)—no violation of the European Convention could be found.

In Romania, the restitution scheme provided for in kind compensations (in the case of lands), or in form of shares, privatization vouchers, and money.[159] The numerous norms that made up the Romanian restitution scheme contain diverse valuation formulas. While the case of in kind compensation seemed relatively straightforward, the law providing that "if possible" the plot should be of the same quality and size, and preferably situated in the same area where the originally taken land was,[160] the case of the other forms of compensation was slightly more controversial. One of the strangest valuation methods was set forth by Law No. 112, which regulated the restitution of dwellings that were transferred into state property on the basis of a title—that is, on the basis of the then applicable legal norms.[161] In these cases, the state's ownership rights to these properties cannot be contested—argued the Romanian Constitutional Court—whilst in those cases where the takings took place without any legal basis (illegal administrative acts, *de facto*

[159] Law No. 18/1991, *op. cit.*, Art. 23 and 44; Law No. 112/1995, *op. cit.*, Art. 2, 12, and 13; Law No. 10/2001, *op. cit.*, Art 1.

[160] Law No. 18/1991, *op. cit.*, Art. 23 and 44.

[161] Law No. 112/1995, *op. cit.*. Scholars have stressed that the simple existence of a normative act in force at the date of the taking—for instance, the property in question is enumerated in the annexes of a nationalization decree, regardless whether the decree itself satisfies the necessary formal and substantive requirements—constitutes "title" in the meaning of the present law (Dumitrache Baias and Nicolae Baias, *Regimul juridic al imobilelor preluate abuziv. Legea nr. 10/2001 comentată şi adnotată*, Rosetti, 2002, Vol. I, p. 73; I. Adam, *Legea nr. 10/2001: Regimul juridic aplicabil imobilelor preluate abuziv*, All Beck, 2003, p. 10; I. Adam, *Drept civil. Drepturile reale*, All Beck, 2002, pp. 319–23). Governmental Decree No. 11/1997 (published in the *Official Gazette*, No. 16, 4 February 1997) refined the definition of "title" so as to exclude also those normative acts which did not respect the requisite formal and substantive conditions.

takings), the state has no ownership rights; thus, as it was already quoted above,[162] the former owners' rights have never been extinguished.[163]

Consequently, as the Court pointed out, in the case of the dwellings falling under Law No. 112, the legislator enjoyed an exclusive and wide margin of appreciation in establishing the conditions of restitution. Therefore, restitution was only an option in the case of those buildings which were empty or had been rented to its former owners. For all other apartments and houses, only compensation was envisaged, but those entitled to have their dwellings returned may also have opted for compensations instead.[164] The valuation method established by the law was identical with the one set forward for the valuation of dwellings for privatization, with the amendment that the coefficient of correction was not to be lower than the coefficient of increase of the medium wages per economy. A general cap was also established, valid for both restituted and compensated apartments and houses, which value could not exceed the arithmetical sum of the medium wages per economy of one person for a period of twenty years, calculated at the date when the compensation was to be established.[165] To make it even more complicated, the law provided that the actual payment had to take place no sooner than twelve months after the compensation was established, and no later than twenty-four months. Due to this considerable delay (and the rampant inflation of that period), it was also stated that the amount of compensation had to be corrected at the date of the effective payment in function of the medium wage per economy of the last month of the previous trimester.[166]

[162] Baias and Baias, *op. cit.*, p. 74; Adam, *Legea nr. 10/2001*, p. 11; Adam, *Drept civil*, p. 319). Law No. 213/1998, *Official Gazette*, No. 448, 24 November 1998, Art. 6(1) contains a further specification of the notion of "title," stating that nationalization acts had to conform at the date of their adoption to the Constitution, international treaties, and the laws in force at that time.

[163] RCC, Decision No. 73, 19 July 1995, published in the *Official Gazette*, No. 177, 8 August 1995. This theory was endorsed by the legislator, which in Law No. 10/2001, Art 2(2) specifically provided that those persons whose property was taken without a valid title retain their ownership status existing at the date of the taking, and are able to exercise their rights after the restitution decision or judgment, has been pronounced.

[164] Law No. 112/1995, *op. cit.*, Art. 2 and 12.

[165] *Ibid.*, Art. 13.

[166] *Ibid.*.

The Constitutional Court, while discussing the constitutionality of the above outlined compensation system, found that while setting the general cap, the existing economical and financial possibilities, as well as other economical and social necessities and priorities were weighed, and added that the legislator had exclusive competence in this respect. As to what concerns the way of establishing and the extent of compensations, the Court recalled the practice of the European Court of Human Rights'—reasonable compensation established through a reasonable valuation method—and found the domestic system to be in line with international standards.[167] However, it appears at least questionable why the value of an immovable is made function of the increase of the medium wage per economy, instead of the increase of the value of real estate. Moreover, as the medium wage per economy in Romania in 1995 was 110 USD,[168] the 24-month wage cap appears extremely reduced, compared to the market value of buildings.[169]

The 2001 Law "On abusively taken immovable property" presented a larger variety of compensations than the previous two acts. Besides privatization vouchers and money, it also contained the possibility of compensation through "other" goods and services offered by the current possessor or stocks. An even more important novelty is represented by the introduction of the idea of equivalent compensation.[170] The valuation method established by this new norm was also not unequivocal. The value of buildings that were subsequently demolished had to be established according to the rules in force at the time of the destruction, updated with the inflation index at the time of the effective payment.[171] At the same time, the value of plots and of unaltered, but not returnable buildings had to be established according to the current

[167] Decision No. 73, 19 July 1995, *op. cit.*.

[168] Silviu Brucan, "Comunism versus capitalism. O falsa problema," quoting Financial Times and Business Central Europe data, available online, at http://www.dntb.ro/sfera/67/dupa_10_ani.html.

[169] The residential palaces and villas in Bucharest were marketed at 130,000–150,000 USD already in 1992, while the most expensive deal to date was represented by the Cantacuzino Palace sold in 1995 for 1,8 million USD (*Bilanţ*, available online, at www.revistabilant.ro/articole.php?art=37). The difference between these and the 26,400 cap USD (110 USD*240 months, according to 1995 data) is formidable.

[170] Law No. 10/2001, *op. cit.*, Art 1.

[171] *Ibid.*, Art. 10(6).

norms of valuation.[172] To make it more complicated, the value of constructions expropriated with the scope of demolishing was established according to the rules in force at the time of the taking, updated with the inflation index, while the value of plots belonging to these buildings was established according to the current norms.[173]

Those who already received compensation under Law No. 112/1995 were granted the possibility to claim the difference between the updated value of the compensation and the value of the property, but they could receive only vouchers or stocks.[174] Finally, in the case of cash compensation, the law provided for a one-year deadline beginning after the expiry of the six-month period established for the filing of notifications by the entitled persons, for a special law to be passed for regulating the modalities and procedures of payment, as well as the quantity thereof, which could be limited.[175]

A number of problems are raised by this valuation scheme. First, there are no reasonable grounds to use different standards of valuation. Second, it is questionable whether the value at the time of demolishing updated with the inflation index is reasonably related to the current market value of the construction. Third, the meaning of the term "equivalent" is not clear under the conditions that a future law may determine the quantity and the limits of cash compensation. Finally, it is also questionable whether this latter provision may qualify at all as compensation, in the conditions that the form and the extent thereof is left to be established by a future norm. This point was also noted by the Strasbourg court, while stressing that the legislator has failed to come up with the promised regulation as of 2005.[176] In a comparable situation, as it was already mentioned *supra* in this section, the Lithuanian Constitutional Court found a provision conferring on the executive the competence to decide upon the terms and conditions of future payments as breaching the principle of the rule of law (the requirements of clarity, certainty, security, and protection of legitimate

[172] *Ibid.*, Art. 10(7).
[173] *Ibid.*, Art. 11(5)–(6).
[174] *Ibid.*, Art. 19(2).
[175] *Ibid.*, Art. 40.
[176] Strain and Others v. Romania, *op. cit.*, para. 56.

expectations).[177] However, in 2005 an extensive revision of the restitution scheme was undertaken, which also affected the above-discussed provisions of Law No. 10/2001. Consequently, the value of constructions and lands—demolished or not—is assessed according to the relevant international standards, on the basis of its market value at the time when the restitution claim was decided upon.[178]

* * *

This subchapter provided a scrutiny of the valuation theories and methods practiced by the post-communist governments as part of their restitution policies. After questioning the substantive justice of the restitution schemes in the previous chapters, the present chapter departed from a minimalist view of the rule of law ideal, projecting procedural justice as the sole requirement to be met by the transitional rule of law.

On the basis of the above outlined valuation methods, the conclusion which can be drawn is that the analyzed restitution schemes have seriously tested this requirement, and in certain cases did not manage to conform even to the minimalist reading of the rule of law. While formulating the relevant European standards of compensation, the European Court of Human Rights held that non-compensation could be justified only in exceptional circumstances, such as political and economical regime changes,[179] but only if no disproportionate and excessive burden is placed upon the former owners. Further, while recognizing the states' wide margin of appreciation in establishing the amount[180] and form of compensation, the Court consistently held that whenever an individual entitlement to receive compensation exists, the

[177] LiCC, Case No. 19/02, ruling of 23 August 2005.

[178] Law No. 247/2005, *op. cit.*, Title I, Art 1, paras. 21, 22, and 28.

[179] The Court's position upon this particular point is inconsistent: in the Former King of Greece (*supra*) it ruled in favor of the applicant, while in Jahn (*supra*) it decided in favor of the government.

[180] A hint was given in Pincová and Pinc v. The Czech Republic, *op. cit.*, towards what might be the limit of reasonableness, when a compensation amounting to one-fifth of the current market value was found unacceptable.

fair balance standard[181] has to be respected in establishing the value of such compensations.[182]

A summary recapitulation of the shortcomings of the various compensation solutions has to highlight the following. The Polish scheme relied on a reasonable solution for the compensation of repatriates from territories outside the country's postwar boarders: it provided that the value of the lost properties can be offset against the value of properties purchased from state funds or the fee for the perpetual use of such properties. In practice, however, the exercise of this right was made impossible by the existing regulations that prevented the entitled persons from acquiring lands from the state funds. The Strasbourg court, as well as the Polish Constitutional Tribunal, has found this burden placed upon the former owners as excessive, contrary to the principles of "protecting acquired rights and citizens' trust in the State as stemming from the constitutional clause of the rule of law."[183] In the Czech Republic, the legislature did not want to leave a certain category of former owners uncompensated; it merely attempted to replace the previously granted entitlement to their full share of property in collective farms with vouchers or shares. The Constitutional Court reacted by striking down the statute, invoking the principles of legal certainty and protection of vested rights.[184] The Slovakian Constitutional Court, emerging as a negative example, has managed to sustain subsequent alterations of previously established entitlements to compensation—unlike the courts of Poland and the Czech Republic—even in those cases where these changes were disadvantageous to former owners.[185] In Romania and Lithuania, in certain cases, the compensation scheme left undefined the modalities and amounts of the indemnification to be paid, leaving the decision up to a future law, respectively to executive decision. While in Romania this provision was left unchallenged until its abrogation, the

[181] This implies that the compensation has to be reasonably related to the current market value of the expropriated good, established through a reasonable valuation method.

[182] Broniowski v. Poland, ECHR, Application No. 31443/96, Judgment of 22 June 2004.

[183] Broniowski v. Poland, *op. cit.*; K2/04, Judgment of 15 December, 2004, *op. cit.*.

[184] CCC, Pl. US 1/98, Coll. Vol. 12, *op. cit., supra.*

[185] SCC, Pl. US 3/00, 24 April 2001, *op. cit., supra.*

European Court of Human Rights has stated *obiter dicta* that such a provision may not be considered as compensation.[186] On the contrary, the Lithuanian Constitutional Court struck down this solution, arguing the breach of the principle of the rule of law (clarity, certainty, security, and protection of legitimate expectations).[187] In Hungary, the Constitutional Court resorted to the doubtful doctrine of "novation," on the basis of which it placed compensations for all previous past property injustices on the same legal ground.[188] This exercise allowed the state to disregard even those obligations arising from international treaties which provided for compensations in different form and to a different extent than the one envisaged by the compensation legislation.[189]

Further, the modality of valuation itself presents questionable features. The Estonian scheme, although in principle it postulated the "continuity of rights of former owners,"[190] it provided for merely a one-tenth compensation of the lost property's value above a general and equal half hectare returnable plot in high-density areas. In Germany, the constitutional scrutiny of the restitution scheme's valuation technique, which applied a gliding scale (compensations inversely proportionate with the value of the lost property), has produced an evenly split decision in the Federal Constitutional Court. The dissenting judges argued that compensations not reflecting the real value of the property and not reaching at least fifty per cent of this are at odds with the Basic Law.[191]

Finally, the voucher solution, comprised in many compensation schemes, has also demonstrated certain incoherence in practice. Generally, when being translated into shares during the privatization process, or sold on the secondary market, the vouchers did hardly reach their nominal value; thus, the compensation received in practice was regularly lower than the amount calculated at the moment of payment. Second, in a low-capitalized economy, recipients were eager to trans-

[186] Strain and Others v. Romania, *op. cit., supra.*

[187] LiCC, Case No. 19/02, ruling of 23 August 2005, *op. cit., supra.*

[188] HCC, AB 28/1991, 1160/A/1991, *op. cit., supra.*

[189] HCC, AB 16/1993, 1378/E/1990, *op. cit., supra* (on the Paris Peace Treaty); AB 45/2003, 960/B/1995 (on the Hungarian-Czechoslovakian population exchange agreement), *op. cit.*, see: *supra*, in *Justice and Restitution.*

[190] Act of 17 October 1991 (as amended), section 2, para. 1.

[191] BverfG 1 BvR 2307/94, *op. cit., supra.*

form vouchers into cash, which generated a secondary market and ultimately hijacked the compensation-feature of the scheme in favor of the speculators. Therefore, as what concerns voucher and stock compensation, it must be emphasized that these did not ensure a reasonable return (mitigation of the loss experienced), but rather represented merely a theoretical possibility of compensation.[192]

2. Timelines

This subchapter is dedicated to another neuralgic point of the post-communist restitution and compensation schemes, namely the time factor. Here, time is present in the form of deadlines, more precisely the periods within which the entitled persons (former owners or their successors) were enabled to file their claims. Further, the analysis will also consider another equally important aspect: the time taken by the competent organs for solving these claims. The central argument of the inquiry is that in many situations the requirements of fair procedure were breached under the above-explained aspects.

2.1 Deadlines

Fundamental tenets of law provide that all claims must be exercised within given deadlines, which, if passed, result in the loss of the possibility of having the specific right enforced. Absent such a principle, insecurity and unforeseeability—in short, chaos—would reign. Predictability and security in vested rights are thus key elements of the rule of law, and in a functional reading are amongst the most important ones. It is enough here to recall Neumann's opinion, quoted *supra*, according to which it does not matter that life is unfair, as long as it is predictable. It was logical, therefore, for all restitution and compensation schemes—regardless whether they recognized the former owners' rights as perpetuating from a certain moment in the past, or whether they es-

[192] It is nevertheless also true that, theoretically, favorable circumstances could have led to the achievement of a return considerably higher than the nominal value of the vouchers or stocks originally received, albeit in the context of the transition economies such outcome was more likely the lucky exception, than the rule.

tablished a new entitlement—to stipulate a deadline for the exercise of the right to claim. As the restitution programs formed part of the entire process of transition from one—political and economic—system to another, and thus the establishment of a stabile new system was a vital question, the entire resettlement of property relationships was envisaged to take place expeditiously. Consequently, the deadlines for filing the restitution claims had to be construed as fast as possible—in any event, faster than the ordinary statutes of limitations did.

This, by itself, does not represent an insuperable problem: it is enough to recall the European Court of Human Rights position on takings, where the Court fashioned a reasonably generous stance towards the states experiencing extreme situations as regime changes.[193] However, when these deadlines are too short, so short as to hamper the entitled person's chances of respecting it, the time frames become problematic. Moreover, excessively short deadlines may become hard to respect not only for claimants, but also for the authorities, with the negative consequences falling of course again on the claimants, as the following Lithuanian case will show.

According to the relevant provisions of the Lithuanian Law "On the Procedure and Conditions of the Restoration of the Rights of Ownership to the Existing Real Property,"[194] houses and apartments were restorable to their original owners only if the tenants presently occupying them were provided with another dwelling place. Finding and allocating the appropriate alternative accommodation for the tenants was the task of the commissioned state institutions or local governments that had a three-month limit to adopt a decision regarding the restitution claim. (Notably, when no alternative dwelling was to be found for the tenants, the former owner had to accept compensation—money and securities—instead.) These legal provisions were challenged before the Constitutional Court, the petitioners alleging that they were *de facto* deprived of the possibility of recovering their former properties since within the three-month period the relevant bodies were not capable of allocating the tenants the required new homes.[195] The Court agreed

193 Jahn and Others v. Germany, *op. cit.*, *supra*, paras. 111–3.
194 Art. 8(2) and Art. 19, *Official Gazette*, No. 37–929, 1996.
195 Ruling "On restoration of the rights of ownership to dwelling houses," 12 November 1996.

that on the ground of a procedural provision, former owners were deprived from the opportunity of having their property restituted. The three-month deadline was held to be "groundlessly short," and therefore altering the fundamental principle of the law, according to which priority should be given to restitution. The Court also mentioned that by the effects of the challenged norm, in fact the priority of the tenants' interests was established over the former owners' right to retrieve their lost properties.[196]

In the Czech Republic, the question of deadlines came up first in the context of a broader challenge against the Law "On extrajudicial rehabilitation,"[197] directed primarily against the citizenship and the permanent residence requirements already discussed in the previous chapter. The applicants alleged among others that the deadlines provided for filing "the call to issue a thing," and for raising the claim before a court became *ex lege*, as interpreted respectively, preclusive in the sense that former owners living outside the country were practically barred from participating in the restitution program.[198] Essentially, the provisions in question required that the conditions of citizenship and permanent residence be met *ex lege* at the time of filing "the call to issue a thing," respectively, according to the interpretation of the courts, on the date when the Law "On extrajudicial rehabilitation" entered into force. The Court went on to quash the provisions requiring permanent residence in the territory of the country, and also the words "from the day this act goes into effect" from the article establishing the deadlines.[199]

The latter was necessary, as the Court explained, because the simple quashing of the above-mentioned requirements alone would not have helped the cause of those living outside Czech territory in any way, as the deadlines were long passed. As to what concerns the time limits themselves, the Court went on acknowledging that the "quite unrealistic" deadlines made it impossible for the persons described above to pursue their rights. Tying these temporal barriers to the entry

---

196 *Ibid.*, part III–IV.

197 Law No. 87/1991, 21 February 1991, Coll. of Laws.

198 CCC, Pl. US 3/94, Judgment of 1 November 1994, part I, section 2.

199 Law No. 87/1991, *op. cit.*, Art. 5, paras. 2 and 4. The respective deadlines were six months for filing the call to issue a thing, and one year for bringing the claim to a court.

into force of the act discriminated against those residing outside the country's borders who might have not or could not learn in time about the situation, and therefore were barred from exercising their claims. This solution was held to be in conflict with the relevant constitutional provisions, the Charter of Fundamental Rights and Freedoms and with the European Convention for Protection of Human Rights and Fundamental Freedoms. However, the Court did not cancel the challenged norms, as on the one hand it was not petitioned to do so, while on the other hand such a cancellation "would deprive both provisions of any material meaning." Instead, it went on holding that the two deadlines should be tied to the enforceability of the Constitutional Court's decision itself. The argument was that this solution sufficiently protected the equal rights of citizens, as even former owners living abroad, it must be presumed, with the passing of time up to the date of the judgment, became adequately informed.[200]

Disputes relating to the deadlines for filing claims of restitution came again, in a different context. The applicant challenged lower courts' decisions, which rejected her restitution claim regarding numerous works of art to be found at two cultural institutions.[201] The applicant's original claim was refused by the respective institutions on the ground that she failed to adequately specify and describe the requested items within the legally established period.[202] The subsequent court decisions also came up with similar arguments. The applicant argued that the interpretation, according to which the claimant had to fulfill the obligation of producing such evidence in relation to the claimed items under the sanction that the claim would otherwise be extinguished, was against the sense and purpose of the respective provision.[203] The Constitutional Court stated that it gave preference to a substantive interpretation of the rule of law, and accordingly could not accept a "too formalistic" reading of the restitution laws. Facing two "equally valid" interpretations, the Court expressed the need for a teleological approach, according to which, taking into consideration the fundamental purpose of the restitution scheme (redress of injus-

200 CCC, Pl. US 3/94, *op. cit.*, part IV.

201 CCC, Pl. US 38/02, Judgment of 24 March 2004.

202 Law "On extrajudicial rehabilitation," *op. cit.*, Art. 5(1).

203 *Ibid.*, part I, para. 5.

tices), the consequences of the past takings could not be interpreted to the detriment of the former owners. Accordingly, if the applicant did not have adequate possibilities to access the various state institutions' archives for gathering the required evidence, then having been obliged to do the impossible, a violation of the principles of fair procedure existed. However, at the same time, the Court considered that it was not convincingly demonstrated that the applicant was indeed unable to specify the necessary details within the given deadline. Still, invoking the principle of minimization of intrusion into the jurisdiction of the ordinary courts, the Constitutional Court satisfied itself to annul only the appellate court's decision because it refused to investigate the other objections and grounds of appeal, finding a breach of fair procedure without having to concern itself with the length of the filing period.[204]

The Romanian restitution program included various deadlines that were usually subsequently prolonged, as they turned out to be impossibly short. Illustrative in this sense were the terms set out by Law No. 18 of 1991, which provided initially a thirty-day period after its entry into force for filing claims related to agricultural lands (and ninety days from its publication for solving the claim).[205] Beyond this unreasonably short deadline, entitled persons were obliged to file their claims with the mayor's office of those settlements where the vindicated plots laid. This deadline resisted about one month, when the first amendment to the law extended it by fifteen days.[206] The second term—pertaining to the establishment of property titles—resisted a bit more, and was extended only the next year by sixty days.[207] In 1997, a new amendment extended the deadline for filing the claim by ninety days.[208] On the second part, however, the government proved to be more prudent, and it merely provided deadlines for the authorities to compile situations with

---

[204] *Ibid.*, part II.

[205] Law No. 18 /1991, published in the *Official Gazette*, No. 37, 20 February 1991, Art. 10, paras. 3–4 (in this case the law entered into force on the date of its publication).

[206] Law No. 29/1991, published in the *Official Gazette*, No. 59, 22 March 1991, single article (prolonging the deadline for filing the claim).

[207] Governmental Order No. 728 of 1992, published in the *Official Gazette*, No. 309, 27 November 1992, Art. 1.

[208] Law No. 169/1997, published in the *Official Gazette*, No. 299, 4 October 1997, Art. 1, para. 3.

the claims, leaving it up to a future law to solve the question of the actual restitution.[209] Only one year later, the law was amended again, but the time limits set by the 1997 law remained untouched.[210] Unsurprisingly, this deadline did not hold out much longer, being extended through an emergency ordinance to one hundred and fifty days.[211] The term was modified again in the same year, when the law for the approval of the ordinance provided that claims had to be filed with the competent authorities no later than 31 December 1998.[212] As these later amendments left untouched the deadlines for the authorities, logically, the next amendment provided for their extension. In the fall of 1999, the deadlines for finalizing the restitution process initiated by Law No. 18 of 1991 were extended until 31 December 2000.[213] In 2001, a new bill was passed for the restitution of agricultural lands and forestry, according to Law No. 18 of 1991. It offered a new deadline for filing the claims—sixty days—and provided a one-year term from the entry into force of the law for issuing the property titles.[214] The latter term was again extended until 31 December 2001, as the authorities were still unable to cope with it.[215]

The most controversial deadline provided for in the Romanian restitution scheme, however, was related neither to the filing of the claims, nor to the length of the subsequent procedure. It was a special deadline for filing claims for annulment of certain transactions, which concerned former religious properties and which were concluded in breach of the

---

209 *Ibid.*.

210 Law No. 18/1991, republished in the *Official Gazette*, No. 1, 5 January 1998, Art. 9(3).

211 Governmental Emergency Ordinancc No. 1 of 1998, published in the *Official Gazette*, No. 26, 26 January 1998, sole article, para. 1. The provisions pertaining to the authorities' obligation to compile and forward situations was kept unaltered (except that the mayor's deadline now started after the expiry of the 150-day limit).

212 Law No. 218/1998, published in the *Official Gazette*, No. 453, 26 November 1998, sole article. The deadlines for the authorities were kept, again, unaltered and started to run from 31 December 1998.

213 Governmental Emergency Ordinance No. 168/1999, published in the *Official Gazette*, No. 536, 3 November 1999, Article 1.

214 Law No. 1/2000, *op. cit.*, Art. 33 and 12(7).

215 Governmental Ordinance No. 69 of 2000, published in the *Official Gazette*, No. 407, 29 August 2000, Art. 4.

norms in force at that time.[216] This provision was challenged in numerous constitutional complaints, but the Constitutional Court rejected every application, arguing that this solution breaches neither the right to property, nor the right to equality. Adopting a positivist attitude, the Court laconically stated that in special cases the legislator might establish special procedural rules, and that the constitutional requirement of establishing rules of procedure through law has also been respected.[217]

2.2 Length of procedure

The European Convention of Human Rights, in its article dedicated to the right to fair trial, establishes, among other guarantees, the entitlement to have one's case heard within a "reasonable time."[218] This provision, also known as the celerity requirement, represents the source of the majority of the Court's judgments in recent years.[219] However, in order to discuss this problem in a restitution context, two preliminary questions have to be answered: first, whether Article 6 of the Convention may find application in restitution proceedings; and second, what the term "procedure" covers.

As to the first question, authors note that the Court's case law is far from being unequivocal in defining the content of the notion "civil rights and obligations." On the one hand, it is obvious that it covers ordinary civil litigation, but the relationship which is of interest to the present analysis is the one between individuals and the state, and concerns the expeditious solving of the specific claims. The Court has yet elaborated a universal criterion, comparable to the one established in Engel for describing a "criminal offence," preferring to decide on a case-

[216] Governmental Emergency Ordinance No. 184, 12 December 2002, published in the *Official Gazette*, No. 929, 18 December 2002, Art. 6, para. 4 established, derogating from *lex generalis*, a six-month term for filing these claims, from the entry into force of the Ordinance.

[217] RCC, Decision No. 542, 7 December 2004, published in the *Official Gazette*, No. 62, 18 January 2005.

[218] Article 6(1).

[219] Clare Ovey and Robin White, *Jacobs and White: The European Convention on Human Rights*, Oxford University Press, 2002, 3rd ed., p. 167 note that approximately one-third of the Court's judgments in 2000 were related to complaints about the unreasonable length of domestic procedures.

by-case basis.[220] Since the Ringeisen case, the Court has been elaborating an increasingly liberal interpretation of the notion of "civil rights and obligations."[221] In deciding whether a case falls under the coverage of this notion or not, the Court looks to the nature of the asserted right, and if its personal and economic nature outweighs the other public law characteristics, Article 6(1) may be found as applicable.[222] It appears that the limit set by the assertability of the right, that is, if it is dependent on governmental discretion, it falls outside the scope of Article 6.[223] As a conclusion, it can be safely argued that applications complaining about the length of the restitution procedures may, in theory, be considered as being covered by Article 6(1) provisions.

As to the second question, it was usually held that the civil procedure starts on the date on which proceedings are initiated (a summons or writ are issued).[224] However, it was also held that the period in question may start even earlier than this, if before the judicial procedure and administrative one had to be undertaken.[225] The end of the procedure is fortunately more easily determined: it coincides with the end of the enforcement proceedings.[226] Still, whether a breach of the celerity requirement is found or not depends usually on the circumstances of the

---

[220] *Ibid.*, p. 145.

[221] Ringeisen v. Austria, ECHR, Application No. 2614/65, Judgment of 16 July 1971, held that the notion covers all proceedings that result in a decision decisive for private rights and obligations, even if one of the parties is not a private person. Similar views were voiced in König v. Germany, Judgment of 28 June 1978; Pudas v. Sweden, Judgment of 27 October 1987; Sporrong and Lönroth v. Sweden, Judgment of 23 September 1982; McMichael v. United Kingdom, Judgment of 24 February 1995, etc.

[222] Feldbrugge v. Netherlands, Application No. 8562/79, Judgment of 29 May 1986: a claim for sickness benefit was considered as falling under Article 6 protection.

[223] Salesi v. Italy, Application No. 13023/87, Judgment of 23 February 1993. Generally claims relating to disability allowance, pension, and salary were found as being covered by Article 6, while in cases where the applicant questioned the authorities' discretionary powers, it was deemed to fall outside the Convention's protection (Ovey and White, *op. cit.*, p. 149).

[224] Ovey and White, *op. cit.*, p. 166.

[225] Pretto and Others v. Italy, Application No. 7984/77, Judgment of 8 December 1998; Sutter v. Switzerland, Application No. 8209/78, Judgment of 22 February 1984.

[226] Ovey and White, *op. cit.*, p. 167.

individual case and the examination of the grounds of the alleged delays, rather than the number of years passed between the start and the end dates of the proceedings.[227] As the cases from the local courts in the countries in focus demonstrate, the domestic constitutions and courts have given a more generous interpretation to the notion of celerity.

The Estonian Supreme Court was petitioned to decide upon the constitutionality of a provision of the Principles of Ownership Reform Act,[228] which provided that applications for return of properties to former owners who left Estonia (within the framework of a population exchange agreement with Germany) would be dealt with through an international agreement.[229] The Court found an infringement of Article 14 of the Constitution, which provides a fundamental right to "organization and procedure." The infringement was identified in the fact that up to the date of the decision, the act in question was not amended so as to conform to the new situation because no international agreement had been entered into, and there was no prospect of concluding it in the future either. Moreover, it was also held that this failure to amend the law amounted to a breach of Article 13(2) of the Constitution, which prohibits the arbitrary exercise of state power. This prohibition was interpreted as giving rise to the principle of legal clarity, which was described through the Strasbourg court's words in Sunday Times v. United Kingdom.[230] While former owners were kept in suspense about their possibility of retrieving the lost properties, their current users were also insecure about the length of their possession and their eventual chance of privatizing the respective dwellings. Legal ambiguity exists, argued the Court, also when some are given the hope of restitution or compensation, and others' prospect to privatize the property in their use is retained for an indeterminate time.[231] Still, through

[227] Győző Szabó and Gábor Nagy (eds.), *Tanulmányok az Emberi Jogok Európai Egyezménye legfontosabb rendelkezéseihez kapcsolódó strasbourgi esetjogról*, HVG-Orac, 1999, p. 115. Also: Jasiūnienė v. Lithuania, *op. cit.*, para. 27.

[228] Principle of Ownership Reform Act of 1991, consolidated text published in the *State Gazette*, RT I 1997, 27, 391, Art. 7(3).

[229] ESC, Case No. 3-4-1-5-02, Decision of 28 October 2002.

[230] Sunday Times v. United Kingdom, ECHR, Judgment of 27 October 1978: a citizen must be able to foresee to a degree that is reasonable in the circumstances, the consequences a given action may entail.

[231] ESC, Case no. 3-4-1-5-02, *op. cit.*, paras. 30, 31, and 35.

an extremely interesting solution, the Court refrained from invalidating the challenged provision, arguing that it has no competence to make such political decisions. Instead, it "obligated" the legislator to bring the said provision in conformity with the principle of legal clarity.[232]

In Lithuania, the Supreme Court has found that the failure of the authorities to adopt a decision upon the applicant's well documented request to restore his property rights within the statutory period[233]—and for nine years since—amounted to a violation of the applicant's right to effective remedy. Interestingly, the Court argued that mere further litigation would breach the European Convention's Article 6 rights; therefore, it ordered the relevant regional administrative bodies to restore the former property rights to the applicant.[234] After that date, the applicant got back a large part of the vindicated lands, and was repeatedly offered compensations for the remainder. An application was filed in the meantime also with the Strasbourg court, alleging violation of Article 6(1) and Protocol I, Article 1. However, the Strasbourg court found no violation of the celerity principle (as a matter of fact, neither the right to property), arguing that the delays in the execution of the Supreme Court's judgment were imputable to the applicants, who neglected the authorities' efforts to finalize the formalities.[235] The Court also noted that the authorities were not required to carry out a one-off action, but an entire process, which required the participation of the applicants themselves.[236] Although it would have been interesting to learn the Court's opinion on the initial delay of nine years elapsing between the filing of the restitution claim with the relevant authorities and the quoted decision of the Supreme Court, the application was filed only after the Supreme Court's decision, and complained only about the failure to execute this judgment.

---

[232] *Ibid.*, para. 37 The dissenting opinion held that the challenged article should have been invalidated, to create a financial obligation for the state, but its entry into force should have been postponed for one year, with regard to the approaching general elections.

[233] Three months from 25 September 1991 (date of the claim's submission).

[234] Supreme Court of Lithuania (hereinafter LiSC), Judgment of 22 May 2000; quoted by the European Court of Human Rights in Užukrėlienė and Others v. Lithuania, *op. cit.*, paras. 17–8.

[235] Užukrėlienė and Others v. Lithuania, *op. cit.*, paras. 28–36.

[236] *Ibid.*, para. 35.

In another case filed on the same grounds against Lithuania, however, the Strasbourg court decided for the applicants. Here, the relevant administrative body issued in time the decision upon the restitution of the claimed property rights without specifying its form, but the decision was never implemented. After taking the case to the courts of law, the applicant eventually secured a favorable judgment on appeal, which obligated the administrative organs to adopt within a specific deadline a decision on the restitution request. But this decision was not executed either, as the applicant refused to accept the alternative lands offered as compensation. Concomitantly, the authorities' option for compensation was motivated by the fact that the applicant failed to submit the relevant documentation for the proof of ownership (which was required by a 1998 governmental instruction); thus, they could not proceed with the decision until these instruments were not presented. The Strasbourg court still found a breach of Article 6(1), arguing that while until 2 June 1999 the applicant's refusal to accept the offered compensation represented an acceptable defense for the government, after that date—when the amendments to Article 18 of the Restitution of Property Act entered into force—the applicant's agreement was not needed anymore. The government's arguments challenging the merit of the property claim, by referring to certain obligations which postdate the ruling in question, were considered only to aggravate the non-execution of the judgment.[237]

Somewhat resembling the above-presented Estonian case, the Hungarian Constitutional Court was also confronted with petitions complaining about failures to afford compensations for certain categories of claimants. However, unlike in the Estonian example, where the target of the challenge was an un-honored domestic commitment to conclude an international agreement, in Hungary the failure to implement international agreements by domestic means was scrutinized. Here, the 1947 Paris Peace Treaty in its Article 27(2) provided for the handing over of heirless properties—of those persecuted under the Nazi regime—to domestic organizations representing such persons. But similar provisions were contained also by previous, still enforceable domestic legislation.[238] Also distinctly from the Estonian case, where

[237] Jasiūnienė v. Lithuania, *op. cit.*, paras. 8–31.
[238] Law No. XXV of 1946.

the application was alleging a breach of the constitutionally protected right to fair procedure, in Hungary the challenge was directed against the constitutionality of the compensation laws' provisions that did not include those covered by the Peace Treaty within the pool of beneficiaries. Still, the Court found it necessary to investigate *ex officio* the question of compatibility with the international agreements.[239] The Constitutional Court found that no normative measures had been taken for the execution of the obligations contained by the above-mentioned article of the Peace Treaty, nor for the provisions of the previous domestic law providing similar solutions. Interestingly, especially in the light of the above-presented Estonian decision, the Hungarian Court confined itself to finding a breach of the constitutional obligation to ensure the compliance of domestic legislation with the state's international engagements.[240] It did not bother to speak about the principle of legal clarity and about the law's ability to guide human conduct. It merely mentioned that an unconstitutional situation had been created due to the partially legislative, partially executive omission to implement the Peace Treaty's relevant provisions, and called upon the Parliament to adopt the necessary measures within a certain deadline.

In spite of the above decision, the provisions of the Peace Treaty stubbornly came back to the center of attention, as non-compliance with another of its article was brought before the Court.[241] This time, the application complained about the failure to compensate those citizens whose properties found on the Allied powers' territory were confiscated on the basis of the Peace Treaty.[242] The Peace Treaty, besides providing for the possibility of confiscation, also contained a provision on Hungary's obligation to afford relief to these citizens.[243] Just like in its previous decision, the Constitutional Court held that this omission to afford compensation amounted to a breach of Article 7 of the Constitution, and called upon the Parliament to adopt the necessary measures by a specific deadline. Again, the complaint alleged an un-

[239] HCC, AB 16/1993, 1378/E/1990, part IV, published in the *Official Gazette*, No. 29, 1993.

[240] Constitution of Hungary, para. 7(1).

[241] HCC, AB 37/1996, 837/E/1995, published in the *Official Gazette*, No. 75, 1996.

[242] Paris Peace Treaty of 1947, Art. 29(1).

[243] *Ibid.*, Art. 29(3).

constitutional situation manifested in the omission to implement the international agreements' provisions, and similarly, the Court did not address the issue of fair procedure.

The latest decision finding an unconstitutional omission was issued in 2003, when the Court held that the failure to afford compensations to the citizens repatriated from former Czechoslovakia, as provided on the bilateral agreement of the two states, is in breach with Article 7 of the fundamental law.[244] The bilateral agreement on the exchange of population provided that compensations above a certain ceiling would be afforded by the receiving state, and this obligation was restated and specified in more detail by a subsequent minute, even though their provisions have never been put into practice.[245] Consequently, faithful to its previous case law, the Court found a breach of the constitutional obligation to ensure the compliance of domestic legislation with the state's international engagements, and set a deadline for the Parliament to take action.

Lastly, it has to be mentioned that a relatively large number of decisions have been recently passed by the European Court of Human Rights, finding Croatia in breach of Article 6 provisions. These applications, resembling to a certain extent the above-presented, complained about the government's failure to enact necessary legislation that would allow for the compensation of wartime property damages. Accordingly, in 1996 the Croatian Parliament amended the Civil Obligations Act, which up until then presented the legal basis for such claims, providing that all proceedings resulting from wartime damages ("terrorist acts") would remain untouched until an appropriate special norm was to be enacted, setting a six-month deadline for this. This of course also meant that no new claims could have been filed, either. The promised norm was only enacted as late as 2003, but it nevertheless provided for the resuming of the halted proceedings.[246] The Croatian Constitu-

[244] HCC, AB 45/2003, 960/B/1995, published in the *Official Gazette*, No. 111, 2003.

[245] Law No. XV of 1946, "On the bilateral agreement upon population exchange between Hungary and Czechoslovakia"; Minute of 1964, published in the "Joint communication of the Hungarian Ministry of Foreign Affairs and the Ministry of Finances," No. 8004/1991.

[246] Mihajlović v. Croatia, ECHR, Application No. 21752/02, Judgment of 7 July 2005, paras. 6–11.

tional Court begun to deal with complaints against this impossibility of obtaining compensation only after the promised act had finally been enacted. Nevertheless, it managed, much like the other constitutional forums cited in this section, to find a breach of the constitutional requirement of trial within a reasonable time and also of the access to court.[247]

The Strasbourg court, on its behalf, has emphasized the Article 6 violation not as much due to the length of the proceeding, but as to the access to court provision, arguing that the former is absorbed by the latter. The Court relied on the length of the period during which the applicants were unable to have their right to compensation determined, arguing that even if the state enjoyed a certain margin of appreciation while enacting necessary regulations in cases where it had to deal with a large number of significant pecuniary claims, Article 6 provisions still were to be observed.[248]

Alas, the European Court of Human Rights gave unfortunate signs of inconsistency as what regards the Croatian apartment cases. In a revolting unanimous first section decision, the Court upheld the domestic courts' rulings[249] upon the application of the Housing Act to the claimant.[250] In fact, the applicant enjoyed a specially protected tenancy of a flat in the town of Zadar, which was terminated by the local court due to the applicant's allegedly unjustified absence from her home for a period of time that exceeded the statutory six months.[251] The domestic

[247] Croatian Constitutional Court (hereinafter CrCC), Decision No. U-III-829/2004, 24 March 2004; quoted in Mihajlović v. Croatia, *op. cit.*, para. 21.

[248] Kutić v. Croatia, Application No. 48778/99, Judgment of 1 March 2002; Acimović v. Croatia, Application No. 61237/00, Judgment of 9 October 2003; Crnojević v. Croatia, Application No. 71614/01, Judgment of 21 October 2004; Friemann v. Croatia, Application No. 5266/02, Judgment of 24 June 2004; Dragović v. Croatia, Application No. 5705/02, Judgment of 28 October 2004; Mihajlović v. Croatia, *op.cit.*, etc. It has to be noted that in many cases the case was struck out of the list, as the parties managed to reach an agreement upon the amount of compensation to be paid by the government.

[249] Zadar Municipal, Supreme, and Constitutional Court decisions all decided against the applicant.

[250] Blečić v. Croatia, ECHR, Application No. 59532/00, Judgment of 29 July 2004; referred to the Grand Chamber, pending decision.

[251] *Ibid.*, paras. 7–26.

courts rejected all the reasons given by the applicant for her failure to return (old age and illness, the escalation of armed conflict and shelling of the town, loss of pension and medical insurance, illegal occupation of the apartment by third persons). The Strasbourg court on its behalf demonstrated an inexplicable deference towards Croatian authorities, and spoke about the margin of appreciation they enjoy in balancing competing social interests.[252] Consequently, it was unable to find violations of Article 8 or of Protocol I, Article 1.

3. Proving the entitlement

Providing evidence for the long-lost title is one of the crucial problems of all restitution schemes. On the one hand, critics of restitution policies stress the difficulty of producing convincing evidence, while on the other hand, the unreasonably short deadlines or the complexity of the required evidence are sometimes the factors that make the burden of proof too heavy to handle.

In a post-colonial context, the question of proof represented a more dramatic question, as the period of time between the takings and the restitution efforts was a lot longer than in the case of post-communist transition. In the United States, Indian claimants before the Commission[253] and the Court of Claims[254] had to produce proof of actual Indian possession before the governmental taking occurred, proof of the dispossession, and finally, proof of the government's responsibility. As the only available redress was monetary compensation, and in many cases the issue was to recoup the difference between the ridiculous prices paid upon the taking and the present value of the land, a lot of wrestling took place to establish the fair market value and the even-

[252] *Ibid.*, paras. 63–71.

[253] Indian Claims Commission Act of 1946.

[254] The Claims Commission was dissolved in 1978 to be replaced by the Court of Claims, which at its turn, was reorganized after five years of activity, in 1982, when the merger of the Court of Claims and the Court of Patent and Customs Appeals resulted in the new Claims Court as part of the Federal Circuit. See also: Nell Jessup Newton, "Indian Claims in the Courts of the Conqueror," *American University Law Review* 41 (1992).

tual interest on "ancient claims."[255] The difficulty to produce evidence is illustrated also by the painfully long time these claims may take to go through the system: for instance, the Gila River Pima Maricopa's claim,[256] filed in 1951, was awarded a final judgment only in 1985. In Australia, the test of continuous traditional connection and usage of the particular land[257] had to be satisfied for obtaining recognition of the native title, but the test turned out to be extremely demanding in practice, as only less than 10% of the Aborigine population became eligible for restitution.[258] Interestingly, the U.N. Draft Declaration on the Rights of Indigenous Peoples contemplated a roughly similar standard of proof, stating that indigenous peoples should have the right to restitution of those lands "which they have traditionally owned or otherwise occupied or used, and which have been confiscated."[259]

A completely different problem arose in a Holocaust-restitution context, where the lack of death certificates for those perished in death camps complicated the fate of their properties. In Norway, for instance, these persons (roughly over 700) were classified as "missing," and their assets were transferred to the public guardian's office, and subsequently to the probate and bankruptcy court. As long as the procedures lasted, mortgage debt, inheritance, and other taxes in connection with administration were charged to the estates, which eventually were almost equivalent to the total payments made to the Jewish

[255] In Sioux Nation of Indians v. United States (448 U.S. 371 (1980)), the Supreme Court clarified the question of interest, considering that a good faith, but incompetent effort to pay the tribe does not amount to a taking, but to a mere breach of trust, for which no interest is owed. In the actual case, the Court found that a "sign the treaty or starve" approach was not the act of a guardian, but of a sovereign. See also: Newton, *op. cit.*, pp. 822–3.

[256] Unpublished opinion; quoted by Newton, *op. cit.*, p. 825.

[257] It does not need to amount to possession as known to common law, neither does it require the exploitation of the lands in question. The question of whether this relationship must be a physical one is giving rise to contradictory positions—in this sense, see: Coe v. Commonwealth (1993) 118 ALR 193 and Mason v. Triton (1994) 34 NSWLR 572, both referred to by Anthony Moore, in Johnston, Hinton, and Rigney (eds.), *op. cit.*, p. 141.

[258] Elazar Barkan, *The Guilt of Nations: Restitution and Negotiating Historical Injustices*, Norton 2000, p. 244.

[259] U.N. Draft Declaration on the Rights of Indigenous Peoples, 1994/45, Art. 27, available online, at http://www.unhchr.ch/huridocda/huridoca.nsf/(Symbol)/E.CN.4.SUB.2.RES.1994.45.En?OpenDocument.

groups.[260] In the Netherlands, this problem was dealt with through the Death Certificate Act.[261] In Great Britain, the Trading with the Enemy Act of 1939 seized all "enemy" assets to be found in Britain (this was especially under the form of bank accounts). The funds were used primarily to compensate those British creditors who were left unpaid by their foreign (enemy) partners after the outbreak of the war, and to a smaller extent, to compensate the victims, in the framework of subsequently concluded Money and Paper Agreements. (For instance, in the case of Hungary, Romania, and Bulgaria, creditors were paid approximately 8 million GBP, while victims received around 1.5 million.) For the victims, a six-month deadline was given to apply for—*ex gratia*—payments (commentators note that funds were not enough even to satisfy the creditors), which was later extended until 1956 for victims of German citizenship, and to 1957 for victims from Hungary, Romania, and Bulgaria. Applicants had to demonstrate that they had been deprived of their liberty (inmates of labor camps qualified only if conditions in the camp were known as extremely harsh), they had left enemy territory, did not act against the Allies, and did not enjoy full rights of citizenship.[262]

Probation-related problems arising in a post-communist context were significantly different from those that can be met in the cases discussed above. Specifically, the restitution claim had to be accompanied by a varying number of documents that mostly had to be obtained from certain state institutions, and, taking into consideration the shortness of the deadlines discussed above, this considerably hindered the applicants' chances of success.

In the case of Lithuania, besides the common practice of repeatedly extending the impossibly short initial deadlines, the difficulties in obtaining the necessary documents allegedly resulted in another peculiar outcome. In the initial phase of the program, decisions were frequently passed without specifying the manner of restitution or compensation, and without acquainting the tenants of restituted homes with their legal rights to alternative housing.[263] To this, as it will result from the follow-

---

260 Beker (ed.), *op. cit.*, pp. 233–4.
261 *Ibid.*, pp. 291–9.
262 *Ibid.*, pp. 212–6.
263 LiCC, Ruling of 15 July 1994.

ing case, it can be added that in certain cases decisions were passed in absence of the required proof of the original title. Attempting to correct this situation, the government passed a resolution directing the relevant authorities to reconsider their previous decisions according to the applicable norms in force at the time of their adoption.[264] The Constitutional Court, in a decision that was already quoted and commented in the previous subchapter, quashed this provision, arguing that once the decision on restitution or compensation was adopted, the beneficiaries were "entitled to the rights of ownership." Therefore, reconsidering this decision is equal to changing the content of ownership rights against their holders' will.[265]

From the fact pattern of the case of Jasiūnienė v. Lithuania,[266] which was also cited several times above, it can be seen that the authorities in charge of deciding upon restitution claims ruled in favor of the applicant, in spite of the fact that the applicant, as the heir of the original owner, did not produce the relevant documentation proving the former owner's right to the plot in question.[267] According to the rules in force at the time, applicants had to sustain their claims with documents confirming ownership (excerpts from mortgage records, contracts on the transfer of property, court decisions, acts on the nationalization of property, or certificates issued by the state archives).[268] Further, they had to submit a document attesting the type, dimensions, and location of the property, the indication of the present manager of the property, and the time and means of their loss.[269] Interestingly, in spite of the—allegedly—incomplete application, the administrative decision was also held up by the courts (in 1996), which merely reprimanded the local authorities for failing to indicate the concrete means of indemnification (restitution or compensation).[270] The series

264 Resolution "On partial amendment to the Government of the Republic of Lithuania Resolution No. 470 (On the implementation of the restitution law)," 17 May 1993, *Official Gazette*, No. 17-440, 1993.

265 Ruling of 15 July, *op. cit.*.

266 ECHR, Application No. 41510/98, Judgment of 6 March 2003.

267 *Ibid.*, para. 19.

268 Law "On the procedures and conditions for the restoration of citizens' rights to the ownership of existent property," 15 November 1991, Art. 9.

269 *Ibid.*, Art. 10 and 11.

270 Jasiūnienė v. Lithuania, *op. cit.*, para. 14.

of strange decisions and instructions in this case did not, however, stop here. In 1998, an official from the Ministry of Agriculture and Forestry asked the local authorities to re-examine the lawfulness of the initial (1992) restitution decision, while the above-quoted 1994 Constitutional Court decision held the re-examination of restitution as being unconstitutional. In spite of this, the local authorities continued to make compensation offers (in form of alternative plots) for one more year, until finally bringing the proceedings to a halt, for lack of evidence as to the ownership of the claimed land. Inexplicably, the administrative decision referred to a 1998 governmental instruction.[271] The Strasbourg court found a violation of Article 6(1), for the failure to execute a final court judgment, considering the invocation of the 1998 governmental instruction (post-dating the court decision) as an aggravation of the breach.[272]

In Poland, the act on the offsetting of the value of property abandoned beyond the Bug River[273] provided that claims had to be filed with the governor of the relevant province, who could confirm the right to credit by way of an administrative decision.[274] The application had to be accompanied by an official description of the property or a compensation certificate issued by the National Repatriation Office, or other, unspecified official documents, including court documents. In the absence of these, the claim might also be based on documents dating before 1 September 1939 (extracts from land and mortgage registers, notary deeds, and court decisions). Interestingly, the law provided also for the admissibility of testimonial evidence, of at least three persons of full age at the moment of the conclusion of agreements with the Soviet Republics, who were not close relatives of applicants and who resided in the settlement where the abandoned property was located.[275] This

[271] *Ibid.*, paras. 19–21.

[272] *Ibid.*, paras. 27–30.

[273] Offsetting the Value of Property Abandoned Beyond the Present Borders of the Polish State Against the Price of State Property or the Fee for the Right of Perpetual Usufruct Act, 12 December 2003.

[274] *Ibid.*, sections 4 and 5.

[275] *Ibid.*, section 5. See also: "The procedures of implementing entitlements to compensation for Bug River property," 24 February 2005, available on the webpage of the Polish Ministry of the Treasury, at http://www.msp.gov.pl/index_eng.php?dzial=34&id=118&poz=6.

particular provision—along with many others—came under challenge before the Constitutional Tribunal in 2004.[276] Applicants complained of the fact that the law excluded the possibility of relying on the testimony of witnesses who were minors at the time of the conclusion of the Republican Agreements.[277] The claimants pointed out that the employment of the evidence was practically unworkable, as the majority of the potential witnesses did not live anymore. Further, as the administrative decision was only issued to confirm the existence of the entitlement, such evidentiary limitations could strip in practice the concerned persons from the possibility of obtaining compensation, contradicting the principle of protecting acquired rights. The Tribunal agreed to this challenge, and found that that this restriction was unjustified in the light of the principle of the rule of law.[278]

In Czechoslovakia, several restitution-related laws established the various documents required for proving the entitlement to restitution. The Law "On the mitigation of the consequences of certain property losses"[279] required the submission of a document from the District National Committee within whose territory the property was located, confirming the expropriation of the item. In absence of this, a document from a ministry confirming nationalization or a decision from the same place concerning nationalization, or an excerpt from a land register or any other "credible" document which stated the legal grounds for the expropriation and the name of the persons from whom the property was taken. But if some compensation was paid, documents had to be presented—either from a District National Committee or the Ministry of Finance, the organization which paid it, or the competent office for property and convertible currency affairs. If the claimant was residing abroad, he additionally had to obtain a document from the latter office certifying that the claimed property was not disposed of through interstate agreements. The same norm also provided that in case of movables, proof had to be produced as to their location at the entry

[276] PCT, K 2/04, Judgment of 15 December 2004, *op. cit.*.

[277] Offsetting the Value of Property... Act, *op. cit.*, section 5(2), point 2, letter (a).

[278] PCT, K 2/04, Judgment of 15 December 2004, *op. cit.*, part III, section 14.

[279] Law "On the mitigation of the consequences of certain property injustices," *op. cit.*, Art. 6.

into force of the law.[280] Another norm, the Law "On extra-judicial rehabilitation," established that proof had to be produced as to how the property in question came into state ownership, and if it was movable, its current place had to be indicated, too.[281]

Surprisingly, the requirements that turned out to be more contested were the ones regarding the restitution of movables. As the same provisions have been challenged in both successor states, a comparison of the two decisions might prove extremely interesting. In the Czech case, the heir of a former owner filed a restitution claim regarding a number of artworks (paintings), furniture, and other valuables located in various castles falling under the administration of several institutes of monuments and museums.[282] In the Slovakian case, the applicant filed for the return of a number of gold and silver coins of numismatic value, confiscated from his father and presumably held by the one of the Public Security Regional Administration offices.[283] In the Czech case, the petitioned institutions turned down the request, on the ground that the claimed items were not sufficiently clearly designated. Both the first instance and the appellate courts later upheld this view, repeating that the claimant failed to fulfill this legal requirement in the required period.[284] In Slovakia, the claim was filed with a district court, which decided in the favor of the applicant, emphasizing that he had no possibility of inspecting the premises of the former Public Security Regional Administration, while the Ministry of Interior did not show any evidence upon the eventual transfer of the claimed items to a different authority. On appeal, however, this decision was overturned under the argument that the applicant failed to show where the coins had been deposited when the relevant restitution norm entered into force. The regional court even undertook some summary investigations on its own initiative, but it did not manage to establish the whereabouts of the confiscated coins. This

[280] *Ibid.*, Art. 13.

[281] Law "On extra-judicial rehabilitation," 1991, No. 87/1991 Coll., Art. 5.

[282] CCC, Pl. US 38/02, Judgment of 24 March 2004, quoted also *supra*.

[283] Kopecký v. Slovakia, ECHR, Application No. 44912/98, Judgment of 28 September 2004, quoted also *supra*.

[284] Pl. US 38/02, *op. cit.*, part I, paras. 1–6.

decision was later upheld also by the Supreme Court essentially under the same argument.[285]

The Czech Constitutional Court, when petitioned to decide upon the lower courts' rulings, stated that it cannot abstract from the fact that a totalitarian state took these properties and disposed of them in arbitrary fashion; therefore, the consequences of its actions cannot be interpreted exclusively on the former owner's detriment. Accordingly, due to the uncommon circumstances of the case, the claim should have been accepted, unless it had been proven without any doubt that it was in her power to compile the detailed list in the statutory period. However, as no such proof was made, and the appellate court did not bother to investigate the details of the case, a violation of the right to fair trial was found.[286] On the contrary, the Slovakian Supreme Court did not find it too difficult to dismiss the appeal, employing exactly that kind of formalism which the Czech Constitutional Court considered to be undesirable in interpreting normative acts. In their view, the law clearly and unequivocally formulated the conditions for the restitution of movable property; therefore, "following from logical and systematic interpretation," a failure to meet them, for whatever reason, must trigger the dismissal of the claim.[287]

Finally, it has to be mentioned that the Strasbourg court did not manage to find a "possession" of the applicant within the meaning of Protocol I, Article 1; thus, it could find no violation of this provision, either.[288] Although, as the dissenting opinions argue, had the Court managed to find a "possession," it presumably must have found a violation of Protocol I, Article 1, too. A group of dissenters ground their opinion in the imbalance created by the disproportionate burden of proof placed on the applicant, while another dissenter emphasized a tendency in the Court's recent case law (since 2000) to subject to supervisory review also the application of national law, and noted that it

285 Kopecký v. Slovakia, *op. cit.*, paras. 15–21.

286 Pl. US 38/02, *op. cit.*, see also: *supra*.

287 Kopecký v. Slovakia, *op. cit.*, para. 21. Similar decision was reached earlier, in Judgment No. 1 Cdo 27/94 of 25 May 1994, interestingly also concerned with the restitution of precious metals and banknotes (*idem*, para. 24).

288 *Ibid.*, paras. 25–61.

regarded formalistic and strict interpretation as incompatible with the principles of the Convention.[289]

In Hungary, the Compensation Law did not specify in detail what kind of evidence might be employed to prove the entitlement; it merely mentioned that in the absence of certifying documents, other means may be used, too,[290] the details of the implementation being left to a future governmental order. Indeed, the subsequently enacted order[291] did contain some more specific rules upon evidence. Accordingly, in the case of immovable property, either the decision of expropriation or a warrant issued by the land office—certifying the taking—had to be attached to the compensation claim.[292] The norm also provided for those cases in which the property rights were acquired outside the registration system (but before the taking), unregistered owners having to submit the "valid" deed proving the transaction or a warrant obtained from the land office.[293] Perhaps the strangest requirement within the Hungarian scheme is the one referring to the compensation for commercial property. As it was already mentioned *supra* and also in the previous chapter, the value of such properties was established in function of the number of employees existing at the time of the taking. Consequently, evidence had to be produced about the employees, under the form of a certificate issued by the (state) social insurance organs. However, for the issuance of such a certificate, applicants had to present a list of the employees from decades ago.[294]

The various Romanian restitution laws formulated rather laconically their evidence-related requirements. The Land Law mentions "documents attesting the right to property,"[295] and in the case of dismantling the agricultural collectives, it enumerates "property documents" and land register or cadastral extracts. Moreover, unlike in Hungary, also other documents as applications for membership in the collectives or extracts from the agricultural register from the date of

[289] *Ibid.*, Dissenting Opinion of Judge Rees, joined by Judges Steiner and Borrego Borrego, section 3; Dissenting Opinion of Judge Strážnická, section 7.
[290] Law No. XXV of 1991, Art. 12(2).
[291] Governmental Order No. 104, 3 August 1991.
[292] *Ibid.*, Art. 18(1).
[293] *Ibid.*, Art. 19(1).
[294] *Ibid.*, instructions for the completion of claim forms.
[295] Law No. 18 of 1991, Art. 9.

entry in the collectives were accepted. Finally, in absence of the above-enumerated, any other means of proof, including witness testimonies were considered acceptable.[296] Most of the other relevant norms[297] merely mentioned "documents attesting the right to property" as basis for the restitution claims. Further clarifications were brought by the 2005 amendments to the restitution scheme. Thus, in the emergency ordinance[298] dealing with the restitution of church properties, new paragraphs were inserted, enumerating the following means of evidence that could be employed: witness testimonies, expert opinions, or any other evidence. Further, in the absence of proof to the contrary, a legal presumption was created that the property right existed in such a way as recognized by the legal or administrative act which ordered the taking.[299] At the same time, the evidence-related provisions of the Land Law of 2000 were amended so as to create the possibility of proof by witness testimony. This was possible in those cases where the former property was restituted within its original boundaries, under the condition that the witnesses were the owners (or heirs) of all the neighboring plots.[300]

Although neither the Hungarian, nor the Romanian probation-related regulation was seriously tested before domestic or international courts, this does not mean that they are free from problematic points. In the case of Hungary, it has to be emphasized that while decisive weight is attached to official documents (obtainable from diverse administrative bodies), the case of unregistered owners is also accommodated if they still possess the original transaction documents (or obtain the relevant certificate from the land office). Unlike Hungary, the Romanian legislation also recognized the admissibility of testimonial evidence—albeit under severe conditions—and provided for a relatively wider range of documents that could be used as evidence of former ownership. At the same time, the Romanian system included certain features that arguably made the use of permissible evidence extremely difficult. Such is the case of those claimants applying for restitution of

[296] *Ibid.*, Art. 11.

[297] Law No. 112 of 1995, Art. 15; Law No. 1 of 2000, Art. 6 (expressly referring to the above quoted Art. 9 of the Land Law); Law No. 10 of 2001, Art. 23.

[298] Governmental Emergency Ordinance No. 94 of 2000, *op. cit.*.

[299] *Ibid.*, Art. 3, paras. 2^1 and 2^2, as modified by Law No. 247 of 2005.

[300] Law No. 1 of 2000, Art. 6, para. 1^3, as modified by Law No. 247 of 2005.

landed property who wished to rely on witness testimonies. According to the relevant normative provisions, this evidence was admissible only if the witnesses were the owners (or heirs of the former owners) of all neighboring plots. Apparently, former owners relying on this form of evidence could successfully apply for restitution only if the neighboring plots were already re-assigned, with the obvious effect that disputes over any of these neighboring lands would necessarily delay also the case of the applicant who grounded his claim on witness testimonies.

4. A footnote: the pitfalls of a formal solution or the case of Prince Hans-Adam II

All through this chapter it was argued that rules of reparations were in many cases at odds with the fundamental requirements of predictability and regularity. In the introduction—and also in the previous chapters—reference was made to authors who maintained that the role of the rule of law is not to produce just outcomes, or that one has to look firstly for predictability in the courtroom. This section is dedicated to a case which demonstrates how a formal solution can fail to yield a just result in a post-communist property reparations context.

The application filed by Prince Hans-Adam II of Liechtenstein against Germany with the European Court of Human Rights concerned the alleged failure of the German State to ensure him his[301] Article 6 and Protocol I, Article 1 rights, during an attempt to recover a work of art confiscated by the former Czechoslovakian authorities from his family under the famous Beneš Decrees. According to the applicant, the artwork in question had been in the property of his father (former sovereign of Liechtenstein) and was to be found on the territory of former Czechoslovakia in one of the properties owned by him there. After World War II, the properties, together with their inventories, were nationalized under Decree No. 12 "On the confiscation and accelerated allocation of agricultural property of German and Hungarian persons and of those having committed treason and acted

[301] Prince Hans-Adam II of Liechtenstein v. Germany, ECHR, Application No. 42527/98, Judgment of 12 July 2001.

as enemies of the Czech and Slovak people."[302] The measure was later upheld against challenge by the former sovereign by an administrative court, under the argument that he was a person of German nationality "on the basis of a finding that this was and had been generally known."[303] As the painting in question was transferred to a museum of arts, and it was—after many years—exhibited also in Germany, the applicant instituted proceedings before the German authorities for having the painting delivered to him. Failing to achieve the desired result, he ultimately turned to the Strasbourg court, claiming deprivation of access to a court and violation of his right to property.[304]

The Strasbourg court accepted the reasoning of the German courts, which considered that the relevant provisions of the Settlement Convention[305] excluded German jurisdiction over measures that were carried out with regard to German external assets seized for the purpose of reparation. Thus, the Court found no disproportionate interference with the applicant's right to access to a court, because the "vital public interest" in regaining sovereignty and reunifying Germany was deemed to outweigh the individual interest in bringing litigation before German courts.[306] On the second prong, the Court employed an argument familiar from several of its other property restitution related decisions, namely first the applicant's interest could not be considered as "possession" within the meaning of Protocol I, Article 1.[307] Second, the circumstances of the expropriation itself could not be scrutinized

[302] *Ibid.*, paras. 10–1.

[303] *Ibid.*, para. 12.

[304] *Ibid.*, paras. 1–3.

[305] The Settlement Convention was a part of the "Bonn Conventions" signed between the Allies and Germany, and which basically ended the occupation regime. During the process of re-unification, a Treaty on the Final Settlement was concluded, by which the united Germany regained full sovereignty; nevertheless, according to an agreement signed subsequently with the former Allied powers, the relevant provisions of the Settlement Convention were perpetuated (*Ibid.*, paras. 23–35).

[306] *Ibid.*, para. 69.

[307] E.g., Jasiūnienė v. Lithuania, *op. cit.*, para. 40; Gratzinger and Gratzingerova v. The Czech Republic, ECHR, Application No. 39794/98, Decision of 10 July 2002, para. 69; Maltzan and Others v. Germany, ECHR, Application Nos. 71916/01, 71917/01, and 10260/02, Decision of 2 March 2005, para. 74(d).

due to the lack of *ratione temporis* jurisdiction,[308] as the nationalization occurred prior to the entry into force of Protocol I.[309]

However, the unanimously entered judgment is beyond any criticism: international agreements, and especially lack of jurisdiction, are strong arguments; the formally correct solution still leads to (or rather perpetuates) injustice. It still remains a fact that Liechtenstein was a formally neutral power during World War II, and Liechtenstein property could not have been therefore considered German or enemy property from a Czechoslovakian perspective. Moreover, the categorization of the applicant's father as German "on the basis of a finding that this was and had been generally known" could have never been considered as acceptable.[310] In the light of these, the formalist standpoint fashioned by the Strasbourg court appears as an easy way out of a painful problem, but at the same time, sadly, a solution that fails to address the injustice suffered by the victims.

5. Conclusions

The previous two chapters of this book departed from questioning the justice of the post-communist restitution schemes, and then turned towards the concrete threats that a distributive or a predominantly distributive approach to restitution can pose to the ideal of the rule of law. It was argued, that through the—personal, temporal, and quantitative—limits imposed on the extent of the restitution programs, the equality of opportunity was denied to those former victims who, at least from the perspective of the losses suffered, were in the same situation. Accordingly, a thick conception of the rule of law, which equates it with justice, rights, or objective equality, is very much at odds with the post-communist restitution approaches. This chapter, therefore, was dedicated to an inquiry from the perspective of a thin version of the rule of law ideal, which proposes not more and not less than predictability

308 E.g., Jasiūnienė v. Lithuania, *op. cit.*, para. 38; Kopecký v. Slovakia, *op. cit.*, para. 35(d).

309 Prince Hans-Adam II of Liechtenstein v. Germany, *op. cit.*, paras. 78–86.

310 See also: Dagmar Brokova v. The Czech Republic, UNHRC, Communication No. 774/1997, UN Doc. CCPR/C/73/D/774/1997 (15 January 2002), quoted *supra*, Chapters 2 and 3.

and regularity.[311] The rule of the restitution laws, however, fell short of fulfilling this requirement from several aspects. As it was demonstrated above, restitution schemes did not manage to ensure beyond criticism the fairness of valuation, application, and evidence-related procedures.

The valuation of former properties for the purpose of compensation was in some cases left by legislation to further governmental regulations (regarding the form and amount of receivable indemnification). This practice was found unconstitutional in Lithuania, for breaching the principle of the rule of law (under the aspects of clarity, certainty, security, and protection of legitimate expectations), but passed unchallenged in Romania. Notably, in a European Court of Human Rights' judgment it was stated that (*obiter dicta*) such a solution could not be regarded as a genuine compensation. In the case of Hungary, the Constitutional Court found it permissible to disregard obligations regarding compensation assumed through international agreements and to afford the very same compensations, on the same legal grounds, also to those whose original entitlement arose from the agreement.

What concerns the deadlines for filing the claims, they turned out to be unrealistically short in most cases. In the Czech Republic, for instance, the Constitutional Courts found such a short deadline to effectively hinder the applicants possibilities to pursue their rights. However, in Slovakia, the Constitutional Court dismissed such claims by stating that in special circumstances the state may adopt special procedural rules. Practically, even in those situations where the deadlines were not challenged in courts, they were subsequently, and sometimes even repeatedly, prolonged so as to make it possible for the applicants to participate in the restitution process.

Another interesting time-related question was the length of the proceedings. The Lithuanian Supreme Court considered that the authorities' failure to adopt a decision upon the applicant's well-documented request to restore his property rights within the statutory period, and even for several years since, amounted to a breach of right to effective remedy. In Estonia, the Supreme Court found that keeping

[311] (Pure) procedural fairness, as I stated in the introductory passages as well, would perhaps be too much to expect from the rule of law, especially in a transitional context, where theorists emphasize the law's transitional (as opposite to foundational) role in mediating the social shift (Teitel, *op. cit.*, pp. 11–27; also *supra*, Chapter 2).

the former owners in suspense about the possibility of retrieving their former properties, as well as the current possessors of such properties about the length of their possession, amounts to a breach of the requirement of legal clarity. The Hungarian Constitutional Court in several decisions pointed towards a constitutional omission, materialized in the failure to ensure the compliance of domestic legislation with the state's international engagements to afford compensation.

As for the problem of proving the entitlement, it has to be emphasized that the relatively large number of documents required—and which were obtainable, as a rule, from certain administrative bodies—, combined with the above-mentioned short deadlines, in practice constituted a barrier for the applicants in pursuing their rights. In some cases, as for example Hungary, it was possible to complete the timely submitted application, even after the deadline passed. However, in Slovakia, the Constitutional Court considered that failure to comply for whatever reason with the legal requirements within the given deadline must result in the lapse of the claim. In other cases, the evidence itself was impossible to collect by the available deadline because the applicants were either refused access to certain sites, or they simply did not have enough time to compile the required lists. This was the case in both Czechia and Slovakia for movable properties, where a detailed description and indication of their current place was required for each movable item. Perhaps not surprisingly, the Czech Constitutional Court demonstrated more sympathy for the claimants and more determination in fulfilling the aims of the restitution laws, while its Slovakian counterpart contended itself by stating that according to the applicable law failure to submit required evidence leads to the denial of the restitution claim.

Another controversial prescription was to be found in the regulation of witness testimonies (which was not, as a rule accepted in most of the analyzed cases). In Poland, it was required that witnesses had to reach the age of adulthood at the time of the taking, which meant that in the case of the Bug River claims, at the time of the adoption of the law, qualified witnesses could not have been younger than 78 years. In Romania, witness testimonies could have been used only in the case of religious properties, but to be valid they had to come from all the owners (or their heirs) of the neighboring plots. However, while the Polish Constitutional Tribunal found the testimony-related conditions as being at odds with the principle of the rule of law, the Romanian provisions are unchallenged up to the present day. A similarly odd rule is comprised by the Hungarian scheme, which in the case of commercial properties required former owners to obtain a certificate from the relevant authority about the number of persons employed at the date of nationalization. However, in order to obtain this, a list of the former employees had to be submitted by the claimant to the certifying authority, which may prove a rather difficult exercise four decades after the taking.

In sum, it can be stated that at least in some cases the restitution or compensation schemes did fall short of the requirement of foreseeability and regularity. While in some cases the constitutional courts came to the individuals' rescue by striking down some of the problematic legal provisions or court decisions, in other cases they remained deferential and upheld the legislative arrangements. In the third instance, some of the problematic provisions passed unchallenged. But a massive involvement of constitutional courts in the restitution process is problematic in itself. As Sadurski notes, a strong judicial review system may send a negative message, obscuring the rights discourse and lifting it from public discourse (deliberation) to the small, specialized world of constitutional experts. And this aspect is considered to be at least as important as the undeniable gains—visible in restitution perspective from the above analysis—of having the legislation monitored by specialized guardians.[312]

[312] Wojciech Sadurski, *Rights Before Courts. A study of Constitutional Courts in Post-communist States of Central and Eastern Europe*, Springer, 2005, pp. 298–9.

Conclusion

1. The current state of art

As of 2006, the restitution programs in Central and Eastern Europe are far from being concluded. In Estonia, the legislature is considering a bill on amendments to the Principles of Ownership Reform Act. Its objective is to eliminate the legal uncertainty surrounding the situation of the unlawfully expropriated property of those persons who left Estonia for Germany between 1939 and 1941. The original version of the act merely mentioned that the question of compensations for these properties would be solved by international agreements. This situation was found problematic by the Supreme Court—as discussed *supra*, in Chapter 4—, which requested the legislature to bring the relevant provisions of the act in line with the principle of legal clarity. As no international agreements have been concluded, argued the Court, former owners and current possessors of the claimable goods are kept in suspense about their possibility to retrieve or to privatize the properties concerned.[1] The proponents of the bill argue for a solution inspired by Alexander the Great's "undoing" of the Gordian knot: as the conclusion of any international agreement in this matter seems highly unlikely, the "theoretical possibility" of compensation shall be eliminated, and thus the problem of legal "unclarity" will be solved.[2]

The Latvian legislature is also considering a bill that would provide for the restitution of communal properties also to non-observant Jewish communities. Under the original 1992 act, only those organizations

[1] ESC, Case No. 3-4-1-5-02, Decision of 28 October 2002.

[2] For details, see: The Parliament of Estonia, Weekly Records, 6–9 and 14 February 2006, available online, at http://www.riigikogu.ee/?id=38455&parent_id=39883 and http://www.state.gov/p/eur/rls/or/64425.htm.

could apply for the restitution of religious items, which were registered and active at the date of filing the request. Nevertheless, many Jewish communities were poorly organized, and therefore missed the deadline, while in other cases communal property was registered as private, which also made restitution problematic.[3] Under this scheme, eighteen property items were restituted (or compensated) to the observant community (made up of approximately 136 people), while the new bill may clarify the fate of a further 200 items, claimed by the significantly larger non-observant community.[4] The Lithuanian restitution scheme is scheduled to end in 2009 in the case of lands, forests, and bodies of water, in the case of houses and apartments in 2011 (i.e., these are the deadlines until which compensations have to be paid).[5]

In Poland, the *Sejm* will consider a new compensation bill in June 2006, which is known to afford compensation amounting to 15% of the current value of the properties lost under the Nazi and communist regimes. It is also known that it will contain neither citizenship, nor residence requirements for the claimants.[6] In the Czech Republic, the deadline for filing claims for looted art expires at the end of 2006, while in Slovakia religious bodies were entitled to file restitution claims targeting agricultural land and forests, and constructions on these sites until 30 April 2006.[7] After the famous "Golden Train" litigation—discussed *supra*, in Chapter 3—Holocaust victims obtained a settlement, which means a compensation around 5 million USD for victims living in Hungary, consisting of contributions to medical, overhead, and

[3] For details, see: "Proposed Latvian restitution law would return Jewish properties," Jewish Telegraphic Agency, 23 January 2006, available online, at http://www.ncsj.org/AuxPages/011706JTA_Latvia.shtml.

[4] For details, see: "Summary of Property Restitution in Central and Eastern Europe," United States Department of State, Under Secretary for Political Affairs, Bureau of European and Eurasian Affairs, 12 April 2006, available online, at http://www.state.gov/p/eur/rls/or/64425.htm.

[5] *Ibid.*.

[6] For details, see: "Private restitution proposal in Poland offers unsatisfactory resolution to some," JTA News Service, 19 May 2006, available online, at http://floridajewishnews.com/articles/index2.php?option=com_content&do_pdf=1&id=430.

[7] For details, see: "Summary of Property Restitution," U.S. Department of State, *op. cit.*.

transportation expenses. The compensations will be paid exclusively to those in need, for a period of 5 years.[8]

Currently, the compensation procedure for property left behind in the former Soviet Socialist Republic of Ukraine is in progression in Romania, the deadline for filing claims ending in May 2007.[9] However, the most controversial restitution-related issue in Romania is represented by the case of the former royal family's assets. The former sovereign of Romania, who was forced to abdicate and leave the country in 1948, has filed claims for the return of the numerous properties of his family according to the provisions of the law providing for the return of the abusively taken properties.[10] Beyond the obvious political implications, the case has also a significant economical aspect—the properties in question are palaces and castles in value of millions of Euro—; the government sought and found an agreement with the former sovereign upon the form and extent of restitution (compensation). The agreement was sanctioned by a 2005 bill, enacted with the purpose of regulating the situation of the former king's properties.[11] The Constitutional Court, however, on preliminary review, found the bill unconstitutional.[12] The Court considered that the bill has an individual character that makes it applicable not to an indefinite number of cases, but a pre-defined situation exclusively, which makes it discriminatory, and therefore unconstitutional. Further, the Court engaged itself in a rather strange argumentation about the alleged agreement between the government and the former sovereign, complaining that on the one hand no details of the agreement are given, while on the other hand the former king could not have validly disposed of his family's former assets, as he was not their owner any more. The second line of argumentation appears especially strange, as the Court in its earlier decisions has already stated that the state may not be considered to be the owner

[8] For details, see: "Megkérdőjelezett igazságosság," MTV, 30 June 2006, available online, at http://www.azeste.hu/este/cikk/6156.

[9] For details, see: Law No. 171/2006, published in the *Official Gazette*, No. 437, 19 May 2006; as well as *supra*, Chapter 2.

[10] Law No. 10/2001, *op. cit.*.

[11] Legislative project PL-x 158/09.05.2005, available online, at http://www.cdep.ro.

[12] RCC, Decision No. 600 of 9 November 2005, published in the *Official Gazette*, No. 1060, 26 November 2005.

of those properties that were transferred to it unlawfully, or in absence of a legal basis; moreover, the individual's rights to these properties were never extinguished.[13]

In addition, the Court also noticed the fact that the bill does not provide for the extinction of the former king's right to restitution for the remainder of the royal family's assets, and warned that at least a theoretical possibility exists that he may subsequently request their restitution. Finally, the Court emphasized that the constitutional way of solving the issue would have been through agreements between the former sovereign and the Ministry of Finances, ratified by a governmental decree, which would have been within the executive's competence of administering state property and organizing the execution of laws. However, argued the Court, the legislative solution in these conditions amounts to a breach of the principle of separation of powers.[14] Eventually, following the Court's decision, the executive opted for restituting the properties in question, and agreed with the former royal family upon the subsequent re-purchase of some of them, in the exchange of the same amount of compensation that was provided by the above bill.[15]

2. On property: creating the monster

Post-communist property reparation programs cannot be separated from the specific circumstances of the transition period during which they took place. These, in their turn, contributed to the peculiar understanding of the right to property that is reflected by the reparation programs. Still, it would definitely be a mistake to bracket the entire transition period, invoking its special nature, when discussing the contemporary notion of property. Therefore, it is not a wasted exercise to shortly summarize the proceeds of the reparation programs from

---

[13] RCC, Decision No. 73 of 19 July 1995, published in the *Official Gazette*, No. 177, 8 August 1995; see also *supra*, Chapter 2.

[14] *Ibid.*.

[15] Accordingly, the former monarch was promised a 30 million Euro compensation for the repurchased items. For details, see: "Peleşul va fi răscumpărat de stat cu 30 de milioane de euro," *Gândul*, 26 June 2006, available online, at http://www.gandul.info/2006-06-07/arte/pelesul.

a property-rights perspective. Obviously, there are no theoretically pure property rights systems in practice, so the interesting point here is to identify the various theories that are reflected within reparation schemes, and to examine whether and to what degree they are compatible with each other.

Firstly, there are two features of the right to property that stand out emphatically in all post-communist reparation programs: the right to own property is a fundamental and a natural right.[16] It is a natural, pre-political right, for it has survived changes of regimes and even of borders: compensation—in any of its forms—was determined in function of the property lost. This Lockean conception of property appears in its strongest form in the case of the victims of post-war population exchanges,[17] where compensation is afforded for an expropriation effected by a different regime and a different state. (Even if the situation is nuanced by the fact that the obligation to compensate was derived not from the expropriation itself, but from the former government's failure to fulfill its constitutional and/or treaty-based duties.)[18]

But then there are also two bothersome features of the reparation programs that are at odds with this natural right conception of ownership. On the one hand, there are some groups whose rights appear to be more natural than others'; in a post-communist context these usually represent the ethnical and/or religious majorities (this having a lot to do with the post-war border-redrafting). Thus, those lacking adequate political leverage faced serious difficulties in their pursuit for redress. This explains the relative success of the Maori restitution in comparison to Native American or Aboriginal claims, and the relative failure of Jewish claims in Central and Eastern Europe.[19] As Avineri emphasized, post-communist reparations had a significant (national) identity-building feature.[20] On the other hand, if property is considered to pre-exist and transcend current political arrangements, it is rather

[16] See, for example: LiCC, Ruling of 27 May 1994, *supra*.

[17] See, for example: the Bug River case discussed in details *supra*.

[18] See, for example: HCC, AB 45/2003, 960/B/1995. (A more or less similar rationale was invoked during the settling of Maori claims in New Zealand.)

[19] On a smaller scale one might consider the situation of the Sudeten Germans or Hungarians in former Czechoslovakia, the Uniate Church in Romania, etc.

[20] Avineri, *op. cit.*.

difficult to accept the limitations and conditions that the compensating governments instituted. Especially so if one considers the fact that—as it was argued in some detail in the previous chapters—limitations created winners and losers of the reparations.

Second, the above summarized critique, which goes right against the core of the notion of natural right, nicely builds up towards neoclassical theories of property. As Douglas North observed—putting aside for the moment the question how initial ownership emerged—the development of property rights is ultimately dependent on the costs incurred and the benefits achieved. Therefore, as we do not live in a transaction costs-free world, institutions and rules are created more according to the needs and interests of those possessing the most bargaining power, and less according to criteria of social efficiency.[21]

Third, perversely, it was exactly the idea of social efficiency that was echoed in most property reparation programs. Lawmakers and courts both used the notion of market economy to explain the necessity of reparations, as if economic reform could not have been implemented in any other way but through compensating former property owners.[22] Moreover, justifications dwelling on the limited financial possibilities of the state,[23] or the interests of the current possessors of claimable goods,[24] or even the interests of the state itself[25] were also rather popular. As attractive as it may be, the utilitarian justification for property reparations falls short at least under two aspects. On the one hand, it cannot explain why redistribution has to rest on former, pre-totalitarian baselines. On the other hand, it cannot justify some of the limitations imposed on reparations—personal limitations for example—, since the exclusion of non-citizens and/or non-residents from the scheme improves neither social equality, nor the conditions of market economy.

---

[21] North, *op. cit.*.

[22] See: Preamble of the Hungarian Compensation Law, Law No. XXV of 1991, *op. cit.*; PCT, K 2/04, Judgment of 15 December 2004, *op. cit.*; ESC, Decision 3-4-1-10-2000, 22 December 2000, *op. cit.*; LiCC, Decision of 8 March 1995, *op. cit.* and Decision of 20 June 1995, *op. cit.*.

[23] See: PCT, K 33/02, *op. cit.*; HCC, AB 28/1991, 1160/A/1991, *op. cit.*; LiCC Ruling of 16 March 1999, *op. cit.*.

[24] Užkurėlienė and Others v. Lithuania, ECHR, *op. cit.*.

[25] See, for example: Estonian Law "On the Fundamentals of Ownership Reform," June 1991, *op. cit.*.

Finally, attempts to defend the inequalities created by the reparation programs might be made from a Rawlsian standpoint, arguing that the program was deliberately designed to benefit the least well off, although this can prove extremely difficult to demonstrate in practice.

Post-communist property reparations definitely lack a coherent theoretical grounding. In spite of this, beyond contradictions and inconsistencies, they do transmit one significant message, namely that the right to own property is fundamental and natural. At least to the extent that it can survive even the harshest dictatorship. For regardless of the reasons that drove governments to implement massive property redistribution programs, in all of the analyzed cases they thought it best to rely on pre-totalitarian baselines, and in all of the cases they achieved wide popular support. The property rights system and the structure of private ownership in the former communist states of Central and Eastern Europe is a consequence of the reparation programs and rests upon the idea of property that was created by this process, with all of its shortcomings. For these reasons, its significance should not be underestimated.

3. On restitution

The post-communist governments of Central and Eastern Europe had two main options in entrenching a new political elite resulting from a combination of the old nomenclature and the leaders of the democratic opposition movements, which was experiencing a pressing need for legitimacy after the fall of the totalitarian rule. One was the political option, consisting in demonstrating allegiance towards democratic values and institutions,[26] to the rule of law. The other was the economic option, the creation of a market economy that carried the promise of a well-being characteristic of the much envied capitalist societies.

[26] Jowitt, *supra*, Chapter 4, makes an argument according to which the most difficult task faced by transition governments was the institutionalization of public virtues. Czarnota, Krygier, and Sadurski speak about the "need to preserve continuity with frameworks of everyday life and law and often with elite arrangements which ushered in the new era" and at the same time the need to "demonstrate an ability to do justice to, and to distinguish themselves from, often vicious past legacies" (Czarnota, Krygier, and Sadurski, *op. cit.*, p. 3).

Unfortunately, the chosen solution was arguably the worst one, as transition governments attempted to achieve both options at the same time, under the false impression that the two totally distinct goals may legitimate and support each other. As this book has argued, it is theoretically untenable to pursue an even (or close to even) distribution of property in the name of reparatory justice on the basis of the argument that this would better facilitate the emergence of a market economy. It is equally wrong to talk about the role of privately owned property in a market economy as an argument that justifies mitigation of past property injustices. Linking reparatory goals with structural reform necessarily requires a distributive justification, albeit the danger in distributive justice arguments rests in the fact that in a post-communist context, distribution is likely to be conceived in substantive equality terms, and this, as Hayek emphasized, easily turns against the rule of law ideal.[27]

As it is argued in Chapter 2, no compelling justice argument can be invoked for the mitigation of past property injustices. Nothing compels governments to rely on the pattern of previous holdings while effecting the redistribution of property, although reliance on arguments of justice may undoubtedly enhance the legitimacy of the reforms. Nevertheless, as it was also shown, a number of significant exceptions demand redress, such as the case of *de facto* (illegal) takings, or when the government failed to fulfill its (international or domestic) promises of compensation. In these cases, it is unjust to derive the right to claim and the corresponding obligation to compensate from governmental gratitude. As a consequence of the above-explained, the priority given to property injustices by the post-communist reparation schemes can be defended solely by reference to the social and economical role and significance of private property.

Chapter 2 undertook an analysis of the normative values that may justify property reparations (past harm, breach of fundamental rights, and political persecution), and concluded that none of them explains convincingly the exclusion of other victims. The idea of past harm is over-inclusive, as property deprivations were only one, although widespread, form of losses that could have been encountered during authoritarian regimes. The principles of violation of fundamental rights and of political discrimination may constitute perfectly defendable

[27] Hayek, *op. cit.*, p. 59.

justifications for property reparations in the context of indigenous or Holocaust restitution (takings as part of a genocidal project), but are rather week arguments in the context of communist-era expropriations. Deprivation of property as a form of political persecution can form the grounds of distinctive treatment from a reparation perspective only if economical reasons are also brought into play.

Having established that post-communist property restitution schemes cannot be unequivocally defended at large and solely on reparative justice grounds, and that the association of structural (economical) reform with the idea of reparations necessarily confers a (at least partially) distributive justice character upon the programs, Chapter 3 inquired whether reliance on private property's economic and social aspects may result in substantive equality concerns in reparations. The very idea of limited restitution, which—to various extents—characterized all the examined schemes, discernable from the person-related, temporal, and property-based conditions imposed on the claimants, betray substantive equality concerns. However, this is only one side of the reparation program's goals (and achievements). The second concern—as it was argued in Chapter 3—was exclusion: the prevention of certain categories of former property owners to benefit from the programs. Conclusively, attempts to substantive equality result in objective inequality: some members of the same pool of victims end up with none, or a lot lesser degree of redress, than the rest.[28] The abovementioned limitations are responsible for the division of the pool of victims into winners and losers.

Citizenship and residence requirements—contained initially in almost every restitution scheme—clearly deny equality of opportunity to those who do not possess them anymore. Their exclusion furthers neither goals of justice nor that of social equality. The Czech Constitutional Court employed an argumentation grounded on the idea of collective responsibility of certain minorities (Sudeten Germans and Hungarians) for the German occupation and its consequences in former Czechoslovakia during World War II, to justify their collective ex-

[28] As Hayek has stated in his much quoted phrase, adherence to the rule of law inherently produces economic inequality, inequality which is unobjectionable, as long as it is not designed to affect particular people in a particular way (Hayek, *op. cit.*).

clusion from restitution (through a combination of person-related and temporal limitations).[29] Beyond the absurdity of the idea of "collective responsibility," the weakness of the argument is demonstrated by the unclear, random, and sometimes malicious procedure by which the ethnicity of the persons concerned was established under the Beneš Decrees, providing for their expropriation.[30]

Cut-off dates also managed to draw a dividing line between the former property owners who have been the victims of various past takings. Obviously, no reparation program can feasibly attempt to redress all past property injustices: objective (economic and procedural) constraints raise insurmountable hurdles. However, in the case of post-communist restitution in Central and Eastern Europe, where the communist regimes often practically followed another (Nazi) totalitarian establishment, the drawing of lines becomes a lot more problematic, and less reasons can be invoked for compensating victims of one, but excluding those of the other oppressor. The differentiated treatment of past property objects, by which certain types of properties were restituted or compensated, while others were simply left out of the scheme, plus a common ceiling that limited the amount of receivable reparation simultaneously produces exclusion of certain victims and equalization of the others.

For the aforementioned reasons, Chapter 3 concludes that post-communist restitution schemes—due to their distributive character—contain at least some features that result in theoretically unjustifiable distinctions between beneficiaries, producing arbitrary outcomes. This constitutes a breach of the criteria of formal equality before the law, and therefore conflicts with the idea of the rule of law. Whatever role the rule of law is considered to have during transition, the consequences of these restitution policies reach far beyond the transition period, as at the same time they perpetuate old, and create and entrench novel property injustices.

As a thick version of the rule of law, which describes it in terms of justice, rights, or objective equality, has proven to be a project too

[29] CCC, Pl. US 14/94, Judgment of 8 March 1995.

[30] See, for example, *supra*, Chapters 3 and 4, the cases of Dagmar Brokova v. The Czech Republic, UNHRC, Communication No. 774/1997, U.N. Doc. CCPR/C/73/D/774/1997 (15 January 2002); and Prince Hans-Adam II of Liechtenstein v. Germany, ECHR, Application No. 42527/98, Judgment of 12 July 2001.

ambitious for the post-communist restitution schemes, Chapter 4 analyzed the programs from the perspective of a thin concept of the same ideal, which demands essentially predictability, coherence, and regularity. Accordingly, procedural aspects were in the focus of the investigation, but unfortunately the conclusion was no less pessimistic than in the previous chapter: under the investigated criteria of valuation, deadlines and evidence there were at least some elements that could not withstand criticism. The practice of leaving the establishment of the concrete form and extent of the compensation to be received up to further governmental regulations was found unconstitutional in Lithuania[31] (for breaching rule of law requirements such as clarity, certainty, security, and protection of legitimate expectations), but was left unchallenged in Romania. In Hungary, the Constitutional Court found the government's reluctance to fulfill international obligations relating to compensation acceptable, holding that the common solution given by the Compensation Law was to be applied also to those whose original entitlement arose from international agreements.[32]

Deadlines for filing claims to reparation proved unrealistically short, and even in those cases in which they were not challenged in court, they were subsequently prolonged—even repeatedly—to make it possible for more applicants to benefit from the project. In the Czech Republic for instance, the Constitutional Court found the shortness of the deadline effectively a barrier for the applicants in pursuing their rights,[33] while in Slovakia similar claims were dismissed on the grounds that special circumstances justify special treatment.[34] The length of the reparation proceedings was also problematic. The Lithuanian Supreme Court found a breach of the right to effective remedy,[35] the Estonian Supreme Court spoke about the violation of the requirement of legal clarity,[36] while the Hungarian Constitutional Court discovered an unconstitutional omission in cases in which the authorities failed to react in reasonable time.[37]

[31] LiCC, Case No. 19/02, Ruling of 23 August 2005; for details, see *supra*, Chapter 4.
[32] See, for example: HCC, AB 16/1993, 1378/E/1990.
[33] CCC, Pl. US 3/94, Judgment of 1 November 1994.
[34] SCC, Pl. US 3/00 of 24 April 2001.
[35] LiSC, Ruling of 22 May 2000.
[36] ESC, Case No. 3-4-1-5-02, Decision of 28 October 2002.
[37] HCC, AB 16/1993, 1378/E/1990.

Evidence-related problems have arisen either in combination with the shortness of deadlines (in Hungary, for example, it was possible to complete the submitted application even after the deadline had passed, but in Slovakia failure to comply with legal requirements was considered to result in the lapse of the claim), or due to the refusal of authorities to allow access to certain sites or documents. Further, certain forms of evidence, such as witness testimonies, were not allowed in the majority of the analyzed cases. In Poland, for example, a witness-related requirement that in practice precluded anybody younger than 78 years of age from deposing in the favor of the applicants was found to be at odds with the principle of the rule of law.[38] However, a Romanian provision that required depositions to be made by all the owners (or their heirs) of the plots surrounding the claimed land remained unchallenged. Similarly difficult to satisfy, a provision of the Hungarian scheme requiring claimants to submit a list of the former employees of the company to obtain a certification about the number of employees from the relevant authority (which was the basis of compensation), also managed to escape scrutiny.

Therefore, Chapter 4 concludes that in many situations it was up to the constitutional courts to come to the former owners' rescue and clarify problematic provisions. However, in a number of cases the courts remained deferential and upheld the government's view, while in other cases the relevant provisions did not even get to the stage of scrutiny, as they were not challenged.

4. On the rule of law

As it was argued in the foregoing passages, the Central and East European post-communist restitution laws posed a series of serious challenges through their intended and unintended effects the (emerging) rule of law. The constitutional review forums of the region were extensively involved in clarifying the compatibility of the various reparatory measures with the constitutions, and managed from case to case to eliminate some of the problematic provisions. However, their approach was far from consequent and conclusive, as they sometimes either up-

[38] PCT, K 2/04, Judgment of 15 December 2004.

held problematic provisions, or contributed, through their decisions, to the enhancement of confusion and perpetuation of injustice. Finally, not all of the relevant provisions were challenged and thus scrutinized; therefore, courts could not become (in this field) champions of the rule of law, even if they very much enjoyed seeing themselves in this role. Arguably, neither did the European Court of Human Rights manage to do a much neater job in sorting out restitution-related claims. As the analyzed case law illustrates, the Court has a rough time dealing with transitional problems. It might appear especially frustrating for applicants that the Court did not come up with a consistent pattern as to which interpretation of the rule of law it finds suitable for adjudication in a transitional context.

On the one hand, under the temporal jurisdiction doctrine, the Court managed to dismiss a serious number of applications for lack of jurisdiction. It is difficult to assess whether this firm refusal can be traced back to the idea according to which issues of transitional justice are not questions of ordinary justice, and therefore should be non-justiciable,[39] or whether it has a prudential basis, according to which the rule of law (in transitions) is best defended if the *status quo* is preserved.[40] This latter view is also echoed by those judgments which condemned the uncompensated (re)taking of properties distributed by the previous regimes (such as the Third Section judgment in the case of Jahn). Here again—seemingly—that view prevails which rejects radical changes to existing rights. However, the Grand Chamber in Jahn departed from this line and seemingly applied the "ordinary" (that is to say, non-transitional) reading of fairness and justice to a transitional case, and overturning the Third Section judgment, considered the uncompensated taking as justified in the given context.[41]

On the other hand, in judgments dealing with the (uncompensated) return of property from the current to its original owners (e.g., Pinchová and Pinch), the Court fashioned a much stricter approach and stressed that old injustices may not be compensated at the price of creating new

[39] Loizidou v. Turkey, ECHR, Application No. 15318/1989, Judgment of 18 December 1996, Dissenting opinion of Judge Jambrek.

[40] Allen, *op. cit.*, pp. 26–7. The argument is that restitution may carry a host of negative effects, which hamper, for example, the economic reform or social cohesion.

[41] For more details, see: Allen, *op. cit.*, pp. 35–8.

ones. The distinction between "ordinary" and transition contexts is obvious, and the Court seems to allow a much narrower margin of appreciation to the states in designing the relevant legislative scheme. Apparently, the emphasis again falls upon fostering stability and legality.[42]

Only a couple of pages above, the complexity of tasks that transition societies had to face were canvassed. Reference was made to Czarnota, Krygier, and Sadurski, who wrote in this context about the burden that has fallen upon "institutions of justice," in the attempt to conceal the competing interests and expectations, a process, which resulted in a transformation of "expectations and the realities on which they are based."[43] This view echoes to a certain degree Teitel's argument—quoted several times in the book—, according to which during transitions the role of the rule of law is not foundational but transitional by "mediating the normative shift in justice."[44] Accordingly, during transition periods, rule of law ideals are applicable only with significant amendments, generated by the tumultuous context of the transformation process. Transitional law, according to Teitel, is a *sui generis* paradigm, a vehicle of social, political, and ideological transformation.[45]

The analysis of the various property reparation processes across Central and Eastern Europe, however, create an uneasy feeling towards the above-delineated conception of the transitional rule of law. For as it was argued, property reparations pursued a number of goals and not all of them were targeting the greatest benefit of the people. A redrafting of power structures took place, a struggle between the elites, which defined to some extent the context of transition, and thus, implicitly, the rule of law ideals, as Teitel correctly noted. Also, as theorists observed, restitution laws were (re)shaping, constructing post-communist national identities.[46]

Obviously, the law had to be responsive to these circumstances of the political change.[47] However, the question that arises is whether

[42] *Ibid.*, pp. 40–1.
[43] Czarnota, Krygier, Sadurski, *op. cit.*, p. 3.
[44] Teitel, *op. cit.*, p. 215.
[45] Martin Krygier, "Rethinking the Rule of Law After Communism," in Czarnota, Krygier, Sadurski, *op. cit.*, p. 267; Ruti Teitel, "Transitional Rule of Law," in Czarnota, Krygier, Sadurski, *op. cit.*, pp. 279–94.
[46] Avineri, *op. cit.*; Pechota, *op. cit.*.
[47] Teitel, *op. cit.*.

one may accept all the outcomes—the distinctions made by reparation schemes, the exclusion of certain groups (of former owners and of types of properties) from the benefits of the program—under the argument that "it is what the law does and it is the reason why law does it."[48] Is the perpetuation of old (and creation of new) injustices justifiable by the *sui generis* nature of transition?

The answer to these questions, in the light of problems analyzed in this book must be a categorical "no." Regardless of the fact how specific the circumstances of transition from authoritarianism to democracy are and regardless of the transitional tasks of the rule of law, a core, a minimum of the ideal must be recognized as invariably surviving in any kind of regime context (transitional or not), for otherwise there would not be much left to talk about. This—in the footsteps of Krygier—I take to be the protection against the arbitrary exercise of power.[49] "Arbitrary," in a property reparations context, equates with unjustified distinctions in the treatment of those placed in an equal situation. Whereas "unjustified" stands for the lack of any convincing argument that may explain how the envisaged scheme does contribute to a better furtherance of the multiple goals that it proposed to achieve. As it was argued, economic reform and mitigation of past injustices are goals which cannot explain and justify each other.

What follows from all this is that property reparations—as a special transition problem—simply do not fit into the logic of property. The obviously strong popular sense of justness, which demanded the undoing of all that was wrongfully done by the overthrown authoritarian regimes, could not have been unequivocally translated into the implacable logic of law. Even if the notions of rule of law or justice are stretched to their very limits (labeled as transitional) in the quest to accommodate the tumultuous processes of regime change, no consistent solutions were met in the analyzed jurisdictions.

The special nature of the problem, given all the circumstances mentioned and analyzed in the foregoing chapters, which distinguish it so fundamentally from any case of proper takings, leads towards the idea that the law is not the most proper device to deal with such large scale historic injustices. With a perhaps perverse symmetry, one

[48] Krygier, *op. cit.*, p. 271.
[49] *Ibid.*, p. 272.

might consider to admit that wrongs committed outside of a rule of law regime could be fully rightened also only outside of a rule of law framework. The Maori restitution, but also the truth and reconciliation commissions that were drafted for dealing with the legacies of the totalitarian past, are arguments for seeking efficient relief outside of the boundaries of legal justice. Further, arguably due to the difficulty of coming to terms with property reparations within a system guided by the rule of law, the entire reparation scheme could have been hijacked and abused by the various interest groups, which transformed it almost in all analyzed jurisdictions into a nation-building tool, giving an undesirable ethnic dimension to reparations.

The amendments to the rule of law ideal, justifiable in the context of transition, can go as far as—for example—to allow governments to decide upon the concrete form of the reparation, the type of wrongs it wants to address, the period in time intended to be covered. As it was shown in this book, there are no clear-cut guidelines either in international law or in legal theory that may shed enough light on these matters. But they may not create winners and losers; they may not distinguish between those placed in the same situation. For transition may come to an end, but the injustices that it entrenched will prevail.

APPENDIX

List of cases

Australia

The High Court of Australia[1]

Coe v. Commonwealth (1993) 118 ALR 193
Mabo and Others v. The State of Queensland (1992) 175 CLR 1
Mason v. Triton (1994) 34 NSWLR 572
Members of the Yorta Yorta Aboriginal Community v. Victoria (2002) 77 ALJR 356
Western Australia v. Ward (2002) 76 ALJR 1098
Wilson v. Anderson (2002) 76 ALJR 1306

The Czech Republic

The Constitutional Court of the Czech Republic[2]

III. US 132/96
IV. US 215/94
Pl. US 3/94, Judgment of 1 November 1994
Pl. US 14/94, Judgment of 8 March 1995
Pl. US 1/98, Coll. Vol. 12, 71–9
Pl. US 24/98, Coll. of decisions 15 (1999 – Part III)
Pl. US 9/99, Coll. of decisions 16 (1999 – Part IV)
Pl. US 17/99, Coll. Vol. 16
Pl. US 754/01, Decision of 23 November 2003
Pl. US 38/02, Judgment of 24 March 2004

[1] Source: http://www.hcourt.gov.au.
[2] Source: http://test.concourt.cz/angl_verze/index_angl.html.

Estonia

The Supreme Court of Estonia[3]

Case No. 3-4-1-10-2000, Decision of 22 December 2000

Case No. 3-4-1-5-2002, Decision of 28 October 2002

The European Union

The European Court of Human Rights[4]

Acimović v. Croatia, Application No. 61237/00, Judgment of 9 October 2003

Basacopol v. Romania, Application No. 34992/97, Judgment of 9 July, 2002

Blečić v. Croatia, Application No. 59532/00, Judgment of 29 July 2004

Broniowski v. Poland, Application No. 31443/96, Judgment (friendly settlement) of 28 September 2005

Broniowski v. Poland, Application No. 31443/96, Judgment of 22 June 2004

Brumarescu v. Romania, Application No. 28342/95, Judgment of 28 October 1999

Crnojević v. Croatia, Application No. 71614/01, Judgment of 21 October 2004

Dragović v. Croatia, Application No. 5705/02, Judgment of 28 October 2004

Feldbrugge v. The Netherlands, Application No. 8562/79, Judgment of 29 May 1986

Friemann v. Croatia, Application No. 5266/02, Judgment of 24 June 2004

Gratzinger and Gratzingerova v. The Czech Republic, Application No. 39794/98, Decision of 10 July 2002

Jahn and Others v. Germany, Application Nos. 46720/99, 72203/01, and 72552/01, Grand Chamber Judgment of 30 June 2005

Jahn and Others v. Germany, ECHR, Applications Nos. 46720/99, 72203/01, and 72552/01, Third Section Judgment of 22 January 2004

---

[3] Source: http://www.nc.ee/?lang=en.

[4] Source: http://www.echr.coe.int/echr.

James and Others v. United Kingdom, Application No. 3/1984/75/119, Judgment of 22 January 1986

Janter v. Slovakia, Application No. 39050/97, Judgment of 4 March 2003

Jasiūnienė v. Lithuania, Application No. 41510/98, Judgment of 6 March 2003

Kopecký v. Slovakia, Application No. 44912/98, Judgment of 28 September 2004

Kutić v. Croatia, Application No. 48778/99, Judgment of 1 March, 2002

L'Association et la Ligue Pour la Protection des Acheteurs d'Automobiles, Ana Abid et 646 Autres c. La Roumanie, Requête No. 34746/97, Décision de 10 juillet 2001

La Paroisse Gréco-Catholique Sâmbăta Bihor c. Roumanie, Requête No. 48107/99, Décision sur la recevabilité de 25 mai 2004

Lithgow and Others v. United Kingdom, Application No. 2/1984/74/112-118, Judgment of 7 August 1996

Loizidou v. Turkey, Application No. 15318/1989, Judgment of 18 December 1996

Maltzan and Others v. Germany, Application Nos. 71916/01, 71917/01, and 10260/02, Judgment of 2 March 2005

Mihajlović v. Croatia, Application No. 21752/02, Judgment of 7 July 2005

Paduraru c. Roumanie, Requête No. 63252/00, Arrêt de 1 décembre 2005

Paulescu v. Romania, Application No. 34644/97, Judgment of 10 June, 2003

Pincová and Pinc v. The Czech Republic, Application No. 36548/97, Judgment of 5 November 2002

Porteanu c. Roumanie, Requête No. 4596/03, Arrêt de 16 février 2006

Pretto and Others v. Italy, Application No. 7984/77, Judgment of 8 December 1998

Prince Hans-Adam II of Liechtenstein v. Germany, Application No. 42527/98, Judgment of 12 July 2001

Ringeisen v. Austria, Application No. 2614/65, Judgment of 16 July 1971

Rucińska v. Poland, Application No. 33752/96, Decision of 27 January 2000

Salesi v. Italy, Application No. 13023/87, Judgment of 23 February 1993

Scordino v. Italy, Application no 36813/97, Judgment of 29 July 2004

Sofletea v. Romania, Application No. 48179/99, Judgment of 25 November, 2003

Sporrong and Lönnroth v. Sweden, Application Nos. 7151/75 and 7152/75, Judgment of 23 September 1982

Strain and Others v. Romania, Application No. 57001/00, Judgment of 21 July 2005

Sunday Times v. United Kingdom, Application No. 13166/87, Judgment of 26 November 1978

Sutter v. Switzerland, Application No. 8209/78, Judgment of 22 February 1984

Széchényi v. Hungary, Application No. 21344/93, Decision of the ECommHR of 30 June 1993

Tandreau v. Romania, Application No. 39184/98, Judgment of 25 November, 2003

The Former King of Greece v. Greece, Application No. 25701/94, Judgment of 23 November 2000

Užkurėlienė and Others v. Lithuania, Application No. 62988/00, Judgment of 7 April 2005

Valová, Slezák, and Slezák v. Slovakia, Application No. 44925/98, Judgment of 1 June 2004

Vasilescu v. Romania, Application No. 53/1997/837/1043, Judgment of 22 May 1998

Wittek v. Germany, Application No. 37290/97, Judgment of 12 December 2002

Zvolský and Zvolská v. The Czech Republic, Application No. 46129/99, Judgment of 12 November 2002

Zwiazek Nauczycielesta Polskiego v. Poland, Application No. 42049/89, Judgment of 21 September 2004

Hungary

The Constitutional Court of the Republic of Hungary[5]

1043/B/1992 AB

1395/E/1996 AB

411/E/1996 AB

707/B/1997 AB

[5] Source: http://www.mkab.hu/en/enmain.htm.

AB 21/1990, 1057/G/1990, published in the Official Gazette, No. 98, 1990
AB 27/1991, 91/E/1990, published in the Official Gazette, No. 53, 1991
AB 28/1991, 1160/A/1991, published in the Official Gazette, No. 59, 1991
AB 11/1992, 2086/A/1991, published in the Official Gazette, No. 23, 1992
AB 15/1993, 1543/B/1991, published in the Official Gazette, No. 29, 1993
AB 16/1993, 1378/E/1990, published in the Official Gazette, No. 29, 1993
AB 4/1996, 1482/B/1992, published in the Official Gazette, No. 14, 1996
AB 37/1996, 837/E/1995, published in the Official Gazette, No. 75, 1996
AB 45/2003, 960/B/1995, published in the *Official Gazette*, No. 111, 2003

The Supreme Court of Hungary[6]
BH1997.507, Kfv. II, 28.205/1996

Latvia

The Constitutional Court of the Republic of Latvia[7]
Case No. 09-02 (98), Judgment of 30 April 1998
Case No. 04-03 (98), Judgment of 10 June 1998
Case No. 04-01(99), Judgment of 20 April 1999
Case No. 2002-17-01 (03), Judgment of 10 January 2003

Lithuania

The Constitutional Court of the Republic of Lithuania[8]
Ruling of 27 May 1994
Ruling of 15 July 1994

---

[6] Source: http://www.lb.hu/english/index.html.
[7] Source: http://www.satv.tiesa.gov.lv/ENG/index_e.htm.
[8] Source: http://www.lrkt.lt/index_e.html.

Ruling of 8 March 1995
Ruling of 20 June 1995
Ruling of 27 October 1998
Ruling of 16 March 1999
Ruling of 2 April 2001
Ruling of 4 March 2003
Ruling of 23 August 2005

The Lithuanian Supreme Court[9]
Ruling of 22 May 2000

Poland

The Polish Constitutional Tribunal[10]
K 33/02, Judgment of 19 December 2002
K 2/04, Judgment of 15 December 2004

Romania

The Constitutional Court of Romania[11]
Decision No. 127 of 16 November 1994, published in the *Official Gazette*, No. 66, 11 April 1995
Decision No. 49 of 19 May 1995, published in the *Official Gazette*, No. 224, 29 September 1995
Decision No. 73 of 19 July 1995, published in the *Official Gazette*, No. 177, 8 August 1995
Decision No. 312 of 19 November 2002, published in the Official Gazette, No. 81, 7 February 2003
Decision No. 542 of 7 December 2004, published in the Official Gazette, No. 62, 18 January 2005
Decision No. 375 of 6 July 2005, published in the Official Gazette, No. 591, 8 July 2005
Decision No. 600 of 9 November 2005, published in the *Official Gazette*, No. 1060, 26 November 2005

[9] Source: http://www.lat.litlex.lt.
[10] Source: http://www.trybunal.gov.pl/eng/index.htm.
[11] Source: http://www.ccr.ro/default.aspx?lang=EN.

The Romanian High Court of Cassation and Justice[12]
Civil Section, Decision No. 2276 of 30 May 2003

Slovakia

The Constitutional Court of the Slovak Republic[13]
Pl. US 23/94 of 12 April 1994
Pl. US 23/98, Coll. 1999, 462–70
Pl. US 3/00 of 24 April 2001

The United Nations

United Nations Human Rights Committee[14]
Adam v. The Czech Republic, CCPR/C/57/D/586/1994, Communication No. 586/1994
Brokova v. The Czech Republic, CCPR/C/73/D/774/1997, Communication No. 774/1997
Drobek v. Slovakia, CCPR/C/60/D/643/1995, Communication No. 643/1995
E.K. and A.K. v. Hungary, CCPR/C/50/D/520/1992, Decision of 5 May 1992
Fábryová v. The Czech Republic, CCPR/C/73/D/765/1997, ICCPR, A/57/40 Vol. II (30 October 2001) 103
Šimůnek and Others v. The Czech Republic, CCPR/C/54/D/516/1992, Communication No. 516/1992
Somers v. Hungary, CCPR/C/57D/566/1993, Decision of 29 July 1996

The United States

The Supreme Court of the United States[15]
Cherokee Nation v. Georgia, 30 U.S. 1 (1831)
Cherokee Nation v. Southern Kansas R. Co., 135 U.S. 641 (1890)
Fuentes v. Shevin, 407 U.S. 67 (1972)

---

[12] Source: http://www.scj.ro.
[13] Source: http://www.concourt.sk/A/a_index.htm.
[14] Source: http://www.unhchr.ch/html/menu2/8/jurispr.htm.
[15] Source: http://www.supremecourtus.gov.

Loretto v. Teleprompter Manhattan CATV Corp., 458 U.S. 419 (1982)
Montgomery v. U.S. 414 U.S. 935 (1973)
Nollan v. California Coastal Commission, 483 U.S. 825 (1987)
Oneida Indian Nation of N.Y. State v. Oneida County 414 U.S. 661 (1974)
Shoshone Tribe v. United States, 299 U.S. 476 (1937)
Sioux Nation of Indians v. United States 448 U.S. 371 (1980)
Tee-Hit-Ton v. United States 348 U.S. 272 (1955)
United States v. Santa Fe Pacific R. Co. 314 U.S. 339, 345 (1941)
Webb's Fabulous Pharmacies, Inc. v. Beckwith, 449 U.S. 155 (1980)
Worcester v. Georgia 31 U.S. 515 (1832)

Bibliography

Books, articles, and talks

Allen, Tom, "Restitution and Transitional Justice in The European Court of Human Rights," *The Columbia Journal of European Law* 13.1 (2007).

Alexander, Gregory S., "The Limits of Property Reparations," Cornell Legal Studies Research Paper No. 05-004, 2002, http://papers.ssrn.com/sol3/papers.cfm?abstract_id=404940.

Alexander, Gregory S., *The Global Debate over Constitutional Property*, University of Chicago Press, 2006.

Amar, Akhil Reed, "Forty Acres and a Mule: A Republican Theory of Minimal Entitlements," *Harvard Journal of Law and Public Policy* 13 (1990).

Aristotle, *Politica*, Clarendon Press, c1957.

Avineri, Shlomo, "A Forum on Restitution: Essays on the Efficiency and Justice of Returning Property to Its Former Owners," *East European Constitutional Review* 2 (1993).

Barkan, Elazar, *The Guilt of Nations: Restitution and Negotiating Historical Injustices*, Norton, 2000.

Bazyler, Michael J., "The Holocaust Restitution Movement in Comparative Perspective," *Berkeley Journal of International Law* 20 (2002).

Bazyler, Michael J. and Amber L. Fitzgerald, "Trading with the Enemy: Holocaust Restitution, The United States Government, And American Industry," *Brooklyn Journal of International Law* (2003).

Berle, A.A. and G.C. Means, *The Modern Corporation and Private Property*, Macmillan, 1933.

Beker, Avi (ed.), *The Plunder of Jewish Property during the Holocaust: Confronting European History*, Palgrave, 2001.

Bentham, Jeremy, *An Introduction to the Principles of Morals and Legislation*, The Athlone Press, c1970.

Birmontiene, Toma, "The Perspectives of Introducing the Constitutional Complaint in the Republic of Lithuania (Report)," http://www.venice.coe.int/docs/2005/CDL-JU(2005)067-e.asp.

Brennan, Sean, "Native title in the High Court of Australia a decade after Mabo," http://www.gtcentre.unsw.edu.au/Public-Law-Review-native-title-as-published.doc+Native+Title+%22rule+of+law%22&hl=hu&start=3.

Bronislovas, Mikuta, "Land Privatization in Lithuania," 1999, http://www.ies.wisc.edu/ltc/live/baseur991115.pdf.

Brucan, Silviu, "Comunism versus capitalism. O falsa problema," quoting *Financial Times* and *Business Central Europe* data, http://www.dntb.ro/sfera/67/dupa_10_ani.html.

Bowman, Margaret B., "The Reburial of Native American Skeletal Remains: Approaches to the Resolution of a Conflict," *Harvard Environmental Law Review* 13 (1989).

Bruzzese, Pamela, "Distributing the Past, Jewish Cultural Property in Lithuania," *New York University Journal of International Law & Politics* 31 (1998).

Carter, Alan, *The Philosophical Foundations of Property Rights*, Harvester Wheatsheaf, 1989.

Cartwright, A.L., *The Return of the Peasant*, Ashgate, 2001.

Cass, Ronald A., "Property rights systems and the rule of law," Boston University School of Law, Working Paper Series, Public Law and Legal Theory Working Paper No. 03-06 2003, http://ssrn.com/abstract_id=392783.

Cepl, Vojtech, "A note on the restitution of property in post-communist Czechoslovakia," *Journal of Communist Studies* 7 (1991).

Cepl, Vojtech, "The Transformation of Hearts and Minds in Eastern Europe," *CATO Journal* 17 (1997).

Chapman, John W. (ed.), *Compensatory Justice*, New York University Press, 1991.

Crowder, Richard W., "Restitution in the Czech Republic: Problems and Prague-Nosis," *Indiana International & Comparative Law Review* 5.

Czarnota, Adam, Martin Krygier, and Wojciech Sadurski (eds.), *Rethinking the Rule of Law After Communism*, Central European University Press, 2005.

Dancaescu, Nick, "Land Reform in Zimbabwe," *Florida Journal of International Law* 15 (2003).

Dekker, Henri A.L., *Property Regimes in Transition: Land Reform, Food Security and Economic Development: A Case Study in the Kyrgyz Republic*, Ashgate, 2003.

Dembour, Marie-Benedicte and Magda Krzyzannowska-Mierzwska, "Ten Years On: The Voluminous and Interesting Polish Case Law," *European Human Rights Law Review* 5 (2004).

Demsetz, Harold, "Toward a Theory of Property Rights," *American Economic Review* 57 (1967).

Dorsen, Norman, Michel Rosenfeld, András Sajó, and Susanne Baer, *Comparative Constitutionalism: Cases and Materials*, West Group, 2003.

Dworkin, Ronald, *Taking Rights Seriously*, Harvard University Press, 1978.

Eizenstat, Stuart, "Justice after confiscation: Restitution of Communal and Private Property in Central and Eastern Europe," *East European Constitutional Review* 6.2–3 (1997).

Eizenstat, Stuart, "Imperfect Justice: Looted Assets, Slave Labor, and the Unfinished Business of World War II (Speech)," *Vanderbilt Journal of Transnational Law* 37 (2004).

Elster, John, "A framework for the study of transitional justice," http://www.media.uio.no/forskning/prosjekter/1945/english/artikler/framework1.shtml.

Elster, John, "On Doing What One Can: An Argument Against Post-Communist Restitution and Retribution," *East European Constitutional Review* 1.2 (1992).

Endziņš, Aivars, "Practice of the Constitutional Court of the Republic of Latvia in the sector of economic rights," Paper presented at Commission for Democracy Through Law's Seminar on "Economic transition: property rights, restitution, pensions and other issues concerning the constitutional protection of economic rights of citizens," Bishkek, 27–8 April 2001, http://www.venice.coe.int/docs/2001/CDL-JU(2001)026-e.asp#_ftn12.

Engerer, Hella, *Privatization and Its Limits in Central and Eastern Europe*, Palgrave, 2001.

Epstein, Richard A., *Bargaining with the State*, Princeton University Press, 1993.

Foster, Frances H., "Restitution of Expropriated Property: Post-Soviet Lessons For Cuba," *Columbia Journal of Transnational Law* 34 (1996).

Francis, Diane, "Who owns what in Eastern Europe?" *Financial Post*, 8 September 1993, available in the Westlaw International News Database.

Frankenberg, Günther, "Critical Comparisons: Re-thinking Comparative Law," *Harvard International Law Journal* 26 (1985).

Frochlich, Norman, Joe Oppenheimer, and Cheryl L. Eavey, "Choices of Principles of Distributive Justice in Experimental Groups," *American Journal of Political Science* 31 (1987).

Fuller, Lon L., "Positivism and Fidelity to Law—A Reply to Professor Hart," *Harvard Law Review* 71 (1958).

Fuller, Lon L., *The Morality of Law*, Yale University Press, 1969.

Glendon, Mary Ann, Michael Wallace Gordon, and Cristopher Osakwe (eds.), *Comparative Legal Traditions*, West Publishing Co., 1994.

Glos, George E., "Restitution of Confiscated Property in the Czech Republic," Czechoslovak Society of Arts and Sciences, 2000, http://www.svu2000.org/issues/glos.htm.

Gray, Cheryl W., "The Legal Framework for private sector activity in the Czech and Slovak Federal Republic," World Bank, Working Paper Series, 1992.

Greenfield, Jennifer, *The Return of Cultural Treasures*, Cambridge University Press, 1996

Grote, Kerstin, "Compensation for East German Victims of Political Persecution," *German-American Law Journal* (April 2000), http://www.amlaw.us/arauf_19.shtml.

Hann, Chris, *The Postsocialist Agrarian Question*, Lit Verlag Münster, 2003.

Hart, Herbert Lionel Adolphus, "Positivism and the Separation of Law and Morals," *Harvard Law Review* 71 (1958), 593.

Hart, Herbert Lionel Adolphus, *The Concept of Law*, Clarendon Press, 1997.

Havemann, Paul (ed.), *Indigenous Peoples' Rights*, Oxford University Press, 1999.

Hayek, Friedrich, *The Road to Serfdom*, University of Chicago Press, c1991.

Hegel, Georg Wilhelm Friedrich, *Philosophy of Right*, trans. by T.M. Knox, Clarendon Press, c1965.

Heller, Ágnes, *Beyond Justice*, Basil Blackwell, 1987.

Heller, Michael, "The Tragedy of Anticommons: Property in Transition from Marx to Markets," *Harvard Law Review* 111.

Henkin and Hargrove (eds.), *Human Rights: An Agenda for the Next Century*, American Society of International Law, 1994.

Hochstein, Robert, "Jewish property restitution in the Czech Republic," *Boston College International & Comparative Law Review* 19 (1996).

Holmes, Stephen, "A Forum on Restitution: Essays on the Efficiency and Justice of Returning Property to Its Former Owners," *East European Constitutional Review* 2 (1993).

Hofmann, Mahulena, "Impact of the views of the UN Human Rights Committee in the national legal order of some Eastern and Central European countries," http://web.abo.fi/instut/imr/ILA/Hofmann.doc.

Howard, Bradley Reed, *Indigenous Peoples and the State*, Northern Illinois University Press, 2003.

Hume, David, *A Treatise of Human Nature*, ed. by David Fate Norton and Mary J. Norton, Oxford University Press, c2000.

Jaskaunas, Paul, "Vilnius lost," *Legal Affairs* 63 (2003).

Johnston, Hinton, and Daryle Rigney (eds.), *Indigenous Australians and the Law*, Cavending Publishing, 1997.

Kartenthaler and Luthardt (eds.), *The Domestic Politics of German Unification*, L. Rienner, 1993.

Kraus, Tomas, Executive Director of the Federation of Jewish Communities in the Czech Republic, "Anti-Semitism, Holocaust Memory, Property Restitution and Related Issues Confronting the Jewish Communities of Central and Eastern Europe," Presentation given at the AJC Conference in Bucharest, March 2002.

Krygier, Martin and Adam Czarnota (eds.), *The Rule of Law after Communism*, Ashgate, 1999.

Kutz, Christopher, "Justice in Reparations: The Cost of Memory and the Value of Talk," *Philosophy and Public Affairs* 32.3 (2004).

Kvetkovskis, Viktor and Edvins Kapostnis, "The legal ways of privatization in Latvia—the State Land Service of Latvia," 1999, http://www.ies.wisc.edu/ltc/live/baseur991124.pdf.

Locke, John, *Treatise of Civil Government and a Letter Concerning Toleration*, Appleton-Century, c1965.

Locke, John, *Two Treatises of Government*, Dent, c1924.

Lucus, Ritchie, "Indian Burial Sites Unearthed: The Misapplication of the Native American Graves Protection and Repatriation Act," *Public Land & Resources Law Review* 26 (2005).

Macklem, Patrick, *Indigenous Difference and the Constitution of Canada*, University of Toronto Press, 2001.

Macklem, Patrick, "1 Rybná 9 Praha 1: Restitution and Memory in International Human Rights Law," *European Journal of International Law* 16.1 (2005).

Marmor, Adrian, "The rule of law and its limits," USC Public Policy Research Paper No. 03-16, http://ssrn.com/abstract=424613.

Mclean, Janet (ed.), *Property and the Constitution*, Hart Publishing, 1999.

Meron, Theodor, *Human Rights and Humanitarian Norms as Customary Law*, Clarendon Press, 1991.

Mertelsmann, Olaf (ed.), *The Sovietization of the Baltic States, 1940–1956*, Kleio, 2003.

Michelman, Frank I., "Property as a Constitutional Right," *Washington and Lee Law Review* 38 (1981).

Mihályi, Péter, *A kárpótlás*, Állami Privatizációs és Vagyonkezelő Rt. Budapest, 1998.

Moriwake, Isaac, "Critical Excavations: Law, Narrative, and the Debate on Native American and Hawaiian 'Cultural Property' Repatriation," *University of Hawaii Law Review* 20 (1998).

Munzer, Stephan R., *A Theory of Property*, Cambridge University Press, 1990.

Nedelsky, Jennifer, *Private Property and the Limits of American Constitutionalism: The Madisonian Framework and Its Legacy*, University of Chicago Press, 1990.

Neuborne, Burt, "Preliminary Reflections on Aspects of Holocaust-Era Litigation in American Courts," *Washington University Law Quarterly* 80 (2002).

Neumann, Gerald L., "The U.S. Constitutional Conception of the Rule of Law and the Rechtsstaatsprinzip of the Grundgesetz," Columbia Law School, Public Law and Legal Theory Working Paper Group, Paper No. 5, 1999, http://papers.ssrn.com/paper.taf?abstract_ud=195368.

Neumann, Michael, *The Rule of Law: Politicizing Ethics*, Ashgate, 2002.

Newton, Nell Jessup, "Indian Claims in the Courts of the Conqueror," *American University Law Review* 41 (1992), 753.

Nissinen, Marja, *Latvia's Transition to a Market Economy: Political Determinants of Economic Reform Policy*, St. Martin's Press, 1999.

Nozick, Robert, *Anarchy, State, and Utopia*, Basic Books, 1974.

Oddie, G. and R. Perrett (eds.), *Justice, Ethics, and New Zealand Society*, Oxford University Press, 1992.

Offe and Bönker, "A Forum on Restitution: Essays on the Efficiency and Justice of Returning Property to Its Former Owners," *East European Constitutional Review* 2 (1993).

Ovey, Clare and Robin White, *Jacobs and White: The European Convention on Human Rights*, Oxford University Press, 2002.

Pechota, Vratislav, "Privatization and Foreign Investment in Czechoslovakia: The Legal Dimension," *Vanderbilt Journal of Transnational Law* 24 (1991).

Penner, James E., *Property in Law*, Oxford University Press, 1997.

Pipes, Richard, *Property and Freedom*, Vintage Books, 2000.

Platzman, Steven, "Objects of Controversy: The Native American Right to Repatriation," *American University Law Review* 41 (1992).

Pogány, István, *Righting Wrongs in Eastern Europe*, Manchester University Press, 1997.

Posner, Eric A. and Adrian Vermeule, "Reparations for Slavery and Other Historical Injustices," *Columbia Law Review* 103 (2003).

Posner, Eric A. and Adrian Vermeule, "Transitional Justice as Ordinary Justice," *Harvard Law Review* 117 (2004).

Preuss, Ulrich K., "A Forum on Restitution: Essays on the Efficiency and Justice of Returning Property to Its Former Owners," *East European Constitutional Review* 2 (1993).

Přibáň, Jiří, *Dissidents of Law*, Ashgate, 2002.

Procházka, Radoslav, *Mission Accomplished: On Founding Constitutional Adjudication in Central Europe*, CEU Press, 2002.

Prucha, Francis Paul, *American Indian Treaties*, University of California Press, 1997.

Radbruch, Gustav, *Rechtsphilosophie*, ed. by Arthur Kaufmann, C.F. Müller Juristischer Verlag, 1987.

Ragnitz, Joachim, "German Unification: Restitution of Nationalized Properties," Presentation at the Goethe-Center Nicosia, Cyprus, 2004, http://projusticia.net/i_009.php.

Rajczi, József, "A földminősítés történeti áttekintése," http://www.magyaringatlanklub.hu/?page=tudastar_foldminosit.

Rawls, John, *A Theory of Justice*, Harvard University Press, 1971.

Rawls, John, *Political Liberalism*, Columbia University Press, 1993.

Raz, Joseph, "Rule of Law and Its Virtue," in Cunningham (ed.), *Liberty and the Rule of Law*, Texas A&M University Press, 1979.

Raz, Joseph, *The Authority of Law*, Oxford, 1977.

Reitz, John C., "How to Do Comparative Law," *American Journal of Comparative Law* 46 (1998).

Romsics, Ignác, "Az újraosztott köztes-európa," *Európai utas* 1 (2000), http://www.hhrf.org/europaiutas/20001/3.htm.

Rose, Carol M., "Property as the Keystone Right?" *Notre Dame Law Review* 71.3 (1996).

Rose, Jonathan, "The Rule of Law in the Western World: An Overview," *Journal of Social Philosophy* 35.4 (2004).

Rosenfeld, Michael, "The Rule of Law and the Legitimacy of Constitutional Democracy," Cardozo Law School Working Paper Series No. 36 (2001), http://papers.ssrn.com/paper.taf?abstract_id=262350.

Sadurski, Wojciech (ed.), *Constitutional Justice East and West*, Kluwer Law International, 2003.

Sadurski, Wojciech, "'Decommunisation,' 'Lustration,' and Constitutional Continuity: Dilemmas of Transitional Justice in Central Europe," European University Institute, Florence, EUI Working Paper Law No. 2003/15.

Sadurski, Wojciech, *Rights Before Courts. A Study of Constitutional Courts in Postcommunist States of Central and Eastern Europe*, Springer, 2005.

Sajó, András, "A részleges kárpótlási törvény által felvetett alkotmányossági kérdések," *Állam és Jogtudomány* 1–4 (1992).

Sajó, András, "Preferred Generations: A Paradox of Restoration Constitutions," *Cardozo Law Review* 14 (1993).

Sampford, Charles, *Retrospectivity and the Rule of Law*, Oxford University Press, 2006.

Sax, Joseph L., "Some Thoughts on the Decline of Private Property," *Washington Law Review* 58 (1983).

Scalia, Antonin, "'The Rule of Law as a Law of Rules,' Oliver Wendell Holmes Bicentennial Lecture, Harvard Law School," *University of Chicago Law Review* 56 (1989).

Seliger, Berhnard, "Ten Years After German Unification," *Central Europe Review* (2001), http://www.ce-review.org/01/4/seliger4.html.

Sened, Itai, *The Political Institution of Private Property*, Cambridge University Press, 1997.

Sharp, Andrew, *Justice and the Maori: The Philosophy and Practice of Maori Claims in New Zealand since the 1970s*, Oxford University Press, 1997.

Shirley, Jonathan, "The Role of International Human Rights and The Law of Diplomatic Protection on Resolving Zimbabwe's Land Crisis," *Boston College International Comparative Law Review* 27 (2004).

Sinn, Gerlinde and Hans-Werner Sinn, *Jumpstart: The Economic Unification of Germany*, MIT Press, 1992.

Szabó, Győző and Gábor Nagy (eds.), *Tanulmányok az Emberi Jogok Európai Egyezménye legfontosabb rendelkezéseihez kapcsolódó strasbourgi esetjogról*, HVG-Orac, 1999.

Szigeti, P. and P. Takács, *A jogállamiság jogelmélete*, Napvilág, 1998.

Swinnen, Johan F.M. (ed.), *Political Economy of Agrarian Reform in Central and Eastern Europe*, Ashgate, c1997.

Tadayuki, Hayashi, "Politics of the Agricultural Transformation in Czechoslovakia: 1990–1991," http://src-home.slav.hokudai.ac.jp/kaken/ieda2001/pdf/hayashi.pdf.

Teitel, Ruti G., *Transitional Justice*, Oxford University Press, c2000.

Teitel, Ruti G., "Post-Communist Constitutionalism: A Transitional Perspective," in Sadurski (ed.), *Constitutional Theory*, Ashgate, 2005.

Treanor, William M., "The Origins and Original Significance of the Just Compensation Clause of the Fifth Amendment," *Yale Law Review* 94 (1985).

Tremblay, Luc B., *The Rule of Law, Justice, and Interpretation*, McGill–Queen's University Press, 1997.

Tribe, Laurence H., *American Constitutional Law*, The Foundation Press, Inc., 1988.

Tribe, Laurence H., "Revisiting the Rule of Law," *New York University Law Review* 64 (1989).

Trope, Jack F. and Walter R. Echo-Hawk, "The Native American Graves Protection and Repatriation Act: Background and Legislative History," *Arizona State Law Journal* 24 (1992).

Ulen, Thomas S., *Rational Choice Theory in Law and Economics*, 1999.

Underkuffler, Laura, *The Idea of Property: Its Meanings and Power*, Oxford University Press, 2003.

Ungvári, Krisztián, "Nagy jelentőségű szociálpolitikai akció—adalékok a zsidó vagyon begyűjtéséhez és elosztásához Magyarországon 1944-ben," http://www.rev.hu/html/hu/kiadvanyok/evkonyv02/ungvary.html.

Varga, Csaba, *Law and Philosophy: Selected Papers in Legal Theory*, Project on Comparative Legal Cultures of the Faculty of Law of Eötvös Loránd University in Budapest, 1994.

Varga, Csaba, *Transition to the Rule of Law*, Eötvös Lóránd University and the Institute for Legal Studies of the Hungarian Academy of Sciences, 1995.

Veraart, Wouter, "'Reasonableness' or strict law? The postwar restitution rights in the Netherlands and in France (1945–1952)," Paper presented at the International Conference on Confronting History: The Historical Commissions of Inquiry, Yad Vashem, 2002, http://www1.yadvashem.org/about_yad/departments/institute/pdf/10.pdf.

Verdery, Katherine, *The Vanishing Hectare: Property and Value in Postsocialist Transylvania*, Cornell University Press, 2003.

Waldron, Jeremy, *The Right to Private Property*, Clarendon Press, c1988.

Weber, Max, *Economy and Society*, ed. by Günther Roth and Claus Wittich, University of California Press, c1978.

Wilson, Paul (ed.), *Open Letters: Selected Writings, 1965–1990*, Alfred A. Knopf, 1992.

Youngblood, William R., "Poland's struggle for a restitution policy in the 1990s," *Emory International Law Review* (Fall 1995).

Zweig, Ronald W., *German Reparations and the Jewish World: A History of the Claims Conference*, Frank Cass, 2001.

Miscellaneous

22, No. 789 of 22–9 April 2005, http://www.revista22.ro/html/index.php?nr=2005-04-21&art=1676.

A II. Vatikáni Zsinat Dokumentumai, Szt. István Társulat, az Apostoli Szentszék Könyvkiadója, 2000, Gaudium et Spes.

Annual Report to Congress on International Religious Freedom, Released by the Bureau of Democracy, Human Rights, and Labor, U.S. Department of State, 2005, http://www.state.gov/g/drl/rls/irf/2005/51550.htm.

Australian Institute of Aboriginal and Torres Strait Islanders Studies (AIATSIS), http://www.aiatsis.gov.au/rsrch/ntru/research/resourceguide/national_overview/national02.html.

Bilanţ Magazine, http://www.revistabilant.ro/articole.php?art=37.

Claims Conference, Compensation—Restitution in Hungary, http://www.claimscon.org/?url=hungary.

Gândul, 26 June 2006, http://www.gandul.info/2006-06-07/arte/pelesul.

European Commission for Democracy Through Law, Opinion No. 277/2004, CDL-AD (2004) 009.

European Commission: The Czechoslovakian Presidential Decrees in the light of the Acquis Communautaire, Summary Findings of the Commission Services, Brussels, 2002, http://www.mzv.cz/servis/soubor.asp?id=3138.

German Unification Case Study, in *Lex Mundi World Reports*, Supplement No. 15, 1992, http://www.foothill.fhda.edu/divisions/unification/restitution2.html.

Institute of Economics, Estonian Academy of Sciences: Review of Structural Reforms, 1995, available on-line at URL: http://www.ibs.ee/economics/esc/part-1.html.

Joint communication of the Hungarian Ministry of Foreign Affairs and the Ministry of Finances No. 8004/1991.

Jurnalul National, http://www.jurnalul.ro/modules.php?op=modload&name=News&file=article&sid=14439.

Materials of the Third Consultative Meeting, Geneva, 29 September to 1 October 2004, http://www.ishr.ch/About%20UN/Reports%20and%20Analysis/CHRWG/Remedy/Remedy-3rdConsultation.pdf.

"Megkérdőjelezett igazságosság," MTV, 30 June 2006, http://www.azeste.hu/este/cikk/6156.

New Zealand Legal System: A Guide to the Constitution, The, Government and legislature of New Zealand, Homepage of the New Zealand Ministry of Justice, http://www.justice.govt.nz/pubs/other/pamphlets/2001/legal_system.html.

Parliament of Estonia, The, *Weekly Records*, 6–9 and 14 February 2006, http://www.riigikogu.ee/?id=38455&parent_id=39883 and http://www.state.gov/p/eur/rls/or/64425.htm.

Proclamation of Timişoara (Romania), 11 March 1990, http://www.timisoara.com/timisoara/rev/proclamation.html.

"Private restitution proposal in Poland offers unsatisfactory resolution to some," JTA News Service, 19 May 2006, http://floridajewishnews.com/articles/index2.php?option=com_content&do_pdf=1&id=430.

"Proposed Latvian restitution law would return Jewish properties," Jewish Telegraphic Agency, 23 January 2006, http://www.ncsj.org/AuxPages/011706JTA_Latvia.shtml.

Realitatea Romaneasca, http://www.realitatearomaneasca.ro/content.php?c=articole&id_categorie=6&articol_id=4630&p=;.

Return of Indigenous Cultural Property (RICP) Program, available on the homepage of the Australian Cultural Ministers' Council, http://www.dcita.gov.au/arts/councils/return_of_indigenous_cultural_property_(ricp)_program.

Stiri.ro, http://stiri.rol.ro/stiri/2004/10/154459.htm; http://news.softpedia.com/news/1/2004/October/9831.shtml.

United States Department of State, Summary of Property Restitution in Central and Eastern Europe, Submitted to the U.S. Commission on Security and Cooperation in Europe On the Occasion of a Briefing Presented to the Commission by Ambassador Randolph M. Bell, 10 September 2003, http://www.state.gov/p/eur/rls/or/2003/31415.htm.

United States Department of State, Under Secretary for Political Affairs, Bureau of European and Eurasian Affairs: Summary of Property Restitution in Central and Eastern Europe, 12 April 2006, http://www.state.gov/p/eur/rls/or/64425.htm.

Új szó, 26 November 2004, http://www.ujszo.com/clanok.asp?vyd=20041126&cl=109302.

Ziua, http://www.ziua.ro/archive/2002/07/19/docs/26089.html.

Legislative and administrative acts

Czechoslovakia

Decree No. 108/1945 Sb.

Law No. 243/1992 Coll. of Laws

Law "On extrajudicial rehabilitation," 21 February 1991, No. 87/1991 Coll. of Laws

Law "On modifying ownership relationships with respect to land and another agricultural properties," 21 May 1991, No. 229/1991 Coll. of Laws

Law "On the mitigation of the consequences of certain property injustices," 2 October 1990, No. 403/1990 Coll. of Laws

Czech Republic

Law of 29 April 1994, No. 116/1994 Coll. of Laws, amending the Law "On extrajudicial rehabilitation"

Estonia

Land Reform Act, 1997, consolidated text published in the *State Gazette*, RT I 2001, 52, 304

Land Valuation Act of 1994, consolidated version in 2002

Principles of Ownership Reform Act, 1991, consolidated text published in the *State Gazette*, RT I 1997, 27, 391

Unlawfully Expropriated Property Valuation and Compensation Act of 1993, consolidated version in 2002

Germany

Compensation for Persons Subjected to Nazi Persecution Act, Official Notice of 27 September 1994

Decree "On registering property claims," 11 October 1990

Settlement of Property Claims Act, Official Notice of 2 December 1994

Hungary

Constitution of 1949

Decree No. 104/1991 for the implementation of Law No. XXV/1991

Decree No. 92/1992 for the implementation of Law No. XXIV/1992

Governmental Decree No. 13.160/1947

Governmental Decree No. 17/1964

Governmental Order No. 104 of 3 August 1991

Law No. LII of 1992

Law No. X of 1997

Law No. XIV of 1992

Law No. XV of 1946

Law No. XVIII of 1947

Law No. XXV of 1991

Law No. XXXII of 1989

Law No. XXXII of 1992, "On the compensation of those unjustly deprived of their life or liberty on political grounds"

Ministerial Order No. 9/1964
Prime Minister's Order No. 12.530/1946
Prime Minister's Order No. 1600/1944
Prime Minister's Order No. 300/1946
Prime Minister's Order No. 3630/1945
Prime Minister's Order No. 5280/1947
Prime Minister's Order No. 6400/1947
Prime Minister's Order No. 7590/1945
Prime Minister's Order No.10.480/1945

Latvia

Law "On land privatization in rural regions," 1992
Law "On land reform in cities," 1991
Law "On the land reform in the Republic of Latvia rural regions," 1990
Law "On the renewal of property rights in enterprises and other property objects," March 1993
Law "On the return of buildings to their legal owners," 1991

Lithuania

Law No. I-1454 "On procedures and conditions for restoration of citizen's rights to the ownership of existent property," 18 June 1991
Resolution "On the partial amendment to the Government of the Republic of Lithuania Resolution No. 470 ('On the implementation of the restitution law')," 17 May 1993, *Official Gazette*, No. 17-440, 1993

Poland

Offsetting the Value of Property Abandoned Beyond the Present Borders of the Polish State Against the Price of State Property or the Fee for the Right of Perpetual Usufruct Act, 2003
Law "On the realization of the right to compensation for property left beyond the present borders of the Polish State," 21 July 2005
Decree of 6 December 1946, "On the transfer from the state of non-agricultural property in the regained territories and the former City of Gdańsk"
Land Administration and Expropriation Act, 29 April 1985

Romania

Constitution of 1948

Decree No. 177/1948

Decree No. 358/1948

Decree–Law No. 126/1990

Governmental Decree No. 11/1997, published in the *Official Gazette*, No. 16, 4 February 1997

Governmental Emergency Ordinance No. 168/1999, *Official Gazette*, No. 536, 3 November 1999

Governmental Emergency Ordinance No. 184/2002, *Official Gazette*, No. 929, 18 December 2002

Governmental Emergency Ordinance No. 83/1999, *Official Gazette*, Nos. 266/1999, 797/2005

Governmental Emergency Ordinance No. 94/2000, *Official Gazette*, No. 308/2000

Governmental Ordinance No. 69/2000, *Official Gazette*, No. 407, 29 August 2000

Governmental Ordinance No. 728/1992, *Official Gazette*, No. 309, 27 November 1992

Law No. 501/2002, *Official Gazette*, No. 561, 31 July 2002

Law No. 1/2000, *Official Gazette*, No. 8, 12 January 2000

Law No. 10/2001, *Official Gazette*, No. 75, 14 February 2001

Law No. 112/1995, *Official Gazette*, No. 279, 29 November 1995

Law No. 169/1997, *Official Gazette*, No. 299, 4 November 1997

Law No. 171/2006, *Official Gazette*, No. 437, 19 May 2006

Law No. 18/1991, (republished in) *Official Gazette*, No. 1, 5 January 1991

Law No. 187/1945, *Official Gazette*, No. 68/1945

Law No. 213/1998, *Official Gazette*, No. 448, 24 November 1998

Law No. 218/1998, *Official Gazette*, No. 453, 26 November 1998

Law No. 247/2005, *Official Gazette*, No. 955, 27 October 2005

Law No. 29/1991, *Official Gazette*, No. 59, 22 March 1991

Law No. 290/2003, *Official Gazette*, No. 505, 14 July 2003

Law No. 9/1998, (republished in) *Official Gazette*, No. 105, 07 February 2002

Legislative project PL-x 158/09.05.2005, http://www.cdep.ro

International documents

Charter of Fundamental Rights of the European Union, 2000/C 364/01

Convention for the Protection of Human Rights and Fundamental Freedoms, Rome, 4 November 1950

International Covenant on Civil and Political Rights, G.A. Res. 2200A (XXI), 21 U.N. GAOR Supp. (No. 16) at 52, U.N. Doc. A/6316 (1966), 999 U.N.T.S. 171

U.N. Draft Declaration on the Rights of Indigenous Peoples, 1994/45, http://www.unhchr.ch/huridocda/huridoca.nsf/(Symbol)/E.CN.4.SUB.2.RES.1994.45.En?OpenDocument.

Universal Declaration of Human Rights, G.A. Res. 217 A (III), 10 December 1948

Index